2000

Between 1580 and 1745 – Edmund Spenser's journey to an unconquered Ireland and the last Jacobite Rebellion – the first British Empire was established. The intervening years saw the cultural and material forces of colonialism pursue a fitful, often fanciful endeavor to secure space for this expansion. With the defeat of the Highland clans, what England in 1580 could only dream about had materialized: a coherent socio-spacial system known as an empire.

Taking the Atlantic world as its context, this ambitious book argues that England's culture during the seventeenth and early eighteenth centuries was saturated with a geographic imagination fed by the experiences and experiments of colonialism. Using theories of space and its production to ground his readings, Bruce McLeod skilfully explores how works by Edmund Spenser, John Milton, Aphra Behn, Mary Rowlandson, Daniel Defoe, and Jonathan Swift imagine, interrogate, and narrate the adventure and geography of empire.

Bruce McLeod gained his Ph.D. at the University of Iowa, where he has also been a visiting assistant professor. This is his first book.

THE GEOGRAPHY OF EMPIRE IN ENGLISH LITERATURE

1580–1745

BRUCE MCLEOD

CAMBRIDGE
UNIVERSITY PRESS

PUBLISHED BY THE PRESS SYNDICATE OF THE UNIVERSITY OF CAMBRIDGE
The Pitt Building, Trumpington Street, Cambridge, United Kingdom

CAMBRIDGE UNIVERSITY PRESS
The Edinburgh Building, Cambridge CB2 2RU, UK   http://www.cup.ac.uk
40 West 20th Street, New York NY 10011–4211, USA   http://www.cup.org
10 Stamford Road, Oakleigh, Melbourne 3166, Australia

Bruce McLeod 1999

First published 1999

Printed in the United Kingdom at the University Press, Cambridge

Typeset in Baskerville 11/12.5pt [VN]

A catalogue record for this book is available from the British Library

Library of Congress cataloguing in publication data
McLeod, Bruce, Ph.D.
The geography of empire in English literature, 1580–1745 / Bruce
McLeod.
p. cm.
Includes bibliographical references
ISBN 0 521 66079 3 (hardback)
1. English literature – Early modern, 1500–1700 – History and
criticism. 2. English literature – 18th century – History and
criticism. 3. Imperialism in literature. 4. Geography in
literature. 5. Colonies in liteature. I. Title.
PR428.I54M38   1999
820.9'358 – dc21   98–53638
CIP

ISBN 0 521 66079 3 hardback

For Naomi

Contents

Illustrations

Acknowledgments

This project had its genesis in a class on the *avant garde* at the University of Iowa. It was there that I was taken aback by Edward Said's essay "Opponents, Audiences, Constituencies and Community." Said critiques the specialization of "fields" and "disciplines" within academia and exhorts us to generalize, to make connections. If we fail to think big we accept and further a situation, in the words of Henri Lefebvre, in which "intellectual labour, like material labour, is subject to endless division" (*Production of Space* 8); a situation where our work is in danger of irrelevance. Thus I set out not only to write a thesis that (originally) studied transatlantic culture and imperialism of the First British Empire (from 1580 to 1815), but to foreground mechanisms of segregation which I felt to be intrinsic to colonialism (even as it forces different cultures into proximity with one another) as well as the brutal spatial "restructuring" throughout the world today.

In this sometimes over-reaching ambition I was fortunate to receive unequivocal support and encouragement from my dissertation committee at Iowa: Rudolf Kuenzli, Wayne Franklin, Alvin Snider, Florence Boos, and Thomas Lewis. Their example as astute and committed critics and as generous and politicized intellectuals has left an indelible mark both on this book and myself. I especially want to thank Rudolf Kuenzli, Wayne Franklin, and Alvin Snider who from the very start offered (non-imperial) super-vision. Their care, hospitality, and humor sustained this project over many years.

I am grateful to Judith Pascoe, Elizabeth Sauer, Balachandra Rajan, Paul Stevens, and Terry Eagleton for their support; and to Josie Dixon at Cambridge University Press and the two spectral readers she conjured up; this book has benefited immeasurably from their critical comments and suggestions. Steven Mathews, Cindy Stretch, Ron Daniels, Tony Kushner, and David Gothard have all had a significant impact on the materialization of this project. Through their own work, intelligence, and desire to make the world a better place, if not overnight then in the foreseeable future, they have proven that intellectual honesty and creativity is alive and well.

Finally, I wish to thank my parents, John and Clare McLeod, for their unconditional support and for showing me the importance of the space of the home; and my brother and sisters, Allan, Julie, and Anne, whose careers in art and medical science and practice have kept my feet on the ground. Nadira, Caitlin, and Tegan continue to show me how to produce and properly inhabit space. Their intense grasp of the everyday and their love made writing and not writing easier and easier. This book is dedicated to Naomi Wallace, in whom I found my space, and the liveliness of her courage. Her example inspired this book, and much more.

CHAPTER I

Introduction: productions of empire

Nothing could be more political than just the way objects are spatially distributed.   Eagleton in Ross *Emergence of Social Space* xiii

I prefer to call this generative doubt the opening of non-isomorphic subjects, agents, and territories of stories unimaginable from the vantage point of the cyclopian, self-satiated eye of the master subject. The Western eye has fundamentally been a wandering eye, a travelling lens. These peregrinations have often been violent and insistent on mirrors for a conquering self – but not always.

Haraway *Simians* 192.

This book is about the production of space. More particularly, it explores the production of an empire, the creation of "Englands out of England" (Purchas *Hakluytus*, 1.xxxviii). The expansive multiplication of certain (extremely unstable) spatial and ideological formulations was as much a question of imagination and myth as hard-nosed calculation and economic realities. My intention is to expose the innards, the facts and fictions, of a society and culture that by 1745 had coalesced into an empire that stood for liberty and commerce. In this project I hope to reinforce Edward Said's contention that the "major ... determining, political horizon of modern Western culture [is] imperialism" (*Culture* 60). I have, perhaps, taken the risky step of applying Said's thesis to the very beginnings of what became, though not inevitably, the British empire. The 1580s is a time when imperialism clearly had more to do with far-fetched dreams than with far-flung territories. In light of this, I will follow the useful distinction made by an historian of Empire, between "Imperial Britain" and the "British Empire." The former "indicates the informing spirit" or "consciousness" that aids and abets, sometimes precedes and often falsifies the territorial materiality of the latter (Cramb *Origins and Destiny* 5). Nonetheless, in the last decades of

1

the sixteenth century the fairy tale of an English imperium began not only to gather pace but seriously take up space.

1580 was a ground-breaking year for "Imperial Britain." As Lesley Cormack has shown in *Charting an Empire*, it was a year that saw the creation of new geographies based on imperial designs. Edmund Spenser's short trip across the sea to Ireland coincided with Drake's triumphant return from circumnavigating the globe. Drake's achievement, and booty, ignited a frenzy of financial and literary speculation (far more of the latter than the former) and attempts at colonizing the New World. The new confidence, though short-lived as far as the Americas were concerned, rejuvenated England's pursuits in the Old World. A precursor of the East India Company, the hugely successful Turkey/Levant Company was founded in 1581, while Pet and Jackman set off to find the North East Passage to China. The world appeared to be within England's grasp, even if its nearest colony, as Spenser discovered, remained a world away. Spatial relations were rapidly being reconfigured through the dreams and nightmares of a renewed global and imperial sensibility – a sensibility given keener definition in the face of the annexation of Portugal by Philip II of Spain. New ways of organizing space on the ground as it were, whether the rise of the slave plantation in Brazil or of an environmentalism in England centred on country estates and progressive agricultural techniques, also mark 1580.[1] The aftermath of Drake's return brought these developments into focus under the lens of England's desire to replicate the success of the Spanish and Portuguese. The next century and a half saw this desire gain systematic form, territorial domination, and cultural legitimacy. The narration of this history is the subject of the following pages.

This book then explores the relationship between "Imperial Britain" and the evolution of the "British Empire" – the former often being at odds with the reality of the latter. Its design is to lay bare the sinews connecting the cultural imaginary to that multifaceted and uneven spatial production, empire-building. One early example of these sinews is the relationship of Thomas More's *Utopia* to the New World. If More was inspired by Spain's exploits in the New World, in 1531 Vasco de Quiroga began to build two cities for Indians in Mexico based on *Utopia* (Benevolo *European City* 119). Spain's experiments in the Americas later spurred England into imperial activity with the second invasion of Ireland and forays to North America. It is this type of transaction and its repercussions within the Atlantic world of European imperialism that this book seeks to examine. But as in the case of *Utopia* there is often a crucial twist to this Eurocentric flow of information. If More's utopia springs from the knowledge produced by Spanish conquesting in the Americas – Vespucci's name appears in the book – then it is more than likely that Amaurotum's urban layout (essentially a square) derives from, as Hanno-Walter Kruft points out, "the influence of the pre-Columbian town plans of Central America" (*Architectural Theory* 229). Was Vasco de Quiroga simply returning to Mexico a Europeanized version of a Central American spatial form, one seen in Europe as original to an Englishman's inspirational vision?[2] Thus, the relationship between literature and colonialism is not only part of Europe's Atlantic world. It is also infused by a transcultural exchange with the colonized, although the latter's influence is usually relegated to a marginal, dependant role, if not erased altogether. My goal, therefore, is similar to that advocated by Gauri Viswanathan when she remarks, "with sustained cross-referencing between the histories of England and its colonies the relations between Western culture and imperialism will be progressively illuminated" (*Masks of Conquest* 169).

More's and Vasco de Quiroga's utopian schemes were part of a growing belief in the ability to manipulate nature and thereby improve the design of the human environment and its productive capacity. New ways of evaluating the environment were, as David Harvey points out, based on a "Cartesian vision of fixed property rights [and] of boundaries in abstract space" (*Justice* 265). Colonialism was the cutting edge of this ideology. Keith Thomas has shown that by the late sixteenth century and with the rise of Natural History nature is no longer seen as something solely to be dominated (*Man and the Natural World* 51). Economic exigencies, the acquisition of social status, and agricultural advances meant that nature was seen more in terms of the market than mayhem or the mysterious. Political changes also led to the production of a new nature. The abolition of feudal tenures and wardships, for instance, and the resultant greater security of landowners at the expense of copyholders, made "possible long-term, planned estate management" (Hill *Intellectual* 288–9). These interdependent forces, fuelled by England's political maneuvers and sense of providentialism, led landowners and merchants to harness and profit from resources in competition with other European powers. Under new structures of investment, speculation, and exploitation nature became a valuable commodity: a piece of property to be secured, a space of control, and the proper distribution of assets. Increasingly segregated and specialized, by the end of the sixteenth century the selling of space, both domestic and exotic, began to unify the British Isles and propel England overseas. As the exploitation became systematic the idealization of the land increased.

Such changes in England lent themselves to the ideology of a natural, hereditary, and meritocratic order, usually sanctioned by God and overseen by a benevolent ruler/landowner. We can trace the benefactors, at odds with the crown but acting as a local monarch, from Jonson's "To Penshurst" to Fielding's Squire Allworthy and Richardson's Sir Charles Grandison. The legitimacy of this superintendent rule was embedded in the space it presided over, most often a landscape centred on an ancient residence, and what Pope describes as "Nature Methodiz'd" ("An Essay on Criticism" *Poetry and Prose* 40). A political and aesthetic methodizing of nature went hand in glove with its economic re-formation by landowners. As Fernand Braudel points out "Cultures . . . are ways of ordering space just as economies are" (*Perspective* 65). Spatial structures were to reflect the subordination of nature to the cultured. Literature became replete with ideal versions of space. Lauro Martines's writing on the fifteenth-century building boom of *palazzi* in Florence is pertinent here. He argues that the elites' awareness of being able to extend and renew their power through spatial forms resulted in an interest in ideal cities and landscapes. Martines sees this as a "politically conservative conception, a response to the rising demand by princes and urban elites for grandeur and show, order and ample space, finesse and finished surfaces" (in Twombly *Power and Style* 17). Finished surfaces were only the most obvious display of the determination of elites to control the theater of social relations. Imbedded in these spatial morphologies is the crucial question of who are the subjects of history and geography, and who are the objects.

Culture, however, has the ability to transform subjects, to elevate or debase them. In other words "Imperial Britain," whether seen through the lens of literature or architecture, transfigures the brutal realities of the "British Empire." As Viswanathan argues, "the split between the material and the cultural practices of colonialism is nowhere sharper than in the progressive refinement of the rapacious, exploitive, and ruthless actor of history into the reflective subject of literature" (*Masks of Conquest* 20–1). The self-conscious, expansionist subject who must wrestle with the nefarious plots that threaten to steal away a civilized, Protestant, and English identity populates culture's empire. Further, "science," art, and literary culture were awash with an imperial mentality. The partnership of the mathematician Thomas Harriot and the

Figure 1   Frontispiece, Thomas Harriot *A Briefe and True Report* London, 1590.

artist John White in the settlement of Roanoke amply displays such a culture. Fittingly, the frontispiece to Harriot's *A Brief and True Report of . . . Virginia* (1590 edition) exemplifies the way in which Europeans and the culture of the elite framed those it sought to dominate. The classical triumphal arch is decorated with Indians who are clearly players, if marginal, in the narrative plot situated at the centre. As ornaments the Indians enrich an English set and design; they may loom large as characters within Harriot's text, but they are subordinates within the world-historical theatre of the English and their vision. The structure neatly embodies the relations of empire mediated through culture, in this case an illustration which invokes the masque, theatre, and classical architecture. Whether in Harriot's scenario or in the masque – both of which portray the bringing of order to confusion – the actors are part of the taming of nature, the transformation of perspective whereby the imperial English self is left in control of space.

As if commenting on the frontispiece, Bruno Zevi states that "architecture is environment, the stage on which our lives unfold" (*Architecture as Space* 32). Colonialism more urgently foregrounded the link between control over the environment and the actors. The theatrical metaphor used by authors like Pope to describe spatial relations and used by spatial designers like Inigo Jones to buttress the power of royalty and patrons points to the constructed and tenuous, even illusory, nature of elite rule. Nevertheless, space was the surest way to ensure control over opposition real or imagined. By studying spatial design – especially in the case of the English, who concentrated on legitimizing imperialism via the occupation of space rather than the subordination of other peoples – we can learn a good deal about the ideologies and conflicts within colonial and metropolitan society. As theorists of architecture from Vitruvius onward have recognized, social order rested on spatial design and vice versa.

The process of culturally framing or coordinating resistant populations for specific economic purposes was however undermined by colonialism itself. As it produces itself, colonial society threatens to unravel because its "natural order" is constantly questioned by the proximity of and interchange with other societies. Its inevitable cross-cultural and territorially uncertain character means that the colonizers' social order is in constant jeopardy. The constructedness of colonial society, hence its flaws and failings, are exposed as it attempts to conceal them in the interests of presenting a natural, coherent, and controled society fit for rulership. Edmund Spenser recognized as much through his years in Ireland: "how quickly doth that country alter men's natures" (*View* 151). Hence, central to the colonial enterprise is the project of working up a dominant hegemonic order which invalidates, dismisses, and renders unimaginable the possibility of counter-hegemonic sites, systems, and societies. As Stephen Saunders Webb has demonstrated, from the beginning England's colonial ventures were as much military as they were mercantile in nature. The military, no matter where they were stationed, carried out disciplinary measures to ensure loyalty to the monarch and subservience to colonial rule (*Governors* xvi–xvii). In order to keep the vulnerable subject in a constant state of check the theaters of war and culture are inextricably bound.

If counter-hegemonic rumblings upset Spenser and the New English in Ireland, the military also had to put its foot down on the other side of the Atlantic. In 1610 "*Lawes Divine, Morall and Martiall*" had to be instituted in the early Jamestown colony in order to dissuade insubordination by colonists (Morgan *American Slavery* 74). It was not only Indians who needed to be set within the proper standards of behaviour. The laws were mainly directed at the blurring of socio-spatial categories by colonists who defected to the Powhatan confederacy. The "natural" rule of the authorities is radically undermined by the "generative doubt" or the "unimaginable," as Haraway puts it in the epigraph above, created by the interaction of different cultural systems. Under such propitious circumstances colonists chose to cross from their own into the space of the Other. Whether in the colonies or in the British Isles, cultural spaces were contested, interactive, and were viewed strategically by all competing groups. Essentially the contest is over resources. As Carole Fabricant puts it, unsettling prospects concerning socio-spatial mobility and stability "inevitably revolv[e] around the question of who has access to land and on what terms" (in Nussbaum and Brown *New Eighteenth Century* 255). Thus Vasco de Quiroga's plans, like those of Thomas More, colonial leaders, and landowners, sought to "improve" land so as to rid it of conflict and disorder; those who did not or refused to be bit players in the drama of Europe's manifest destiny were casualties of history. Because so many resisted becoming casualties, the ideal or paradisal and the fortified are inseparable. Colonial utopias, which are so often invoked in one form or another in the texts studied in the following chapters, plot the great master-narrative of (benevolent) imperialism battling numerous "great master-mischief[s]." In Edmund Burke's day these were identified as Jacobinism coupled with that timeless imperial illness "Indianism" (*Works* vi, 58).[3]

The authors and texts that I examine exemplify the interaction between literary culture and the developing world of Britain's first empire. Few of the major authors during this period did not invest either financially, politically or bodily in colonial ventures, and this must surely tell us something about who became established writers, how they saw themselves as writers, and what constituted literary subject matter and culture generally. Edmund Spenser, John Milton, Aphra Behn, Mary Rowlandson, Daniel Defoe, and Jonathan Swift (as well as a slew of other "colonial surveyors") imagine, interrogate, and narrate the adventure and geography of empire. Yet more than being inextricably part and parcel of an imperial culture these particular writers have a personal stake in colonialism: as colonists (Spenser, Behn, Rowlandson, and Swift) and as enthusiasts or ideologues (Milton and Defoe). Their investment is especially significant given the canonical status of many of the texts they penned, and serves to underscore the central question of my book: how does literature function in relation to imperialism?

I argue that a great deal of national culture during the seventeenth and eighteenth centuries was imbued with a geographical imagination fed by the experiences and experiments of colonialism. In *The Staple of Newes*, for instance, Ben Jonson reproduces Captain John Smith's description of Pocahontas verbatim. As Anthony Pagden has pointed out, culture was shot through with the "language of empire" (the core of which changed little over the centuries), the sense of a new geography, and the lure of the Americas (*Lords* 6). This imaginary, which effectively normalizes empire, brought the sight and sound, if not the touch and taste, of imperial adventure into everyday circulation. Hence when Charlotte Smith, in the 1780s, wants to celebrate "Harriet" and her "friendship's cheering light," she does so via the recounting of a captivity narrative set in North America, where, like Mary Rowlandson, the English captive, pursued by "torturing, savage foes" and "reptile-monsters" of the "waste," finally "hails the beam benign that guides his way" to a fort and civility (Smith *Poems* 50). Empire was the stuff of common sense as well as daydreams and infinite possibilities, casually conjured up by members of the colonizing nation: "he dreamt of becoming a trapper in America, of entering the service of a pasha in the East, of signing on as a sailor" (Flaubert *Sentimental Education* 101).

The empire did not capture the collective imagination of British literary culture. The cultural imagination was never outside the geopolitical development of empire. Indeed, as will become clear, some of the great works of English literature are inconceivable without imperialism. Referring to imperial "structures of location and geographical reference" within which culture is always-already situated, Said argues that "these structures do not arise from some pre-existing . . . design that the writers then manipulate, but are bound up with the development of Britain's cultural identity, as that identity imagines itself in a geographically conceived world" (*Culture* 52). To argue for the existence of an imperial culture is not to reduce imagination to a reflex of imperialism. On the contrary, imagination is active, as much agent as antagonist. The point is that the development of British culture is inseparable from that historical project and seemingly unending source of wealth, both in goods and knowledge, known as planting abroad. In other words, English (and after 1707 British) culture only came to knowledge of itself through the accumulation and "cultivation" (economically and culturally) of territory inhabited by populations deemed backward, inferior, or worse.

Imperialism is the global extension of and solution to the driving and often dissonant forces of early modern capitalist society forever in search of markets and profit margins. Spurred on by an unstable and ever-evolving ensemble of forces (most of which were unique to England in the seventeenth century) – new agricultural practices, urban expansion, population growth, property rights, a centralized state, and mercantilism – imperialism reproduces and reinvents spaces for capitalism, its managers, soldiers, and labor. More than this however, imperialism produces the naturalization of thinking about space in a certain way.

Culture uses the volatile arena of colonial space to air pressing social issues, and at the same time colonialism *structures* culture with its imaginative and material results. Space undergoing the uneven, fraught, and never complete process of colonization offers up to inspection the most naked forms and forces of the metropolitan society's development, just as it seems to provide amelioration for social problems. It provides a discourse for evaluating and imagining, as well as re-forming society, its progress, success, and ills. A constellation of forces from providentialism to empiricism fuse in the hothouse of colonial space, producing material perfect for the analysis of questions of authority, property, and individual rights. This occurs as English society moves from a late feudal society of deference and obligation to the mercantile and agrarian capitalist order of individual autonomy and the values of the marketplace. Imperial expansion was the very hallmark of progress and was eagerly affirmed by the cultural elite. Rev. Samuel Purchas couched his 1625 collection of colonial and trading narratives in the following terms: "here Purchas and his Pilgrimes minister individuall and sensible materials (as it were with Stones, Brickes and Mortar) to those universall Speculators for their Theoricall structures" (*Hakluytus* 1.xl). My project interrogates this kind of analogy between discourse and building materials, between cultural and concrete spatial productions.

Culture, as Said has argued in *Culture and Imperialism*, has often been the vanguard for empire, preparing the ground, providing the conceptual apparatus and imaginative repertoire, and predisposing the metropolitan pioneers for the tasks and territory that they encounter (9). Although literary culture voiced criticism of imperial designs, empire was often viewed in a progressive light, its magnetism throwing established orthodoxies and institutions into disarray. Spurred on by the potential to form "new" societies from scratch, the literary imagination explored the notion of sovereignty within the auspices of nascent capitalism, working through the different spatial scales ranging from the autonomous individual and the "primitive," to the nation and its colonies. The question of how to parcel out rights and how to control them, who fits the bill and who is to foot the bill is a central theme within the literature I analyze.

As post-colonial studies has shown, the often progressive nature of imperial culture, as it promoted utopian plans (from More to Coleridge), economic and social mobility, individualism, the communication of ideas due to inter-national trade (Lefebvre *Production* 217), and the rationalism of the Enlightenment, presented the colonized peoples with the short, sharpened end of the stick. Radicals at home were often imperialists abroad. The imperial culture which presented new realities and subjectivities, and critiqued the old, was underwritten by several assumptions. England's status as the chosen nation destined to export liberty and commerce was seldom questioned. Nor was the central legitimation for English colonialism seriously challenged. The Roman law or "agriculturist" argument known as *res nullius*, which rendered unimproved and unowned land (by English standards) empty and thus available for colonization (Pagden *Lords* 76–9) was rarely critiqued. That the Spanish bloodily imposed "colonies" while the English acquired "plantations" (though they were capable of slipping into Spanish behavior) became a sort of catechism. Empire was a fact of everyday life or, to use Raymond Williams's evocative phrase, a "structure of feeling." It was a way of life, its definition and future open to debate but not its existence. Not only were the English self-conscious heirs to the classical empires, but Christian providentialism, whether as guiding beacon or as the power behind Britannia's throne, remained the "ideological taproot" of England's national and imperial character (Marshall *Eighteenth Century* 233).[4] Like God, empire was a force akin to the "direction of *nature nurturing*," to appropriate a phrase from Defoe (*Best of Defoe's Review* 126).

At the end of his essay entitled "Empire as a Way of Life" William Appleman Williams states, "I think often these days about the relationship between those two words – imagination and empire – and wonder if they are incompatible" (102). He concludes that they are and exhorts us to imagine our way "out of the imperial idiom" in which both the US and Britain are mired. As I have argued above, imagination can never be exempt from empire because empire is intrinsic to our way of seeing, and in order to combat the imperial idiom, with its race, class, gender, ethnic, and national inflections, we must recognize empire's pervasiveness within our lives. At the same time we must recall from history and try to imagine in the present, along with Williams, a reality that counters the systems, technologies, and logic of imperialism. To this end, my project foregrounds the imperial idiom and imagination; it defamiliarizes or makes strange, as Brecht might put it, empire's presence in the literary and public sphere of the seventeenth- and eighteenth-century transatlantic world.

If at the time of writing *Orientalism* Said could argue that a "serious study of imperialism and culture is off limits" (13), since the late 1970s the topic of empire has become an increasingly popular and fertile area of study.[5] This has prompted Michael Sprinker to speak of "an explosion of writing about colony and empire and their aftermath," and an awareness of the "need to come to terms with imperialism as a phenomenon that continues to dominate, often in occult ways, our understanding of culture both theoretically and empirically" (in De la Campa, Kaplan, and Sprinker *Late Imperial Culture* 7, 1). The "field" of post-colonial and transnational cultural studies has established literature's participation in the service of colonial expansion and domination.[6] Said's magisterial *Culture and Imperialism* is his answer to the academy's blind eye to the legacy of empires past and the lethal presence of imperialism in the present. Reaffirming Said's work, the editors of *Cultural Readings of Imperialism* argue for the significance of "how imperialism generated altered metropolitan modes of apprehending time and space, which impinged on perceptions of the domestic geography, inaugurating an exorbitant lexicon to construe an imperial mission and destiny, and stimulating new tropological ruses to explain, validate and enhance the west's global reterritorializing project" (24). Cultural theorists such as Mary Louise Pratt and Robert Young have forcefully analyzed imperial eyes and desires, and the way the colonial experience is imbricated in the culture of the metropole, whilst Laura Brown's *Ends of Empire*, Moira Ferguson's *Subject to Others*, Felicity Nussbaum's *Torrid Zones* and the

Margo Hendricks and Patricia Parker anthology, *Women, "Race," and Writing in the Early Modern Period* explore the role that women, gender, and sexuality played in imperialism and its ideological make-up. The editors of *Subject and Object in Renaissance Culture* support the "recent tendency to periodize around the concept of the 'Colonial' rather than the [Early] 'Modern'" (de Grazia, Quilligan, and Stallybrass 5). Arguing that the imperial constitution of US culture has been by and large neglected, the editors of *Cultures of United States Imperialism* set as their goal "the multiple histories of continental and overseas expansion, conquest, conflict, and resistance which have shaped the cultures of the US and the cultures of those it has dominated within and beyond its geopolitical boundaries" (Kaplan and Pease 4). Gauri Viswanathan and Simon Gikandi have shown how colonized cultures helped to invent Englishness, its traditions, and dissemination. Thus empire-building, with its constituents of colonial and post-colonial resistance, the inter-infiltrating relationship between different cultures, and the West's capitalist, patriarchal, and racial overdetermination of the body and knowledge, is firmly on the agenda.[7]

Yet this work has focused primarily on the "high" imperialism of the nineteenth century or on colonial discourse.[8] When it does deal with empire, New Historicism, for instance, favors the exploration of labyrinths of power and symbolism, where the real meaning ultimately resides on a psychological level. While a growing number of studies explore how the novel or a particular author and text relate to empire they fail to explore the ways in which metropolitan writers and their equivalents in the colonies engage with the material practices and forms created by the project of building new societies or reforming the old. In this project I go beyond existing studies of imperial relations by demonstrating how the forms and fantasies of early English/British culture are saturated with the geopolitical designs and daring-do of colonialism. I do this by studying how that culture envisions geographical space at home and abroad. Although critics such as Douglas Chambers, Simon Varey, John Bender, and John McVeagh have examined the relationship between literature and space in the seventeenth and eighteenth century, the "First British Empire" up to 1745 has yet to be fully incorporated into an understanding of literary culture's spatial politics.

Aijaz Ahmad has critiqued Said for implying that imperialism is "*mainly* a cultural phenomenon to be opposed by an *alternative discourse*" (*In Theory* 204). Although Ahmad misrepresents Said's goal of showing how culture, hand-in-glove with economic imperatives, helps build empires, he is right to bring to our notice a general over-emphasis on discourse as opposed to a more materialist theoretical approach – the privileging of the cultural subject over its economic sibling. Keeping in mind Marx and Engel's dictum that "The nature of individuals ... depends on the material conditions determining their production" (*German Ideology* 42), I have tried throughout to refer the symbolic (re)formulations of contested territory to the material productions and processes within Britain's first empire. In doing so I assume (as did many an imperial ideologue or city planner) that the way space is regulated and reproduced is central to a hegemonic and expansionist culture. Further, the process in which hegemony is "continually ... renewed, recreated, defended, and modified" as well as "continually resisted, limited, altered, [and] challenged by pressures not at all its own" (Williams *Marxism* 10) is one that often takes place in the spatial realm. As John Urry notes, "some class conflicts are in fact caused by, or are displaced onto, spatial conflicts" (*Consuming Places* 14). Conflicts stemming from colonialism and its ideological ramparts are of course inherently predisposed to be spatial. Hence my attention to geographical information, architecture, rural and urban design, networks of places, groups, and ideology, aesthetic representations of the natural world, and to the narratives organizing space into the categories of the Godly, civilized, and productive as opposed to the temptational, degenerate, and wasteful.

My approach owes a great deal to two general and inter-related areas of theoretical work: feminism's focus on the colonization of the bodies and subjectivities of women and the gendered differentiation of public and private space, as well as the rise of cultural geography, which has also hugely benefited from feminist scholarship (while not always incorporating its major concerns). Derek Gregory points out that even the most exemplary literary theorists writing about empire and geography, like Edward Said, Timothy Mitchell, and Paul Carter, have often given far too little attention to gender or to non-European agency in the face of colonialism (*Geographical Imaginations* 175–7). Contested geographies are synonymous with contested/contesting bodies. Moreover, it is far more unsettling when whoever lurks or wanders outside empire's design – be it native, rebel, defector, or hapless colonist – is female. If, as Barbara Duden says, "the geometrization of space in the seventeenth century [is] expressed in new body disciplines" (*Woman* 32) and "the human body," as Harvey observes, "is a battleground within which and around which the focus of production of spatio-temporality are perpetually at play" (*Justice* 279), the struggle for clear lines of demarcation most often takes place within and over the female body.

Feminist geography, through the work of Doreen Massey, Gillian Rose, and Alison Blunt among others, has complemented, and often critiqued, the better known representatives of cultural geography like Edward Soja, Neil Smith, and David Harvey.9 Combining the insights of this general interdisciplinary scholarship allows us to map "metropolitan nature." I use this phrase to indicate four interdependent spatial relationships: first, it refers to the environment and ideology of countryside or colony that serve both city and imperial centre. Secondly, it refers to how the colonizer and colonized interact as "*inter*-societal systems" along "time-space edges" (Urry *Consuming Places* 16). Thirdly, it invokes how the imperatives of property and capital accumulation produce socio-spatial relations. Finally, I take "metropolitan nature" to involve the processes through which the masculinist project of empire uses the female to signify coveted property as well as the covert danger posed by unruled space. In many of the texts that I analyze women represent the ebb and flow of empire, its lightening conductor and handmaiden, its Britannia as well as its Errour and Sin.

Felicity Nussbaum defines "women of empire" as encompassing "European women in their complicity in the formation of empire *and* in their being scapegoated as the focus of luxury and commercial excess" (*Torrid Zones* 2). And Laura Brown sums up women's status, whether as antithesis of masculinist adventure or pioneer herself in the following terms: "as figures of difference, women are connected with sexual insatiability, class instability, natives, the colonized, and the potentially threatening, unassimilable other" (*Ends of Empire* 19). Writing in the late seventeenth century Ned Ward confirms Nussbaum and Brown's thesis of how interwoven misogyny and imperialism are. He describes London's prostitutes as "Beasts of America"; their disorderly ways and life-threatening, sexual voraciousness are similarly embodied by a devilish "*Negro Woman*, and an *Irish Woman*" that the London Spy discovers at St. Bart's Fair (*London-Spy* 42, 244). Degeneracy, seduction, and chaos are the prime negative coordinates that conflate women, the colonized other, excessive consumption, and the hellish. Indian women are particularly fond of torturing captives, Catholic Irish women pose the greatest danger to the English colonist, whilst the honor of the English woman abroad legitimizes domination but, being more prone to fall for the extravagances of empire, she is also a figure of possible degenerative contamination at home. These issues are specifically explored in chap-

ters two and four. As Mark Wigley points out, referring to the Renaissance spatial theorist Leon Battista Alberti, the female and feminine, like
colonized peoples generally, represent a fluid and disruptive force; a
force that transgresses civilized boundaries and hierarchies ("Untitled"
335). Alberti pits harmony – all things assigned their proper place –
against ornament, mobility, and disengagement from the controlling
socio-spatial regime. Yet even when domesticated or "housed" this
(feminine) excess threatens to "imprison" the patriarchal order and blur
the most personal divisions of spatial power. The female colonist and
native, the potentially emascualting realms of country house and wilderness, and the anxieties over luxury, independence, and exchangeability,
particularly as it impacts on or is exhibited by women, are concerns and
characters populating the narratives from Spenser's cast of women
warriors and wanderers through to the irrepressible female of the
Swiftian imagination.

However gendered, the threat to civility at home or overseas ema-
nates not just from the corrupting wealth and social mobility produced
by the empire, but also from the undisciplined spaces of the laboring
and unemployed poor. As chapter four argues, England itself came to be
known through imperial eyes. If the countryside had always been a
colonial space, the cities, as they mushroomed, were soon represented as
terra incognita and thus in need of tactics learnt abroad. Again Ned Ward
provides ample evidence in his secret surveillance of the capital.
"[E]very two or three Steps," he informs us of the area between
Salisbury Court and Fleet Street, "we met ... *Corrupt Carcases*: for
nothing could be Read but *Devilism* in every Feature. *Theft, Whoredom,
Homicide*, and *Blasphemy*, peep'd out at the very Windows of their *Souls*."
Ward "fanc[ies]" the inhabitants of this wilderness "a Colony of *Hell-
Cats*, planted here by the *Devil*, as a Mischief to Mankind" (*London-Spy*,
156–7). This reverse colonialism is also to be found in the area of
White-Fryars near the Temple, which is mapped as "the very *Theatre of
Sin*" and "*Infernal Territories*" (160). Ward invokes a fundamentally colo-
nial spatiality where the Devil's territory abuts civilization (with its
all-seeing, all-roving imperial private-eyes), tempting the obedient into
"Mischief." This is the world, examined in the following three chapters,
that Spenser, the Puritan colonists, Milton and Rowlandson inhabit,
and Behn problematizes. We might also keep in mind the words of
Defoe's Preface to the first volume of the *Review* in February of 1705:
"My design is plain: to tell you the strength of your enemy that you may
fortify yourselves in due proportion" (*Best of* 4).

If we are to fully understand how imperial and hegemonic culture negotiates or manages, what Terry Eagleton calls, "a rebarbative world which threatened to unmask Britain's own civility," we need to insert this "secret materialist history" (*Heathcliff* 8–9) into "the *long history of space*" (Lefebvre *Production* 116).[10] If, as Henri Lefebvre contends, "ideologies . . . intervene in space in the form of *strategies*" (101–2) then I would like to posit that the authors analyzed in this project are *strategic writers*. That is to say, they are relational to, situated, and invested in the flows of knowledge, power, and opposition that course through the capillaries of Britain's empire. Recognizing the "role of space, as knowledge and action" (Lefebvre 11) means we explore how a work like *Paradise Lost* and its global subject(ivity) is involved in the production of the spatial politics of an imperial world. It is a stratified world, to use Lefebvre's formulation, produced as a "tri-faceted institutional space": it is *global*, where issues of sovereignty predominate; it is *fragmented*, where space is differentiated in order for it to be controlled and negotiated; and it is *hierarchical*, where space is made up of the "lowliest places to the noblest, from the tabooed to the sovereign" (282). If the social sciences and humanities have of late become rife with spatial metaphors and issues of mobility, positionality, hybridity, encounter, translocation, and so forth, this project attempts to go beyond both metaphor and situated identity politics to a more materialist and historical understanding of space and its ideological forces. In other words, I try to present a different spatial history to that of "imperial history," which, in the words of Paul Carter, "reduces space to a stage, that pays attention to events unfolding in time alone" (*Botany Bay* xvi).

Three general, interconnected cultural and historical forces underlie the following chapters and play a significant role in the naturalization of empire: the ideology and economic theory of mercantilism, the Horatian ideal and spatial politics of the country house, and a republicanism stemming from James Harrington and the English Revolution. With his vision of colonizing and collecting the knowledge of a finite world for the glory of God and England, Francis Bacon unites these three forces when he states: "certainly the great multiplication of virtues upon human nature resteth upon societies well ordained and disciplined" (*Essays* 116). The great multiplication of virtues – the expansion of knowledge, trade, material wealth, and Christianity – stemming from the discovery of the New World and the potential for its exploitation had to be worked into the general but unstable outlook dominating the seventeenth and eighteenth centuries known as English mercantilism. In

The Contours of American History William Appleman Williams argues for the hegemonizing force of this *"Weltanschauung"* where agrarian and mercantile capitalism were to be kept in check by traditional religious and social customs. Underwriting the set of ideas and policies making up mercantilism

> was the Biblical injunction to promote the general welfare and common good of God's corporate world and its creatures. The second [theme] was the growing propensity to define God's estate as the civil society in which the individual Christian resided. In this fundamental sense, therefore, the rise of mercantilism is the story of a struggle to retain and adapt an original Christian morality during the dynamic secularization of a religious outlook as an agrarian society was transformed into a life of commerce and industry. (33)

With the state as the none-too-invisible hand assuring some sort of balance between commonweal and capitalism, it became clear that "the best – if not the only – way to get wealth and welfare was to take them away from somebody" (35). Corporate Christian welfare, under the pressures of modernization, the evil of other (Catholic) empires, and the necessities and enthusiasm behind imperialism slid into a zealous internationalism to spread the bounty of England's innate liberty and enlightening trade practices. Drawing upon just this sort of potent brew, that inspired imperialist Philip Sidney legitimizes "Plantation," according to Fulke Greville, as "not like an *Assylum* for fugitives, a *Bellum Piraticum* for *Banditi*, or any such base *Ramas* of people; but as an *Emporium* for the confluence of all Nations that love, or profess any kinde of vertue, or Commerce" (*Life* 118–9). As the fugitives and pirates went about founding the English empire, Sidney's notion of an emporium dispensing universal beneficence carried down to the English Revolution and James Harrington's influential ideas, including the notion that "the buds of empire ... with the blessing of God, may spread the arms of your commonwealth like an holy asylum unto the distressed world" (*Political Works* 323). Conflating the notion of patrician stewardship of the corporate welfare so dear to the country-house ethos with that of the world, Harrington further states that "if the empire of a commonwealth be patronage, to ask whether it be lawful for a commonwealth to aspire unto the empire of the world is to ask whether it be lawful for her to do her duty, or to put the world into a better condition than it was before" (328). This statement unites the essentially progressive and general outlook of Milton, Defoe, and Swift. Republicanism can be traced out of the feudal ideologies of the country-house ethos, which as Virginia

Kenny shows has at its core a concern "for the right use of wealth" (*Country-House Ethos* 211) in the face of rapid social change, and out of mercantilism's combination of patronage and expansion.

Mercantilism, Republicanism and country-house ideology: the focus of all three is the regulation of liberty and property, both landed and mobile, in the interests of those who are virtuous and labor as opposed to those who are unpropertied, idle, and/or insubordinate. If the independent, liberty-loving, and propertied yeoman farmer stood as the backbone against tyranny, then the (idle) poor, who rarely made it into the category "the people," were only an ever-present danger to the social order, a "multitude of People which in England Cheat, Roar, Rob, Hand, Beg, Cant, Pine, and Perish" (quoted in Morgan *American Slavery* 320). Edmund Morgan has shown how the rise of Republicanism coincided with a growing contempt for the poor (381). Along with the other and the colonized, the poor always represented tyrannical forces that, if they were not to sweep away civility, had to be kept in a permanent state of regimentation and active ideological bombardment. The "scumme" and Indians and Africans were effectively excluded from the commonwealth and the "protectorate" of empire since they secured little or nothing for its welfare by their own virtue. Forever deficient in virtue and civility, they must pay the price and labor under their social/racial superiors. As with the dispossessed today under capitalism's commodifying domination of global space, the "scumme" must defer to, if not disappear for, those who, in the words of the Patent for Virginia in 1606, "shall have all the Lands, Woods, Soyle, Grounds, Havens, Ports, Rivers, Mynes, Minerals, Marishes, Waters, Fishings, Commodities and Hereditaments whatsoever" (Purchas *Hakluytus* XVII.401).

In light of the Virginia Company's spectacular failure to deliver anything worth writing home about for twenty years, the patent's wishful vision of total domination needs to be set alongside the realities of England's "empire" and the rather more profitable trade with Europe, the Baltic, and the Far East. As I signaled by beginning with the distinction between "Imperial Britain" and the "British Empire," empire is a problematic term. Indeed, words such as empire, colonialism, space, mercantilism, and Britain are so heavily freighted with variable meanings, and they can loom so large and abstract that historicity suffers.[11] Can one really talk of the English having an empire before the eighteenth century rather than a sprinkling of colonial outposts and privateers who roamed high seas ruled by the Dutch to feed off the Spanish empire? If one argues in the affirmative, aren't we simply looking back through the chauvinist-tinted spectacles of the Victorians? By pursuing empire's beginnings in the period between 1580 and 1745 are we in fact simply chasing a chimera?

An "empire nowhere"[12] interpretation of early modern English history highlights the failures, the lack of territory and economic returns, and the compensatory literature that is full of anxiety masked by a thin layer of bravado. To write of a colonial empire before 1700 would be to privilege the big talk of a small group of dreamers and desperadoes; it would be to privilege the illusionary over the real. However, as Patrick Brantlinger cautions, "the invented fictions of nationalism and imperialism have had ... very 'significant material consequences'" (*Fictions of State* 20). Obviously, I do not subscribe to an "empire nowhere" thesis; it strikes me as both a misreading of what constitutes an empire and a misreading of history, specifically Britain's unique evolution. It *is* all too easy to play fast and loose with these terms, subsuming all under the rubric of a totalizing, ahistorical colonialism without recognizing contradictions. One aim of this project is to show that colonialism is not a bulldozer leveling or shaping everything in its path. Another aim, underlined by the book being framed by Spenser's Ireland and the Jacobite Rebellion, is that imperialism and colonialism begin and end at home.

A complex web of strategy, adaptability, chance, and exchange as well as appropriation developed between the different groups involved. The cultural spaces of indigenous populations were not simply buried into the ground of English rule. A spatial history challenges any tendency toward an undifferentiated colonialism. For example, the reverse side to the exploitation of agricultural "improvement" in England and abroad was a concern about its ecological costs. This complicating of blind colonization (which always had its detractors on ethical grounds) should not prevent us from the larger picture. As Richard Grove admits "nascent environmental anxieties were soon overwhelmed by ... rapacious capitalism, contemporary medical prejudices and the dictates of an imported landscape fashion" (*Green Imperialism* 70). Moreover "conservationist ideology," however it may counter "monolithic theories of ecological imperialism" (7), had more to do with sustainable exploitation than a wholesale critique of what Carolyn Merchant calls a "colonial ecological revolution" that mortally wounded Amerindian socio-environmental practices (*Ecological Revolutions* 2).

Just as literary theorists have traditionally been loathe to place Spenser or Milton, Wordsworth or Austen in an imperial context, there has been opposition to the notion that England was imperialist before the eighteenth century. Writing in 1979 Stephen Saunders Webb argued that generally historians had been reluctant to see Britain as imperial before 1763, preferring to argue that "England's had been a 'commercial and colonial policy'" before that date (*Governors* xvi). Yet can trade, internal colonization, and the piecemeal colonial expansion to the west really be separated from empire? Webb convincingly argues that "from the beginning, English colonization was at least as much military as it was commercial." He shows how the military under the "governors-general" knit together a coherent system under their "imperial influence": "the empire that they organized originated almost two centuries before 1763" (xvi). Their imperial ethos was introduced to Jamestown through the "*Lawes Divine . . .*" (in 1610). Webb equates empire with garrison government imposing upon others the prerogative of metropolitan power and monarchy. The process of conquering began at home: "to the army's domestic police function and its American ambition [which was inspired by witnessing Spain's power during the wars in continental Europe], the reconquest and colonization of Ireland between 1550 and 1622 added agrarian and societal duties" (437). The soldier-farmer settling a plantation under garrison government was exported to the Americas. However small and unprofitable, an outpost like Plymouth – a "village" fortified and patrolled by Captain Standish – was exactly that: an outpost of a military and imperial system bent on the "spread of crusading Christianity and English authority over conquered territories and 'native' people." It is within this system that Webb uncovers the "elements of empire" (438).

To these elements, that indeed constitute an imperium, we can add others. Although England was obsessed with duplicating the Spanish empire it nevertheless was forced to evolve in quite a different fashion through a process of experimentation, interloping, ideological groundbreaking, domestic cohesion, and in competition with the other European powers. This process began in earnest with the Great Fishery and the flood of literature promoting New World colonies. As D. W. Meinig states, "the English had formalized competitive imperialism in [North America] by laying claim to Newfoundland in 1583" (*Atlantic America* 64). The steady colonization of the Atlantic ocean spawned the "long revolution" of England's empire where privateering and outposts, fully backed by the state after 1650, gelled into a well-equipped navy and merchant marine that finally surpassed the Dutch by the last decades of the seventeenth century. As one historian puts it, "the sea war of the 1580s and 1590s helped forge the tools of Empire, developing the ships, men, and capital needed for seaborne expansion" (Appleby in Canny *Origins* 68).

Yet, one might argue that pompous claims, pirates, and precarious outposts pale into insignificance next to the profits of trade. This line of argument somehow disengages commerce from the requirements of capitalism to seek and *control* new markets. It also begs the question of how to define "trade." Michel de Montaigne conflates trade and conquest: "Whoever else has ever rated trade and commerce at such a price? So many cities razed to the ground, so many nations wiped out, so many millions of individuals put to the sword, and the most beautiful and the richest part of the world shattered on behalf of the pearls-and-pepper business! Tradesmen's victories!" ("On coaches": *Essays* 344). Raleigh argued that "whosoever commands the sea, commands the trade; whosoever commands the trade of the world, commands the riches of the world, and consequently the world itself" (Hill *Intellectual Origins* 150). The shift around 1600 to a preoccupation with trade as integral to national power, and therefore the need to be less reliant on other nations, coincided with the forming of the Viriginia Company and other similar ventures. Colonialism was seen as intrinsic to trade and national sovereignty. Exemplifying this view, Matthew Craddock, one of the merchant princes, added colonial trade to his Levant and East India investments.[13] Many a court masque and Lord Mayor's Show celebrated trade through symbols of imperial domination. Seventeenth-century political economists like William Petty, Thomas Mun, Edwyn Sandys, and Josiah Child agreed on two points. First, according to the dictates of mercantilist theory, in order to sell more to strangers than one buys from them and be self-sufficient in a world of finite resources one had to colonize other markets. And second, one should invest in colonialism. Shaftesbury "launched a campaign to consolidate the affairs of commerce with those of the colonies and produce an integrated and balanced system" (Williams *Contours* 54). Locke took it a step further essentially arguing that individual freedom and wealth depended upon imperial expansion. By 1700, Linda Colley informs us that the benefits and "cult" of trade were inextricable "from Britain's ruthless pursuit of colonial markets" (*Forging the Nation* 56). Hence, John Gay repeats Raleigh's dictum in a more succinct fashion: "Be commerce then thy sole design, / Keep that, and all the world is thine" (quoted in Colley

60). As Kathleen Wilson has shown, by 1715 imperialism was coursing through the heart of England's culture and politics.

Colonialism and commerce are then two sides of the same coin. The much heroicized colonial privateers serve as a fitting symbol of this. Commerce was revolutionized or shall we say imperialized by the opportunities presented by the Americas. From the first we should recognize that the British Isles were part of a global economy – a "world-system" as Wallerstein terms it. Thus England's economy and cultural perceptions registered the effects of the Americas in real terms way before Roanoke with the importation of precious metals and the unprecedented scale of pillage (Beaud *History of Capitalism* 23). An estimated one third of Brazilian gold made it into England's economy. Similarly, the slave trade had its impact even when England's participation had been limited to John Hawkins's entrepreneurial skills. As Robin Blackburn puts it "the oxygen required by the European furnace of capitalist accumulation, if it was not to succumb to auto-asphyxiation, was supplied by the slave traffic and the plantation-related trades" (*New World Slavery* 376). Given that the English were late arrivals and only participated on any real scale around 1650, the fact that they were dominant in the slave trade by 1670 shows that a great deal of groundwork had already been laid (Canny *Origins* 440). Although trade was dominated by the established companies – the Merchant Adventurers, the Levant and East India Company – Robert Brenner emphasizes the "fundamental transformation of the English commercial world" wrought by a new breed of merchants willing to take risks in the Americas (*Merchants* 92). The economic system that was evolving out of a stable and unified England was shaped by the burgeoning pressure to open up trade to new merchants, to create a freer market for novel, often exotic commodities. This system fed colonialism and vice versa, or as Marx put it, "the colonial system ripened, like a hot-house, trade and navigation" (*Capital* 1.753).

The period before 1620 and the rise of this "new breed of traders," who connected planters in Virginia with shopkeepers in London (Blackburn *Slavery* 227), does look bleak in terms of colonialism. Little was achieved by 1585 in the New World, though trade with Asia was far from promising either. To see the period of 1580 to 1604 as simply one of incubation (Quinn and Ryan *Sea Empire* 45) is to underestimate the internal colonization of the British Isles by the governors-general and the imperial ethos they represented. Internal colonization led England into a unique position of economic development and national integration centred around London and the market. Progressive agriculture and estate management, which included coal mining, released capital and labor to fund and feed urbanization, industrialization, and overseas expansion (Marshall *Eighteenth Century* 57–9).[14] Moreover, the energy, resources, and lessons drawn from colonizing Ireland and struggling against Spain were instrumental in forming a coherent nation and empire. In the twenty years of peace following 1604 the cloth trade still dominated and the "commercial-imperialistic ventures" (note the terminology) of East India and Levant Companies received the bulk of investments (Quinn and Ryan *Sea Empire* 157). But it was not all a story of the Older trades and new commerce in Asia (159). Carole Shammas sees the period from the turn of the century to the Revolution as a transitional period for colonialism and western trade, where privateering "demonstrated ... what markets were available for sugar, tobacco, and other exotic commodities" (*Consumer* 170). She goes on to underline what she calls the "commercializing of colonization" and shows how vital the imperial work of the last decades of the sixteenth century was to later trade and colonialism: "What the new emphasis on markets did for American colonization was to restore its plausibility and underline its desirability"(170).

Colonization, therefore, was reignited and made viable because rather than inspite of the market. Migrants landed in the Americas and wars were fought over that territory because of consumer products: "Whatever way one looks at it, the demand for tobacco, sugar products, and caffeine drinks – what contemporaries referred to as groceries – has to be a big part of the answer [to migration]" (3). By 1660 London was overtaking Amsterdam as the entrepot of Europe. In 1694 the commercial revolution symbolized by the founding of the Bank of England promised even greater investment in colonialism and colonial trade, as writers like Defoe recognized. Indeed colonialism made this revolution possible; for instance "the operations of the Bank were to be underpinned by an influx of Brazilian gold" (Blackburn *Slavery* 261). As J. M. Blaut concludes, "colonial capital ... new capital" accumulated from the new extra-European markets generated the development of capitalist enterprises (*Colonizer's Model* 199–200). From the sixteenth century on, colonialism fired the socio-economic and imaginary relations of Europe.

The Americas and their colonization, even on empirical terms, were therefore not of little importance before 1700. It is significant that an influential consultant to the Muscovy Company, as well as to African and Far Eastern traders, came out in favor of the west on economic

grounds. The lawyer Richard Hakluyt argued that the American lati-
tudes could provide England with all that was currently supplied by
Europe, the Baltic, and Iberian lands. The new merchants, who bought
Hakluyt's vision, were on a continuum with sixteenth-century privateers
and those who served the land-hungry, lesser nobility, who turned to the
New World and Ireland for the spoils no longer available to them in
Europe. These men, as soldier-colonists, traders, mathematicians, or
artists, balking against monopolies or the conservatism of the status quo,
represented a dynamism that is encouraged and reimagined by literature. Often, as with Spenser, those who captured this spirit in literature
were the same men who claimed territory and resources in the name of
millennial dreams, Baconian science, mercantilist ideology, and the
premier Protestant nation. It is of course true that "New World colonization appealed to a very narrow segment of the Tudor population"
(Shammas *Consumer* 153), but that is really beside the point. The question
is who did it appeal to? This small group was (and remained) the leaders
in science and the arts. Their promotional zeal, their imaginative leaps
of faith, their concrete knowledge had an impact out of all proportion to
their numbers. To focus on the Americas and figures like Walter
Raleigh is not to somehow obscure the economic importance of, for
instance, the Baltic trade. Raleigh and men like him do not serve as an
ideological smoke-screen for England's imperial impotence. Rather,
they represented a fundamental sea-change in English society as capital
accumulation forces a turn to the west. They epitomized the fitful
beginnings of a process whereby the established imperial network was
catapulted across the Atlantic by a revolutionary class and new economic relations.

Finally, even though I have gone to some length to outline economic
developments, this is a study of culture and its representation of (colonial) space. In this book I argue that culture, particularly literary culture,
similarly catapulted back and forth across the Atlantic and processed the
new spatial and social relations. There are some critics, however, whilst
not being interested in defending the sanctity of Great English Literature, nonetheless argue that the connection between literature and
nascent imperial expansion is more a recent figment of academia's
imagination than sound history. In the first volume of *The Oxford History
of the British Empire* David Armitage argues that rather than the Victor-
ian's invention of literature and empire's glorious alliance from
Raleigh's day onward a "counter-orthodoxy" has arisen accepting the
same historically inaccurate thesis but from a critical stance. In Armit-

age's view post-colonial studies has spawned proto-colonial studies which liberally paints early modern history with a myriad of anachronistic notions starring race, gender, sexuality, and even "literature" (Canny *Origins* 101–2). In short, the "mid-Imperial complacenc[y]" of the nineteenth century is simply one side of the coin, the other side features today's "post-Imperial demystifications" (102).

Thus the literature that supposedly interacted with colonialism, Armitage would have us believe, inhabits that same non-place frequented by the "empire nowhere": both are at best of a spectral nature. In short, empire and its literature are of little consequence during the early modern period of English history. Putting aside his commendable desire to warn against ahistorical methodology and foreground an "anti-imperial strain within European humanism" (109), Armitage provides evidence that appears to contradict his general argument, and give space both to imperialism and a literature directly involved with its welfare.[15] He acknowledges that Raleigh, Sidney, Donne, Hobbes, and others were indeed dynamic agents of English expansionism, but that it is "easy to mistake the significance of their involvement." Wishing to sever a direct connection between two imaginary categories called "empire" and "literature," Armitage instead posits the importance of "financial opportunities offered to the gentry and nobility by overseas ventures, of the close connection between arms and letters in Elizabethan culture, and of the role played by humanistically trained secretaries in the expanding opportunity state created by their patrons in the new overseas companies" (102). It is unclear how the roles and opportunities Armitage outlines in anyway contradict the argument that the literature produced by said secretaries and their patrons was informed by the westward push of capital and a cultural–military complex bent on expansion and confident of heaven's backing. Furthermore, Elizabethan culture with its powerful brew of humanism and providentialism was acutely conscious of empires past and present: history *was* a story of empires.

As I have said, it is true that those promoting imperialism were few and through canon formation have perhaps become larger than life. On the other hand, Sidney, Spenser, Donne, Milton, Behn, Defoe, and Swift were not obscure writers. Even if we accept Armitage's contention that the literature (and its colonial context) we study did not command a wide audience, then popular tracts such as John Foxe's *Acts and Monuments* (1554), with its depiction of England as the chosen nation whose destiny it was to combat Catholicism on a global scale, certainly fits the bill. It went through six editions before 1600, and was enlarged in order to keep abreast of England's struggle against the anti-Christ. Conceding that both Spenser and Milton dealt with empire, Armitage attempts to rescue them for a critical humanist tradition, even though Spenser "presented perhaps the most ambitious and hard-line British imperial vision of its time" (115). As we shall see in the following chapters Spenser's "Aristotelian programme of moral re-education" and Milton's "commitment to the political programme of English humanism" (116, 120) do not place them in an anti-imperialist camp. As will become evident in this book, before English Literature beatified some and banished others, literary culture was indeed forged in the enthusiasm and experience of England's relation to empire-building.

You cannot roam far in literary culture produced between 1580 to 1745 without bumping into considerations of empire and, more than likely, its Atlantic venue (McVeagh *All Before Them* 34). In terms of real spatial experiments, England's colonies and fantasies in the Americas were where literature traveled to imagine and find the measure of different societies and individuals; and travel it most surely did, imprinting a vivid geographic empire on its readers' minds. I want to retain the services (the connotations of physical and hegemonic domination) of the word "empire" for two simple reasons. First, because of its ideological significance in English culture, and secondly because imperialism did indeed descend upon the heads of the non-English near and far. This book is about how literature produces geographical space for specific purposes. It is also an attempt to put the empire back into books we love. Often empire is what makes a piece of writing tick or hum with energy. There is a real need to further theorize "empire" past and present, and to not let the post-colonial become the post-imperial. None of this is cut-and-dried; the imperial narrative that I explore is set within ever-changing circumstances, and authors often occupy ambivalent positions. As Braudel warns, "we shall be walking over quicksands indeed" (*Perspecticve* 19).

In chapters two and three I describe the mapping of new and inter-related social systems – the expansionist colonial settlement and the local power of the ascendant gentry centred on the country estate – as they are enshrined in poetry. In chapter two I demonstrate how European imperialism and the development of an English Atlantic world impact upon the colonization of Ireland and its literary representation, specifically in *The Faerie Queene*. Edmund Spenser serves to encapsulate

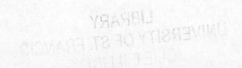

the contradictions and ambiguities of imperial ideology and colonial space. As a colonist advocating settlement (rather than conquest) in order to combat the corrosive cultural system of the Irish, Spenser articulates a staunch, if not fraught, advocacy of the Elizabethan state and subjecthood. At the same time, however, he criticizes inadequate policies to achieve such an end – inadequacies represented by the lack of control the English have over Ireland's cultural and physical landscape. I have, therefore, taken to heart Christopher Hill's suggestion: "Should we not come to terms with our imperial history starting with the history of Anglo-Irish relations?" (*Nation* 4).

Chapter three then traces how technologies of categorization and control – the cartographic project of representing the nation and colonialism – relate to the country-house ethos and its promulgation of a natural authority. I connect the politics of the country estate to the local scale of urban expansion and to the global scale of early settlement in North America, specifically via William Bradford's account of the Plymouth colony. Here I posit the small "world," though vast Atlantic network, of capitalist entrepreneurs and colonial elites, and demonstrate how, for instance, the New England blend of "moral capitalism" and redemptive community are intimately connected – through trade, family, and colonial discourse – to the immoral capitalism and decidedly ungodly communities in the West Indies.[16]

Affirming an interactive transatlantic culture system, where different ideologies "contract" and commodify socio-spatial relations, chapter four is framed by the global homogenizing of space under a growing, self-conscious empire. As space is fragmented and "pulverized," enclosed, and mapped in the interests of capital accumulation, Milton, Behn, and Rowlandson explore the relationship between individual liberty and command over new and dangerous cultural spaces. In this chapter I turn to the notion of the female body as an index and instigator of imperial relations. On a more general level I also explore what it means to be a member of a colonial society and, in the absence of discipline over oneself and space, to suffer dismemberment. To stray into the "wilderness," whether it be in rebellious Ireland, Surinam, or New England is to undergo cultural and physical alienation, if not mutilation and death.

Chapter five focuses on pan-Atlantic interchanges, specifically the way the nation-state tests out "new institutions of state power" in its contact arenas or along its frontier zones (Cronon, Miles, and Gitlin *Open Sky* 16) which are then imported back to Britain. This is what W. J.

T. Mitchell calls a "double movement," wherein empire's "'develop-ment' and exploitation" abroad "is typically accompanied by a renewed interest in the re-presentation of the home landscape, the 'nature' of the imperial center" (*Landscape* 17). Real and imaginary South-Sea adven-tures and the experiences of Britain's continental and Caribbean pos-sessions find their way "home" to Swift's Ireland and Defoe's "Whole Island of Great Britain" as these spatial histories, myths, and formations are processed in *Robinson Crusoe* and *Gulliver's Travels*. In this chapter I pay particular attention to developments in urban planning, estate management, agrarian enclosure, property rights, and colonial design in order to show how these spatial concerns structure the two novels.

In chapter six I look ahead to the crisis of empire leading up to the American Revolution and the Romantic movement. "Britain's" victory at Culloden in 1746 is, I argue, a turning point for the empire. The subjugation of the Highlands heralds a systematizing of imperial forces and policies that provokes revolution yet ultimately is vital to building the Second British Empire. Both the militarism and codification of the natural that London uses in an attempt to regulate the vast proportions and instabilities of the British Empire, especially after the Seven Years War (1755–62), are reproduced in the cultural realm. If the cleansing of the Highlands boosted the machinery of empire, the wasted landscape and the lost world of the clans either directly provide (in the case of Sir Walter Scott) or resemble the mythical and deserted natural worlds favored by the Romantics in the face of industrialism and imperial belligerence. The debate over the nature of empire was settled by lauding empire's natural world. Ironically, it is the colonized landscape (or the colonizer's desired landscape, the "wilderness" and the exotic) that is used as a foil against the imperial state.

The authors I examine are not simply tools of empire, lauding Britannia's sway overseas. They seek, as James Harrington wrote in the seventeenth century, to "put the world into a better condition," to combat misgovernment by arbitrary rulers, and to implement what Burke called "judicious management" of imperial social relations (Eag-leton *Heathcliff* 37). They all exhibit an awareness of writing from within the "fault-lines" of an imperial or colonial society. Put another way, they write from the interstices of empire, never comfortably at "home" yet positioned socially so as to be particularly astute about the machin-ery and metamorphozing nature of empire. Articulating critiques of imperial practice, Spenser and Swift are representatives of a colonial elite caught between rebellious natives and irresponsible metropolitan policies. Occupying tenuous positions in England, Milton, as a regicide, and Defoe, as a dissenter (and debtor), envision a purified version of *imperium britannicum* whilst admiring its boundless, anarchic energy. Behn and Rowlandson vigorously support Royalist/Puritan politics whilst being intensely aware of belonging to two groups whose status vis-à-vis the imperial center is ambiguous. As women and as colonists they are deemed doubly susceptible to corruption. Both interpellated by and interpreting empire, these writers reveal a sense of attempting to find one's place, one's home in social circumstances that are riven with the processes and promulgation of the imperial enterprise.

Exhibiting "the enduring preoccupation with the deleterious consequences of over-extension [of empire]" (Pagden *Lords* 161), the authors attempt to fathom and fix the amorphousness of empire. Like the wealth generated by consumer and luxury items – wealth that seemed to appear out of nowhere and threatened corruption – empire itself was viewed as too intangible, unaccountable, and changable. For the metropolitan writer especially, empire's illusory nature called forth strategies and narratives to "ground" it. More than this, the authors studied here work through what Fredric Jameson terms a "spatial disjunction" between metropolis and colonies, a disjunction that splits the identity of the imperialized subject:

a significant structural segment of the economic system as a whole is now located elsewhere, beyond the metropolis, outside of the daily life and existential experience of the home country, in colonies over the water whose life experience and life world – very different from that of the imperial power – remain unknown and unimaginable for the subjects of the imperial power, whatever social class they may belong to. Such spatial disjunction has as its immediate consequence the inability to grasp the way the system functions as a whole. ("Modernism and Imperialism" 50–1)

Obviously Jameson is referring to a later period but his insight, I think, can be applied as early as Spenser. In all the texts studied there is a desire to survey, know, and grasp the totality of England's territorial expansion and providential future; a desire to (re)locate the self in a new geography. In the face of enormous displacing forces, it is in essence a struggle, voiced by all the authors, to remain a unified subject of history (as determined by England) rather than its object or, worse, become lost between England and *terra nullius*.

While acknowledging the radicalism or revolutionary nature of Milton, Swift, and Behn, I argue that their antipathy to certain aspects of empire-building does not preclude endorsement of imperialism. Their normalization of empire takes place due to a fundamental assumption that the British Isles has a special duty to benevolently replenish and subdue the globe. Similar to what Mary Louise Pratt labels the "anti-conquest" (*Imperial Eyes* 7), often the authors studied here articulate what I call the "anti-empire" – where empire's excesses rather than its existence, or potential as a civilizing force, are attacked. The anti-empire is not a hypocritical move, but born of deep reservations and ambivalent attitudes created by contact with other cultures. It recognizes that colonialism is in a constant state of flux, its ideological and physical parameters continually under construction. It negotiates the impact of having an empire, especially when consumer culture kicks in and social divisions appear to wobble precariously.

The authors with which we are concerned are alive to this (de)generative process; they *see through* colonialism and empire and anxiously look upon the other side and its myriad possibilities. However, their respective social critiques and alternative visions – for example Behn's attack on mercantile capitalism – utilize a discourse and imagination that are deeply indebted to imperialism and its cultural diffusion. In short, the writers work out of an imperial culture whose hegemonic sway – structured as it is by the common sense of spatial politics – they only partially perceive. Hence, an imperial subjectivity based on "the *idea* of having an empire" (Said *Culture* 11) and certain "code[s] of space" (Lefebvre *Production* 269) are the common denominators that these writers share despite their obvious differences. By studying how a text deals with space we will see how the dominant culture is shot through with and constituted by the practises and products of appropriating "foreign" territory. We may also discover how spatial agency, thus historical and geographical integrity, is denied the colonized.

Literature and its dissemination, then, should not be separated from techniques and technologies of surveillance, theatrics, categorization, containment, and division used to transform unruly nature(s) into productive, if not virtuous and civil plots of empire. I have tried to show how nature is more often than not a synonym for the lower orders of society and other societies that differ from the social structures and goals of Britain's elites. The "scumme" and "savages" were all together too natural in that they stood in the way of capital's civilizing thrust to partition, market, and parcel out resources and energies. They therefore had to be put into and taught their place by the culture of their superiors. This essentially violent territorial, geographical process is at the heart of imperial culture. Moreover, this book attempts to show that the "scumme" and "savages" resisted, as well as wilfully interacted with, systems of empire through their own insubordinate conceptions of social production and spatial forms. To recognize these counter-hegemonic forces is to turn upside down the story of the imperialists, and imagine other ways of social interaction. The Catholic Irish poet Geoffrey Keating (ca.1570–ca.1650) lamented after the Flight of the Irish Earls: "long have they stood as a hedge against hostile trash" (quoted in Deane *Irish Literature* 20). Here the (new) English are predators bringing with them their wasteful ways into a productive and organised landscape, which, as an obstacle to the march of civility, must be violently wrenched into a different social order and its imagination's sway.

CHAPTER 2

Thinking territorially: Spenser, Ireland, and the English nation-state

[We] need to understand how a place on the map is also a place in history.

Rich *Blood, Bread, and Poetry* 212

before newe building were erected the olde should have been plucked downe. ffor to think to joyne and patch them both to gether in an equalitie of state is impossible and will never be without daunger of a great downefall such as nowe is hapened. Howe then? should the Irish have ben quite rooted out? That were to bloudie a course: and yet there continuall rebelliouse deedes deserve little better.

Spenser *"A briefe note of Ireland"* (*Works* IX.240)

PLOTTING IRELAND

Geoffrey Keating termed the New English "foreigners," thereby erasing his own foreign status as a member of the Old English who had come to dominate the Gaelic Irish after the Norman invasion. The Old English had undergone the metamorphosis that became, to the ideologues and planners of the Elizabethan phase of conquest, the key to understanding Ireland's unsubjugated state and England's impalement. If Keating "forgets" this metamorphosis, testifying to the hegemonic victory of an Irish cultural system over the first round of English invaders, the New English colonist Edmund Spenser is at pains to recall the workings of this terrifying mutation and set forth strategies to ensure the hegemony of the Elizabethan state and that slowly evolving imaginary thing, the English nation. In other words, Irish rhymers like Keating now faced England's chief rhymer, Spenser. Both contested for the power to "plot" Ireland – define its history and geography. In that "plot" at this time could mean either plan, strategy, or parcels of property, and as a cartographic term obviously could incorporate all of the above, it can also be seen as a particular narrative and ordering of space that seeks to reterritorialize the seemingly incoherent and the often resistant.[1] In *A View of the Present State of Ireland* Spenser has Irenius recall that there have been "diverse good plots" to bring the Irish to heel but, as Eudoxus remarks, the "unsoundness of the . . . plots" (1) has meant that none have had sustained success.

This chapter will explore the ways in which Spenser believes "soundness" can be brought to the project of colonizing Ireland and how the plot of the New English depends upon nothing less than hegemonizing Ireland's entirety into an English design. As Spenser went about his aim, in his policy papers and *The Faerie Queene*, of exposing and ruling out the metamorphozing culture of the Irish, similar projects undertook to pin Ireland down, to enmap it. This prerequisite for any attempt at hegemony – obtaining a workable, accurate knowledge of territory and its value – came up against a resistant population and landscape, full of deception, danger, and unreadable sites and signs. Spenser might well have shared his frustrations with the surveyor Arthur Robins, who wrote that the natives were

such as will do nothing else but misinform and seek to interrupt and hinder the service which also chiefly consisteth in a waste county, the people for the most part discontented with the course to be observed, and therefore dangerous with the adventure of life by reason of the stratagems that may be laid by the evil disposed. (Quoted in Andrews *Plantation Acres* 38–9)

Surveying at this time mainly meant officially delineating and valuing the property of landowners like Spenser, who acquired estates or "seignories" from the confiscated lands belonging to the rebel Earl of Desmond after 1583. Thus plotting the Munster plantation, for instance, also meant obtaining first-hand observation about lands only recently controlled by Irish landowners. As an instrument of colonial occupation such an operation was as vital as it was dangerous.[2] Hence it is no surprise that a continual complaint of the Elizabethan administration was about the lack of accurate, detailed maps of Irish territory. As far as plotting Ireland went, there were too few surveyors and far too much left unclear(ed). Into this large gap in the colonist's knowledge Spenser inserts his stratagems toward turning "waste country" into sound plots serving the political economy of England.

The plots Arthur Robins did make secured him a seignory, "Robin's

Rock," in County Cork. Spenser spent eighteen years trying to secure a profitable estate in Ireland, producing a number of literary plots – texts that are informed by strategies concerning the domination and dangers of colonial space – with which he attempted to ensure and understand his precarious situation. His writings have at their core the proper use of space, written by a poet and colonist intensely aware of geographic relations. The geographic imagination through which Spenser understands his position in Ireland at once serves the project of English/West Country colonialism and shows how very uncertain an undertaking that was. Or as Eudoxus summarizes, underlining Spenser's attention to a spatial orderliness aimed at straightening out the "evil plotted" state of Ireland:

in all this your discourse, ye suppose that the whole ordinance and institution of that realm's government was both at first when it was placed evil plotted, and since through other oversight, run more out of square, to that disorder which it is now come unto, like as two indirect lines, the further they are drawn out, the further they go asunder. (*View* 93)

Since around 1980 Spenser's imperial narrative and colonial plots have received increasing attention. Stephen Greenblatt has called Spenser "our originating and pre-eminent poet of empire" (*Renaissance* 174), Lesley Cormack argues that *The Faerie Queene* is one of the founding texts of English patriotism ("Good Fences" 652), and an increasing volume of work has appeared placing Spenser and *The Faerie Queene*, usually via *View*, in their colonial habitat.[3] Book length studies by Andrew Hadfield and Willy Maley have explored how colonizing Ireland fractured Spenser's perception of himself, fissuring his loyalty to Elizabeth beyond salvage.[4] It is widely agreed that Marx's characterization of Spenser as "Elizabeth's arse-kissing poet" is inaccurate, albeit a healthy approach to revered poets. However, notwithstanding Louis Montrose's anxious claim that the "cultural politics that are currently ascendant within the academic discipline of literary studies call forth condemnations of Spenser for his racist/misogynist/elitist/imperialist biases" (in Margreta de Grazia, Quilligan, and Stallybrass *Subject and Object* 121–2), Spenser's colonial experience is rarely set in the continuum of European imperialism.[5] I do not intend to offer a systematic interrogation of Spenser's works, but rather a survey of how selected pieces fit into the system of north-west European imperialism. My particular emphasis will be on the ideologies and strategies of space with which a colonizing power attempts to represent and maintain itself – secure "plots" for itself.

Spenser recognized the central fact that, as Terry Eagleton puts it, "For any state, the greatest test of its hegemonic powers is posed by its colonial subjects" (*Heathcliff* 28). Spenser attributes the failure in Ireland not just to a lack of resolution and resources forthcoming from London, but also to the lack of a systematic domination of space; space being the material history, geography, and practices within and through which hegemony takes or forms "place." However, Eagleton's resilient "colonial subjects" can also include the restive colonist who occupies an unstable relationship to the cultural space of the colonized as well as to the society he or she is representing. Spenser occupies such an ambiguous, in-between position, reproducing and writing-in-large Elizabethan rule while simultaneously aware of his marginality to state power and his proximity to Irish society.

If, as Irenius informs us about the difficulties of hegemonic rule, "the Irishman ... fears the government no longer then he is within sight or reach" (*View* 133), it is also the case that the colonist can wander out from under the "sight or reach" of the colonial administration. Whilst advocating greater surveillance and domination in *A briefe note of Ireland* (1598) and his better known *A View of the Present State of Ireland* (1596), Spenser explores "this darksome neather world" (*Faerie Queene* II.vii.49) that lies outside England's imperial "sight or reach" and one that the colonist is exposed to, not least within his or her own psyche. This other world, which continually invades the tenuous cultural space of the colonist, is the world of *The Faerie Queene*, where England and Ireland intermingle.

Spenser makes an important distinction, and a decidedly colonial one, between the processes of mingling and degeneration. The latter is the metamorphosis that occurs when English hegemony fails to dominate, structuring the lives of both English and Irish in secured colonial space. The former is this process of structuring, and is part of God's plan for reforming those that are barbarous (*View* 47–8). In short, there has not been enough mingling – the English living amongst the Irish – and Ireland's present problems (perhaps too far gone for "mingling" now) stem from the Irish living "out of sight by themselves" where "all their evil customs are permitted unto them" (6, 9).[6] The fate of the Old English is put down to them having had too much liberty, being "governors for the most part of themselves" (63). The adoption of Irish names leads Eudoxus to again exclaim in amazement, "Is it possible that any should so far grow out of frame that they should in so short space quite forget their country and their own names?" (64). As we shall see Spenser's aim is to reinsert a "frame" of cultural reference and spatial regulation thereby forestalling not only a cultural and spiritual, even racial deformation but also a sexual transformation. The Old English suffer also from being "degendered" (66), a fate Sir Turpine and other unfortunate knights undergo in *The Faerie Queene*.

On the cusp between mingling and degeneration (if not death) it is no wonder that Spenser, especially in his two policy papers, objectifies and subverts the ideologies and techniques so busily constructing the Elizabethan state's "natural order." This might explain why *View* did not appear for thirty-five years after is was penned.[7] His position as a civil servant and colonizer places Spenser in a critical relationship to consensus. The building of colonies begs the question of the general constructedness of social orders. The colonizer's job is a constant process of (re)formulation, with a great deal of adaptability required to hold the "newe building" together. The sovereignty of the humanist's individual is not spared during this process, but, as Spenser warns, becomes malleable, subject to forces other than those serving the Elizabethan state. Spenser examines this complicated social process of expatriation due to the claims of another cultural space, and as such exposes competing and relative social systems, ideologies, and relations of power.

The outcome of such a demystifying "view" of social formation and colonialism, in the words of Cornel West, "is to lay bare the complex ways in which meaning is produced and mobilized for the maintenance of relations of domination" (*Keeping Faith* 89). The epigraph from Spenser above exemplifies the colonial relations of domination: they are ultimately concerned with the re-organization of space and the regulation of social bodies in space in the interests of the colonizer. "The spatialising description of discursive realities," Foucault reminds us, "gives on to the analysis of related effects of power" (*Power/Knowledge* 70–1). The in-house policy papers and *The Faerie Queene* are significant contributions to, as well as creations of, a particular politics of space: that of the production of the early nation-empire. What Spenser shows is that though the nation-state and its imperial domain violently strive for "closure around one dominant cartography of meaning and power" (Pile and Thrift *Mapping the Subject* 5), it is never attainable. The techniques, technologies, and tacticians striving for this closure in late sixteenth-century England are worth reviewing briefly before looking at Spenser in greater detail.

THE "ISLANDISH IMPIRE"

The emergent space-economy and geo-strategic forces in the sixteenth century were revolutionary: new worlds of knowledge, social relations, trade, and violence came into being. As Robert Sack summarizes: "Merchant capitalism led Europe away from a fragmented, cellular, feudal economy and polity to a global economic network based on a handful of national political and economic systems seeking new markets, new transportation routes, and enlarged territorial jurisdictions" (*Human Territoriality* 129). England, on the eve of the seventeenth century, was a society both in tumultuous flux and officially inscribing itself as its state consolidated power. England's commercial and landed elites invested their money, learning and energy into the control of global trading routes and overseas expansion, subscribing to an ideology of adventure.[8] Fuelled by the "progressive" force of Protestant imperialism and conscious of the Spanish and classical empires, culture was bent to the task of forming a nation built upon "ideologies of separateness and empire" (Cormack "Good Fences" 640). Refugees from the continent brought vigor and vision to expansionary projects (Meinig *Atlantic America* 48–51), as England's economy, seeking and responding to new markets, jolted into agrarian and mercantile capitalism. The vast majority of the population experienced unsettling upheavals in their social relations. Mobility, either of an increasingly feared wandering population or in terms of class, was rife (Kriedte *Peasants* 32–60). "All change is perillous" (*Faerie Queene* v.ii.36) Spenser rightly averred. Spenser played a significant role in plotting the relationship of this evolving nation and the attendant uncertainties to its nearest overseas colony, Ireland.

If the nation was imagined as an exclusive "*hortus conclusus*, an enclosed garden walled off from its enemies" (Samuel *National Fictions* III.204), it was simultaneously an "IMPERIAL SHIP" (Dee *General and Rare Memorials* 53) pursuing God's mandate and, as Sir Thomas Smith argued, "the price of the universal market of all the world" (*Discourse* 87). Both images trade on a notion of independence that often stood in for empire (Canny *Origins* 1–2). The participation in an international economy and protecting one's own "market" whilst gaining access to the "commodities of others" (Smith *Discourse* 61)[9] expresses the mercantilist balancing of *laissez-faire* profiteering with the general welfare.[10] Colonialism not only secured one's market, independent access to resources (formerly deriving from one's competitors), and profits, but also appeared to be the perfect panacea for the maintenance of social stability – for hard-pressed nobility as well as the unemployable. Hence Secretary of State Smith was an enthusiastic advocate of Irish colonization. His failed Roman-style venture, led by his son, intended to simply impose his monarch's power centred upon the city of Elizabetha.[11]

In spite of the failures that marked England's forays into colonialism in the late sixteenth century, the groundwork for its later dominance was being laid. As Christopher Hill points out, the quixotic pursuit of the North West Passage produced and galvanized a more progressive section of the elite and their intellectual pursuits.[12] As if mirroring the shift from the fantastical allure of Cathay to the practical adventure in an Atlantic world and the Northeast coast of America, science (mathematics, navigation, geography) and literature flourished under the sun of imperialism. Sir Thomas Gresham, merchant, financier, and builder of the Royal Exchange, epitomized this progressive and imperial spirit. He endowed Gresham College, in opposition to the introverted Oxford and Cambridge, with the explicit purpose of facilitating the exchange of practical knowledge in the interests of trade and colonialism.[13] Leading mathematicians such as Henry Briggs, Thomas Hood, John Dee, and Thomas Harriot were at the heart of imperial ventures. They joined the literati of Sidney, Spenser, and the Leicester circle, city of London merchants like Gresham and Thomas Smith, and the West Country adventurers, Raleigh, Gilbert, and Grenville, in the development of a militant Protestant humanism geared to imperial expansion, a culture inseparable from empire.

What was continually foiling Spenser's notion of a permanent plantation, a secured "plot," was the success of England's maritime conflict with Spain, which culminated in the defeat of the Armada. The "nation" came into being based on maritime power (Andrews *Trade* 248) providentially directed against Catholicism and Spain's imperialism. This particular narrative of national consciousness, its geographical imagination of itself, was expressed through Richard Hakluyt's *Principal Navigations* (1589) and William Camden's *Britannia* (1586), the latter having a major influence on Spenser (Hadfield *Spenser's Irish Experience* 100). The "dilute and pervasive" naval force, with its "creeping invasion" of the Caribbean (Andrews *Trade* 252), and its extremely successful privateering countermanded the other commercial strategy linked to England's agrarian growth: the formation of settlements in its colonial possessions. The formation of new societies abroad was on the board, as Thomas Harriot's *Briefe and True Report* shows, but the privateering that filled the coffers and dreams of both merchant and aristocratic adventurer time and again undermined this development.[14]

Although the colonization of Ireland was a continuation of a general European push west, out of the arenas of the Mediterranean and the Baltic, as well as the *reconquista* of the Iberian peninsular and the colonization by Northern France of its southwest, English imperial ventures differed substantially from the Spanish model. Due both to the power of the Spanish empire and its own historical and geographical circumstances, such as its proximity to the Great Fishery off New Foundland, England focused its energies on seafaring and plunder. Rather than Spain's "formalized system of conquest" the Northwest European countries developed a "flexible system of commerce" (Meinig *Atlantic America* 50). The flexibility of the system fulfilled the needs of profit-hungry merchant companies. It also suited plunder seeking aristocrats. Raleigh specifically rejected any formalized system, commercial or agriculture, for the piety, glory, and honor of colonial adventure beloved of the aristocracy (Pagden *Lords* 67). If the emphasis on plunder and gaining social status and material wealth certainly fit the knightly, courtly ideology Spenser rehearses in *The Faerie Queene* and the heroic code his patrons lived and, like Philip Sidney, died by, I want to suggest that Spenser, due to his class and practical experience, saw the failings of such an unstable predatory scheme. He envisioned a system of permanent plantation that would go beyond the awarding of large estates to loyal English subjects, set adrift in a sea of hostile Irishness, as was the case in the Munster plantation.

If the English usually succumbed to smash-and-grab policies, they were aware of more institutional ways of obtaining wealth from others. Here we might cite the influence of the administrative system of the Spanish evident in their *reconquista* and the conquest of America. In addition, not only were the Huguenots an extremely important resource of experience for the English in terms of colonizing the New World, but they had also been part of the colonization of Southwest France from the thirteenth century on. The Spanish with their rigid code for urban colonial development and the Huguenots with their knowledge of fortified towns, *bastides*, offered blueprints for permanent plantation. Their examples would surely have confirmed Spenser's argument in favour of Roman-style garrison-towns throughout Ireland (*View* 125) to bring about "intermingling" and the "translating of them [the Irish]" into English subjects or at least subjects of England (153). The interdependence of subjectivity upon the proper reproduction of social space echoes the "Great Transformation" that Alvar Nuñez Cabeza de Vaca discovers at the end of his captivity narrative (in 1542). His (Spanish) identity, so unsettled and de-formed by his years with Indians of the southwest of North America, is re-secured through his commitment to the project of building churches for the Indians and a program for exchanging bows for crosses (132–3). As we shall see later, Spenser, like another colonist-poet Sir John Davies, also advocates a great transformation of space in order to maintain one's self against deformities. This is not to dismiss Spenser's attention to the selective use of "the sword" and other "violent means" like induced mass starvation to whip the Irish into line (*View* 95).[15] Rather it is to yoke violence to the production of colonial space.

Referring to the Spanish-American colonial town and its code of urban space set out in *Orders for Discovery and Settlement* (1573), Henri Lefebvre argues that violence, and its monopoly by the state, constitutes a major component of creating and controlling the new forms of social space: "the main point to be noted . . . is the production of a social space by political power – that is, by violence in the service of economic goals. A social space of this kind is generated out of a rationalized and theorized form serving as an instrument for the violation of an existing space" (*Production* 151–2). In order to reverse the loss of profitable land for the Queen (*View* 23) Spenser advocates the division of space into holdings for which the inhabitants will be responsible. "Each new form of state," according to Lefebvre, "each new form of political power, introduces its own particular way of partitioning space, its own particular administrative classification of discourses about space and about things and people in space" (*Production* 281). Citing partitioning and settlement as King Alfred's solution for dealing with outlaws – the latter literally ran out of room in a landscape hierarchically divided into shires, hundreds, "rapes or wapentakes," and "tithings" (*View* 143) – Spenser sees the strict control of space as the key to profits, a loyal populace, and the deterrence or detection of rebels. His attention to the hegemonic details of spatial organization could be taken from the pages of the *Laws of the Indies* where Philip II laid out the basic strategy and subsequent power relations of Spain's colonial settlements. The *Laws* state that the spatial arrangements of the colonizer should be such "so that when the Indians see them they will be filled with wonder and will realize that the Spaniards are settling there permanently and not temporarily. They will consequently fear the Spaniards so much that they will not dare to offend them and will respect them and desire their friendship" (quoted in Reps *Town Planning* 30). Harriot's conclusion that "discreet dealing and governement" and proper settlement will bring the Indians "to honour, obey, feare and love us" (*Briefe and True Report* 29) echoes the *Laws*. Just as Cabeza de Vaca's identity is repatriated by the plan to build churches, the *Laws* state that churches must be spaced out "so that the teaching of religious doctrines may be evenly distributed" (quoted in Girouard *Cities* 235). How culture and people are distributed is what colonialism is all about. The control of resistant native populations is dependent upon strategic space; a spatiality that will naturally – because of its overdetermination – provoke fear and friendship. At the core of this spatial restructuring of the world was the *permanent* violence implied in Philip II's plan for a successful settlement.

What Spenser recognized, along with imperial theorists like John Dee,[16] was that successful imperialism depended upon a systematic strategy, especially given the lures and wiles inherent in colonial space: "O who may not with gifts and words be tempted?" (*Faerie Queene* v.xi.50). The year after Hawkins published the narrative of his third slaving voyage in 1569, Dee set forth in his *Preface to the English Euclid* the scientific means by which to discover, measure, profit by, and command – both in terms of having knowledge about and physical control over – geographical space.[17] In the *Preface* Dee is concerned with the standardization of England's "Situation" in relation to the Other. The application of the sciences, especially navigation and geography, is defined in terms of England's well-being in trade and power. As Cormack summarizes: in the late sixteenth-century "the utility of geography shines through; part of this utility ... involved the development of a definition of things and people English, one that would aid the nation in its imperial and national strivings" ("Good Fences" 641). Hence, the use of "Art Mathematicall" for Dee is its ability to give English merchants and army the edge over their foreign competition. The project of institutionalizing the "Situation" of the British Isles, which also produced such map-making projects as Christopher Saxton's *Atlas* (1579), meant defining everything from "general Rules for exchange of money" to the "measuring and surveying of Land or Woods" (Dee *Preface* 7, 15) in the service of God's "Glory and the Commodity of our Country" (38).

Dee's call in his *General and Rare Memorials pertayning to the Perfecte Arte of Navigation* (1577) for an aggressive enforcement and defence of "this Island Empire" (28) was taken up with gusto as commercialized plunder.[18] This ultimately "produce[d] the new wave of enterprise which broke with the new century upon the East and West Indies, North and South America" (Andrews *Trade* 253). Spenser was not averse to American ambitions and the promotion of Dee's "Islandish Impire" that

Figure 2   Hermetic symbols urge Elizabeth to expand overseas. Frontispiece,
John Dee, *General and Rare, Memorials, Pertaining to the Perfecte Art of Navigation*, 1577

would rule the Atlantic ocean, so that "the Fame, Renown, Estimation, and Love, or Fear, of this British *Microcosmus*, all the whole and Great world over, will speedily be spread, and surely be settled" (Dee *General and Rare Memorials* 10). But the Atlantic appeared to come between Ireland and English settlement. As the capital accumulated via privateering financed the East India Company and the Virginia Company (among others), Spenser struggles to turn London's policy to one of sustained settlement in the microcosm of an untamed and partially unknown Ireland.

SOBER GOVERNMENT AND IRELAND

Thus the system that Dee proposed was channeled into seafaring and not brought to bear on Ireland, a place Spenser might call a "puddle of contagion" (*Faerie Queene* v.xi.32).[19] Therefore Spenser offers his own hegemonizing scheme, combining a knightly ideology of adventure with an adherence to the cold calculations of the merchant's or bourgeois glorification of colonial commerce. What I want to suggest is that Spenser, along with many of the Leicester circle like Sidney, is part of a fundamental shift from the plunder-and-glory school of the feudal nobility to a colonialism of settled commerce and societal hegemony more characteristic of nascent capitalism and its elites. Although separated socially, Spenser as an upwardly mobile scholar/civil-servant[20] and Philip Sidney as financially strapped lesser nobility, both have Ireland in common and take it as their cultural bearing in defining their status and that of England. *The New Arcadia* and *The Faerie Queene* work through, what Michael Nerlich terms, the "courtly–knightly allegory of [the] fairy-tale epic" toward the "justification for colonialist primitive accumulation" (*Ideology of Adventure* 132). The latter is expressed in Sidney's *Discourse on Irish Affairs* (1577) and Spenser's policy papers.[21] In other words, the natural right to conquest is supplemented with the national right of the commercially civilized to rule over those of more barbarous disposition.

Secure settlement and commerce, however, presupposed a sound plotting of Ireland: exercizing control and knowledge of the land. This the English never had. On his 1576 campaign and in not-so-hot pursuit of two sons of the Earl of Clanrickarde, Henry Sidney, with his son probably in tow, acknowledges this fact. Hoping "to make an Ende of the Matter," to bring closure and coherence to his task, Sidney admits failure "by Reason of their often Flitting from Place to Place, in soch secrete Sorte, as I cannot have trewe Intelligence of theim, and where they lurcke" (quoted in Bradshaw, Hadfield, and Maley *Representing Ireland* 77). In other words, the English don't *know* how to view, use, or think their way around Irish space. Indeed, they are without a clue. Just as the Irish "misinform" surveyors, here the English are similarly lacking information and a structure within which to use it. Outside the Pale lies a strategic space within which the English do not own a strategy. The key to winning in contested space is "trewe Intelligence" – a subset of hegemony. Talus, the brutal Iron man of book five of *The Faerie Queene*, combats the blindness of which Henry Sidney complains.

In tackling the project of "how to reforme that ragged common-weale" Spenser offers part of his overall strategy: "that same yron man which could reveale / All hidden crimes, through all that realme he sent, / To search out those, that usd to rob and steale, / Or did rebell gainst lawfull government" (v.xii.26). But this is only half of Spenser's prescription for a recalcitrant and "soch secrete" Ireland.

Philip Sidney articulates just this lack of domination. His eye on the Lord Deputyship of Ireland, Sidney put a common argument at this time to his Queen.

> The second consideration was that lenity were better to be used than severe means. Truly, the general nature of all countries not fully conquered is against it. For until they find the sweetness of due subjection, it is impossible that any gentle means should put out the fresh remembrance of their lost liberty. And that the Irish man is that way as obstinate as any nation with whom no other passion can prevail but fear, besides their story, which plainly paint[s] it out, their manner of life, wherein they choose rather all filthiness than any law, and their own consciences, who best know their own natures, give sufficient proof of. For under the sun there is not a nation which live[s] more tyrannously than they do, one over the other. (*Discourse* II)

Sidney usefully summarizes a number of colonial debates and strategies. Accompanying the colonizer's usual inversion of power relations, whereby the invader is enrolled as both liberator against tyranny and victim of savagery, Sidney weighs up the "leniency" of piecemeal reform against the "severe means" of total military domination. Spenser poses the same question in *brief note* (*Works* 243). But as Sidney surely knew from his father's experience the latter was, even with greater resources, well nigh impossible, not to mention economically nonsensical. Realizing that reactive and alternating policies of the sword and laws were proving useless, Sidney begins to articulate a different plan for Ireland, one that Spenser more fully develops. Implicitly acknowledging a conflict between two different cultural systems, Sidney advocates colonization through the coercion and consensus-building of hegemony: the "story," "manner," "filthiness," tyrannical nature, and structures of remembering as well as the "liberty" of Irish society must be supplanted by fear and "the sweetness of due subjection." Sidney has Astrophel refer to the ongoing reformation of Ulster: "How Ulster likes of that same golden bit/ Wherewith my father once made it half tame" (*Selected Prose and Poetry* 30). As Sidney recognizes the untamed remainder retained their cultural space or the freedom to make their own "story."

The key to this shift from the plunder–purge–possess mentality to one that could envision a total cultural and economic reformulation of existing conditions is the phrase "all filthiness." Most obviously "filthiness" could refer to contagions like those of 1582, when plague, famine, and the Desmond Rebellion devastated Ireland. But it is Spenser, perhaps more than any other colonist, who recognizes the more nefarious component of Irish filthiness: indigenous social structures that are not only resistant but attractive enough to turn English heads. Thus Palmer, after a recently saved man wishes to return to a bestial state, comments in disgust yet also knowingly: "The donghill kind / Delights in filth and foule incontinence" (*Faerie Queene* II.xii.87). Such contagions necessitate the English placing the country under a state of permanent and structured "fear," something similar to the spatial domination Philip II envisioned. And this I would argue is Spenser's great contribution to the ongoing debates about Irish policy: like the maps Saxton was producing, where a government could know and control ownership, mobility, and resistance, Spenser encapsulates a detailed, everyday *integrative* approach to subjugation based on the facts of living cheek-by-jowl with a vibrant and worryingly magnetic Irish culture. Hence his emphasis on spatial regulation as inextricable from the sovereignty of the state and selfhood.

This is not to lose sight of Spenser's later call in *briefe note* to "bring [Ireland] all under," rather than reform parts, with a "greater force" (*Works* 243–4). More specifically: "great force must be the instrument but famine must be the meane for till Ireland be famished it can not be subdued" (244). Such a death-dealing strategy is partly the product of a dispossessed and desperate colonist. Before the Munster rebellion of 1598, Spenser advocated a different policy; he writes of the time when the "province was planted" and it was then that the Irish should have been "framed and fashoned ... [and] disarmed" and "garrisons sett over them" (240). To plant a colony, we may see, is to violently regulate space: to "bring it all under" the geographical and governing eye of the colonizer. Stallybrass sees this suppression and unification in terms of "Protestantism and empire [which] are but two names for the same thing: the restoration of Godly enclosure through the process of one-ing" (in Samuel *National Fictions* 203).

Without denying Spenser's defence of (and probable participation in) the Smerwick massacre and the brutal policies that spawned such atrocities,[22] I want to move to the specifics of his vision of socio-spatial "one-ing" – a process as much concerned with framing and fashioning English colonists as with the Irish, if not more so. Analogous to the

Blatant Beast who roams the terrain of *The Faerie Queene* spewing forth poison, the temptational space of Ireland works its "horrible enchantment" turning the English mind into "the mind of beastly man, / That hath soone forgot" England; so much so "That now he chooseth, with vile difference, / To be a beast, and lacke intelligence" (*Faerie Queene* II.xii.80, 87). Spenser's major concern is with this contamination; it undermines boundaries separating Irish and English cultural spaces, as well as rendering hard-won or not so hard-won estates useless.[23] Consequently he saves his fiercest condemnation for those who have been corrupted, or, to use an apt spatial phrase, gone over to the other side, since they are living examples of the relational instability built into colonial spaces. Such instability, which is part and parcel of a colony evolving at a remove from its metropolitan governors and regardless of "native" interference, demands constant, omnipresent policing. As Nicholas Canny puts it: "this insistence upon the inevitability of decay might suggest that Spenser and his associates were being influenced by a Calvinist pessimism that evil would always prevail over good unless godly people remained constantly vigilant against it" (in Coughlan *Spenser and Ireland* 20). To be constantly vigilant of an expanding colonial space, one must surely dominate that space – take the physical as well as cultural high ground.

In Ireland the apparatus of civility has fallen prey, according to Spenser, to "wastfull luxuree" (*Faerie Queene* II.xii.80) and the "delight of licentious barbarism" (*View* 11). As every humanist knew from the Romans, empire is always at risk from the suffocating embrace of decadence. The "delight" has created English who "are degenerated and grown almost mere Irish, yea and more malicious to the English than the very Irish themselves" (48). There follows the disturbing question that worried many a colonial administrator and ruler worldwide: "is it possible that an Englishman brought up naturally in such sweet civility as England affords could find such liking in that barbarous rudeness that he should forget his own nature and forgo his own nation?" (48). Some of the traitors "have quite shaken off the English names and put on Irish" (64) – essentially trading their national subjecthood for the sensual and licentious "story" of the colonized. As much a product of colonial knowledge as religious belief, Spenser argues that if man, God's finest creation, is not "kept in sober government" corruption is only as far as the next thicket: "But none then it, more fowle and indecent, / Distempered through misrule and passions bace: / It growes a Monster, and incontinent / Doth loose his dignitie and native grace"

(*Faerie Queene* II.ix.1). The loss of "native grace" is not a little feared by (and attractive to) Spenser himself. Indicative of this anxiety is the violence with which "*Guyon* broke downe, with rigour pittilesse" the society of "bestial" pleasures: "Their groves he feld, their gardins did deface, / Their arbers spoyle, their Cabinets suppresse, / Their banket houses burne, their buildings race, / And of the fairest late, now made the fowlest place" (*Faerie Queene* II.xii.83). Recognizing that social systems are fabricated entities and that *controlled* mingling is the key to permanent settlement, Spenser is keenly sensitive to the osmotic way that one can cross from one system to another, from civility to the "bestial" yet beckoning world of the non-English. Fortunately the problems of converting the Irish into productive subjects and returning the wayward Old English nobility to the fold have a precedent which ended in success: the civilizing of England. Displacing contemporary Ireland onto ancient Britain and comparing both to the "mightie empire" of *his* England, Spenser reconstructs a lesson in historical evolution that a colonist can learn from and actively work toward:

> The land, which warlike Britons now possesse,
>   And therein have their mightie empire raysd,
>   In antique times was salvage wildernesse,
>   Unpeopled, unmanured, unprov'd, unpraysd,
>   Ne was it Island then, ne was it paysd
>   Amid the *Ocean* waves, ne was it sought
>   Of marchants farre, for profits therein praysd,
>   But was all desolate, and of some thought
> By sea to have bene from the *Celticke* mayn-land brought.
>
> (*Faerie Queene* II.x.5)

The country was inhabited by a "salvage nation" similar to the Irish: "halfe beastly men" who "like wild beasts lurking in loathsome den" and "fen" "farre in land," the natives lived unsettled, instinctively violent and unproductive lives: "By hunting and by spoiling lived then" (II.x.7). In *View* we learn that the Irish "naturally delight ... in spoil, though it do them no good" (105). Toward the goal of converting the "salvage wildernesse" of Ireland into English property, the Roman precedent of spatial division is particularly useful: "they planted some of their legions in all places convenient, the which they caused the country to maintain, cutting upon every portion of land a reasonable rent ..." (125). In short, Spenser advocates a sustained military-settler occupation to force Ireland into the modern age of English mercantile and agrarian capitalism.

Befitting a property owner amidst the violent vicissitudes of colonial space, Spenser structures *The Faerie Queene* through episodes of negotiating a plainly anarchic geography. Throughout, knights and damsels-in-distress are subject to and attempt the coordination of spatial chaos; a chaos which breeds chase and captivity, loss and savage lusts, disorientation and death. Anarchic geography is of course synonymous with the mobile mayhem of insubordinate groups like the Irish and the lower orders throughout the British Isles. Whenever a group of people are seen on the horizon in the poem, significantly *not* in an urban setting, they inevitably turn out to be trouble. In book five we see the starkest example of Spenser's advocacy of a general social hierarchy, an order more acutely needed in the unstable, amorphous arena of a colony. Hence Talus brutally deals with "the vulgar" who "flocke" about a giant preaching "equality" and that "all the wealth of rich men to the poore will draw." The "lawlesse multitude" hope for "uncontrolled freedome to obtaine" (v.ii.32–v.ii.52). The danger of and answer to such levelling cant is as appropriate for Ireland as England: "that every one doe know their certaine bound" within a natural hierarchy (36, 41). This argument is supplemented by the dispatching of the giant by Talus and, when the people "gan to gather in tumltuous rout, / And mutiny, to stirre up civill faction" (51), the dispersal of the "rascall crew" as if they were "a swarme of flyes." The class politics has a significant spatial, and in Spenser's case colonial, context. Pernicious doctrines are promulgated beyond the "sight and reach" of "justice" and the colonizer. If a certain social order is to be instituted and maintained then even the "holes and bushes" where the rebels hide from Talus, "from his vew" (53), must be stopped up, erased or incorporated into the geography of the colonizer. As long as the Irish "lurketh in the thick woods and straight passages" (*View* 52), the English will have no "peace."

"The first thing," therefore, "must be to send over into that realm such a strong power of men as that shall perforce bring in all that rebellious rout of loose people which either stand out in open arms or in wandering companies do keep the woods spoiling and infesting the good subject" (*View* 96). The enemy is unsettled and unsettling (contagious), and, as Henry Sidney discovered, as elusive, wild, and unremarkable as untamed nature. Therein the Irish have an advantage over "civilized" soldiers: "it is well known that he is a flying enemy, hiding himself in woods and bogs, from whence he will not draw forth but into some strait passage or perilous ford where he knows the army must needs pass, there will he lie in wait, and if he find advantage fit, will dangerously hazard the troubled soldier" (98). Spenser's answer, in part, is to impose a "garrison upon his country." The more civilian spatial order envisioned for Ireland is based on this military principle. Artegall, Talus and sundry other knights "pricking" their way across a terrain full of unpleasant surprises are the "provost marshal[s]" Irenius proposes: "I would wish that there were a provost marshal appointed in every shire which should continually walk through the country with half dozen or half a score horsemen to take up such loose persons as they should find thus wandering" and punish them (or save depending on whose side the person is on) (159–60). This plan, with its invocation of English division of space into "shires," its justices of peace, and Poor Laws, is aimed at demobilizing and rooting out spaces of Irish resistance and culture. The English must erase not only the kernes and galloglass soldiers but also those who promulgate Irish culture – the "bards" (71–5), horseboys, "carrows," and jesters. The latter are "privy to many traitorous practices, and common carriers of news." These carriers are the way "the Irish are fed" (76). Starvation is a double tactic, aimed at food and cultural production.[24]

Unlike many of his contemporaries, Spenser realized how massive an obstacle indigenous cultural practices presented to the colonizer. Emphasizing the clash of cultural spaces, David Beers Quinn has pointed out that Ireland's mainly pastoral society, with its considerable mobility, flexible agricultural practices, and diffuse system of property rights struck the English as backward (*Elizabethans* 8–11). Not only did the Irish eat, drink, farm (although, that they farmed at all was often denied), dress, and speak in a "primitive" manner, they also conceived of space in a way inherently subversive to the Elizabethan state with its standardizing, classifying, and unifying projects. Ireland's social hierarchy was alien enough, especially in terms of primogeniture and the status and mobility of its intellectual class, that the English saw it as a threat to a stable society. Different cultural systems in a constant state of friction (as well as interaction) mirror well the constant state of assault in *The Faerie Queene*. In *View* alternative modes of social organization are death-dealing to Elizabethan society.

Spenser is very specific about the sources of Irish independence. He details the "wilderness" where the colonizer lacks knowledge/power and a native cultural system asserts its hegemony. Thus he attacks "folkemotes" or as he puts it "place[s] for people to meet or talk of anything that concerned any difference between parties and townships" (*View* 77). As if this display of an indigenous form of government was not bad enough, these "great assemblies" on "a Rath or hill" – which echo the meeting of the giant and his "rascal crew" – were inherently sites of opposition to the English: "in these meetings many mischiefs have been both practised and wrought. For to them do commonly resort all the scum of loose people . . . many Englishmen and other good Irish subjects have been villainously murdered" (77). Counter-hegemonic spaces are both culturally and physically "forts" holding out against English occupation, as Spenser indeed acknowledges: "it is very inconvenient that any such [meetings and places] should be allowed, specially in a people so evil minded" (79). Like the adding of O' or Mac to one's surname (155–6) – a mark of ancestral history and community – such signs of Irish culture are "best to be abolished" (79).

"Bollies" are also anathema to Spenser. Again they are a spatial practice that represent complete freedom from English customs, spatiality, and vigilance. The bollies allow the Irish to "live more licentiously than they could in towns" and to formulate opposition or "combinations" against the English government (50). Flying in the face of English attempts to promote tillage and husbandry (158), or rather agricultural production and property rights serving English markets, the Irish live "in herds": they "keep their cattle and . . . live themselves the most part of the year in Bollies, pasturing upon the mountain and waste wild places, and removing still to fresh land as they have depastured" (49). Without bollies (and similar cultural spaces), Spenser reasons, "great enormities" would be reduced and "outlaws or loose people" would starve, i.e. there would be no place for them to take refuge, receive nourishment, and aid. English "enclosures" will initiate reform by clearing away indigenous habitus (Bourdieu); eradicating their "swinsteads" is paramount because Irish culture's own spatiality "is the chiefest cause of his so beastly manner of life and savage conditions" (82–3). In other words, Spenser envisages a laying bare, an exposing of the country to the commanding gaze and structures of the colonizer; only then the thief, "the rebel or open enemy . . . either at home or from abroad shall easily be found when he cometh forth, and also be well encountered withal by a few, in so strait passages and strong enclosures" (83). *The Faerie Queene* offers us numerous examples of this accessing of enemy territory. The destruction of Pollente's bridge, his daughter and castle, the latter two "quite raced," gives both control over the area and disallows "memory thereof to any nation" (v.ii.7–v.ii.28). A site/sight of collective opposition, a cultural rallying point, is wiped from history.

Instead of these rallying points Spenser seeks to have the space of

Ireland produced through what Louis Althusser would call the Ideological State Apparatus: the schoolhouse and church and their "civil conversation," "principles of science," and "discipline" (*View* 158–9): "Therefore I would wish that there were order taken to have them [ruined churches] built in some better form according to the Churches of England, for the outward show, assure yourself, doth greatly draw the rude people to the reverencing and frequenting thereof" (163). Mobility between markets, ports, and towns, essential for economic development and effective colonial law, must be provided. If the market is to flourish and the Irish be forced to "labour ... for their living, and to apply themselves unto honest trades of civility" (124), dangerous spaces must be *disclosed* and dominated (emptied of their threatening content), while vital places and networks, such as towns and highways, need to be *enclosed*: "and first I wish that order were taken for the cutting down and opening of all paces through woods, so that a wide way of the space of a hundred yards might be laid open in every of them for the safety of travellers, which use often in such perilous places to be robbed and sometimes murdered" (164). Particular attention has to be paid by the colonizer to the geographical points that have strategic value (outside the Pale) or are removed from immediate colonization; spaces such as woods, bogs, hills, river crossings, and "blind" routes that discount English army tactics and knowledge are of greatest danger. River crossings and, more importantly, trade are to be regulated by bridges sanctioned by the English and

every bridge [is] to have a gate, and a small gatehouse set thereon, whereof this good will come, that no night stealths, which are commonly driven in byways and by blind fords unused of any but such like, must be conveyed out of one country into another as they use, but that they must pass by those bridges where they may be either haply encountered or easily tracked or not suffered to pass at all by means of those gatehouses thereon. Also that in all straits and narrow passages, as between two bogs or through any deep ford or under any mountain side, there should be some little fortilage or wooden castle set, which should keep and command that strait ... Moreover, that all highways should be fenced and shut up on both sides, leaving only forty foot breadth for passage, so as none should be able to pass but through the highway. (164)

The way that the three evil foresters – "whose Knowledge of those woods, where [they] did dwell" (*Faerie Queene* III.v.14) gives them an edge – are able to ambush Arthur by controlling "his passage through the ford" (17), is a clear case for bridge-building. If the "narrow foord" had had Spenser's "little fortilage" Arthur would have ridden on unmolested. The point for Spenser of this omniscient power, however, is economic improvement and profits. The (English) town guarantees exchange value as well as civilized values. Hence, Spenser argues that "civil manners" are created via secure markets: "nothing doth sooner cause civility in any country than many market towns" (*View* 165). As the colonizer's power base and nodal point in his imperial network, the town must be secure, with "their inhabitants well and strongly entrenched or otherwise fenced, with gates at each side thereof to be shut nightly, like as there is in many places in the English Pale, and all the ways about it to be strongly shut up" (165). More explicitly, the "corporate town'[s]" function is to "both strengthen all the country round about them, which by their means will be the better replenished and enriched, and also be as continual holds for Her Majesty, if the people should revolt and break out again" (165).

Dependency upon the market and thus the value system of the English will, Spenser seems sure, destroy the independence of the Irish. The town will hopefully subdue and convert its environs to its market economy, and "the countrymen will also be the more industrious in tillage and rearing all husbandry commodities, knowing they shall have ready sale for them at those towns" (165). The eventual upshot of socio-economic re-orientation is that "in a short space," Spenser promises, "[Ireland will] yield a plentiful revenue to the crown of England" (167). Ireland should be, in short, subject to the partitioning and homogenizing that distinguishes the capitalist spatial order. Spenser represents, as Lefebvre states in relation to nation formation, "a political power controlling and exploiting the resources of the market or the growth of the productive forces in order to maintain and further its rule" (*Production* 112). Spenser's politico-strategic dialogue represents the attempt to "control ... the unknown and the intractable by mapping it" (Coughlan *Spenser and Ireland* 78). Abstract partitioning and plotting of the land works, in part, to systematize what Spenser knows to be a mutable and miasmal situation. Hence we learn that Ulster "doth contain nine thousand plough lands, every of which ploughlands, containeth six score acres, after the rate of eleven foot to every perch of the said acre ... every of which plough lands I will rate at 46s. 8d. by the year ... (*View* 126–7). Pages and pages of this evaluating of territory, the homogenizing of land under the sign of exchange value, was as important to the city investors and commerce as it was to estate-conscious landowners. In this respect Spenser is fulfilling a similar role to the major figures from the fields of map-making, surveying, cartography, and military architecture who were employed to design and give scientific substance to the Munster plantation of 1587.[25] As Spenser shows, although the English were familiar with Ireland and its geography in comparison to North America, they treated Ireland as though it were *terra nullius* and thus easily and geometrically subdivided into territorial units. The conception of space as *absolute* – as an empty field or container – derives from Euclid's geometry, which John Dee had recently introduced to England for the stated purpose of enhancing imperial power. Hence, Karl S. Bottingheimer describes

> how the Desmond lands were to be divided up into seignories of twelve, ten, eight, six, and four thousand acres, each full seignory to be planted with eighty-six families, forty-two of them copyholders (at one hundred acres each), six freeholders (at three hundred acres each), six farmers (at four hundred each), and thirty-six families as tenants on one thousand five hundred acres of demesne. (*English Money* 11)

Absolute and abstract, the geography of Ireland became so much property value, a quantity more readily dealt with and dealt out by the English.

To fail to "translate" Ireland into proper English can only result in loss of life.[26] If the Irish "Knock" fails to become an English "Mount," then the Irish retain cultural, if not physical, control over this portion of the country. The practice of personalizing, thus anglicizing, one's estate, for instance "Inchiquin Raleigh," represented geography dominated by a new history (MacCarthy-Morrogh *Munster Plantation* 249). In *The Faerie Queene*, after a lengthy survey of English rivers and their characteristics, Spenser seamlessly, befitting the colony's supposed union with England, moves on to Irish rivers. The survey is incomplete however; knowledge is wanting because of Irish barbarity: "And baleful Oure, late stained with English blood:/ With many more, whose names no tongue can tell" (IV.xi.24–IV.xi.44). Earlier Spenser admits that he is unable to give us a full picture of the Irish rivers "nor tell their hidden race, / Nor read the salvage cuntries, thorough which they pace" (40). The failure to dominate the geography of Ireland is particularly galling when distant climes are yielding to Europeans: for instance, "Rich Oranochy, though but knowen late; / And that huge River, which doth beare his name / Of warlike Amazons, which doe possesse the same" (21). If colonization is about acquiring free movement for the colonizer, officially being able to label and map, to produce *the* knowledge about the colonized, then undoubtedly the "simple" ability to name, say, rivers is in an index of the colonizer's success or failure. The act of naming is to give space a specific history: a history that naturalizes the rule of the colonist. Spenser's inability to furnish the reader with all the names of Irish rivers is testament to both England's tenuous occupation of a limited area as well as Ireland's symbolic emptiness. In light of this failure to register a clear plot and England's backwardness in imperial resolution, Spenser rallies the forces: "But this to you, ô Britons, most pertaines, / To whom the right hereof it selfe hath sold; / The which for sparing litle cost or paines, / Loose so immortall glory, and so endlesse gaines" (22).

Ireland's unsettled state is testimony that the English, like the men confronted by "those warlike women," the Amazons, "quaile in conquest" (22) and must correct such *unmanliness* forthwith. Using the Amazons to bolster the masculinist project of colonization, Spenser argues that if the Irish rivers are not to run with English blood but rather *under* English names, Elizabeth must act more princely: man herself in order to man Ireland with her subjects.

THE DEEP SPACE OF IRELAND

As far as the control over space is concerned Spenser presents us with a record of failure; his poem is replete with abduction, degeneration, and alienation. Ireland tended to swallow the English. In light of this "unmanning" Spenser implicitly urges Elizabeth to better man (and manage) Ireland. The consequences of unregulated space is emasculation, where English, Protestant, and patriarchal identity slides into something else. Artegall resists such a demise through his commitment to "virtuous government" (*Faerie Queene* v.viii.3). Virtue and self-will are no longer enough, especially against a threat so opaque (IV.vii.30). That book five begins with history's great emasculations and follows with the violent imposition of patriarchal justice, shows Spenser's fears, in later years, of degeneration. In the topsy-turvy world of Ireland/fairy land gendered spaces are blurred: unattended women exist in the male realm of strategic/"public" space while men run the risk of imprisonment in the female realm of enclosed, domestic/"private" space. Sir Turpine's forced effeminacy, a degendering that parallels the decay of the Old English, flies in the face of a natural order that is both patriarchal (v.v.25) and geopolitical. Ireland is not so much passive female territory to be conquered but an elusive female space that conquers, especially via the dissolution of abstract space that privileges the male and the English. The befrocked Turpine is the result of unbounded space. The wasting away, malleability, and "otherness" that manifests itself in the face of another cultural system calls for more than English nobility and their martial glory. Spenser advocates a fortified subjectivity and social system to combat the entropic forces that lead lusty Englishmen to go native.

In seeking a subjectivity adequate to dangerous though potentially profitable social relations, where ambiguity and marginality work hand in hand, Spenser articulates the friction between the colonial subject and the English nation-state, symbolized by the absolutist authority of Elizabeth. As he makes clear, degeneration comes in the shape of a woman. Radigund, Queen of the Amazons, who is "halfe like a man" (v.vii.36), may or may not be a barb directed at Spenser's prince, but she is one of the many women who represent the endangering and/or corruption of English manhood and purpose. Like Radigund's (and Elizabeth's) androgynous state, the ambiguous or the unfixed is a threat. Sclaunder, who is the antithesis to wholly victimized Amoret, is all fluid hate, living to corrupt the virtuous with her "streames of poyson and of gall" (iv.vii.24). Her fluidity fits into the tradition of defining women as naturally transgressive, over-running proscribed areas or boundaries, and destabilizing patriarchal hierarchies. Amoret's fellow prisoner, Æmylia, is not in fact as innocent as she. She is captured by the "wilde and Salvage man" because she defied her father. Independent of patriarchal authority, she wanders, errs, and pays dearly. In short she acts in an uncivilized way and thus falls prey to savagery. With Hellenore we are taken a stage further: she wanders, is caught by Satyres (iii.x.36), usually a synonym for the Irish, and becomes assimilated into their "lewd / And loathsome life" (51). So much so that she refuses to be rescued by her erstwhile lover, Malbecco. As we shall see with Serena and Florimell, Hellenore is not a rebel but the victim of an "evill guide" (iv.viii.21) – in this case her own judgement. Like English authority, the female's place in colonial space has yet to be established.

The threat to the masculinist project of colonization is linked to spatial mobility. Elizabeth, unlike the chaste and martial Britomart, fails to "move" in a decisive manner, thereby ceding the majority of the land to the Irish. The mobility of the Irish, their spatial irregularities outmanoeuvring and challenging the English, finds its most virulent form in Irish women, who are, in opposition to manhood, like Duessa "falshood" personified. If Irish clothing and hair, mantles and glibs function as tools of resistance, accoutrements analogous to the spaces they inhabit and foster (*View* 50), the behavior and dress of the women only goes to show how barbarous Irish society really is. The archetypal representative of Irish space for Spenser is of course the female Errour; the antithesis of the House of Holiness is "the wandring wood, this *Errour's den*" (*Faerie Queene* i.i.13). Inseparable from an elusive *and* invasive landscape, she induces a wandering from the straight and narrow course of Protestant civility. The sexism that relegates English women in colonial space to pawns and penitents represents Irish women as seditious prostitutes and, at worst, the extreme misogynistic figures of Errour or Duessa. The former is so much vicious waste, "Most lothsom, filthie, foule, and full of vile disdaine" (14), spewing out her (reproductive) poison, while the latter is the embodiment of deceit and treachery, seemingly seductive but when disrobed is a deformed woman "Whose secret filth good manners biddeth not be told" (i.viii.46). True to form Spenser then details at length her unwomanly, unEnglish appearance.

Purveyors of "secret filth," the English endeavored to eradicate, as I have argued above, the vital and wandering culture which unified and strengthened Irish society. Spenser identifies the "*Monashut*," worn by "these wandering women," as not only a "coverlet for [their] lewd exercises" and unseemliness but also a sign of non-domestication or a lack of servitude to English economic practices (*View* 52–3).[27] Wandering women, whether lost or licentious, English or Irish, represent an affront to political, cultural, and economic order. For the English the unnatural and mutable state of Ireland is figured through the chased rather than the chaste female. *Virginia* on the other hand signifies the proper social, specifically gendered, order with its chaste label representing territory that has had its (re)productive capacity secured. Like Florimell, North America is the "bountiest virgin" (iii.v.8), which will help maintain a particular social order. Indicative of how Ireland has yet to secure subordinated space and people, and benefit from manly force, Florimell spends book three either fleeing danger or resisting temptation and illusion in the "thicke forest" or "desert wildernesse" (ii.vii.2). The constant assault upon Florimell's "stedfast chastitie and vertue rare" (iii.v.8) underlines the fact that in colonial space the chaste and chased are one in the absence of a strict regimentation that secures as it subdues. How does the colonizer preserve the one whilst dealing with the latter threat?

Given Ireland's rampant insubordination Florimell is right to be so vigilant: "Long after she from perill was release: / Each shade she saw, and each noyse she did heare, / Did seeme to be the same, which she escapt whyleare" (iii.vii.1). She does not know she has been saved by

Arthur: out alone in the wilderness Florimell is essentially and always chased. This points to a central gendered ideological configuration at the heart of colonial discourse: not only is the female colonist used as a register for the state of the overall enterprise, but her waywardness legitimizes both the subjugation of chastity-chasing natives as well as the superiority of the male colonists who are needed to protect her with their strength and knowledge. Further, for the female colonist to wander in the wilderness is to become less feminine: the threat to chastity stands for the fear of behavior and ways of seeing usually considered manly, the loosening of her bonds to patriarchal society, and an in-between, indefinite status.[28] Aphra Behn will later embody this wayward, unaccountable woman in the face of, as Maureen Quilligan points out, the growing sexual differentiation of labor and supportive role for women in the family (*Milton's Spenser* 177–8). Hellenore stands as a warning against dissolution, a fate or betrayal Una narrowly escapes. If a knight like Guyon is sorely tested in the temptational space of that "uncouth, salvage" Mammon (II.vii.3–II.vii.49), wherein "Disloyall Treason" resides (22), then Florimell or Serena, to cite but two symbols of potential defeat, are even more likely to succumb to the deceptive wilderness. It is clear that women's already tenuous relationship to geography and history is further threatened, if not canceled altogether, by what the male colonist deems anarchic space.

In a formula that foreshadows the "captivity narratives" of early colonial North America, Serena becomes lost and bewildered in an untamed landscape which is both hostile and deceptively safe:

> Through hils and dales, through bushes and through breres
> Long thus she fled, till that at last she thought
> Her selfe now past the perill of her feares.
> Then looking round about, and seeing nought,
> Which doubt of daunger to her offer mought,
> She from her palfrey lighted on the plaine.   (VI.viii.32)

"Seeing nought" in such a landscape tells us that Serena is not an accomplished colonial surveyor; she has not learnt the first colonial lesson, which Spenser labors to express in *View*: an unrecognizable landscape is hostile territory. Vigilance is not enough. Indeed, to be in a foreign landscape and see no sign of danger is to misread that space. An unfamiliar landscape is by definition threatening. It should bear the marks of the erasure of danger. Of course, that Serena fails to see savagery, does not mean savages are not always already watching her.

Afterall, the Other is more often than not indistinguishable from "alien" nature. Even Arthur is, on one episode, "blinded" by space that is "wild": the "woody glade / . . . stopt his further sight," and also obscures his enemies, "shrowded in guilefull shade" (vi.v.17). Like Serena Arthur is vulnerable to "invasion" because he is bereft of colonial vision provided by a colonized landscape. Since Arthur/the English have not enclosed the wood, the enemy "dangerously did round about enclose" (20). When rescue comes, the enemy cannot be pursued because "The covert was so thicke, that did no passage shew" (22).

Serena's episode reveals that savagery is also malleable. Since Calepine's absence Serena has been cared for by a "wylde" or "salvage man." Una is first rescued by a "salvage nation" (1.vi.11) and then by the half savage knight, Satyrane. If on the one hand one's identity is at risk of dissolving (into savagism) or being devoured (by savages), Spenser also allows for beneficial interaction. Afterall, Irish nobles were recognized by Elizabeth. Central to Spenser's conception of the reformed savage is a reorientation toward (English) spatial order; as Bernard Sheehan notes: "Spenser saw the Salvage Man's major defect in his heedlessness, his inability to manage his environment" (*Savagism and Civility* 77), or at least manage the environment for others. Among such environmentally inept peoples are the "monstrous rabblement" that worship Una (*Faerie Queene* 1.vi.7–1.vi.13) and the "brutish kynd" who exhibit "So milde humanity, and perfect gentle mynd" (vi.v.29) that Serena discovers. Spenser thus offers the noble savage, a figure all too willing to obediently serve in his superiors' economic system. The "milde humanity" translates into cheap Irish labor of the sort Spenser illegally employed on his 3000 acres estate (forfeited by the rebel Earl of Desmond) in County Cork.[29] Unfortunately for Serena, she runs across the not so mild type; those who have too much of the "Blatant beast" in them.[30] As she sleeps, out of the wilderness materialize a transatlantic hybrid of bestial Irish and Indians:

> In these wylde deserts, where she now abode,
>   There dwelt a salvage nation, which did live
> Of stealth and spoile, and making nightly rode
> Into their neighbours borders; ne did give
> Them selves to any trade, as for to drive
> The painefull plough, or cattell for to breed,
> Or by adventrous merchandize to thrive;
> But on the labours of poore men to feed,
> And serve their owne necessities with other need.   (vi.viii.35)

Here, the savages are undoubtedly Irish, with the two last lines referring to the practice of coign and livery or "cuttings" and exactions by the chiefs upon the "churls," with the bad neighborliness a reference to the continual incursions, from the colonizer's view, along the "border" of the Pale.[31] Utilizing transatlantic notions of savagery, in the next stanza Spenser invokes cannibalism which displaces Ireland into the wider colonial world. Instead of producing food stuffs and goods, the savages steal, spoil, and seduce in order to eat. Incapable of productivity they are wholly destructive: "Thereto they usde one most accursed order, / To eate the flesh of men, whom they mote fynde, / And straungers to devoure, which on their border / Were brought by errour, or by wreckfull wynde" (36). Unable to control a "wreckfull wynde," the colonizer can however – behind exaggerated tales about cannibalism – wipe out "errour" by redrawing territorial divisions. Before her rescue by Sir Calepine, Serena's situation represents the consequences of porous and neglected borders. Analogous to Queen Elizabeth and her territories, Serena is laid bare and dispossessed (of economic value): the cannibals "spoile her of her jewls deare, / And afterwards of all her rich array" (41). Symbolically raped and devored visually – Spenser's sa-lacious description also serving as a violent referral back to Elizabeth – Serena is on the point of being cannabilized when Sir Calepine dis-patches the "feends": "swarmes of damned soules to hell he sends" (49).[32] The function of this captivity narrative, as for the later North American versions, is fourfold. It acts as a warning against sympathies for or even defections to the Other side. Women's proper socio-spatial place is confirmed. The danger of undominated space and the barbarity of the natives is proven. And therefore, lastly, the colonizer has justifica-tions for the expropriation of land and, if needs be, the extermination of its inhabitants.

The stripping and near devoring of Serena, as well as the author/ reader complicity with, even titillation over her torture, encapsulates the precarious state of the English (and their loyalty) in Ireland. Ultimately "faire Irene," who encompasses both the fluxive, seductive female body and Ireland, like the other female characters is on the brink of unnatu-ralness. This predicament is borne out by the "headlesse Ladie" who first marks Artegall's trail (v.i.13). The English are faced with forces of deformation. Behind the cannibal, who "with his shamefull lust doth first deflowre, / And afterwards ... doth cruelly devoure" (IV.vii.12), is a reference to the deformed state of Ireland's non-productive agricultural and social system. Rather than England's economic system the Irish lay waste with their "ungodly trade" (12). The danger is not limited to Ireland. Spenser intimates that his Queen is directly under threat. This point is established early on in the poem: in book one the "royall virgin" is nearly attacked by a lion who appears from the "thickest wood" and "at her ran greedily, / To have attonce devour'd her tender corse" if, one monarch recognizing another, the lion had not bowed down to his superior (1.iii.5). How long before such obedience from those naturally loyal to the monarch is eroded by Ireland's attrition?

Spenser extends the danger of devoring from the scale of Elizabeth's body[33] (and the bodies of her subjects) to the spatial scale of her outposts in Ireland, i.e. the castle. Alluding to the unstable state of affairs in Ireland, implicitly criticizing Elizabeth for the lack of "sober government," Spenser juxtaposes the possibility of the individual's degeneration in Ireland "through misrule and passions bace" (11.ix.1) with a besieged castle. The castle, significantly set "in a pleasaunt dale" (10), represents the power, history, and wealth of England and its beleaguered state in Ireland. Sir Guyon and the Briton Prince "found the gates fast barred long ere night, / And every loup lockt, as fearing foes despight" (10). The watch tells them that the castle has been under a state of siege for seven years and as good as his word, the surrounding landscape erupts with "deformd" rebels:

> Thus as he spoke, loe with outragious cry
> A thousand villeins round about them swarmd
> Out of the rockes and caves adjoyning nye,
> Vile caytive wretches, ragged, rude, deformd,
> All threatening death, all in straunge manner armd,
> Some with unweldy clubs, some with long speares,
> Some rusty knives, some staves in fire warmd.
> Sterne was their looke, like wild amazed steares,
> Staring with hollow eyes, and stiffe upstanding heares.   (11.ix.13)

Possibly referring to his own, albeit ruined, castle at Kilcolman, County Cork, Spenser depicts a valiant outpost of civility besieged by a geography infested with blood-thirsty assailants. The price paid for Ireland remaining "evil plotted" is that the English have their backs to the wall: "their cruell Captaine / Sought with his raskall rout t'enclose them round, / And overrun to tread them to the ground" (15). Reduced to this enclosure, England's innate and historical superiority underscores the severity of the present situation. Echoing Spenser's advocacy of territorial partitioning carried out by Alfred and the Romans (*View* 125, 143), Guyon and the Prince learn in the library that conquest is based on the domination of space; they read "An auncient booke, hight *Briton moni-ments*, / That of this lands first conquest did divize, / And old division in to Regiments, / Till it reduced was to one mans governments" (II.ix.59). It also appears that "Glorian['s]" ancestors ruled both the East and the West: "The first and eldest, which that scepter swayed, / Was *Elfin*; him all *India* abayd, / And all that now *America* men call" (II.x.72). But for now they are reduced to a tight spot in Ireland. After Guyon and the Prince leave the siege resumes: "So huge and infinite their numbers were, / That all the land they under them did hide" (XI.5). Like locusts or army ants depriving the English of safety and sustenance, the enemy goes through terrifying metamorphoses; half animal, half human embodiments of the seven deadly sins, they are a powerful, almost natural force. Spenser represents these (Irish) beasts as agents of a fluid disorder, issuing from the more hostile regions of the natural world, bent on destroying the static and noble order of the castle: "Like a great water flood, that tombling low / From the high mountaines, threats to over-flow / With suddein fury all the fertile plaine" (18). The assailants' relationship to the land, like that of the Irish, is transient and non-productive.

The Amerindian–Irish conflation comes to the fore when we meet their captain, Maleger, who is clearly of mixed blood:

> And in his hand a bended bow was seene,
> And many arrowes under his right side,
> All deadly daungerous, all cruell keene,
> Headed with flint, and feathers bloudie dide,
> Such as the *Indians* in their quivers hide.   (II.xi.21)

Plugging into the common imperial practice of categorizing in the same taxonomic group Scythians, Tartars, Picts/ancient Britons, and Amerindians, Spenser later likens Maleger to "the *Tartar* by the *Caspian* lake, / When as the *Russian* him in fight does chace" (26). In 1596 Sir Richard Bingham stated that "the wastes [in Ireland] [are] no other than a Tartarian waste" (quoted in Quinn *Elizabethans* 36). In *View* Spenser manages to trace Irishness to Scythian – which in the racial terms of the English colonizer is close to Tartarian – as well as Spanish *and* Moorish roots (they are both Papists and "infidels"). In turn, the Spanish are mentioned in the same breath as Gauls, Africans, and Goths (39). In the poem Sansloy, Corflambo, and Souldan all represent the infidel, who conquer through violation and infection. A similar threat is embodied in Grantorto who represents not just the threat of

Spain and Catholicism, but significantly endangers the sanctity of property. The hybrid, transterritorial Maleger and his troops of natural catastrophe neatly encapsulate the flexibility inherent in the discourse of colonialism and the totalizing global consciousness of imperial nations. England's trials and tribulations in Ireland become, through the channels of an imperialized culture, part of a wider colonial world. Spenser not only describes his poem as "the wilde fruit, which salvage soyl hath bred," but explicitly places its spatial politics within the haphazard world of transatlantic empire-building and England's manifest destiny: "From th'utmost brinke of the *Armericke* shore,/ Unto the margent of the *Molucas*?/ Those Nations farre thy justice soe adore:/ But thire owne people do thy mercy prayse much more" (v.x.3). The gaping disjunction between the ideal empire of Mercilla/Elizabeth and England's ongoing attempts to form stable colonies serving the nation is the subject of Spenser's poetry and the source for his own tenuous, fragmented sense of subjectivity.

IRELAND AND NORTH AMERICA

Spenser wrote with a wider imperial world in mind. Behind the record of failures is a manual of how to carry the providential fight to the world of Catholicism and barbarism. His poem may be the swan song of an obsolete social order by one on the edge of its circles, but within its contours is a new way of occupying colonial space. Spenser articulates the adventure of Faery Land, which speaks as much to bourgeois temperance as the glory-greedy nobility, with all the excitement of contemporary imperial pursuits:

> And dayly how through hardy enterprise,
> Many great Regions are discovered,
> Which to late age were never mentioned.
> Who ever heard of th'Indian *Peru?*
> Or who in ventrous vessell measured
> The *Amazons* huge river now found trew?
> Or fruitfullest *Virginia* who did ever vew?
>
> ((*Faerie Queene* II.) Proem. 2)

But this invocation of new empires, with its recurring questioning, seems to undercut the reality of such places. The reality of "Faerie lond" coupled with "Moones" and "other worldes" calls into question the reality – the settled space rather than a mere name-tag – of Virginia

Figure 3   A knight like Sir Grey De Wilton/Arthegall or figure of degeneration?
Portrait of Captain Thomas Lee, (1594) Marcus Gheeraerts, II

(Proem.3, 4). This would be in keeping with Spenser's view of England's control over its Irish lands, and lack of stable colonies elsewhere. He is all too aware of the illusory and unstable nature of the colonial project. What did not exist yesterday, exists today; what existed yesterday has disappeared today. The settlement of Roanoke, which vanished in 1590, might well have been on Spenser's mind as he worked on the poem's first three books. England's imperial possessions remain in the violent realm of fitful and fanciful possibility, evading real substance due to the lack of resources for secure, hegemonizing settlement. However, the Proem is ultimately concerned with lessons in strategy: in that Elizabeth can see "thine owne realms in lond of Faery," she can learn from this land with its adventures and dangers which are commensurate with "other worldes."

If Ireland's precarious state is represented by the wandering female, if socio-spatial disorientation promotes degeneration regardless of sex, then all is not lost. These problems, via spatial regimentation, can be rectified. Indeed, Spenser offers a good deal of non-lethal interaction between two antagonistic cultural realms (for instance, savages that are not only gentle and adoring but can provide knights of Satyrane's quality) that promises well for England. But Ireland must become a function of thinking rather than an object for conquest. Arthegall, who most likely represents Sir Grey de Wilton, is not so much a Salvage Knight but a knight who thinks, understands, and can perhaps pass as his foe. He can inhabit their space and see through their eyes, and thus is able to deliver justice and reformation (a task he would have completed if not called away [*Faerie Queene* v.xii.27]). In a space that is as lethal and mutable as the metamorphozing Malengin, the key to domination is "To understand that villeins dwelling place" (viii.7). The trick is to turn Malengin's subterranean labyrinth into secure terrain. These principals apply in any colony, and Spenser purposely links Ireland to a wider sphere of colonization, in order to bring some system to the haphazard and often contradictory colonial pursuits of England.

The American arena provides Spenser with greater imaginative and political substance for a more coherent Irish colony, although, as I have already argued, Virginia/El Dorado constantly undermined serious settlement. His referral in the Proem to the Spanish empire invokes the reality of the well-knit web of knowledge shared between imperial groups. Spenser's notion of savagism clearly connects the Irish to the larger project of colonizing the Americas.[34] John White (in partnership with Harriot), Jacques Le Moyne, Theodore de Bry and John Speed followed Lucas de Heere in linking Amerindians and ancient Britons (and the Irish) in the colonizer's natural history (Kupperman *America* 42). The overlapping of colonial spaces and knowledge, for purposes of propaganda and to lend the English colonial policy consistency, could take absurd forms. Indicative of how an imperial imagination shrinks or compresses time and space, Fynes Moryson (in 1617) referred to Ireland as "this famous Island in the Virginian Sea" (*Itinerary* 185). Hakluyt the younger claimed that "the people of America crye oute unto us their nexte neighboures to come and helpe them" (Taylor *Original Writings* 216). Whether good or bad neighbors, the imperial nations in Europe influenced each other with their various experiences and strategies. Most of the adventurers in Ireland were well-traveled and read, and saw themselves as conquistadors – a self-image that fit with their knightly ideology of adventure. Henry Sidney's familiarity with the plans and realities of Spanish colonial settlement may have led "him [to] enlarge the scope of English colonization plans" (Quinn *Elizabethans* 106). The French Huguenots' colonial experience played an essential role in determining English initiatives toward America. Hawkins, Gilbert, Drake, and Raleigh all had direct involvement with Huguenot colonial circles. The Cambridge geographer, Richard Eden, was in Huguenot service in 1562, and introduced into England "a substantial body of information on the new age" via his translations of Spanish colonial accounts. One of Hakluyt's first and most famous publications was an account of French Florida (Meinig *Atlantic America* 28–9).[35]

The extremely tight-knit, mostly West Country gentry who straddled and struggled in Ireland and Virginia, and with whom Spenser identified and found patronage, underline the transatlanticism of any view of colonial undertaking and space. Sir John Davies stated in 1609 that Ulster was "heretofore as unknown to the English here as the most inland part of Virginia as yet unknown to our English colony there" (quoted in Canny *Elizabethan Conquest* 1). That Ireland remained largely alien and lamentably illusory as a coherent part of an English empire, as Spenser would agree, only reinforced its connection to the Virginian venture. Hence, in light of Davies's comment it is no surprise that John White, Harriot's surveyor-artist companion to Virginia (and later governor of Roanoke), probably surveyed Raleigh's Mogeely farm in County Cork.[36] The last we hear of White is as planter in Munster (in 1593 he wrote from Hugh Cuffe's estate in County Cork), and we find Harriot in 1589 settled as one of Raleigh's tenants at Molana Abbey on his Munster estate (Quinn *Elizabethans* 115). To give another example of this interlocking of arenas, strategies, and soldier–settlers, Ralph Lane left off from "mopping-up operations after the Desmond wars in County Kerry, [where] he had also begun to carve himself an estate" (113–4), in order to be the first governor of the Roanoke colony in 1585. Lane returned to Ireland in 1592, as a Knight, and spent the rest of his life in "Irish service." Whether military postings or desperate attempts to garner wealth and status, this sort of toing and froing shrunk the Atlantic into an English world, fusing experiences, myths, and spaces into an accessible, albeit elastic narrative.

Ireland was as much on the way to America as it was on the way back, not to mention en route from the experiences of the Huguenots, the Spanish conquistadors, and Englishmen fighting in European wars. Besieged but real and vast estates in Ireland, possible riches in Virginia, and bases from which to plunder the Spanish treasure fleets make up a triangular spatial network of colonial expeditions, adventurers, impulses and informants. Hakluyt bound all the people, movements, and narratives together as a sort of master-editor and cultural stock exchange; Philip Sidney affirms such a pivotal role: "We are haulf persuaded to enter into the journey of Sir Humphrey Gilbert *very* eagerly whereunto ... M*aster* Hakluit hath served for a very good Trumpet."[37] It is true that, as Michael MacCarthy-Morrogh claims, "The differences between the two places were infinitely greater than the similarities" (*Munster Plantation* 214). This however does not prevent Ireland serving as a "convenient practice area" (214) nor rule out how the two were perceived and culturally assimilated as similar projects and problems. Ancient Britain, Ireland, and North America are associated as part of a continuum by Spenser in the representation of their inhabitants:

> At last by fatall course they driven were
>   Into an Island spatious and brode,
> The furthest North, that did to them appeare:
>   Which after rest they seeking far abrode,
>   Found it the fittest soyle for their abode,
>   Fruitfull of all things fit for living foode,
>   But whole wast, and void of peoples trode,
>   Save an huge nation of the Geaunts broode,
> That fed on living flesh, and druncke mens vitall blood.
>
> (*Faerie Queene* III.ix.49)

Spenser conjures a transterritorial image akin to the giant Indian "weroan" on the map of Virginia inserted into Harriot's report and its enormous reproduction in John Smith's 1612 map of the same. The known and the promised were also represented in almost identical tried-and-tested, generic formulas. In terms just as readily used to describe Virginia, the younger Thomas Smith promotes Ireland in 1571 as "a land that floweth with milk and honey, a fertile soil truly if there be any in Europe, whether it be manured to corn or left to grass. There is timber, stone plaster, and slate commodious for building everywhere abundant, a country full of springs, rivers, and lakes, both small and great, full of excellent fish and fowl" (quoted in Quinn *Elizabethans* 58). Within the user-friendly gloss of most promotional literature, depicting a bountiful and passive nature impatiently waiting to be exploited, with alienated natives somewhere off in the margins of the picture, there is always reference to the geo-strategic situation of both the place and its indigenous peoples. Harriots's text, for instance, is a prime example of this. Young Smith had been advised by his father, Sir Thomas, to plant as if Ireland were "all in warre."[38] The glowing report of resources to be had, cited above, are almost a post-victory scenario: after the Irish have been defeated. Smith's fairly domestic ideal is amplified by Spenser in *View*.[39] He identifies the stakes of the imperial game of which England was becoming a player. He rehearses standard rhetoric of a paradise for the taking, but then enlarges the spatial scale of expropriation and domination to mention the ease of building ships and the many "good ports": "if some princes in the world had them [ships], they would soon hope to be lords of all the seas and ere long of all the world" (18–19). Here Spenser echoes the desires of imperial ideologues and city investors alike who, aided by piracy, were intent on increasing England's share in Europe's world-wide trading system. And we should remind ourselves that England, though seemingly split between its East-bound, London-based mercantile companies and its West Country elites who adventured and plundered in Ireland and the Americas, also represented a single system, intertwined, and interdependent.

It is this interdependence, and how it promotes or hinders old-style plundering and "trafficke," that underwrites Spenser's work. If Ireland obstructed Virginia's development, the reverse was also true. The general lack of convenient plunder opportunities and easy estate-building in Virginia and the proximity to Spanish sea routes and bases not only frustrated attempts to find new markets (especially for woolens) and raw materials (dye stuffs, naval stores, timber), but also fueled the conquesting spirit in Ireland. Within Ireland's already existing social structure lay the "glittering opportunity" (Bottingheimer *English Money* 48) of acquiring thousands of acres of forfeited lands, booty, and social status. *The*

Faerie Queene is perhaps a last link with an order (and loyalty) that Spenser deems unworkable, even if he is dependent upon it. The recurrence of loss and rescue, of alienation and reparation (or repatriation) underlines this. The ideal but ineffectual nobles defending honor and righting wrongs are of the past, whereas Spenser is part of a new social and economic order which consigns the "knightly" to the grave. If the poem is a last tour of feudalism it is also a cover for Spenser's subversive project, even subversions of his loyal identity. His project is pragmatic, city rather than court bound, and capitalist. Along with the Hakluyts he calls for a more systematic colonization, emphasizing the importance of the geographical and state intervention. It is a project as specific and inglorious as town planning, where authority – as shown by the Spanish in America – is extended through spatial forms and institutions (Meinig *Atlantic America* 236). Similar to Spenser's plans for market towns civilizing Ireland in conjunction with military force, in *Inducements to the Liking of the Voyage Intended Towards Virginia* (1585) Hakluyt the elder urges for peaceful planting and "trafficke" with the natives; if needs be, however, "we will proceed with extremitie, conquer, fortifie, and plant in soiles most sweet, most pleasant, most strong, and most fertile, and in the end bring them all in subjection and to civilitie" (Taylor *Original Writings* 330). Spenser's is an American as well as Anglo-Irish vision, and he works to fuse the practicalities of Spanish conquest with England's commercial bent.

Crucially, the different development between Ireland and Virginia was determined by the type of society and resistance that confronted the colonizer. In Ireland the feudal society complemented the colonizer's training and ideology. Virginia, however, with its recently decimated Indian populations and alien social structures, offered no such convenient spatial "handles": the colonists had no support system but for the Indians.[40] Until Puritans, tobacco, sugar, and slaves, and long-term trading interests arrived in the 1630s and 40s, peripheral trading forts, fishing ports, and plunder – ocean-facing projects – almost always won the day rather than sustained settlement. Sizing up the difference, in 1587 Richard Hakluyt wrote "that one hundred men will doe more nowe among the naked and unarmed people in Virginea, then one thousande were able then to doe in Irelande against that armed and warrelike nation" (Taylor *Original Writings* 377). Hakluyt expresses a similar frustration felt by Spenser that even after the deputy-ship of Sir Henry Sidney (1565–78) and Sir Humphrey Gilbert's brutal military campaigns, the Irish were still rebelling and Ireland remained an unproductive and contested space.

The overwhelming similarity between the two areas was the view that whatever resources, human or material, the colonies had were to serve the English nation-state and economy. Further, colonization, besides producing "merchantable commodities," was seen as a method of social engineering, stabilizing society at home. The colonies were generally viewed as perfect receptacles for England's mobile, seditious and/or unemployed people, few of whom wanted or were the slightest bit prepared to be "colonists" and were effectively "transportees." In a *Discourse of Western Planting* (1584),⁴¹ the younger Hakluyt repeated the common wisdom that in order to "deliver our common wealthe from multitudes of loyterers and idle vagabonds," who like their cannibalistic Indian neighbors "are readie to eate upp one another," and who are "either mutinous and seeke alteration of the state" (Taylor *Original Writings* 234), they must be displaced abroad. Safely contained, the poor and the discontented, might then be converted into cheap labor for the colony and the making of English goods. England's surplus people could, the elder Hakluyt envisioned, be exchanged for the surplus resources in America, which would be transformed into commodities by their labor: "since great waste Woods be there ... many of our waste people may be employed in making of Ships" (331). These "supurfluous people" were the most threatening part of the lower orders whose lives and spaces were being rapidly standardized to fit the new economic and spatial order of wage labor. Moreover, English felons, disbanded soldiers, vagrants, unemployed, social undesirables, and common settlers were conceived of in the same way as unreformed Irishmen and resisting Indians. In a letter to Philip Sidney in 1585, Ralph Lane complains about the "wylde men of myne owne nacione" and their general "unrulyness" (quoted in Andrews, Canny, and Hair *Westward Enterprise* 34). The unruly and previously masterless English men and women abroad then posed the threat of identifying with or going over to the "natives," as frequently happened. Perhaps the rabble that the Giant exhorts to rebel in *The Faerie Queene*, another counter-plot, contain disaffected English colonists.

Ultimately this inconstancy threatened the production of commodities and commodious space, or in other words the reproduction of the English nation-empire. As in accounts of North America, classifying resources is a strategy aimed at making space enclosed, intelligible, and attractive to the colonizer and merchant in the face of numerous risks. It is also a way of defining the role of the colonist, commodification being as much about labeling natural resources as about delimiting a person's activities. Spenser's catalogue of trees in book one represents a cognitive mapping of the colonizing subject, a siting/sighting of one's position, and a protective encompassing in the face of *"Errour's den."* Thus, identifying the "sayling Pine" or the "fruitfull Olive" enacts a spatialization to ward off the danger every colonist fears: "They cannot finde that path, which first was showne, / But wander too and fro in wayes unknowne." It is a process of alienation "That makes them doubt, their wits be not their owne" (*Faerie Queene* 1.i.8–1.i.10). In order to ensure one's wits fit the proper identity, a spatialization borne of commodity production is necessary, where natural resources are identified in terms of an English economy. As Robert Sack describes this colonizing practice:

> naming things of value to be taken from the land makes it clear that the land was valuable primarily insofar as it contained resources and commodities... The changing nature of commodities and their fluctuations in value fosters the notion that space and its places at one time can be filled with things of value, and at another time, be void of value; that space is merely a framework in which commodities are located; and that place and events are contingently related. This notion is reinforced by the unencumbered means of owning property, and by the abstract metrical system of describing property and political territory. Together these present space as an abstract system, conceptually emptiable and fillable. (*Human Territoriality* 144)

Just as the increasing monetary value of land is reflected in the importance and techniques of surveying, the economic value of people came to delineate their subjectivity. Colonial space is made up of two interdependent, though often seemingly separable, *strategies*: the space produced through the accumulation of commodities and the space produced through domination and opposition – the arenas of economic production and the battlefield. When Barnaby Rich recorded how the Irish "live like beasts, voide of lawe and all good order" (quoted in Canny *Elizabethan Conquest* 127), he was repeating the central tenet in the colonizer's creed of justifications: when necessary colonial spaces were suddenly unpeopled.[42] This dehumanizing or disappearing of native inhabitants, the dissolution of their culture and spaces of hunting, agriculture and settlement, appears in *The Faerie Queene*, skilfully merging both American Indian and Irish barbarism.

Thus similarities between Virginia and Ireland are based on the abstraction of space: with profits, investment returns, and commerce in mind, Harriot saw the Virginian trees as ship masts just as Henry Sidney invited leading merchants over to Ireland to look into Ulster's timber which was needed for mining in England. Timber was a quick cash-crop and a vital resource, especially for an expanding navy, wherever it was found. In order to extract untapped resources, the cultural spaces of the colonized had to be discounted. That the Indians in Virginia were plainly sedentary, had settlements and fields, and had territorial jurisdictions was either ignored or played down. Similarly, the Irish were also portrayed as nomadic, even though Henry Sidney states that there was tillage, corn, and his campaigns purposely ruined settlements and produce (Canny *Elizabethan Conquest* 13). The oft cited transhumance in Ireland, evidence of nomadism and disorganization, was regular and controlled, with a settled community at its centre. Even in mountainous areas oats were sown. As Canny states "all of this [evidence] suggests that every piece of land that was suitable for tillage was, in fact, under cultivation in Gaelic Ireland, unless the area was particularly open to attack from a neighbouring lord" (14–15). Although the social and spatial systems encountered by the English on both sides of the Atlantic differed, the ideological tools with which dispossession of indigenous inhabitants was justified were extremely malleable and migratory. Religious metaphors and secular arguments of enclosing, pruning, and cultivating the wasted whilst combating and civilizing the traitorous and contagious formed an overarching (and evolving) repertoire of colonial discourse from which all groups involved could draw to serve their interests. Francis Jennings offers the bottom line: "a basic rule was that any given Englishman at any given time formed his views in accordance with his purposes" (*Invasion* 59). A vast and various cultural machinery was rapidly put in place to promulgate the purposes of the English nation-state as it forced its way into a global commercial network.

''STRAGGLING PLOTS''

The problem was, as Spenser saw it, that this network lacked coordination; a coordination that was not forthcoming until the English Revolution placed the state firmly behind empire-building. The absence of a clear "plot" led to the disappearance of the second colony on Roanoke, an erasure similar to the uprising in Ireland that destroyed Spenser's estate and severely threatened the whole English enterprise. This absence of fixing a robust colonial social system allows Ireland, Roanoke, and even the British Isles generally to "wander" like the ones Spenser describes in *The Faerie Queene*:

> For those same Islands, seeming now and than,
> Are not firme lande, nor any certein wonne,
> But straggling plots, which to and fro do ronne,
> In the wide waters: therefore are they hight
> The *wandring Islands*.   (II.vii.11)

Such places present a "most deadly daunger and distressed plight." Though they, like Roanoke and the milk-and-honey version of Ireland, might appear paradisal, "Both faire and fruitfull," they are but a trap for the unwary who "wandreth ever more uncertein and unsure" (12). This "*Whirlpoole of decay*," where mercantile capitalism also founders, merchants losing their "precious merchandize" (19–20), is like the unregimented or non-hegemonized colonial space of Ireland, where Spenser appropriately called his estate Haphazard.

The last three books of *The Faerie Queene* clearly show, in relation to the first three,[43] that by 1596 Spenser was increasingly frustrated with English policy in Ireland and the general lack of sustained and large-scale commitment of direct government. This frustration leads Eudoxus to pose the question: "But if that country of Ireland . . . be so goodly and commodious a soil as you report, I wonder that no course is taken for the turning thereof to good uses, and reducing that savage nation to better government and civility" (*View* 1). Sir John Davies, in his *A Discoverie of the True Causes why Ireland was never entirely Subdued* . . . (1612), argues that the failure to conquer Ireland was primarily a matter of geography: the "first Adventurers . . . were deceived in the choice of the *Fittest places for their plantation*" (160). Whilst the English settled "in the *Plaines and open Countries*," vulnerable to attack, the Irish withdrew "into the *Woods and Mountains*" where "they made their Assemblies and Conspiracies without discovery" (160–1). The description of the threat of counter-hegemonic space is the same as Spenser's, as is the underlying geographical answer to Eudoxus's puzzle.

Spenser, however, is more aware of the subversive, metamorphic nature of the relationship between colonist, colonial space, and colonized. To return to his passionate denunciation of the Old English who have "gone native," part of that passion is an acknowledgement of his own precarious social and psychic position. It was a position adrift of spatial and clear-cut ideological moorings; or as Spenser states his case in "The Teares of the Muses" (1591), he "Is like a ship in midst of tempest left / Withouten helme or Pilot" (*Poetical Works* 141–2). The sense of abandonment, of being without a plot is palpable in much of Spenser's poetry and is only tempered by the latent threat to turn coat. For someone who worked all his life for inclusion and permanence, the sense of exclusion in a country where nothing could be taken for granted must have been particularly painful. His legal wranglings over his estate with Lord Roche[44] and the indignity of a boycott by the Irish against him (MacCarthy-Morrogh *Munster Plantation* 131) only reinforced his exilic mentality. In this light, Serena's loss of way, abduction, and symbolic rape also function as a release of tension for Spenser and as a threat from the colonist to his monarch: if Ireland is not completely subdued, the savages that capture Serena might well be former colonists.[45] In short, "no earthly thing is sure" (*Faerie Queene* II.ix.21). He is torn between his position as a civil servant fiercely loyal to the crown, advocating direct government in Ireland, and being a private colonist whose interests not only coincide with colonial elites restive under the crown's distant rule, but bear similarities to those of the Old English and Irish landowners. Thus, Spenser is caught between, as Simon Shepherd argues, "the colonial apparatus and the patronage apparatus" (*Spenser* 108). Officially and poetically he is at the centre, privately and as a landowner he is at the margins.

Spenser is a willing agent of colonialism, but, as he anxiously recognizes once the door of mutability is open, unless there is strict regulation of who goes in and out, there is no telling the havoc that might be caused – to one's own identity as well as to the state. Although Ireland and the colonizer's position is to be as "given" as the empirical truth of a map, Spenser is radical in his awareness of the uncertainty of mastery over colonial space; he recognizes "the overwhelming power of processes operating beyond the conscious control of individual agents, and . . . the inevitable fragility of taken-for-granted notions of self-hood" (Bondi "Locating Identity Politics" 85). Book two is most overtly about the self-control necessary for empire-building (Quilligan *Milton's Spenser* 67). Fearing the dangers of an unfixed social, psychic, and spatial order, he advocates, in compensation, total military occupation and a policy of starving the Irish into submission. *The Faerie Queene* may have functioned as a means of reigning himself in (through aesthetic "release"), since the colony could be a "space of transgression, of the seeping away of 'Englishness,' rather than a site of national enclosure" (Stallybrass in Samuel *National Fictions* 211). National enclosures, whether on land or sea, are never as sovereign, secure, or solid as their myths would have it.

Whether in transgression or, more likely, as a repressive force, national enclosures bleed copiously into other spaces and continually receive transfusions that alter their social and spatial hierarchies.

In the final canto of *The Faerie Queene* Spenser again uses the metaphor of a ship for his Irish project. In this instance, he retains a plot, halting though it may be, of loyalty to the crown and his English identity. Appropriately for the poet laureate of a nation whose imperialism rested on sea-power, Spenser likens himself to a ship "Whose course is often stayed, yet never is astray" (vi.xii.1). It is also an ironic self-identification given that England's focus on seafaring undermined a commitment to settlement and tested Spenser's loyalty to his prince. Spenser concludes with the failure to hegemonize Ireland. The "Blatant Beast" is still at large:

> So now he raungeth through the world againe,
> And rageth sore in each degree and state;
> Ne any is, that may him noe restraine,
> He growen is so great and strong of late,
> . . . .
> Ne spareth he the gentle Poets rime,
> But rends without regard of person or of time.   (vi.xii.40)

The symbol of the metastasizing nature of colonial space and its subjects as well as the plotlessness that threatens the Queen, the "Blatant Beast" must, before all else is secure, be ruled out and mapped in. The colonized must be re-placed and thus re-formed into productive subjects: "it is in vain to speak of planting of laws and plotting of policies," Spenser politely admonishes his readers, "till they be altogether subdued" (*View* 12). The last months of his life were spent fleeing from Tyrone's rebellion, first to Cork, then London. Ireland returned to a place where "Wolves and Thieves abound / Which too-too true that lands in-dwellers since have found" (*Faerie Queene* vii.vi.55). The sound "plot" Spenser sought, an estate within the hegemony of the English state, failed to materialize. Geographically the English failed: Arlo Hill, the "high ground" from which Spenser was to survey his property, had returned to being a "rath." It is also significant that Ireland is returned to a wasteland – after Faunus is caught spying on Diana – through a transgression of (gendered) space.

Spenser is one of the first in a long line of colonial "surveyors." The "gentle Poets rime" (vi.xii.40), like those of the persecuted Irish poets, had everything to do with strategies of power. Spenser *was* a "penpusher in the service of imperialism" (Shepherd *Spenser* 4), but this by no means rules out his antagonistic relationship to Elizabeth and an attraction to the allures of Irish society. In short, Spenser was also a threat to empire. If "Ireland is the place where Elizabeth/Diana is seen naked, exposed like Serena before the salvage nation, the mysterious power of her regal body rendered helpless" (Hadfield *Spenser's Irish Experience* 195), the reality of English authority uncovered, Spenser is conscious both of being in a position to take advantage of this weakness as well as his own vulnerability as Elizabeth's servant.

Spenser incorporates this conflicted relationship along with the "empirical eye" of his *View* of Ireland into *The Faerie Queene*.[46] Anne Fogarty has rightly argued that the two texts "should be seen in a continuum, as mutually defining intertexts … [which] are vitally concerned with constructing and working out the internal contradictions of a discourse of colonialism" (Coughlan *Spenser and Ireland* 77). More specifically Spenser attempts an adequate cultural response to the Irish problem, seeking to fuse the pastoral world of courtly ideology, its formulaic myths, monsters, and knights geared to serving Elizabeth's power, with a colonial world dominated by the pragmatics of mercantile capitalist ideology, its real estate deals, urban development, and industry serving colonial elites. Thus Spenser's writing is the crucible in which are played out the tensions between mother country and colony, court and city, neo-feudalism and nascent capitalism, conquesting and commerce as they are represented in Ireland.

In seeking to secure a "plot" of Ireland, to depict a narrative of empire commensurate to the task of geographically imagining an anglicized Ireland, Spenser captures the ground rules of capitalism's ordering of space as they are imposed. The production of capitalist space is most visible in the volatile context of the colony. Spenser, therefore, articulates a new conception of space, its relativity and relationality, and its unremitting violence. If, as Lisa Jardine has stated, "Spenser consistently takes his cultural bearing from Ireland" (in Bradshaw, Hadfield, and Maley *Representing Ireland* 70), then *The Faerie Queene* and Spenser's importance lies in exhibiting an imagination engrossed with and riven by the everyday strategies of colonialism.

CHAPTER 3

Contracting geography from the country house to the colony

So good a Country, so bad people.   Purchas *Hakluytus* ıxx.231

Colonists were moved to transform the soil by a property system that taught them to treat land as capital... The existence of commerce, however marginal, led them to see certain things on the land as merchantable commodities.

Cronon *Changes in the Land* 77

Europe undertook the leadership of the world with ardor, cynicism, and violence. Look at how the shadow of her palaces stretches out ever further!

Fanon *Wretched* 311

GARRISONS OF GOOD ORDER

There is little "contented bliss" (*Poetical Works* 311) in Spenser's life – the kind of bliss eulogized in the country-house poem for example – but he does offer moments, or places, in his poetry where "bliss" does interrupt, as he puts it in *Colin Clouts Come Home Againe*, "this barrein soyle, / Where cold and care and penury do dwell" (655–6). Thomas Butler's unique and "brave mansione" set amidst Ireland's "barbarism" is one such place (*Faerie Queene* Dedicatory Sonnet: To the Right Honourable the Earle of Ormond and Ossory). The country house plays a key role in Spenser's spatial and political imaginary. In keeping with the Elizabethan belief that architecture reflected the social order, Spenser offers us two views of the country house (though they are obviously more fortified than their cousins in England) which indicate the state of Ireland and display the problems of taming the untamed. In doing so he exemplifies not only traditional concerns of the country-house poem –

its overblown "bliss" containing traces of anxiety about off-stage threats – but also the colonialism at the core of the country house and its ethos.

Spenser's treatment of the country house differs somewhat from that of Philip Sidney. Symbolic of a place between England and Ireland, perhaps the Pale, in *The New Arcadia* (1590) Sidney contrasts Kalander's Arcadian estate with the "wasted soil" (*Prose and Poetry* 256) and strife of Laconia. Kalander's estate embodies many of the standard country house tropes that mark it as a moral economy: hospitality, thrift, lack of artifice, and so forth (257).[1] The utility of field and orchard and the aesthetics of the garden form a seamless unity of prospect and purpose, the sum of which is "making order in confusion" (261). The lodge of Basilius might be criticized as too artificial and solitary, but it is to be noted that "it gives the eye lordship over a good large circuit ... of the country" which has been made into "a pleasant picture of nature" (341). The image of proprietorial domination without artifice, fertile order juxtaposed to wilderness, and the implicit justification for the former to "rejuvenate" the latter is missing in *The Faerie Queene*.

The country-house genre is fairly self-conscious about the relative absence of the ideals it promotes, ideals completely out of place in war-torn Ireland. However, the poetry's formula tells us a great deal about actual socio-spatial relations, desires, and anxieties as they developed under nascent capitalism and colonialism. In a similar fashion to Jonson in "To Penshurst," Spenser criticizes the country house resplendent in its artifice and usually owned by the newly risen gentry whose wealth derived from trade and the state. Evoking the Prodigy Houses of Longleat, Wollaton Hall, or Worksop Manor, Spenser describes the House of Pride, with its "goodly galleries farre over laid, / Full of faire windowes," as "A stately Pallace build of squared bricke, / which cunningly was without morter laid" (*Faerie Queene* i.iv.4). Just as Duessa embodies artifice as corrosive deceit, the palace is built on a "sandie hill" and "all the hinder parts, that few could spie, / Were ruinous and old, but painted cunningly" (5). Spenser underscores the inherent instability of the (gendered) palace by its promiscuity; "Great troupes of people" enter in and out (3). Spenser links this social anarchy to the openness, "commerce," and conspicuous wealth of the palace. Its boastful situation, based on the tricks of the trade, engenders a dissolution of socio-spatial hierarchy.

Rather than a structure that reflects honesty, utility, a moral economy, and "a natural order, with metaphysical sanctions" (Williams *Country and City* 29), the House of Pride, like the proud piles criticized in country-house poems, deals in dissembling and waste. Taken a step further, and placed in the context of a burgeoning English nation-state, artifice, deceit, and inhospitality converge into an attack on the foreign and the disloyal. The inhospitable stands for both irresponsible gentry and the rebellious areas/peoples of the kingdom. As false nobility and demonic rebel, Duessa fits the bill, and it comes as no surprise that she "from the world that her discovered wide, / Fled to the wastfull wildernesse apace" (*Faerie Queene* i.viii.50). Predictably the House of Temperance is "all so faire, and sensible with all" (ii.ix.21). Resembling Kalander's house, and perhaps Penshurst itself (McClung *Country House* 52), this "goodly castle" is solidly of Britain: "Of hewen stone the porch was fairely wrought, / Stone more of valew, and more smooth and fine, / Then Jet or Marble far from Ireland brought" (*Faerie Queene* ii.ix.24). The value(s) of the castle are manifested in its role as repository of British history; the structure is a microcosm of Britain itself. The flaw in its design rests not within its construction or materials, but in its isolation and its inability to spread the history it embodies.

Spenser's fairy/Irish Penshurst lacks the hegemonic dominance that would link houses of power in the country to urban centers and the forces of the state. Security might be first class, thereby reducing internal friction – in contrast, the House of Pride employed a porter "who entrance non denide" (i.iv.6) – but the House of Temperance is doomed because it does not control the countryside around it. It has been under siege for seven years. Spenser is, however, clear about the remedy: enclose or be enclosed by "villeins." The answer is spelt out in Temperance's library: peace is only achieved, "straggling plots" (ii.xii.11) only become a prosperous landscape when space is regimented under an iron hand of governance (ii.ix.59). Arcadia is delightfully disciplined and prosperous so long as it can keep the helots and their "contagion" under control (Sidney *Prose and Poetry* 286). This is as much a colonial story as it is a domestic one.

Perhaps Raleigh best sums up the ideology and spatial *practice* of the country house when he observes that "[the gentry] spread over all, are the garrisons of good order throughout the realm" (quoted in Hill *Reformation* 30). Such household garrisons reflected the martial ethos of the real garrisons that controlled the country and its colonial possessions (Webb *Governors* 4). The implicit network and systematizing nature of these garrisons was part of a wider division of space – whether through urban planning, enclosure or "planting" overseas – under nascent capitalism. It was part and parcel of the consolidation of a fully functioning empire – from the Puritan's "citty on a hill" to the West Indian plantations – and the tremendous social upheavals throughout the British Isles.

THE "GREAT REBUILDING"

I begin with Spenser and Sidney's country houses because I wish to argue in this chapter that the country house should not be seen simply as the symbol of quiet, if tense, power in pastoral England. On the contrary, this relatively new "country" institution is inseparable from colonialism as well as its supposed antithesis, the "city." I hope to show that the rationale for and experiences of colonization underlie the development both of the country house as an ideological signifier and spatial form as well as that of urban planning. Such interdependence is reflected in the cartographic representation of the nation at this time. What immediately catches the eye when looking at John Speed's county maps, published in 1612, is his innovation of including town-plans alongside the coat of arms of important gentry. On the maps themselves deer parks (thus estates) are one of the most prominent features. Speed was an historian and like Spenser articulates a geography that privileges the history of natural, propertied, and *national* rulers. Speed's work issued from the rapid development in technologies of surveying between 1560 and 1600, a development that coincided with England's first wave of colonial pursuits, including the establishment of its own unity. And it is Speed who provided the first detailed map of Ireland. His work, *The Theatre of the Empire of Great Britain*, implies the underlying imperial impulse to the spatial politics at the turn of the century.

If, as Palladio stated, "the city is as it were but a great house, and, on the contrary, a country house is a little city" (quoted in Varey *Space* 28), the colony can be seen to be a mix of country house and city. Voicing this concatenation of different spatial scales, Francis Bacon likened a colony to "a besieged town" (*Essays* 163). The gentry and monarchy struggled for supremacy over "this manor of England"; and as the nation was being resignified as an essentially private realm, the world seemed to revolve around, as Thomas Carew puts it, "This Island Mansion" ("To my friend G.N. from Wrest" *Poems* 79). The shadow cast by England's palaces, to paraphrase Frantz Fanon's evocative image (*Wretched* 311), stretches out to the colonies via the center's cities. The ever-stretching shadows of empire, from the accession of James I up to the English Revolution, acquire the substance of a vital commercial and ideological network linking the ethos and estate of the English country house to the colonies in North America, the Caribbean, and Ireland. Indeed, the shadows of these palaces and places are "the lines of force" that knit together and further create a colonial world which Fanon characterizes as "a world divided into compartments" (37).

If it was increasingly clear that a certain social order now presided over a space made in their image, a culturally naturalized space where the mansion was both a local and imperial signifier, the socio-economic connection of the order was just as certain. On the one hand, there was an increase in foreign commerce and circulating capital, spurred on by joint-stock companies and the pursuit of overseas possessions; on the other hand, development of agrarian capitalism, estate management, and the demands of a growing urban population produced both new ways of using and seeing geography. As capitalism increasingly integrates space, dissolves age-old ties to place and work, unleashes production and laboring people, two general issues become paramount: how to gain control of land and, subsequently, control over the dispossessed populations. Put another way, country house, colony, and expanding town, with their well integrated elites, begin to grapple in earnest with the project of enclosing and controlling space contested by "outsiders," usually those who used to inhabit and use it. In search of justifications for the wholesale expropriation of "common" land, standards of defining space in the interests of private property and capitalist production rendered contested land "vacant" and those who would not or could not fit into the new order "vagrant" – idle, dangerous, mobile, and detached from civil society.

Early seventeenth-century England witnessed a knitting together of the nation-state and fledgling empire through "The Great Rebuilding" (1570–1640); a phrase which aptly evokes the general cohesiveness among a "national" ruling class. This "explosion of architectural construction," Laurence Stone observes, included "the biggest boom in country-house building in English history" (quoted in Fitter *Poetry, Space, Landscape* 240). It also represented a conscious effort by the monarchy, urban oligarchies, and the gentry – usually in competition with one another – to assert control through the standardization of explicit spatial zones and material forms of power. "Architecture has its political use," stated Sir Christopher Wren, "public buildings being the ornament of a country: it establishes a nation, draws people and commerce, makes a people love their native country, which passion is the original of all great actions in a commonwealth" (Wren *Parentalia* 351). The new building –

in both public and private realms – which had at its centre the country house, represented just such a conscious unifying force under a specific social and topographical hierarchy.

The general regularizing of urban space can be seen, for example, in London's expansion where building materials were limited to official designs; James I aimed to bring uniformity to the city and wished to be remembered as the monarch who found the "City and suburbs of stickes, and left them of Bricke" (quoted in Summerson *Architecture in Britain* 94); a Commission on Buildings was founded in 1618 to oversee development; panoramas and bird's eye views proliferated offering the impression of a controlling authority and overall schema; enclosure accelerated; poetry celebrated the country house, its noble occupants, and the traditional communal values that supposedly revolved around a Penshurst or Saxham; and while the monarchy attempted to extend royal power into the countryside, promoting rural "sports" and order-ing the gentry back to their estates,[2] the gentry were establishing their growing social and political power, advertizing this prominence through estates that boasted national authority and challenged the monarchy. At the centre of this will to survey and control and the shift in political architectonics – where the self-contained spaces of feudalism gave way to the state-constrained space economy of capital accumulation – is a contest between privatized and common space.

With the end of the sea war with Spain and the accession of James I, which unified England and Scotland, an era of economic boom, invest-ment, and an excited sense of national enterprise was reflected in the large number of subscribers to the Virginia Company (1606) and the publicity around the Londonderry Plantation (1608/9). The adventure of El Dorado was replaced with a flurry of colonialism as England seriously entered the Atlantic world: settling Jamestown and Sagadahoc, Maine (1607), Newfoundland (1610), Bermuda (1612), and Plymouth (1620). At the same time, however, V. G. Kiernan has noted the dissolution of social ties and the resulting instability, which manifes-ted itself in the rise of nationalism, religious zealotry, and tension among the classes, especially those at the top. It was, in Kiernan's words, a time of "unprecedented transformation... From having been a random growth here and there in the economy, capitalism was turning into a whole social-economic system" (*Eight Tragedies* 19). The havoc caused by the new economic regime, as well as its revolutionary productivity, was clear to its beneficiaries. The impoverishment of the many, the cause of which was so clearly represented by the growing

number of homeless and transient, reached unprecedented proportions. The new spatial forms of this period both caused and were an
attempt to alleviate the worst excesses. Neil Smith and Cindi Katz
summarize the general pattern in the production of space in the late
sixteenth and seventeenth centuries:

> The inauguration of private property as the general basis of the social economy,
> and the division of the land into privately held and precisely demarcated plots;
> the juridical assumption of the individual body as the basic social unit; the
> progressive outward expansion of European hegemony through the conquest,
> colonization and defence of new territories; the division of global space into
> mutually exclusive nation-states on the basis of some presumed internal homo-
> geneity of culture...: these and other shifts marked the emerging space-
> economy of capitalism from the sixteenth century onwards. ("Grounding
> Metaphor" 75)

Thus the fraught and fluid society of early seventeenth-century Britain,
with the gentry's grand monuments to power lording it over the dislocations and grinding poverty of the great majority, produced a new
geography as well as a new cultural history. The two of course go hand
in hand. The Oxford geographer Peter Heylyn asserts as much when, in
Microcosmus or A Little Description of the Great World (1621), he writes: "as
Geography without History, hath life and motion, but at random, and
unstable: so History without Geography, like a dead carcasse hath
neither life nor motion at all" (16). The new geographies of the British
Isles and of the colonies breathed life into a new history; it had as its
chronology the inexorable inheritance of national dominance by the
landed gentry and merchant-princes, and a future of commercial and
imperial glory. Inigo Jones put this vision into material form with an
architectural classicism that bespoke Britain's imperial desires; an architecture that embodied and sanctioned command over time and space.
In short, Jones initiated a spatial form commensurate to the nation's
new global confidence.

   Out of literature's geographic bent during this period a more aggressive conception of mastering space develops. Shakespeare not only
plundered new maps and atlases, but also articulated *strategies* for controlling space. The "colony" in *The Tempest* exemplifies how Prospero's
magic has not a little to do with manipulating what happens where and
to whom, hence utilizing techniques of spatial segregation increasingly
pertinent to the new worlds of capitalism and colonization. He controls
shipping as well as any forms of exchange on the island. He looms as

large as Elizabeth standing on a map of the British Isles in the Ditchley Portrait. The expropriation of resources is dependent upon Caliban's segregation. The island is compartmentalized, and Caliban segregated from the new owners: "and here you sty / me / In this hard rock, whiles you do keep from me / The rest o' th' island" (1.ii.342–5). "The first thing which the native learns," Fanon reminds us, "is to stay in his place, and not to go beyond certain limits" (*Wretched* 52). Transgression of these limits results in the loss of rights. Caliban suffers such a fate. Shakespeare confines Caliban to the logic of the colonizer, here summed up by Robert Johnson in *Nova Britannia* (1609): "And as for the supplanting of the savages, we have no such intent: Our intrusion into their possession shall tend to their great good, and no way to their hurt, unlesse as unbridled beastes, they procure it to themselves" (quoted in Andrews *Trade* 320). Shakespeare's colony is as much about Britain as it is England's imperial potential: in dealing with rebellious nobles and lowlife, Prospero is putting his house in order. It is a house whose shadow now extends to islands like the "still-vexed Bermoothes" (1.ii.229). The strategies of colonialism, as they filter back to Britain around the turn of the century, are as useful in Bermuda as they are in Bristol. And the command over the new geography, as well as old, will only bring more territory:

SEBASTIAN   I think he will carry this island home in his pocket and give it his son for an apple.
ANTONIO   And, sowing the kernels of it in the sea, bring forth more islands.

(*The Tempest* II.i.94–7)

THE COUNTRY HOUSE AND ITS WORLD

In 1599 Joseph Hall describes a countryside in crisis. Rural society is decaying because of absenteeism, which leaves in its wake the cold fireplaces and empty halls of once vibrant country houses.[3] Besides displaying a geopolitics that has a timeless paternalism as *the* life-force for the countryside, Hall accurately has the gentry off in the city where they were busily immersing themselves in commerce and real estate transactions. This sense of crisis is somewhat addressed by the country-house poem, which also expresses an anxiety over the repercussions of changing economic conditions.

The Elizabethan and Jacobean country house exults in being conspicuous and exclusive, indulging in a show of wealth and a confident new order that clearly signals the power of the gentry whilst paying homage and playing host to the monarch. These power houses and their voracious consumption of the land stood in stark contrast to the increasing deprivation of many old communities. The country-house poem, however, celebrates the ideology of natural rulers steeped in organic social traditions, presiding over the fruits of the land, spurning luxury, pomp, and commercial pursuit of wealth. The two versions are of course connected, the latter being less about a nostalgia for a pre-mercantile society than a mystification of the thoroughly capitalist political economy projected by the former. That is not to say that Jonson and the Cavalier poets were not lamenting the passing of a particular social order. Rather, it is to argue that the romanticization of the country house as a place of uncorrupted community was inextricably part of the *rise* of the gentry (and capitalism) rather than the *demise* of nobility. The Sidneys of Penshurst were both the archetypal "ancient" nobility and relative newcomers to the ranks of the gentry, who were energetic in enclosure, imperial expansion, industrial development, and trade.

"The interests of a new kind of society: that of a developing agrarian capitalism," wrote Raymond Williams, "... [are] relocated, in a new ideology, in the country-house" (*Country and City* 22). Famously Williams left empire relatively untouched in his eloquent exploration of this new society in *The Country and the City*. If the country house replaces the castles and fortified manors as "visible centres of the new social system. A more settled and centralized order – a system of social and economic rather than directly military and physical control..." (39) and military control is exported to the colonies, there are aspects that more closely bind plantation to English estate. Indeed, the word "plantation," used purposely to set England apart from Spain and her colonies, nicely conflates country house and colony, benign domestic estate management and re-fertilizing settlement abroad. In both cases the term obscures intensive spatial ensembles producing for the market, its religiously inflected reproductivity displacing real relations of expropriation.

As strongholds of civility, displaying its right use of land in the face of emptiness, even unEnglishness, the representation of the country estate, as in Hall's equation, is an essentially colonial paradigm. James Turner likens the country house to "a new colony, [where] the land is cleared of its troublesome natives and planted with a new and more loyal population... There is virtually no mention of land-clearance" (*Politics of Landscape* 185, 165). This "magical extraction of the curse of labour ... achieved by a simple extraction of the existence of labourers" (Williams *Country* 32) renders to the landowner both the fruits of the land and the uninhabited land itself. The righteous appropriation of resources and the implicit right to dictate terms to land and labor structures the ideology of the country house. I would now like to explore a number of crucial elements within country-house poetry that exemplifies this expansionist creed: command over the land, the organicism of the house and proprietor, the representation of abundance, as well as the labor relations inherent throughout.

The "vogue for prospect" (Fitter *Poetry, Space, Landscape* 268), so characteristic of country house design and poetry, confirms property rights. Æmilia Lanyer's possessive gaze or "proud survey" of Cookeham, or rather the Duchess of Cumberland's domain, portrays a natural world subservient and protective of those born to dominate: "The very Hills right humbly did descend" (line 35 in Woudhuysen *Renaissance Verse*). Indeed nature only signifies via the Duchess: "And all things else did hold like similies" (22). In conjunction with God's "perfit Law" (78) the Duchess and her palace hold sway over "A Prospect fit to please the eyes of Kings: / And thirteen shires appear'd all in your sight" (72–3). No phraseology better conveys the rise of the gentry and their prerogative to rule an officially divided-up landscape. The familiarity, born of ownership and class hierarchy, inherent to this scope and scan of topography, is also expressed by Sir John Denham. He brings his prospect into a particular ideological focus: "My eye, which swift as thought contracts the space / That lies between" ("Cooper's Hill" 11–12). The plot of this contract has "natural" landmarks prescribe royal and imperial power.

The gentry's domination is also a matter of providential blessing, a result of primitive and patriotic election rather than social engineering, politics, and exploitation. That Jonson describes Penshurst as "ancient" articulates this sense of natural rulers as well as an *original* social and spatial order superior to contemporary corruptions. The authenticity of the Sidney family gives them an almost predestined and inalienable right to their property and to the land about them, a claim that echoes territorial rights based on first discovery. Behind this organic authority also lies a colonial logic of appropriating land due to superior status and (re)turning that land to its natural state. In other words, operating within the ethos and material form of the country house is a manifest destiny giving a general precedence over the British Isles to the elect.

Penshurst stands outside the temporality and instability of social construction, as represented by the artifice of other centres of power. Hence "To Penshurst" is framed by claims to the natural (as resources and authority): "Thou joy'st in better markes, of soyle, of ayre, / Of wood, of water: therein thou art faire" (lines 7–8: *Complete Poems*). The "better markes" signify a genealogy that leads back to a natural superiority. In comparison to "Those proud, ambitious heaps, and nothing else," which "their lords have built," the Sidneys "dwell" in Penshurst (99–102). The power of the Sidneys is not imposed, objectified, or even opposed, because it is associated with nature and geography rather than society and history. Witness the intimacy with the natural world: "The painted partrich lys in every field, / And, for thy messe is willing to be kill'd" (29–30). The fish are equally enthralled: "Bright eeles, that emulate them [carp and pike], and leape on land, / Before the fisher, or into his hand" (37–8). A similar submission of overly abundant nature, that recognizes its true masters, appears in the propaganda for the New World.

If God and nature intend certain elites to rule over paradise at home, indeed their rule creates paradise, then it only follows that other places that can be cultivated into a paradisal state are rightfully theirs: original rulers matched to originary places. In the preface to his survey of Great Britain Speed renders the country in colonial terms, fit for the taking: "Seas and Rivers so stored with Fish, and her Fels and Fens so replenished with wild Foule, that they even present themselves for ready prey to their takers: briefly, every soile is so enriched with plenty and pleasures, as the Inhabitants thinke there is no other Paradise in the earth but where themselves dwell" (B3). Chris Fitter identifies four explanations for the seventeenth century's representation of the countryside as paradise: a pervasive millenarianism; the separation of the urban from rural labor and production, thus creating the "mirage of self-producing nature"; the Cavalier representation of the countryside as a place of luxury and leisure; and the destabilization of and conflict over landownership, which produced "nostalgias of 'true' possession and settled rural security" (*Poetry, Space, Landscape* 235). Although Fitter goes on to link millenarian optimism to an expansionist spirit (236) he fails to include colonialism and the representations of colonial space in promotional pamphlets as an element in England's pursuit of the paradisal. In order to maintain, if not expand, their estates, the ruling elites have to deal with the brute realities of capitalism's advent; that meant strategically regimenting space at home and, even better, overseas in colonies.

The cornucopian flow of nature's bounty does signify, as Fitter argues, the division between country and city, the latter perceiving the former as "self-producing nature"; and there are also all sorts of utopian, nostalgic, and millenarian implications in this mystification of labor relations.⁴ However, this abundance also invokes the colonial space of promotional literature, the new found paradise of the Americas: streams clogged with fish, skies darkened with birds, park-like landscapes stocked with deer, and soil that virtually seeds, weeds, and harvests by itself. Moreover, the natural abundance implies the vacancy of people, cultivation, and social structures that differ from the gentry's bucolic and patrician landscape. Common people do exist in country-house poetry but they are divorced from their commons and laboring activities. As would quickly become the case for Amerindians, the dispossessed are only allowed to the table with the implicit acceptance of and allegiance to the landowner's property rights. Under these conditions the food overflowing the table is for all to share, regardless of status: "But all come in, the farmer and the clowne: / And no one empty-handed, to salute / Thy lord, and lady..." (Jonson "To Penshurst" lines 48–50: *Complete Poems*). Following the feudal script of mutual obligation, Jonson has the abundance of produce brought by the common folk happily met by their landlord, "whose liberall boord doth flow, / With all, that hospitalitie doth know! / Where comes no guest, but is allowed to eate" (59–61). If, ideally, the fruits and beasts are for all to share, the land, however, remains solely the landowners. This hospitable and thoroughly loyal environment reflects the ideal of total, justified, and accepted domination.

Yet clearly there are cracks in this benign command economy. Like maps the country-house poem proffered an image perilously balanced between reality and illusion. For all his infatuation with maps Donne seems to warn that just as the globe maker "quickly makes that, which was nothing all" ("A Valediction: Of Weeping" line 13) the opposite can also occur. Just as maps are an attempt to fix space under a particular code, a similar project is at work in the country-house poem. The ideal code is presented but not without an ominous instability haunting its design. While on the one hand Penshurst is an open house because its environs have been made safe and regulated by its owner; on the other hand, these property relations are precarious. Jonson obliquely refers to the "class struggle without class" (Thompson) and the general crisis of the seventeenth century produced by enclosure when he observes:⁵ "And though thy walls be of the countrey stone, / They'are rear'd with no man's ruine, no man's grone, / There's none, that dwell about them, wish them downe" ("To Penshurst" lines 45–7). We find similar lines protesting the ideal a little too hotly in Robert Herrick's "A Panegerick to Sir Lewis Pemberton," where, because the house wasn't built "by the

Poore-man's fleece," "Safe stand thy Walls, and Thee, and so both will" (*Hesperides* 159). This sort of antagonism is the result not only of upstart *parvenu* gentry and their conspicuous and all-consuming drive for wealth, but also because of an absence of effective socio-spatial controls. The country-house poem mystified exploitation just as surely as "To Penshurst" obscures the fact that the Sidney family's success is partly due to the sale of timber and that Philip composed poetry on recently enclosed land. Whether ancient or new, the landed gentry were increasingly involved in estate management and racking rents, in the enclosure and clearing of land for wool production, in the leasing of land for mining rights, harvesting forests, as well as in joint-stock companies and colonial ventures. Thus Raymond Williams interprets the emphasis on eating and drinking as a sign of the "insatiable exploitation of the land and its creatures – a prolonged delight in an organized and corporative production and consumption" (*Country and City* 30). This representation of satiation coexisted with an estimated one quarter of the population on the edge of starvation (Innes *Work and Labor* 5).[6]

Folded into the abundance and happy hierarchy is indeed a recognition of the opening of the Pandora's box of capitalism. But the displacement of starvation, homelessness, waged labor, and the consolidation of capitalist social relations under the ascendancy of the gentry in the city and country alike, is not simply one of mystifying reality.[7] As I have attempted to show, inscribed within country-house poetry is an ethos of colonizing territory, enclosing land under the auspices of a superior social system. Carew's sojourn at Wrest in 1639 underscores this point. After a grueling campaign in Scotland, Carew views Wrest as an outpost of civilization; it is a representative of a social system that must aggressively challenge, as indeed Carew had so recently been doing, the barbarism found in England's colonies.

The country estate and its hegemonic landscape was indeed duplicated abroad, albeit with adaptations conforming to local circumstances and the readiest way to wealth. We may of course cite the great estates that grew up in Greater Virginia by the end of the century, the never quite successful neo-feudal manors of aristocrats like Gorges in Maine and Baltimore in Maryland, Locke and Shaftesbury's design for Carolina, and the patrician families in New York. But for the earliest and most successful duplication of the country house we should look to the sugar-planter class in the Caribbean.[8] Richard S. Dunn observes that "the chief distinguishing features of island society in the seventeenth century was the rapid rise of a cohesive and potent master class" (*Sugar and Slaves* 46). They dominated the land, culture, social relations, and workforce, some owning as many as two hundred slaves, most about a hundred. Such was this plantocracy's domination that one contemporary observer, Richard Ligon, notes that "their houses, many of which are built in manner of Fortifications, . . . have Lines, Bulwarks, and Bastions to defend themselves, in case there should be any uproar or commotion in the island, either by the Christian servants, or *Negro* slaves" (*True and Exact History* 29). These houses, built by and for unhappy labor relations, stored their water in cisterns which "serves them to drink whilst they are besieged; as also, to throw down upon the naked bodies of the *Negroes*, scalding hot; which is as good a defence against their underminings, as any other weapons" (29). This serves to reiterate that the "palaces" and country houses of the ruling elites were always–already in relation to domination of and "underminings" by the populace. The country house ethos is part of an imperial ethos imposed by the garrison government of governors-general throughout the British realm (Webb *Governors* xvii). A figure like Sir Ferninando Gorges exemplifies how the two overlap.

Thus the highly regimented space of the colony, directed at African slave, indentured Irish servant, non-conformist Puritan, or Amerindian, is not a million miles from pastoral estates in England. Both are created and maintained by the appropriation of human and natural resources. Both must defend themselves, physically and ideologically, against opposition to this exploitative system. Recognizing the turbulence created by nascent capitalism, Bacon argues in "Of Sedition and Troubles" that

The first remedy or prevention is to remove by all means possible that material cause of sedition . . . which is want and poverty in the estate. To which purpose serveth the opening and well-balancing of trade; the cherishing of manufactures; . . . the improvement and husbanding of the soil; the regulating of prices . . . *the increase of any estate must be upon the foreigner (for whatsoever is somewhere gotten is somewhere lost)*. (emphasis added; *Essays* 104)

Bacon articulates what William Appleman Williams describes as "a cardinal tenet of mercantilist thought: The best – if not only – way to get wealth and welfare was to take them away from somebody" (*Contours* 35). The well-being of the nation-estate (to which Bacon is referring here) or the country estate is dependent on the same thing: expansion.

"BARBARIANS, BORDERERS AND OUT-LAWES"

In the pursuit of dominated space, the fundamental problem is the same for centre and periphery alike: how to reorganize social and spatial relations whilst controlling both the process and those dispossessed. Just as colony, city, and country estate employ similar ideologies and strategies to gain effective order over turbulent social conditions, they all find themselves confronted by the "savage." Michael Drayton informed George Sandys that Virginia had no special monopoly on barbarism: "But you may save your labour if you please, / To write me ought of your savages. / As savage slaves be in great Britaine here, / As any one that you can shew me there" (*Works* III.206–8). Everard Guilpin warns that if the city explorer "observe[s] the sundry kindes of shapes" by St. Paul's, "Th'wilt sweare that London is as rich in apes / As *Affricke Tabraca*" (Woudhuysen *Renaissance Verse* 186).[9] Caliban is not only a "monster," "a strange beast," "a lame beggar," "a dead Indian," "islander," and commodity (*Tempest* II.ii.25–38), but also part of a "foul conspiracy" with "his confederates" Stephano and Trinculo (IV.i.139–40). Here Shakespeare articulates both savagism and the threat from an alliance between the lower orders and the colonized, such as demonstrated in Ireland.[10] Caliban, as omnipresent as Prospero, is a thoroughly resistant body, to be ignored neither in the colonies nor at home.[11] In contrast to the hospitality of the country house, the savages display an "in hospitality," as Fynes Moryson puts it in his *Itinerary* (1605–17). In Ireland, the traveler is "not without danger to be ill intertained, perhaps devoured of his insatiable Host" (203).[12]

As one of the principal architects of the Londonderry project, Bacon noted that inhospitality was not simply an Irish problem; in 1606 he wrote that "internal troubles and seditions" due to a "surcharge or overflow" of masterless men threatened the very in-habitability of the nation. Like many others before and after, Bacon recommended in *Certain Considerations Touching the Plantation in Ireland* that populating colonies with undesirables would "have a double commodity, in the avoidance of people here, and making use of them there" (*Works* 184). In other words, imperialism has the "double commodity" of replenishing at home and abroad – "commodity" as usefulness overlaps with "commodity" as the product of the economically useful. The surest way to ensure stability was to turn the marginal and the periphery to the production of commodities for the centre. After citing a list of "such commodities as we saw . . ." in Virginia, John Brereton states the case as follows:

These commodities before rehearsed, albeit for the most part they be gross, yet are the same for the State of England especially, aswell in regard of the use of such commodities, as for the employment also of our people and ships; the want whereof, both decay our townes and parts of England, and causeth the realm to swarme full with puss and idle people. (*Briefe and True Relation* 17)

A generalized colonial mentality is apparent if economic exigencies are set alongside the ideology of the country house and its real spatial relations. The reigning geography of the early seventeenth century is made up of zones of exclusion and attendant prerogatives, where one is either a commodity or a member of exclusive space. This territoriality stems as much from colonial desires as from the management of estates. Progressive agriculture, conservationist ideology, and requirements of agrarian capitalism place a premium on expansion and controlling resources and their distribution. Improving the uncultivated linked land (and people) management at home and abroad. The exploitation inherent to such a project was veiled by the trope of paradise, a place at once exclusive and communal.

The "revival of the paradisal motif of nature as commonality" (Fitter *Poetry, Space, Landscape* 252) had communitarian as well as colonial implications. If the brief spark of the Diggers and radical Levellers was the inevitable result of such an ideology, the colonization of North America, that great commons of uncultivated and unpossessed land, was its chief inspiration and target. Nature as commonality was not to be a permanent state, however, but rather an imperfect one waiting to be set to rights through private ownership. If the recalcitrant laborer was absented from the English countryside, a labor theory of value was inexorably becoming the justification for expropriating land inhabited by others. Due to different conditions but also to distance themselves from the Spanish, English theoreticians of land appropriation were "predominantly concerned with securing rights not over peoples but over lands" (Pagden in Canny *Origins* 41). That land was "unimproved" became the keystone of their argument. The Roman legal argument of *res nullius* was as pertinent to England as in the colonies. In the 1580s England challenged Spain and its use of the "law of nations" which awarded ownership on the basis of discovery. England argued that actual property rights should be based on purchase or settlement (Arneil *John Locke and America* 71). These relations of private property ensured power at home for the landowners and attracted investment, if not settlement, abroad. More specifically, Hugo Grotius argued (for the Dutch) that the use of something in its natural state, "hitherto uncultivated," is enough to make it your property (Arneil 50–1). Thus wilderness and commons alike were essentially up for grabs since both lacked the organizing principle of private property and the "landskip" formed by European agricultural practices.

On a spiritual plane, God's grace guaranteed dominion which in turn underwrote property rights. In the country-house poem to oppose the lord would be to go against a natural order of things. So it was with the Lord in the colonies. However, even after the 1622 massacre in Virginia and the sanctimonious declarations against the "savages," a debate over the right to dispossess took place. This was due to the power of the Indians and the colonist's need for them as trading partners and suppliers of food, not to mention a genuine desire to differentiate England's from Spain's methods of colonization. Nonetheless, it was a debate with serious implications for the transformation of the British countryside. Donne posed the question in St. Paul's on Easter Day 1626:

> we dispute in the school, whether infidels have any true dominion, any true propriety in anything which they possess here: And whether there be not an inherent right in the Christians, to plant Christianity in any part of the dominions of the infidels, and consequently, to despoil them even of their possession, if they oppose such plantations, so established, and such propagations of the Christian religion . . . (*John Donne* 378)

He concludes this part of his sermon by arguing that the redemption of (foreign) land for the exclusive use of Christians is a process endorsed "by his higher Law, by his prerogative, as Christians against Infidels," and in a stunning tautological display ends with the claim: "*All things are yours* [1 Cor. 3:21], says the apostle; By what right? *You are Christ's*, says he, *And Christ's is God's*; Thus is a title conveyed to us, All things are God's, God hath put all things under Christ's feet; And he under ours, as we are Christians" (378). The question of "title" is crucial here since it invokes the growing legislative weight of property rights, the growing demand for freehold ownership in the colonies (Canny *Origins* 235), as well as the cultural power of those with "ancient" lineage, those who can trace a genealogy which entitles natural and historical prerogatives. A year earlier Purchas drew attention to the innate "tenure" that the Christians and colonists have, "whereof Hypocrites and Heathens are not capable" (*Hakluytus* IXX.219).[13] One upping Donne in exquisite logic, Purchas adds for good measure: "all things are ours, and wee Christs, and Christ Gods" (221). But God's grace is supplemented by possession through a particular type of socio-spatial arrangement structured around ownership; the "natural right to replenish the whole earth" means that "every man by Law of Nature and Humanitie hath right of

Figure 4 "The Town of Secota" by John White (ca. 1585), as engraved by
Theodor de Bry for Thomas Harriot's *A Briefe and True Report*

Plantation . . . especially where the people is wild, and holdeth no settled possession in any parts" (222). John Winthrop argued in "General Considerations for Planting in New England" (1629), that an absence of property rights engenders dissolution: "that which is common to all is proper to none. This savage people ruleth over many lands without title or property." He justifies "appropriat[ing] some parcels of ground by enclosing" by arguing North American Indians make no attempt to improve, thus own, nature: "for they enclose no ground, neither have they cattle to maintain it" (quoted in Arneil *John Locke and America* 109–13). For Francis Higginson the Indians don't have "any ground as they challenge for their owne possession, but change their habitation from place to place" (*New-Englands Plantation* 317). Or, they have no grounds upon which to argue for their rights.

In all these early promotional tracts the aim is to represent the land as essentially devoid of civilized markers and the people as nomadic, contradicting God's command to replenish and subdue. Hence *Mourt's Relation* (1622) describes a land that is "spacious and void, and there are few and do but run over the grass, as do also the foxes and wild beasts . . . [the Indians don't] use either the land or the commodities of it, but all spoils, rots, is marred for want of manuring, gathering, ordering . . ." (92). Without European "ordering" the land is "undressed" and in "chaos" (93). However, *Mourt's Relation* appears contradictory: earlier the authors note "a great deal of land cleared, and hath been planted with corn three or four years ago" (53) and, as opposed to William Bradford's later version of feeling blinded and oppressed by the woods, "the trees stand not thick, but a man may well ride a horse among them" (64). Purchas was well acquainted with John Smith's accounts of a "hundred houses . . . togither inhabited" by Indians ("A True Relation" *Works* 51) and "sandy cliffes . . . so planted with Gardens and Corne fields" ("A Description" *Works* 330). In fact it was recognized that, contrary to dominant ideological formulas, the colonists settled on the waste land, often "wasting" it further with inefficient European husbandry, whilst the Indians inhabited and produced fertile land.[14] Some Indians did commute (Jennings *Invasion* 71), but as many were as "settled" as the English were, which Edward Winslow recognizes when in 1624 he writes that every sachem knew "how far the bounds and limits of his own country extendeth" (quoted in Jennings *Invasion* 67).

This apparent contradiction – recognizing Indian territoriality and labeling the land *terra nullius* – is resolved because of Indian violence. Hostility toward the English, who were simply appropriating common land, removed the Indians from any legal or moral claims. As the struggle over the rights to land showed, the difference between the English and the Indians was not one of savage versus civilized, though this was how it was coded, but, as Jennings argues, "between effective colonial jurisdictions and effective tribal jurisdictions" (*Invasion* 180). By the actions of 1622 *all* Indians had removed themselves from *any* juridical system. Thus Purchas may simultaneously make a show of legality while reducing the Indians to a state "more brutish then the beasts they hunt, more wild and unmanly then that unmanned Countrey, which they range rather than inhabite" (*Hakluytus* IXX.231).[15] Further, the Indians do not conform to a universal law of nations, part of which means welcoming trade and other European systems. Here, "trade" is a tool of legitimizing conquest. "Not worthy of the name of a Nation," the Indians are now the invaders, without history in territory measured by English standards; they are "yet as slaves, bordering rebells, excommunicates and out-lawes lyable to the punishments of Law, and not to the priviledges; So is it with these Barbarians, Borderers and Out-Lawes of Humanity" (224). Returning us also to the country-house poem and its loyal subjects, Purchas charges the Indians with "disloyall treason"(229). Finally, resistance vacates the land; according to lawyer Winthrop, the land was *vacuum domicilium*, and therefore ready for a new geography and history.

LOCATING ENGLAND WITH "A NEW COMPASS"

If the culture of the early seventeenth century is geographic (Gillies *Geography of Difference* 156), then it is also a culture struggling over the spatial design of history's narrative. *Whose* history personifies the land is the central struggle of both internal and overseas colonization. In order to lay claim to land and its productivity and at the same time resist the crown's intervention, gain local allegiance, and govern a national economy, the gentry had to also lay claim to *the* land, *the* country, and its territories. They needed their history inscribed on the very landscape in order to gain national hegemony. Like Ortelius, court, city, and country recognized that "Geography is ... the eye of history" ("Abraham Ortelius ... to the courteous Reader" in Skelton *Theatre*). The mini-histories of the country-house poem segue with the national chorographical projects of the time. Just as nature seemed to recognize their legitimacy, the gentry became the heirs to an authentic history extending back to before the "Norman Yoke," or as Herrick puts it to Sir Lewis in "A Panegerick": "Thou do'st redeeme those times; and what was lost / Of antient honesty, may boast / It keeps a growth in thee" (*Hesperides* 159). A reclaimed indigenous and non-monarchical tradition coalesces around notions of England as an elect nation and empire. Saxton's *Atlas* began the privileging of the gentry's property rights as the major landmark. This representation of the nation via county maps "was, in effect, a pictorial title-deed; an imprimatur of power" (Gillies *Geography of Difference* 46). Maps were overrun with the gentry's genealogical/ heraldic information as well as the etymology of place-names (Mendyk "*Speculum Britanniae*" 24). As already discussed, Speed included an inno-vation that heralded the rising and cohesive power of local elites: town plans. Camden's *Britannia* (1607), Michael Drayton's *Poly-Olbion* (written between 1612 and 1619, both parts published by 1622), and William Browne's *Britannia's Pastorals* (1613, 1616) gave pictorial materiality to the sense and reality of national unification. If British nationalism grew out of the incredible influence and size of London, joint-stock companies, a dependency on the market, Britain's insular natural geography, the development of its waterways and coasts, anti-Spanish sentiment, and peace for the first two decades, it also was fuelled by the intellectual production represented by chorographical projects.

These hugely popular projects achieve a resituating of the state and nation through, in the words of Lefebvre, "the rational and political principle of *unification*, which subordinates and totalizes the various aspects of social practice ... within a determinate space; namely, the space of the ruling class's hegemony over its people and over the nationhood that it has arrogated" (*Production* 280–1). With its emphasis on local description within an historical gloss, chorography nationalized the country(side) under the sign of the gentry's power. This surveying of the nation "strengthened the sense of both local and national identity," as Richard Helgerson asserts, "at the expense of an identity based on dynastic loyalty" (*Forms of Nationhood* 114). The multiplication of sovereig-nties, the patriotism associated with local autonomy, and the increasing attention to the genealogy of individuals and families "foregrounded" the gentry and "Country" thereby demoting, indeed opposing, the monarchy (131, 141). The construction of local history as the foundation of a stable, patriotic, and socially responsible nation served this shift in political power and socio-economic organization. Wallerstein describes the situation well:

When the local dominant strata are threatened by any incipient class-con-sciousness of lower strata, emphasis on local culture serves well to deflect local internal conflict, creating instead local solidarity against the outside. If, in addition, these local dominant strata feel themselves oppressed by higher strata of the world-system, they are doubly motivated to pursue the creation of a local identity. (*Modern World-System* 353)

As the most politically motivated of the related branches of geography in the late sixteenth and early seventeenth centuries (Cormack "Good Fences" 641), chorography had as much to do with localizing power relations as it had with defining Britain in relation to the globe. Chorographical descriptions enact a resignification that implies a formerly vacant topography. In what is clearly a colonial move, the new maps displaced other representations of the nation in order to make space for a more authentic design. Drayton's *Poly-Olbion* is the counterpart of his poem in celebration of colonialism, "To the Virginian Voyage." The process of accumulating land via naming and measuring, parceling and privatizing is succinctly put by Lesley Cormack when she writes that: "The improvement of surveying techniques and practices was motivated by attempts at political and economic aggrandizement on the part of the middling gentry and merchant families ... Chorography classified time and place in an effort to reduce their surroundings to a manageable and controllable object" ("Good Fences" 656). Thus we find in the map accompanying his *A Description of New England* ... (1616) John Smith making his reader feel at home in the New World by strewing the New England coastline with familiar English place-names. Well might Smith say in *A Map of Virginia* (1612) that, along with the colonial surveyor, "heaven and earth never agreed to better frame a place for mans habitation being of our constitutions" (*Complete Works* 114). The framing of land is crucial, in Bacon's words, "for keeping the country in bridle" (*Works* 190). The "Topo-chrono-graphical Poeme" of *Poly-Olbion* is just such a framing; it performs a "radical renovation" (Greene *Intellectual Construction* 50) of "this manor of England."

National supremacy and territorial aggrandizement are written into the chronicling of Drayton's large two-volume work. One might indeed look a second time at the curious Indian-like figures, with head-dress, sporting bows, and arrows, and emerging from woods in the Dorset and Hampshire maps. These "Wood-Nymphes" seem to beckon to internal colonization and symbolically remind the reader of further civilizing work to be done elsewhere. Time and time again the "Genealogie" of the nation connects the local to the world: the people around Plymouth "from their anchoring Bayes have travailed to finde / Large *Chinas* wealthie Realms, and view'd the either *Inde*, / The pearlie rich *Peru*..."

(*Poly-Olbion* 40: *Works*). Following the trajectory of a good deal of the Puritan emigration, Drayton's description of Ipswich leads to a song celebrating Britain's colonial adventuring. In keeping with the re-entitling of the nation in favor of the gentry, a "British Empire" (184) issues from and returns to the social relations of the country house; sturdy yeomen "even in the hart of *France*," fight beside their "Land-lord," who "in warre, . . . spent of his estate; / Returning to his home, his hospitable gate / The richer and the poore stood open to receave . . ." (219–20). Inexorably England's destiny seems to lead back to the doorstep of the gentry and their world-historical significance.

Recalling John Dee's rather imaginative stretching of Britain's historic imperial sphere, Drayton delineates Arthur's "Ancient Empire." "His awfull Empires bounds" included Iceland, Lapland and Greenland; and "our Argonauts shall lead" us to similar acquisitions (401). Drayton celebrates the small group of lesser gentry and soldiers who represented the dynamism that fueled the later colonial successes of merchant-planters in the 1620s. Sir Hugh Willoughby's ventures to numerous exotic and "wealthy" places (402) heads off a lengthy list of adventurers – "Globe-engirdling *Drake*," "Industrious *Rawleigh*" – and places fit for "our" empire. The re-membering (uniting as one) of national glories continues including Ralph Lane "Who in *Virginia* left, with th' English Colony," had to deal with "those Barbarous, brute, and wild Virginians . . ." (405–6). Via "rich *Guiana*" and the Caribbean we return, quite without transition, to Suffolk's coasts and rivers. Since this is a small section of *Poly-Olbion*, this whirlwind tour through Britain's imperial narrative is not a brochure for colonialism. Rather, expansionism is an intricate part of naming the realm; it is a natural extension of recording the history and topography of England's shires.

The "projections" of Drayton's chorography find their distillation in his promotional poem "To the Virginian Voyage" where the "Countries Name," so painstakingly enumerated in *Poly-Olbion*, spells out: "Goe, and subdue" (lines 2, 4 in Woudhuysen *Renaissance Verse*), an appropriate injunction for "VIRGINIA, / Earth's onely Paradise" (23–4). In a similar fashion to that poet of spatial scales, John Donne, Drayton forges the personal and domestic to the global and a manifest destiny. Hence "brave Heroique Minds"(1) facilitate this *taking possession* of all levels of space: "And in Regions farre / Such *Heroes* bring yee foorth, / As those from whom We came, / And plant Our name" (55–8). If the world is to be reduced to the prerogative, the entitlement, the naming of the English, then "brave Heroique Minds" must be created. Thus

Drayton, Donne, and others argue for a change in perspective, in how the individual views his place in a world of imperial struggle where old certainties have been destroyed. The new world is not just America but a global condition, and England must encourage a subjectivity commensurate to this novel space. A new individual, whose body is inseparable from foreign territory, will find selfhood, discover what it is to be English through action in the world.

It is Donne through his personal "chorography" ("An Anatomy of the World" for instance) that most clearly promotes the adventurous individual who is part of an entrepreneurial, national, and imperial elect. The "worlding" of the individual will create a unified personal and national identity; empire is one of the elements of a "magnetic force" which can "draw, and fasten sundered parts in one" (lines 221–2). It is a force "Which, from the carcase of the old world, free, / Creates a new world; and new creatures be / Produced..." (75–7). In language privileging landowners, Donne yokes religious duty, self-fulfilment, and national well-being to expansion: "God gives men good estates from their parents at first; yet God's purpose is that they should increase those estates" (*John Donne* 286). In "Of Goodness and the Goodness of Nature" Bacon articulates both the imperial sensibility and mercantile pursuits of the more modern "Heroique Mind": he "is a citizen of the world, and ... his heart is no island cut off from other lands, but a continent that joins to them" (*Essays* 98). This citizen is the backbone of Britannia, "She to whom this world must itself refer, / As suburbs" (Donne "An Anatomy" lines 235–6). But as so often, such a scenario, stocked with citizen-imperialists, is wishful thinking.

However much Bacon, Drayton, or Donne might envision imperial expansion, the frustration and persuading tones are evident as empire is thwarted by cautious monarch and merchant alike. Donne is a particularly good example of the cultural elite and their allies in the lesser gentry and military attempting to change the basic reluctance of company merchants and landed gentry to risk investments in settlement abroad (Brenner *Merchants and Revolution* 111). Donne was one of empire's most avid and poetic supporters, and was bitterly disappointed when William Strachey was chosen over him for the secretarial post for Jamestown.[16] For Donne, like Milton, the new world of battling empires is as everyday, intimate, and private as a lover's nakedness. Publicly he did his best, as in his sermon to the Virginia Company in 1622, to show that ills at home, such as "idle persons" (321), could be turned into benefits through colonialism. If he sermonizes about replenishing and dominating foreign territories (285–6) and believes, as the poem "Cales and Guiana" suggests, that the Old World is in decay, Donne just as passionately believes that Britain will be rejuvenated through empire: all the ruling elite "needed [was] a new compass for their way" ("An Anatomy" line 226). Until the 1620s those elites studiously refused, after some initial investments around 1600, the new compass directing them westward.

That is not to say that the gentry were disinterested in colonial ventures in the Americas, but historians such as Theodore K. Rabb have "overestimated the landed class[es] contribution to the colonizing movement" (Brenner *Merchants and Revolution* 106–7).[17] Land management, especially the extraction of higher rents, and southern and eastern trade was where the landed classes invested. Yet the distinction between landowning gentry and merchants was an increasingly porous one: "The predominant pattern was one of landed interests involved in trade – and vice versa" (Williams *Contours* 49). The surest way for the merchant to invest his profits was to sink it into land. As far as colonialism went, the merchants were the "chief pillar of the entire undertaking" (*Merchant and Gentry* Rabb 52), but the gentry flooded joint-stock companies with the capital from higher rents and agricultural prices, and "transformed a series of commercial undertakings into a great national enterprise" (69). These developments were, according to William Appleman Williams, part of a "spirit of . . . maturing mercantilism" (*Contours* 41),[18] which, as the country house ethos exemplifies, sought a strong state to balance corporate Christian responsibility with the commercial cut and thrust of *laissez-faire* individualism. This ideological balancing act which the gentry and merchants championed, and which, for survival, depended on the overseas expansion, was also *the* basic framework for the evolution of and struggles within the colonies.

In 1688 the revolution that came to a head in 1641 but began in the first decades of the century was completed. The victorious alliance is described by Robert Brenner as

an anti absolutist, Protestant, and agrarian capitalist aristocracy favoring a strong state for international military and commercial power and for defense against the Catholic powers [and] a dynamic maturing entrepreneurial merchant class, oriented toward making the most of the growing opportunities that could be derived from the long-distance trades and an expanding colonial empire, as well as from war finance. (*Merchants and Revolution* 713)

Literary culture had prepared the ground for this victory, whose hallmarks were the freeing of the landed classes to exploit and expand their holdings and a powerful state willing and able to support predatory trade and colonization.[19] The literature advocating and imagining the growth of colonization and colonial trade between 1600 and 1630 was a vanguard. Through the country-house poem, chorography, and the ideal of a heroic individual investing his all in risky ventures, it gave an imperial inflection to the gentry's attention to estate management and trade. Drayton's urgent phrase to "plant Our name," with its religious, imperial, agricultural, and hegemonic connotations, well describes what England and her elites were doing in the British Isles and were increasingly interested and equipped to do abroad.

PLYMOUTH COLONY AND COLONIAL NETWORKING

Having explored the links between colonialism and the country house, I now want to see how the town and its evolution participates in the Great Rebuilding and the expropriation of common land at home and abroad. As we have seen with Spenser and Bacon, who likened a new settlement to "a besieged town" (Bacon *Essays* 163), urban development was viewed as fundamental to colonialism. The task of transforming socio-spatial chaos into a productive society aligned to the rigors of the market was the chief problem faced in town and colony alike. More specifically, the standardization sweeping the towns in Britain similarly structures the spatial developments in the colonies. Like the boom in building in the countryside between 1570 and 1630, urban centers especially London began to reorganize their layout. The classical formality that Inigo Jones introduced into England, even though of a limited influence until the eighteenth century, was indicative of a uniformity and control required as pressures on urban land increased. Jones's work on large country houses as well as his development of estates and geometric planning of London's fringes points to spatial practices that can at once be seen in an urban, rural, or colonial context.

Not only does Jones design the innovative gateway into the private garden, bounding nature's reserve with an essentially urban and public form, but he also introduces the essentially sub-urban, even colonial, into the city in the form of Covent Garden. In this case, a private estate on the edge of London is transformed into a city piazza for profit. It is a reaction to a chaotic city already deemed monstrous, and is designed with segregation and easy surveillance at its core. In short, Covent Garden is about money and controlling the development of space.

Moreover, its design – around a square dominated by institutions of power (the church and the Bedford estate) – resembles numerous colonial designs. Perhaps it is the Vitruvian Tuscan style that Jones incorporates into the church that most clearly gives us an idea of the ideology behind the gentry's Great Rebuilding at home and overseas. "The Vitruvian Tuscan," John Summerson observes, "was the furthest an architect could reach to the 'natural' beginnings of architecture" (*Architecture in Britain* 126). Jones's "handsomest barn in England" represented both the primitive purity of Protestantism as well as the organicism of British society and its leaders. It is a form that speaks of a superiority based on authentic rights and an ancient inheritance, which was utilized by the gentry and colonist to expropriate alien(ated) land.

As Peter Clark and Paul Slack repeatedly remind us in *English Towns in Transition 1500–1700*, England was an overwhelmingly rural nation, but the development of towns had an impact disproportionate to their populations or political power. Lefebvre claims "The West was ... turned upside down" by the development of the town as it "overtook the country in terms of its economic and practical weight, in terms of its social importance; landownership lost its former absolute primacy. Society underwent a global change" (*Production* 268). Towns and cities sought independence in opposition to the monarchy and local oligarchies; charters become the site of the struggle for control over urban space (Clark and Slack *English Towns* 133). At the core and in every contour of the early modern town is the facilitation of commerce; the accumulation of capital, private property, and the control of labor structure determine the lineaments of urban design, whether in England, Ireland, or New England. *Lawes Divine, Morall and Martiall* were imposed on Jamestown in 1611 because disorder had become so rife that colonists, rather than laboring, had taken to bowling in the streets.

The gigantic wave of immigration into the towns due to enclosure and new agricultural methods, and the subsequent poverty and unsanitary conditions led to equally gigantic problems of social control for the authorities. Swollen urban areas continually threatened and often delivered epidemic and riot. Older and/or more "desirable" citizens complained about disorder, crime, ungodly living, and a generally unprofitable state of affairs (95). Town corporations, like the owners of landed estates, had to face the threat of the de-forming of their spatial order by highly mobile, highly dispossessed "foreigners" or "immigrants." The outsiders became the large pool of expendable human resource that migrated to the colonies along with defeated and dispossessed Irish and Scots. The migration from the country to the city, and from both overseas, was one movement in an increasingly coherent market-place. Or as Bernard Bailyn puts it: "The Atlantic became a highway like the Great North Road" (*Peopling of America* 26). The experience and lessons of urban space also migrated abroad to the colonies.

In Ireland, not only did the plantations of Elizabethan adventurers like Raleigh and Grenville develop in the seventeenth century into manufacturing towns (Canny *Kingdom* 94), with links to new towns and important trading and manufacturing centers such as Derry and Coleraine in Ulster, but even new towns built on older sites were part of "a conscious effort . . . to provide them with a regular shape, organized about a central diamond or square, and to construct serried rows of stone and slated houses" (48). Nicholas Canny notes that "Bandonbridge in Munster was probably the first English overseas settlement organized on the grid system that was later to become popular for new towns in British North America" (49). The re-formation of Ireland via civilized towns, roads, and bridges, the like of which Spenser and Bacon had called for, proved to be a success, especially in Munster.[20] This reorganization of the colonial space, often in partnership with Irish landowners, and the development of towns in England, was reflected in English America, where the same desire for secure and profitable spaces existed.

North America seemed to offer an unprecedented opportunity for a coherent rather than chaotic social order. This meant a very disciplined regulation of spatial relations. As an export of immeasurable significance, the "Great Rebuilding" or, as it is sometimes known, the housing revolution in England – with its uniformity, symmetry, commercial efficiency, and "complex machinery" for imposing social division and control (Clark and Slack *English Towns* 124) – was installed in the colonies. The sense of the rightness of regimented space smoothly flowing into a global trading network is conveyed by Edward Johnson's view of Boston in 1631. The buildings of the "Metropolis" are "orderly placed with comly streets, whose continuall enlargement" pushes back the "yet untilled Wildernesse" (*Providence* 51). Witness his description of the very young city:

The forme of this Towne is like a heart, naturally scituated for Fortifications, having two Hills on the frontice part thereof next the sea, the one hill fortified on the superfices thereof, with store of great Artillery well mounted, the other hath a very strong battery built of whole Timber, and filled with Earth . . . all three [hills] like over-topping Towers keepe a constant watch to fore-see the approach of forrein dangers . . . [there is] also store of Victuall both for their owne and Forreiners-ships, who resort hither for that end: this Town is the very Mart of the Land, French, Portugalls and Dutch come hither to Traffique. (71)

As one historian has remarked, the "prototypical colony looked more like a garrison or a fortified trading factory than any of the communities that eventually developed" (Cressy *Coming Over* 38). At once entrepot, garrison, and metropole of a growing area, Boston represents civilized and Godly development.[21] If Johnson sees rather more than is there, his view is important for the urban model he depicts; a model typical of colonial settlement. Virginia's production of space through the cultivation of tobacco is an exception, as we shall see later. If we focus on the general spatial pattern of New England's towns we find a production of an anglicized landscape which was coercive, market-oriented, privately owned, commodity-based, and rigorously partitioned. In *New England's Prospect* (1634) William Wood uses language exuding quantifiable and possessive space when he describes "one of the neatest and best compacted Towns in New England" (43). "So rude and unmanaged a country" (52) is properly organized by the town's "many fair structures, with many handsom contrived streets." He continues:

The inhabitants most of them are very rich, and well stored with Cattle of all sorts; having many hundred Acres of ground paled in with one general fence, which is about a mile and a half long, which secures all the weaker Cattle from the wild beasts. On the other side of the River lieth all their medow and marsh-ground for Hay. (43)

The settlement's coherence, corporate nature, and security is fore-grounded. Such a community is part of a rapidly developing communication/transportation system, a network of which Spenser would have been proud. Thus Johnson celebrates: "The constant penetrating farther into this Wilderness, hath caused the wild and uncouth woods to be fil'd with frequented wayes, and the large rivers to be over-laid with Bridges passeable, both for horse and foot" (234). The lands formerly inhabited by Indians[22] are given meaning as they are "overlaid" with the abstract and "Mart"-dependent space of the English: "Thus hath the Lord been pleased to turn one of the most hideous, boundless, and unknown Wildernesses in the world in an instant – to a well-ordered Commonwealth" (248).

Such a process occurs throughout the "Common-wealth and Empire" of Britain (Heylyn *Microcosmus* 464). The essentially urban "garrisons of good order" and "frequented wayes" accumulated into the world-wide trading and colonial network. An Atlantic society evolved and was exemplified by the "many marriages that illustrate the gradual joining of mercantile and planting families of the West Indies with New England and the Low Countries, as well as with Britain" (Bridenbaugh and Bridenbaugh *No Peace* 132). Lest it seem that the sometimes radical differences between colonies are being conflated, I want to stress the *interdependence* of colonies and the similarity of their situations when we speak of who was free, who was not, how a minority ruled, how the majority was ruled (and resisted), and the system of exploitation that all were involved in. Two brief examples will serve to underline the cohesion of this small world. The expansion of the garrison government of the governors-general brought a certain uniformity to Atlantic society. Familial and ideological connections traversed the seas: "From frontier forts, the garrison patrols could seek the native rebels in their 'fastnesses, bogs, and woods,' as, in the 1640s, Sir John Berkeley's men did in Connaught and his brother Sir William's soldiers did in Virginia" (Webb *Governors* 40). A direct beneficiary of such a network is what I call the "Winthrop Triangle" or the colonial power and property of the Winthrop family in New England, Antigua, and Ireland. Like the Downing family, they are an exemplary case of how individuals of a particular social standing and ideology connected an inter-colonial, transatlantic cultural sphere, despite vast differences in local conditions and developments.[23]

Similarly, we should recognize how the colonies, however different in founding principles and populations, interacted with one another and London. For instance, New England was an indispensable General Store for its seeming opposite, the English West Indies.[24] The trade and mutual emigration began in the 1630s leading Governor Winthrop to proclaim: "it pleased the Lord to open to us a trade with Barbados and other Islands in the West Indies" (quoted in Dunn *Sugar and Slaves* 336). Even the most "socially primitive" colonies, especially the early seventeenth-century Chesapeake and the West Indian ventures, were, as Carole Shammas observes, "commercially sophisticated, possessing close market ties with the metropolis, London, and enjoying, by pre-industrial standards, a high per capita output" (in Andrews, Canny, and Hair *Westward Enterprise* 152).

I now want to re-situate an example of colony formation, which is inseparable from reterritorializing projects in the British Isles that we have studied so far. Clearly New England still retains its very political prominence in the history of the British Empire and, of course, North America. This prominence not only runs counter to the low priority of New England to British interests, underscored by the vast majority of emigrants going either to the Caribbean, the Chesapeake, and Ireland, but to the importance of North America as a whole to Britain.[25] The investments and dividends were in the East and in the Caribbean. We might then heed Hugh Kearney's criticism of 1978, that: "the southern colonies, in which, along with the West Indies and Ireland, capital investment and economic exploitation set the tone of society, have largely been ignored" (in Andrews, Canny, and Hair *Westward Enterprise* 300). The work of D. W. Meinig is the leading example of an attempt at righting this distortion and producing an understanding of an "Atlantic America." At the risk, however, of perpetuating a still latent privileging of New England, I now want to turn to William Bradford's representation of colonial space and place-formation in *Of Plymouth Plantation 1620–47*. I do so precisely because of New England's cultural and political influence, and also because the New England settlements might at first appear to have less to do with the voracious exploitation and production of space that characterized Virginia or Barbados.   The Pilgrims and the Puritan migration to New England represented a distinct break in the conception of colonies – nowhere else had the idea of a corporate community really taken root, or indeed been intended. They did however come close to Bacon's ideal in "Of Plantations." Written after the Pilgrims had disembarked, after the 1622 massacre in Virginia, and in light of the public criticism of colonies and companies, Bacon argues against furnishing colonies with "the scum of people and wicked condemned men" (*Essays* 162). He describes the founding of a more certain cultural space than that which had been so nearly erased in Virginia. The opposition between the corporate settlement and the "unsettled" company outpost, was becoming resolved in the former's favor (though Virginian planters large and small ignored such advice). Meinig describes the "empire" around 1630 as

a geographic type of empire that was therefore fragmentary, shallow in continental impact, irregular in territorial hierarchy. Because a large share of the
Europeans came as sojourners rather than settlers, assigned for a tour of duty or
attracted by the hope of profit, it was a system that tended to foster spatial and
class segregation rather than the integration of European and local peoples.
Such geopolitical systems were also unusually flexible and unstable... (*Atlantic
America* 62–3)

Bacon writes to stabilize the system, even urging his countrymen to "use them [Indians] justly and graciously," though he adds "with sufficient guard nevertheless" (*Essays* 164). He warns against inflated hopes of immediate profit and instead emphasizes the need to establish self-sufficient, long-term communities. He argues for communities based on land held in "a common stock," government by "noblemen and gentle-men" wielding "martial laws, with some limitations," as well as the need to allow these settlements free trade: "Let there be freedoms from custom till the plantation be of strength, and not only from custom, but freedom to carry their commodities where they may make their best of them" (163–4). The synthesis of hierarchy, consensus, corporate welfare, self-sufficient agriculture, trade, and discipline (i.e. carefully selecting inhabitants) closely resembles the priorities and social ordering of many Puritan settlements.

Bacon's ruling elite, however, may not seem to fit Plymouth. His ideal leaders have more in common with the Massachusetts colony, particu-larly the personage of John Winthrop, who was of the landed, politically involved gentry, who often traveled to London and "knew firsthand how a country community operated" (Breen *Puritans and Adventurers* 21–2). A great number of the emigrants during the 1630s were persons of substance and, more precisely, shared an ideology of paternalism, independence, and a moral economy to check commercial pursuits. The substance might have been less apparent in those who organized Plymouth, but not the basic ideology. Meinig describes the surprisingly homogeneous group who sailed to New England as

well educated (virtually all were literate), skilled, and prosperous. In England most had been artisans and tradesmen, but some had been farmers and a number were mercantile entrepreneurs of considerable means and influential connections. They emigrated as nuclear families, some bringing along a few servants, and many families came as members of a congregation under the leadership of a minister. (*Atlantic America* 103–4)

This of course contrasted sharply with the Chesapeake or West Indies, where one was "either an exploiter or a resource" (Breen *Puritans and Adventurers* 113). The point is that Bradford and his vision of a closed, corporate, and fortified "commonwealth" surrounded by a dangerous wilderness is virtually identical to Winthrop's grander (befitting his higher social status) vision of an equally structured "Citty upon a Hill," and not dissimilar from the country-house ethos. Indeed, we may add John Smith's "prospect, for an invincible strong City" (*Complete Works*

81). In short, the Puritans viewed space and community from the ideological stand-point of yeomen, artisans, and gentry. Moreover, most subscribed to notions of social contract and control derived from direct – many emigrants came from urban origins and turned farmers – or indirect experience of English towns. The local history or chorography that Bradford writes is about the attempt to create a better social space, with Plymouth an embattled ideal, and the Pilgrims naming, subdividing, and commanding "a hideous and desolate wilderness" (*Plymouth Plantation* 70) into a new geography and history which bespeaks the authority of a civilized and godly order.

Amongst the first things that strike Bradford's congregation when in Holland (their first place of exile) are the "many goodly and fortified cities, strongly walled and guarded with troops of armed men" (16). Already feeling alien and that the congregation had "come into a new world" (16), it is this sight/site of a secure and well-regulated community that Bradford always feels is denied his congregation. Keeping in mind the retrospective heroicizing of Bradford's project, written ten years after the founding of the colony, *Plymouth* initially locates the Pilgrims between "savage barbarians . . . readier to fill their sides full of arrows than otherwise" (70) and the sea. Whichever way they turn their backs are up against a wilderness: "the whole country, full of woods and thickets, represented a wild and savage hue. If they looked behind them, there was the mighty ocean which . . . was now as a main bar and gulf to separate them from all the civil parts of the world" (70). Biblically they are let down: there is no barbarian community to offer them succour and no "top of Pisgah to view from this wilderness a more goodly country to feed their hopes . . ." (70). Two points are worth remembering here: the first is that the colonizer draws from the pool of colonial (and biblical) codes, signifiers, and representations whatever tool will serve the project at hand or the ends desired. And second, Bradford's rewriting, however distant from the reality of a decade before, reflects the ongoing struggles over colonial space and the ongoing subjugation, removal and extermination of Indians: "the place they had thoughts on was some of those vast and unpeopled countries of America, which are fruitful and fit for habitation, being devoid of all civil inhabitants, where there are only savage and brutish men which range up and down, little otherwise than the wild beasts of the same" (26).

Bradford's account of the congregation's debate about the merits and dangers of Guiana and Virginia (the danger of "savages" is a possibility in the latter [27]) has absorbed the ideological turning point of 1622.[26]

Before the massacre in Virginia, relations between the Indians and the English were determined by the needs of the English to survive, explore, and to learn from the Indians, as well as by the mutual desire for trade. Before 1622, Hakluyt, Purchas, and the Virginia Company all recommended respectful relations with the Indians or natives; the term "savages" was rarely used (Jennings *Invasion* 76–7). But as settlement and specifically the land-consuming tobacco cultivation began to override trade with the Indians, the diplomatic and entirely pragmatic relations broke down, and the Indians in Virginia rose up in 1622. Reflecting the new attitude to the now vicious savages and beasts, Bradford erases the oft reported park-like aspect of the countryside and virtually any trace of the cultural space and institutions of the Indians which had saved his colony, and in their stead imposes the "hideous and desolate wilderness" teeming with temptations and ways for one to be ambushed, consumed, and disappear. The scene of the Pilgrim's ransacking Indian graves and dwellings (73–4) – implicitly recognizing the cultural space of the Indians whilst desecrating it – epitomizes this erasure. Invoking Purchas (*Plymouth Plantation* 91) and the wolf-like Indians of the first encounter on this continent of "unpeopled countries" (76–7), Bradford is squarely within the post-1622 logic and the right of conquest even though he recognizes the hospitality of the first Thanksgiving and the Caliban-like Squanto who "directed them how to set their corn, where to take fish, and to procure other commodities" (79).

What soon becomes clear, however, is that the Indians were not the most urgent problem for Bradford and other colonial rulers. As far as the Indians were concerned, they were relatively few due to a recent plague, and the English held a monopoly of violence. At this stage the threat of the Indians was more of a ploy to keep the colonist in line. As always fellow colonists were a greater threat to the security and social structure of the colony. The story of the colonists who lose their way in the woods, "falling into such thickets as were ready to tear their clothes and armor in pieces" (73), serves both as a lesson about the threat of Indian ambush in untamed space *and* about the need to stick together. Self possession is conflated with space possessed and secured under the proper regimes of signification and power. The lesson of *placement*, socially and spatially, is crucial to the success of the colony and, as Bradford's tedious notes about the colonies' business affairs testify, financial returns. The number of times questions of discipline (and insubordination) arise shows that the governors had their hands full in trying to teach this lesson.

What connects Purchas, Plymouth, and Penshurst is the conflation of fidelity to one's superiors and one's "place" (the anarchic alternative always lurking in the wings) with the subjection of nature through the harnessing of paradisal abundance for God and country. The domination of nature so clear in the lists of accessible natural resources which appear in the country-house poem and many surveys of America, presents itself in Bradford's text as the heroic labor of replenishment in marked contrast to the "derangement" waiting for those who wander without the right compass. The discourse of disease is used to shore up the ideological and physical enclosure and enclosing of the colonizer. The detailed account of the Indians suffering from "small pox" (302) and the immunity of the charitable English, with its implicit divine privileging of the latter over the former, resonates throughout the text. It serves to show how nature rejects the indigenous population, just as they reject nature through their lack of (European) cultivation. At the same time, there is always the potential of "catching" an infection which will destroy oneself and threaten the community: dissenting religious doctrines cause "infection" (353). And there was always the threat of defection: to another colony or to the Indians. A "very profane young man ... [who had] lived among the Indians as a savage ... used their manners ... got their language" could still fall back into "evil courses" (242). In other words, wasting away and infection, waste and defection always lie outside strictly regulated colonial space. Like Spenser, Fynes Moryson castigates the "English Irish [who] forgetting their owne Countrey, are somewhat infected with the Irish rudenesse" (*Itinerary* 236). The English colonist in New England was also prey to forgetting his or her "Countrey": one's identity, duty, and social relations.

In the face of "Barbarisme and desolation," people like "wilde Beastes" and "Canniballes," Sir John Davies proposes for Ireland's replenishment "Parke[s] stored with Deere," "Maritime Citties and Townes," and that colonists "plant Gardens or Orchards, Inclose or improve their Lands, live together in setled Villages or Townes" (*Discoverie* 163–71). But most important of all to Davies is the need to have everything out in the open: disclosed to surveillance and regulation. Bradford, in a backhanded recommendation for the organization of a colony, agrees with Davies on the divulging of space, the better to recognize (and defeat) "wickedness":

here people are but few in comparison of other places which are full and populous and lie hid, as it were, in a wood or thicket and horrible evils by that means are never seen or known; whereas here they are, as it were, brought into the light and set in the plain field, or rather on a hill, made conspicuous to the view of all. (*Plymouth Plantation* 352)

Opening up, however, meant the enclosing of colonial space in the interests of the colonizer. Not surprisingly, Bradford is at his most upbeat when the coordinates and ordnance defining a corporate and secured community are established:

[The colonists] agreed to enclose their dwellings with a good strong pale ... everyone had their quarter appointed them unto which they were to repair upon any sudden alarm ... to prevent Indian treachery... This was accomplished very cheerfully, and the town impaled round ... in which every family had a pretty garden plot secured. (*Plymouth Plantation* 107)

The struggle is between fluxive "evil courses" and the structure of the "garden plot secured" within the "town impaled." To seek more than this cautious spatial regimen is to court dissolution. Echoing the disparagement of showy mansions in the country-house poem and a critique of *laissez-faire* individualism, Bradford derides the fantasies of those who came to build "great houses" and become wealthy "all of a sudden" (146). In contrast, Bradford takes great pleasure in detailing his community, built with the example of the Romans in mind: "And to every person was given one acre of land, to them and theirs, as near the town as might be; and they had no more till the seven years were expired. The reason was that they might be kept close together, both for more safety and defense, and the better improvement of the general employments" (160–1). Bradford dismisses those pursuing "castles in the air" (146) in order to stress the corporate castle on the ground, spatially wary of social unrest and threats from the wilderness. In 1634, William Wood is very clear that one cannot successfully colonize a wilderness without a monopoly of violence and defences: "because security hath been the overthrow of many a new plantation, it is their care according to their abilities, to secure themselves by fortifications, as well as they can" (*New England's Prospects* 58–9). As we shall see, however, Bradford's community came to grief not due to Indians but at the hands of fellow colonists and capitalists, as the subtitle "Prosperity Brings Dispersal of Population" (*Plymouth Plantation* 281) implies.

Like Spenser, Bradford finds colonialism intensely unsettling (literally and figuratively): "so uncertain are the mutable things of this unstable world" he complains (131). But for Bradford it was not the allure of an alien society that threatened; it was the dynamism of capital accumulation coursing through the Atlantic world. He would have felt any sign of disintegration keenly since he was part of an experiment to mitigate the excesses of capitalism as well as combat the weaknesses of Anglican Protestantism. Bradford's anxiety about the dissolution of community has its scenario confirmed in the chaotic, competitive, and all-devouring expansion of Virginia. Like Ireland, the government of Virginia, up until the middle of the century, was controlled by unregulated and unscrupulous planters. Moral and spatial dissolution resulted in both places, though more so in Virginia because tobacco cultivation exacerbated haphazard land-grabbing and exploitation of land and labor.[27] Such an exploitative, shifting, and dispersed social order was anathema to Puritan leaders like Bradford and Winthrop. But one suspects, especially in Winthrop's case, the anathema had rather more to do with unstable power relations, and less to do with a minority controlling large amounts of land and seeking profits and exports on the world market. As if issuing from the spatial chaos of Virginia, Thomas Morton of Merry-Mount embodied subversion itself. Bradford labeled him the "Lord of Misrule," a label Morton would probably not have disputed. Both Bradford and Morton viewed those at "Ma-re Mount" as having "become Masters, and masterless people" (Morton 94). This was a specter that haunted England and New England alike.

In fact, Morton simply saw space and social relations differently from colonial authorities in general, and Bradford in particular. Not that Morton was against colonization; on the contrary, he approved of the project "to inlarge the territories of his Majesties empires by planting Colonies in America" (*New English Canaan* 42). He reproduced the shopping list of commodities – the white pines would give England superiority in navigation and so on – as did all colonial surveyors. Nevertheless, while Bradford's men ransacked the graves and stores of corn placed in the ground, Morton noted that "their [the Indians'] Barns are holes made in the earth" (22). This simple but revealing observation hints at the topsy-turvy way Morton, and others, viewed the geography and cultural spaces of New England. Turning upside down the dominant perspective of spatiality usually goes along with counter-hegemonic views and practices. What really bothered the Puritan authorities was Morton's relations with the Indians, who he argued were more humane than the English (15, 77). This sort of behavior in Bradford's eyes set a dangerous example of "a dissolute life" (*Plymouth Plantation* 227).[28] It is logical to Bradford, therefore, that Thomas Weston's renegade colony, with its "disorder" and "keeping of Indian women," ends in thievery and dissolution, the hapless colonists "scattered up and down in the woods" (128). Plymouth's strict segregation from the Indians, selection of its own "congregation," and the organization of land around the town "seek[s] to keep the people together as much as might be" (209).

More than anything else, by establishing a counter-hegemonic place where a cultural exchange between the English and Indians seems to exist on a more equal basis, Morton threatened the "commodiousness" of colonial space: he might reduce the *advantage* (over the Indians) and *productivity* of the English colonists. An alternative cultural space and set of social values might loosen the hierarchy and mercantilist ideology of the Plymouth as well as the Massachusetts Bay leadership. If "inviting the Indian women for their consorts" was not enough of a crime, Morton traded guns with the Indians: "he taught them how to use them, to charge and discharge, and what proportion of powder [to use] … [he] told them how gunpowder is made, and all the materials in it, and that they are to be had *in their own land*" (emphasis added 228–30). That the Indians might utilize the resources of their land in ways that potentially oppose the English, seems to Bradford particularly outrageous. The guns will allow the Indians to claim and protect their land, to claim rights.

Bradford records that something had to be done by the colonists "before their colonies in these parts be overthrown by these barbarous savages … [and] traitors to their neighbors and country". The "terror" of "meeting the Indians in the woods armed with guns" was too much (230). The wilderness, in effect, is changed from a space awaiting anglicization to an indianized territory. Just as important, the lack of segregation and organized social and spatial relations boded ill for the disciplined hierarchy of the colony: significantly Morton "kept no servants" and attracted "scum" and "discontents … from all places." "This mischief would quickly spread over all," argues Bradford, "if this nest was not broken" (230). "The country could not bear the injury he did" Bradford concludes (231). Which of course may have been true.

That "nest" was broken, others were not. But the type of dissidence represented by Morton and his blurring of the division between races and classes did not ultimately break up the corporate community of Plymouth. Market forces were far more effective and impossible to contain. As Boston and its outlying areas grew in population and the trade with the West Indies, England, and Ireland increased, the pressure and profits of producing foodstuffs led New Englanders to look to larger farms as well as real-estate speculation. Bradford records the process with clarity:

> the people of the Plantation began to grow in their outward estates, by reason of the flowing of many people into the country, especially into the Bay of the Massachusetts. By which means corn and cattle rose to a great price, by which many were much enriched and commodities grew plentiful . . . as their stocks increased and the increase vendible, there was no longer any holding them together. (281)

Bradford sees the triumph of *laissez-faire* individualism as a great "hurt" to the scattering colonists, dividing them from one another and of course from their social responsibilities; corporatism, as embodied in a compact town is now left "almost desolate" (282). The three offshoots of the Plymouth church, Duxbury, Marshfield, and Eastham, came out of Bradford's attempt to compromise over the desire of so many of leave:

> to prevent any further scattering from this place and weakening of the same, it was thought best to give out some good farms to special persons that would promise to live at Plymouth, and likely to be helpful to the church or commonwealth, and so tie the lands to Plymouth . . . But, alas, this remedy proved worse than the disease. (282)

Bradford associates dissolution of community with deranged living: New England will be ruined (283) by the free-for-all that market forces and possessive individualism represented. Plymouth's social order did not, however, disappear. Hierarchical and religious bonds were loosened but only to better colonize surrounding areas. Plymouth's elite usually controlled, through shareholding, the new towns. Significantly, the dissolving of bonds between the individual, his or her "place," and the traditional authorities by capitalism, is part of the very same process that brought the Puritans to North America and drove Puritan leaders to speculate in real estate, encourage trade, and set up new towns.

Bradford's text might symbolically fade away on the note of dissolution (369), but other colonial leaders continued to articulate the dangers of unregulated expansion. Winthrop's legal logic regarding ownership was aimed just as much at expropriating Indian land as controlling the expansion of the English (Jennings *Invasion* 136). The authorities' fear of "scattered" colonists identifying with the Indians or other European powers rather than obeying the elite of their own social system threatens to objectify the hegemony of the natural rulers.[29] Although most leaders were heavily invested in expansion, it was a process that they recognized had to be mystified and overseen. Thus there was the constant need for the leadership to keep the colonists ideologically primed: to be "vigilant," to fear the wilderness and blood-lust of the Indians, and to regiment the landscape to serve piety, property, and profits. The social space of the English is (always) under threat from Catholic and Indian barabarism alike. As Bradford in one instance puts it: the French "encroach" and arm the Indians "to the great danger of the English, who lie open and unfortified living upon husbandry, and the other closed up in their forts, well fortified, and live upon trade in good security" (312).

Of Plymouth Plantation ends with the departure of one of the original "Pilgrim Fathers": Edward Winslow leaves in 1646 for England and into military service for Oliver Cromwell. In 1655, as one of the commanders of the expeditionary force, Winslow helped conquer Jamaica.[30] Winslow's duties and journeys remind us of the imperial cartography within which Plymouth was one small node. From *that* locality of power, we can follow the "lines of force" back to the English Revolution and Cromwell's imperial designs, and thus to the Highlands, Ireland, and the West Indies. Traveling through this network, accompanying Winslow and colonial violence, were company directives, goods and profits, entrepreneurial zest, and migrants of all stripes. The colonies were outposts, but outposts of a world-wide market.

John Fredrick Martin has convincingly shown how entrepreneurs were "at the heart of the effort to settle the wilderness" (*Profits in the Wilderness* 3). The "cream of New England society" – men like John Winthrop Jr., John Hull, the Hutchinsons, James Fitch and Thomas Pynchon[31] – were speculators in land (127). In other words, New England for many of the Puritan leading lights was little more than an unparalleled opportunity to gain wealth through the subdividing of expropriated lands, especially, in this period, the lands of the Pequot and Narrangansett Indians.[32] Similar to the gentry in England, the Puritan leaders used idealized social values to mystify and support the marketing, managing, and production of space for their ownership, prestige, and profit. They preached welfare and community, but practiced exploitation for their individual gain. These entrepreneur colonists were wealthy, well-connected, educated, urban, and usually in the government and military; they were absentee landholders or nonresidents in numerous towns; they might launch five to twenty towns in several regions or colonies;[33] they were often related to one another and conducted business along an intricate grid (46). Nearly one third of Plymouth colony towns in the seventeenth century were established by individuals who didn't settle them. All the Plymouth leaders, including Bradford, invested in real estate (79–80).

A sure method of controlling expansion and the social order was to base the whole system on a network of shareholders. Importing from England their business acumen and their ideological conceptions about space and its organization, the colonial elites maintained power by making "inhabitancy" within a town and the subsequent rights, responsibilities, taxation, division of land, and voting dependent upon shares (185). Space and place were "splintered," socialized, staked, and parceled out by shareholders.[34] "Whether it was a town or company, whether the asset was land or lumber," asserts Martin, "land corporations tightly controlled admissions and distributed assets with extraordinary vigilance" (227). The Puritan emphasis on bringing order and fixity to chaotic social change now takes on a different hue. Like their class in Virginia and Barbados, as well as in Old England, the New England elite profited from the ownership and management of real estate. No wonder Thomas Morton's unlicensed goings-on disturbed the authorities; his Maypole threatened the carefully choreographed (and chorographed) expansion.

The authoritarian Bradford protecting his community and the anarchic energy of Morton's overtures to the Indians are part of a single, dynamic system. It was a system, as Martin describes it, that compressed space in the interests of the profit margin:

It was a long distance from the joint-stock companies of England to the wilderness of New England. But the plantation companies, those corporations created in the early seventeenth century to colonize America spanned the distance, carrying English business experience to the New World. They also brought a special view of land, which to them was not so much a time-honored place as a transferable asset: a dividend to be paid to shareholders, a commodity to be sold to settlers. (135)

The deforestation and competition for grazing lands,[35] the roads, the fences, and property laws all derived from the conception of space as a commodity to be sent to market. The chorography of the land underlines this: Indian place names reflected the use or value of a certain place, calling to mind "the things that were on the land during the various seasons of the year" (Cronon *Changes in the Land* 65), while English place names reflected abstract possession. As William Cronon puts it: "Once transferred into private hands ... [the] lands became abstract parcels whose legal definition bore no inherent relation to their use: a person owned everything on them, not just specific activities which could be conducted within their boundaries" (74). Thus the English settled on top of the former sites of Indian villages and fields (90–1) and reterritorialized the landscape: the Pequot tribe and settlements were erased and reborn as New London, Connecticut, on the Thames river, where John Winthrop and his progeny were granted the "priviledge and Right of ordering and disposing all publick Building and affairs of this towne, now and for the future" (quoted in Innes *Labor* 174).

CONTRACTING SPACE

The "priveledge and Right of ordering and disposing" of space is, I would like to suggest, the ideological mortar and practice uniting the various British elites throughout the Atlantic world. To suit the expansionist desires and economy of the British elites, space that could be colonized became *terra nullius* for the taking by those who would cultivate it properly: "Nor are his Blessings to his banks confin'd, / But free, and common, as the Sea or Wind" (Denham "Cooper's Hill" lines 179–80). Like John Locke, John Winthrop Jr. compared the state of America (and founding towns in that "wilderness") to "the beginninge of the world" (quoted in Martin *Profits in the Wilderness* 113–4). Embedded in the millenarian thrust of so much of colonial discourse is this rendering of colonial space as common land awaiting an owner. The manifest destiny of England announced itself as an empire that "Cities in deserts, woods in Cities plants. / So that to us no thing, no place is strange" (Denham "Cooper's Hill" 186–7). Sir John Denham's prospect poem, "Cooper's Hill," roots this millennial and imperial desire to the entrepot of London, "the worlds exchange" (188). Together, this notion of supremacy contracted space into slices of property, grids of communication, flows of capital, people, and knowledge coordinated by networks of ideologically and economically affiliated groups.

The control over space and the distribution of resources is played out at every level, from one's valuables to vast tracts of continental geography. The popularity in the seventeenth century of the "cabinet" which holds one's most prized objects serves as a microcosm of the country-house poem and the idyll of a "citty on a hill": all convey the strict control over one's possessions. "The ubiquitous motif of plenitude delectably contracted into narrow bounds and privately owned," as Fitter describes the cabinet, "is thus a structure of feeling much fed by the appetite for liquid capital and enclosing fields" (*Poetry, Space, Land-*

scape 265). At the bottom of representations and realities of enclosing objects or space is the belief in the legitimacy of owning natural and human resources. The privatizing and consumption of the world's riches by an elect group is part of a general contraction (homogenization and legislation) of space by colonialism at home and abroad. As Denham puts it, nature has no other master than the English: "When Natures hand this ground did thus advance, / 'Twas guided by a wiser power than Chance; / Mark't out for such a use, as if 'twere meant / T'invite the builder, and his choice prevent " ("Cooper's Hill" 53–6). Yoking England's ancient (Arthurian) power to a cosmopolitan culture of *Pax Britannica*, Denham has the Thames and the territorial waters of the British Isles lead to the "Worlds extreamest ends" (107), a journey that "makes both *Indies* ours" (184) – as if one could just place them in a display cabinet.

As the United Colonies of New England "embarked upon a career of expansionist conquest" between 1637 and 1663 (Jennings *Invasion* 254) from, as it were, their "Citty upon a Hill," Denham's journey from Cooper's Hill reflects a global space increasingly compressed by the English and their colonies.[36] The view from both hills is the same: land either subordinated by its rightful patron(s) or crying out for such ordering. Such a prospect proclaimed a new contract for society: in the British Isles the English Revolution decided which contract succeeded, while the colonies negotiated with London over their different charters. Whether colony or metropole, property rights and the production of "merchantable commodities" was the decisive factor. The market governed the social "contracts" of the country house in Suffolk, the plantations in Virginia or Barbados, and the towns of New England; it ruled out the Indians and kept the laboring populations in servitude; and it re-formed land and natural resources into a calculation and a category of private property. As capital created the "commonwealth and empire," the national enterprise became dominated by the task of making space commodious enough for the production of commodities. It was a task that quickly saw results even in the most unpromising areas. Edward Johnson in his *Wonder-Working Providence* marveled "that this Wilderness should turn a mart for Merchants in so short a space" (247).

The *contracting* of space, where land and people are converted into a new geometric, highly disciplined, and market-oriented social order, is basically the working out of sovereignty: who will be subject to whom, and on what terms. In the face of mass unrest and mobility, the struggles over national/colonial power, and the definition of a productive cultural space, sovereignty, and subjecthood are produced through the coercion and containment of space. A consensus on the shape of this brave new world was not easily come by when, in the very creases of the unfolding map of capitalism, colonial expansion, and the formation of a new ruling elite, so many counter-hegemonic notions and spaces presented themselves.

CHAPTER 4

Overseeing paradise: Milton, Behn, and Rowlandson

[D]iscipline proceeds from the distribution of individuals in space.

Foucault *Discipline and Punish* 141

[B]y the Fundamental Law of Nature, Man being to be preserved . . . one may destroy a Man who makes War upon him, or has discovered an Enmity to his being, for the same Reason, that he may kill a *Wolf* or a *Lyon*; because such Men are not under the ties of the Common Law of Reason, have no other Rule, but that of Force and Violence, and so may be treated as Beasts of Prey, those dangerous and noxious Creatures, that will be sure to destroy him, whenever he falls into their Power.   Locke *Second Treatise* 278–9

But you cannot plant an oak in a flowerpot; she must have earth for her root, and heaven for her branches.

Harrington *Oceana* 320: *Political Works*

SPATIAL CONTESTS

The cross-fertilization of English literary culture and colonialism produced a number of texts which are structured by an imagination seeking to unite and secure the English in their essentially global and contested spaces. Hakluyt saw his project as the embodiment of such a strategic imaginary. His encyclopedia of colonial tales were to form a national narrative upon which England could build an empire. The alternative, so Hakluyt implies in his Preface to the second 1589 edition of *Principal Navigations*, is for the Elizabethan nation to be dispersed to the four winds and be consumed by her predators: to disappear from history. In the face of "the greedy and devouring jawes of oblivion" Hakluyt sees it as his task "to gather likewise, and as it were to incorporate into one body the torne and scattered limmes of our ancient and late Navigations by Sea, our voyages by land, and traffiques of merchandise by both: and having (so much as in me lieth) restored ech particular member, being before displaced, to their true joynts and ligaments" (xxxix). What I want to explore in this chapter is how, almost a century later, John Milton, Aphra Behn, and Mary Rowlandson are conscious participants, even protagonists in the historical effort to protect members of an elect nation against the "devouring jawes of oblivion" even as they support expansion into the traditional haven of dissipation, the "wilderness." They warn against the forfeiture Hakluyt seeks to counter with his unifying epic: dissembling ideologies that cause the dis-assembling of English social structures. Hence, the anti-Christian and noxious doctrines that seduce Eve, that provoke the slave rebellion in *Oroonoko*, and that cause the backsliding of New England Puritans jeopardize the new design of society rapidly being implemented by mercantile capitalism under a militantly imperialist Protestant England.

The texts analyzed in this chapter are more than conductors of colonial discourse and explorations of devolving social designs and desires; they are in and of themselves acts of composition – "by the helpe of Geographie and Chronologie" (xxxix) – that respond to actual or threatened decomposition by the forces of evil, corruption, and tyranny. In those spaces where the providential and imperial geography of the Prophetic Protestant or secular colonist do not hold sway, the forces of degeneration threaten mental or physical dismemberment. Moreover, Milton, Behn, and Rowlandson, like Hakluyt, are re-membering, reconstituting a history (and geography) that sees the English as an elect body politic destined to rule over others. Their writing imagines the unification of England's colonial domain under the aegis of God, benevolent trade, settlement, and the natural historical trajectory of civilization.

The imperative to protectively enclose and render visible and coherent is not, however, defensive; the imagination that defines England's growing imperial ligaments no longer has the *hortus conclusus* as its geopolitical model. Milton and Rowlandson share a millenarian mindset with, as Chris Fitter describes it, "its expansionist, centrifugal sensibility, its enthusiasm for paradisal holiness as overflowing beyond enclosed precincts" (*Poetry, Space, Landscape* 236). Behn subscribes to a secular vision of the same colonizing imaginary. The biblical tropes of garden and hedge were more concerned with fortifying oneself against corruption rather than any geographical introversion. Milton and Behn might privilege the English garden and its exclusionary coordinates, but both see it as the coordinating centre of an expanding social order. Rowlandson's narrative underlines the dangers that Milton and Behn so clearly identify: the elect must subdue the ever-resurgent wilderness if they are to survive and fulfil their duty to God and country.

The massive acts of dismemberment known as the Virginia Massacre (1622) or the 1641 uprising in Ireland confirmed such a thesis. The actual walls proposed in the wake of the devastation were not meant to permanently segregate, but to regulate both expansion and subjugation.[1] The threat from the heathen to England's value-system was clear; for John Temple 1641 proved that the Irish, like the American Indians, "were generally devoid of all manner of civility, governed by no settled laws, living like beasts, biting and devouring one another, without all rules, customs, or reasonable constitutions either for regulation of Property, or against open force and violence" (*Irish Rebellion* 5). Without the strict enforcement of these codes of propriety and property, which in colonial terms equals "felicity and great prosperity" (14), the colony spins into a hellish state. The attention to a more systematic regimentation of space after these uprisings or after King Philip's War (1675–6) are but exaggerated instances of a more fundamental, ever-present concern with keeping both the natives *and* colonial population, especially indentured servants and slaves, in their prescribed economic locations.

The walls, hedges, and fences, both physical and metaphoric, invoked by preacher, politician, or patriarch had as much to do with expelling oppositional natives from colonial space as it had to do with regulating the geographical and ideological mobility of the mass of colonials and slaves. Colonial space was organized with one eye fearfully fixed on this population. George Wyatt, sometime planter in Ireland, advised his son, Francis Wyatt, governor of Virginia from 1621–6,

[to] look with Janus two waies on your own contrime[n] Christians, and on the salvages infidels, ... to better cherishing of the former and to the wining of the latter. Yet so as you keepe Cesars rule to his Romans unto your memory, that you reccon more of the danger of one Christian your patriot, then of numbers of pagan infidels. (Quoted in Andrews, Canny, and Hair *Westward Enterprise* 25)

As we shall see, this emphasis on the foe within and the need for constant vigilance against the forces of corruption is at the heart of the narratives this chapter explores. To combat dangers that are disguised, *superintendence* is required. The viewpoint of Milton and Behn is especially pertinent in this respect. The desire to efficiently survey and order all the components of a colonial world manifests itself in the authors' typically imperial dream to be anywhere and anything, to move uninhibited in all realms, and to possess superior knowledge. Similarly, Rowlandson is able to rise above and provide a narrative structure to her dislocations. From such an empowered position, at once in the thick of things and able to stand outside events, the authors are able to demonstrate the need for the elect to frame space. In "Bermudas" Andrew Marvell has the once feared island transformed into a refuge "temple" brimming over with natural abundance – an "eternal spring" (14) – due to the "frame" established by the English and Marvell's promotional writing. It is a framing that heralds further expansion ("Bermudas" lines 35–6: *Complete Poems*).

Hence, colonial domination depends upon who gets to "frame" colonial space: who is a member and on what terms. To wander, by accident or intention, outside the framework of membership is the prelude to "cannibalism" – the negation of one's self and one's own society. The attention to eating habits and food in Rowlandson's account clearly signals her proximity to cannibal-like behavior. In other words, the "wanderer," rebel, dissenter, and captive is liable to be either punished by one's former community or "consumed" by the wilderness. Ultimately, in the non-colonized or dis-organized space the property of one's body is up for grabs – nothing is sacred or secure. Further, it is usually the female body that represents "maps of power and identity" (Haraway *Simians* 180) issuing from the always unstable and uneven expansion of empire. The location and treatment of the female body, as we shall see shortly, is read as compass and barometer of civilization's progress.

Traditionally associated with access to and the excesses of empire, colonial women pose a threat in some ways worse than that of the Indian or Irish, since they are an internal foe who can ruin the reproduction of civilization. They are more easily "infected" with the contagion of degenerate behavior and spaces. A pamphlet in 1620, "Hic Mulier," attacked desirous "Mer-Monsters" and cross-dressing women, "all Odious, all Devil," as more than "barbarous, [since they] make the rude Scythian, the untamed Moor, the naked Indian, or the wild Irish, Lords and Rulers of well-governed cities" (quoted in Hendricks and Parker *Women, "Race" and Writing* 33). Clearly, the dissolution of gender roles is equated with spatial anarchy, and vice versa. Non-conformity, whether imposed or "voluntary," is something the youthful colonist Behn, the captive Rowlandson, and the corrupted Eve share. They need to be carefully observed since they are an indication whether space is controlled or chaotic. Rowlandson's account is an act of post-trauma self-observation. It is the necessity to organize, survey and, ultimately, police the domains of empire that inform *Paradise Lost* (1676), Rowlandson's "The Sovereignty and Goodness of God" (1682), and Behn's *Oroonoko: or The Royal Slave* (1688). These texts are conveniently positioned at the interstices – both spatially and ideologically – of an interconnected and unstable space demarcating the English imperial theatre of the Atlantic World. In this light, we might posit a general question that each of the authors seem to imply: what does it mean to be a member of a society whose social spaces and identities are radically contested or are on the verge of dissolving?

SUBSERVIENT BODIES

If imperialism is about producing subservient economic and political bodies of space, it is also concerned with bodies in space. As the bourgeois and possessive individual makes its place in history, Milton, Rowlandson, and Behn grapple with the insecurity and radical possibilities of this subject in new and unstable spaces. They represent the struggle to discipline the body and its location in conditions bubbling with issues about and occasions for liberty, individual rights, and degeneration. In just such a situation John Winthrop in 1630 preached that individuals must resign themselves to their stations in life; wandering from God's design endangers the entire community: "If one member [of the body of Christ] suffers all suffer with it" (in Gunn *Early American Writing* 110). Eve, Rowlandson, and Behn are that one member. There had been no fundamental change in this perception of the consequences of individual corruption since the 1630s, except that the tensions and stakes were greater by the 1670s and '80s. What becomes apparent is that the sovereignty of the individual is dependent upon adhering to a specific social contract *within* the space(s) of empire. By the late 1670s this contract became the "Imperial Revolution" of the British Monarchy. In the face of numerous rebellions a "Great Britain" effectively took control of the colonies as a whole and usurped the local elites who had been struggling against both metropolitan power and the centrifugal forces below them.

Part of the centrifugal pull was identified as the many anarchic bodies circulating in the realm. The individual body, especially that of women, has a direct correlation with the health of the "body politic," economic relations, the lay of the land, and the ideology of colonization.[2] William

Petty, aptly both a Professor of Anatomy and Surveyor-General of Ireland, evaluated appropriated lands in "The Political Anatomy of Ireland" (1672). When Petty writes that his survey is to "attempt some Rule in nature, whereby to value and proportionate the Lands of Ireland" (*Economic Writings* 180), his categorizing of land is also clearly about the sorting out of the role of colonists and Irish alike within England's economy: "I would hope to come to the knowledge of the Value of said Commodities, and consequently the Value of Land, by deducting the hire of Working-People on it" (180–1). The new anatomy of the English empire thus relegated the defeated and dispossessed to a value within the equation of mercantile capitalism.

But as the new social order constructs membership based on subservience and wage labor it also creates the dismembered: the "hands" and "many-headed" mob of the laboring classes. Forced into dehumanizing yet vital roles in the new system, laborer, servant, and slave are seen as a potentially dismembering force. That is to say, the new body politic cannot help but create or come into contact with (as is the case with the Irish or Amerindian) its own means of destruction. If Petty notes Ireland's "spare Hands and Lands" (192), he is also keen to stress the new anatomy's potential metamorphosis into a corrupt form. The partitioning of space, time, and movement, as Foucault has pointed out, served to maneuver "each individual [into] his own place" (*Discipline and Punish* 143). In colonial spaces regimentation was essential. "Discipline," observes Hill, "and especially labor discipline, was felt by the non-working classes to be a national necessity, preached now by economists with the same zest as by theologians" (*Century of Revolution* 253). In the British Isles as well as the more fluid space of the English colonies it was paramount to "eliminate the effects of imprecise distributions, the uncontrolled disappearance of individuals, their diffuse circulation, their unusable and dangerous coagulations" (Foucault *Discipline and Punish* 143).[3] The threat of Satan and the fate of Adam and Eve; King Philip's War, Mary Rowlandson's captivity, and her "removes", and the complex relationship between Oroonoko, the slaves, the English, and the Indians are all part of this historical process of fixing people in their right(ful) places.

While Milton and Rowlandson delineate Godly/Satanic spaces, Behn blurs the dividing line of social, territorial, and racial segregation by examining the central contradiction of the production of colonial space: the exposed constructedness of a supposedly natural social order. In all three texts, however, the natural is reconfigured as the (English) subject secure in her surroundings. If Behn is seen as the one who most problematizes the dominant socio-sexual-economic system, she nonetheless remains a "litmus test" of the control the English rulers exert over the most unsettled of spaces.[4] Rather than dispensing with chastity as a sign of submission to the social order and its metonymic parallel of chastened land (as opposed to wasteland), Behn updates the notion of chastity to signify the independent management of oneself (and the Other) in order to secure the social hierarchy. This then repositions women as trusted agents of the state at home and abroad. While Eve and Rowlandson are evidence that improvement in the methods of socio-spatial regulation is required, Behn would be a method of improvement herself. Rather than a symbol of a breach in the line between civility and barbarity, Behn is willing to put her body on the line as a crafty guardian.

As Laura Brown has forcefully argued, although the female figure has always been a component of colonial domination, the late seventeenth and early eighteenth centuries see the "feminization of imperialist accumulation" (*Ends of Empire* 13): "The female figure, through its simultaneous connections with commodification and trade on the one hand, and violence and difference on the other, plays a central role in the constitution of this mercantile capitalist ideology" (3). Women represent a map of sorts, leading either to the rewards of colonization or into deprivation. Again Brown eloquently summarizes this cultural dynamic when she writes: "in the paradigm of heroic romance, women are the objects and arbiters of male adventurism, just as, in the ideology of imperialist accumulation, women are the emblems and proxies of the whole male enterprise of colonialism" (47). More specifically, the female body is spatialized: its whereabouts and orderliness serve as an indication of how "settled" and well managed the space of the nation or colony is at a particular time. Eve wanders and thus begins the displacement of paradise; Rowlandson's "removes" underscore the backsliding of the Puritan errand to discipline the wilderness; Behn's movements and contacts allow her to map out the possibilities of English colonialism in Surinam. In all three texts the female body is a register for social equilibrium. Ultimately she represents the confirmation or wrecking of relations of property and labor, and the ownership of settled and productive territory. As Steve Pile succinctly puts it, "the body becomes a point of capture, where the dense meanings of power are animated, where cultural codes gain their apparent coherence and where the boundaries between the same and the other are installed and naturalised" (Pile and Thrift *Mapping the Subject* 41).

The negotiation of boundaries and the valuation of the wandering body is central to Milton's 1634 poem "Comus (A Masque Presented at Ludlow Castle)." While Catherine Belsey notes the political and social function of "Comus" as "a model of worldly control divinely endorsed" (*John Milton* 48), she fails to pursue the spatial implications at work in this model of colonial control.[5] Comus does indeed stand "for lechery [and] also for the abuse of wealth and power" (48) as opposed to true nobility, but he also symbolizes the dangers of uncontrolled space and its threat to the security of a ruling family such as that of the Earl of Bridgewater. As President of the Council of Wales and Lord Lieutenant of Wales, he would of course be aware of the distinction between civilized and uncivilized territory. Hence, as Belsey puts it, "'Comus' is about rape" (46), but rape mediated, in time-honored fashion, by issues about the domination of land and the threat to the social order by those areas deemed wild. It is telling that the nymph Sabrina, a Welsh border-spirit of justice, is reformed by Milton into a placeless protectoress of young (English) virgins (Kendrick "Milton and Sexuality" 69). The spirit of Wales is recruited to serve English claims to domination.

In this colonial fable Milton has the "Imperial rule of all the Sea-girt Isles" ("Comus" line 21: *Complete Poems*) threatened by the "hideous wood" where Comus dwells (519). As they travel to visit their father, the children face the domain of Comus that "Threats the forlorn and wandering passenger" (36–9). The distinctly unEnglish Comus tempts and entraps travelers with a potion that, significantly, leads to "foul disfigurement" (74). As the signifier for controlled and unpolluted space, the wandering virgin, whose "unacquainted feet / In the blind mazes of this tangl'd Wood" (179–80) lead her into a "close dungeon" (348), underscores not only the potential to lose one's integrity in "situations" beyond civilized social structures, but also the potential for the hierarchy of the authorities to be subverted or "ravished." It is via the indeterminacy of unregulated space that Milton articulates his contradictory support for, on the one hand, the Lady as the bourgeois individual struggling to maintain propriety over an errant (even adventurous) subjectivity and, on the other, the discipline of a stable social hierarchy (Kendrick "Milton and Sexuality" 66). However we interpret Milton's conception of hierarchy, the value of the Lady is in her ability to reproduce the social order. Rape threatens to ruin the virtue/unity of woman and society; it represents the usurpation of property rights over women and by extension territory, identity, and those who rule by virtue of integrity (rather than pure blood). Just as the "disfigurement" can transform the chaste into a member of the "wild surrounding waste", the waste, both human and geographical, can become "chaste." Chastity here is synonymous with domination.[6] Thus when the Lady's brothers vouch for her virginity they also vouch for the superior spatial order from which she hails and obeys. Moreover, they issue a threat suitable to those used to command space: "No savage fierce, bandit, or mountaineer / Will dare to soil her virgin purity" ("Comus" lines 425–6).

On the other hand, Eve's loss of "chastity" via a disfigured Satan results in expulsion into the wilderness. Though Rowlandson wrestles to preserve her own physical and mental chastity she seems permanently scarred. And Behn's chastity – sexual and patriotic – is in a constant state of ambiguity and jeopardy. Like the social formations emerging at home and abroad in the latter half of the seventeenth century, the female figure is subject to the threat of being pulled apart by the competing and contributing forces of race, gender, religion, nationality, and class. Bunyan captures the social forces of early modernity as they are imagined through the female body: "Mansoul! her wars seem'd endless in her eyes, / She's lost by one, becomes another's prize / And he again that lost her last would swear, / 'Have her I will, or her in pieces tear'" (*Holy War* "To the Reader" lines 28–31).

GEOGRAPHY AND VIGILANCE

Bunyan's fraught vision was central to the Puritan and imperial imagination; from the body to the cosmos an historical contest was taking place, pitting the saintly against the anti-Christian and anti-English. What was essentially an imperial struggle played itself out within what Stallybrass and White call a "system of extremes which encode the body, the social order, psychic form and spatial location" (*Politics and Poetics* 3). The opposition of "chaste" versus waste serves as a neat example of this system. They go on to stress the interdependency of these "domains" and "how each extremity structures the other, depends upon and invades the other" (3). For Milton, Rowlandson, and Behn the individual's conscience and body are inextricably part of a dangerous spatial contest that binds the local to the global, even to the universal.

It is this contest, where boundaries are severely tested and often transgressed, that Cotton Mather describes during King Philip's War.

The Puritans have been thrust into the domain of Comus: English women face "violations by the *Outrageous Lusts* of the Salvages" (*Decennium* 241); disfigurement rears its head in the form of "Half Indianized French and Half Frenchified Indians" (46); and English captives suffer barbaric tortures by "our Enemies" who retreat into "those *Inaccessible Thickets*, where we despair ever to *Find 'em out*" (245). Similarly, planters in Barbados are faced with their adversaries disappearing into wilderness. In 1655 it was recorded

that several runaway Negroes and some Irish servants were out in rebellion . . . in an area known as The Thicket . . . The rebels were said to be behaving in a "rebellious and arrogant manner," "making a mockery of the law, and attempting to draw other slaves into their design." (Beckles *Black Rebellion in Barbados* 34)

As Petty noted, value (the security of one's property and investment) depends on making bodies and territory visible to the eye of the master. This accountability – the capacity to monitor, place or contain groups for one's profit – eludes colonists on Barbados as well as in New England. As Richard Ligon in his *A True and Exact History of the Island of Barbadoes* (1673) recounts: "in the night [runaway slaves] range abroad the Countrey . . . and the nights being dark, and their bodies black, they scape undiscern'd" (98). In other words, value instead of accumulating was vanishing. For Mather, a violent promiscuity renders the whole Puritan mission insecure, its very integrity threatened by invisible or unrecognizable foes. It is the danger of bodies merging or fusing with the wildness that Milton, Behn, and Rowlandson explore.

The period between the 1640s and 90s was one of revolution and rebellion. The accelerating economy and radical doctrines of liberty were barely checked by a revolutionary bourgeoisie seeking the reins of state power. The English Atlantic world was riven at every level with the reverberations of republican ideology, political revolution, colonial autonomy, and economic instability. James Lang notes "a recurrent pattern of imperial centralization and colonial resistance" (*Conquest and Commerce* 152). Milton, Behn, and Puritan society in general critiqued the satanic energy of mercantile capitalism and its doctrine of *laissez-faire* individualism; they saw it as a force not only of moral corruption and antithetical to a corporate community, but also one that threatened to ignite the ever-inflammable multitude.

T. H. Breen documents the well-founded fears of the governing bodies in the colonies during the 1660s to the '90s, due to the increasing use of slave labor, the growth of population and secular values, the strain of war and resentment against taxes, and the rise of local merchant elites demanding a greater say in the running of the colony (*Puritans and Adventurers* 84). The generalized instability is revealed by the nervous remarks of Virginian leaders on Culpeper's Rebellion in Carolina: "being exceeding sensible of the dangerous consequences of this Rebellion, as that if they be not suddenly subdued hundreds of idle debtors, theeves, Negros, Indians and English servants will fly unto them" (quoted in Breen *Puritans and Adventurers* 139). The 1670s, especially 1676, saw numerous rebellions of the "giddy multitude" against wage-labor, bond-servitude, slavery, and dispossession. The struggle to impose and maintain a socio-spatial hierarchy conducive to commodity production pitted the "outlandish" against the landed. In the most advanced colony of the English empire Hilary Beckles observes that "persistent slave resistance and white reactions represented the most noticeable features of early Barbadian society" (*Black Rebellion in Barbados* 25).

The garrison mentality of the land-holding whites led to the creation of "a police state" and the imposition of repressive codes like the 1661 "Act for the Better Ordering and Governing of Negroes" (31). The same year saw the Servant Code passed – "An Act for the Good Governing of Servants, and Ordaining the Rights between Masters and Servants" – which effectively enforced both racial segregation and the rule of the propertied. As Steven Saunders Webb argues, a garrison mentality was common throughout the Atlantic world because "the governmental institutions of England's colonies, whether in Ireland, the West Indies, or North America, [ ] were shaped by military men" (*Governors* 438) who were intent on imposing an "imperial ethos [of] social order, political loyalty, economic discipline, [and] military preparedness" (xvii). In 1675 the retitled "crown colonies" returned to the rule of military governors. As we shall see, an intrinsic component of paradise is discipline; Milton states in *The Reason of Church Government* (1642), "the state of the blessed in Paradise, though never so perfect, is not therefore left without discipline, whose golden survaying reed marks out and measures every quarter and circuit of new Jerusalem" (*Complete Prose Works* 1.752). It is a militarism that not only echoes Heaven's state "Of Hierarchies, of Orders, and Degrees" (*Paradise Lost* v.591), but Milton's plan for a Commonwealth put forward in *The Readie and Easie Way*. However, the compartmentalization of space, which structures *Paradise Lost* as much as the environments described by Behn and Rowlandson, is not guarantee against subversion. For the colonial elite, surveillance coupled with segregation was the name of the game, especially when the aim of an aborted revolt by *servants* on Barbados in 1673 was "to fall upon their Masters, and cut all their throats, and by that means, to make themselves not only freeman, but Masters of the Island" (Ligon *True and Exact History* 46).

Cotton Mather identifies two strategies with which to combat such designs. "Self-Reformation" (*Decennium* 253) and the expansion of "the English Empire" (*Magnalia* 172):"*Geography* must now find work for a *Christiano-graphy* in Regions far enough beyond the Bounds wherein the *Church* of God had through all former Ages been circumscribed" (118). If this well describes the Protestant empire Milton supports – a "supreme power without limits" (Pagden *Lords* 26) – a more scientific front for the same ends was being formulated by many of those whom associated with the poet. The network made up of Samuel Hartlib, Petty, Boyle, and Gerard Boate (center of the Invisible College in Ireland) among others, set about re-forming and improving the world. This grand project ranged from more efficient estate management to reconstituting Ireland's history and geography. The shift from subjective geography (chorography) to a more scientific mode (cartography) is part of a movement to catalogue, classify, and quantify the obscure, the subversive, and the unknown (Chambers *Reinvention of the World* 21–3). In other words, a culture of surveillance and surveying, of rendering the invisible/insidious legible developed in order to match reality to the image and standards of Protestant and imperial England. Gerard Boate's *Irelands Naturall History* (1652), for instance, attempts to map a new English plot onto the insubordinate spaces of Ireland. If the mapping projects of Saxton and others "took effective visual and conceptual possession of the physical kingdom" (Helgerson *Forms of Nationhood* 107) then Milton, for example, institutes a similar possession of the globe in the name of an elect nation. Behn and Rowlandson struggle to retain their conceptions of space in the face of shifting and non-English geographies. Moreover, the visibility "in a real-life theatre of power" crucial to the monarch's authority is in Milton, Behn and Rowlandson transferred to the individual-in-the-world struggling to hold one's own in the contests over space (152). If republicanism and colonialism are to succeed the authority traditionally invested in the crown must be distributed to the adventuring individual.

To be in a position to survey, secretly or publicly, is a requisite of colonial power. Unless the colonizer has a monopoly of sight/site, domination is impossible. For a good part of *Paradise Lost* it is Satan who enjoys this power. When Adam is finally shown the world it is to counter

Satan's godly eye. In Behn's and Rowlandson's accounts hostilities are able flourish because the enemy is able to organize, watch, and mount operations out of sight. They write to confirm the integrity (and righteousness) of their sight, their point of view, or their conception of a colonial community. We might say that a sort of ichnography is sought after: what is important about recording or creating the ground-plan of any given place is that it enables one to keep a track of bodies, trace movements and communications. The near universal fear of masterless men and women turned mobility and "wildernesses" into targets of regulation.[7] Thus the strategic geography developed during the seventeenth century was aimed at Ireland, at Amerindian and African revolts, and at the "transatlantic class conflict" (Rediker "Stout Hands" 137), which was fueled by what Behn calls the "Fury of the *English* Mobile" (*Oroonoko* 71).[8] The ability to move undetected and to rebel were confronted with a battery of techniques of control. The texts invoke these in the face of Satan's peregrinations, the uprisings in Behn's Surinam, and Rowlandson's ever-moving Indians, whose mobility the Puritan poet Benjamin Tompson described as: "From farms to farms, from towns to towns they post, / They strip, they bind, they ravish, flay, and roast" (in Slotkin and Folsom *So Dreadful a Judgement* 219).

In order to prevent such deadly peregrinations one had to *check* bodies and their whereabouts. The committee set up to investigate the aborted revolt of 1675 on Barbados "noted that much of the rebels' planning and discussions had taken place while they were traveling about the island, both on legitimate plantation business and while attending their own socio-cultural functions" (Beckles *Black Rebellion in Barbados* 38). The resultant act of 1676 stated that "it is absolutely necessary for the safety of this place, to restrain the wandering and meetings of Negroes at all times especially on Saturday nights, Sundays, and other holidays" (quoted in Beckles *Black Rebellion in Barbados* 39). Toward similar ends, the plague legislation of 1666 "had behind it the ambition to regulate and direct much more than plague itself" (Slack *Impact of Plague* 304). "Lewd women" and those who frequented inns and alehouses – the wild places of the city – were particularly targeted. (And in this light it is significant that Behn and Rowlandson are careful to document their movements.) Spatial regulation was instituted under the Settlement Act of 1662 in England, and through restrictions on community membership and the "warning out" of undesirables in the American colonies, and the passes servants and slaves needed for travel in Virginia and Barbados (Breen *Puritans and Adventurers* 136). The workhouse, the ship as factory, John Ogilby's road maps,[9] and the plantation all share this fundamental regulation of communication, labor, and undesirables. On the scale of empire, William Penn's "Holy Experiment," with its grid designed to organize everyday business in the wilderness and as the largest urban project in the West since the Roman empire (Girouard *Cities* 248), matched the imperial enclosure envisioned by the Navigation Acts (1650–1, 1661–3). The latter were to make London *the* commercial entrepot, Dryden's "famed emporium" ("Annus Mirabilis" line 1205: *Selection*).

Nonetheless, outside England's fraught web of contract and control – whether the hedge-enclosed garden of the Puritan congregation or the enclosure of land and sea into private parcels by Acts of Parliament – roamed the threat of dismemberment. "God is round about his own: a wall encompassing, enclosing them around," Peter Sterry assured the faithful, but he is ". . . a wall between us and a sea of blood" (quoted in Hill *English Bible* 134). The blood-lust stems from, as Bunyan saw it, the "wild faith . . . and other wild notions [that] abound" in the wilderness (*Miscellaneous Works* xi.67). In *The Holy War* Bunyan gives us an overview of (a spiritual) empire and its peril. Uncannily articulating the imperial metropole and its periphery, Bunyan states that Mansoul is "to have dominion over all the country round about. Yea all was commanded to acknowledge Mansoul for their metropolitan, all was enjoined to do homage to it" (8). "Mansoul" is, however, always under attack by "Diabolus," a "giant" who is "King of the Blacks or Negroes" (9). In the context of the English Atlantic world, Diabolus can be read as a signifier for the African, the Indian, the Irish, and the unruly English. As Roger Williams accurately pointed out in "The Hireling Ministry" (1652), the forces of colonization also played themselves out in the British Isles: "We have Indians . . . in Cornwall, Indians in Wales, Indians in Ireland" (quoted in Hill *English Bible* 138). The many diabolians on both sides of the Atlantic would qualify for Hobbes's "Confederacy of Deceivers, that to obtain dominion over men in this present world, endeavor by dark, and erroneous Doctrines, to extinguish in them the Light, both of Nature, and of the Gospell; and so to dis-prepare them for the King-dome of God to come" (*Leviathan* 627). For Milton, the dissembler is both Satan and the "savages" of the colonial world: like Satan the Samoeds are "great Talkers, Lyars, Flatterers and Dissemblers" (*Complete Prose Works* viii.495). The battle of (Protestant) truth against (antichristian) "Lyars" is mirrored in the accurate geographical knowledge displayed by Milton.

MILTON'S IMPERIAL IMAGINATION

If in the preface to *A Brief History of Muscovia* Milton states that "The study of Geography is both profitable and delightfull" (*Complete Prose Works* VIII.474), this study is of a more critical nature in *Paradise Lost*. Eve's seduction is not only proof of the vulnerability of the individual will, but also a lesson in geopolitical insecurity. To forestall dissolution geography, interpreted through both the lens of apocalyptic Protestantism and contemporary science, must become the possession of the English. With the imperial oversight of a geographic eye, Milton roams the globe uncovering the spatial codes of God's "vast Design," a design foretelling England's bright future. It is also a design indebted to colonial discourse and structured by the conviction that an historical clash of empires will lead the elect into the Millennium.[10]

When Milton's relationship to empire has been raised it is usually with an eye to his anti-imperialism. The critique of imperialism in *Paradise Regained* as but an excuse to "rob and spoil, burn, slaughter, and enslave / Peaceable nations, neighboring, or remote" (III.75–III.76: *Complete Poems*), and the condemnation of worshipping those "who count it glorious to subdue / By conquest far and wide" (71–92) is, however, thrown into relief by Milton's belief in England's divine status as an elect nation with global duties to perform, such as the subjugation of Ireland.[11] Imperialism does not have to be the "Plagues of men" (*Paradise Lost* XI.697); there is the possibility of conquering mildly, "By deeds of peace, by wisdom eminent" (*Paradise Regained* III.91: *Complete Poems*). If on the one hand Milton lacerates those "Who having spilt much blood, and done much waste / Subduing Nations, and achiev'd thereby / Fame in the world" (*Paradise Lost* XI.791–3), on the other he gestures toward the destiny of "one peculiar Nation to select / From all the rest" (XII.111–12). Eve's fate stands at the core of how Milton imagines, locates, and gives substance to the "peculiar Nation" of England. I will argue that in light of his *Observations on the Articles of Peace* Milton maintains a belief in an ideal of English imperialism, expressed in *Paradise Lost* both from the globe-consuming gaze of the "Lordly eye" (III.578) and the planter's garden-containing or colony-constructing perspective.

As an instrument of providential history-making, the elect nation of the English Protestant tradition embodies both an egalitarian *and* imperial mission. In the same spirit Milton could be, like Cromwell, at once anti-monarchist *and* imperialist. Protestant expansionism is the antithesis of Catholic territorial aggrandizement, where empire is oppressive not liberatory. Further, the *imperium britannicum* is inseparable from the Christian world and thus, in Anthony Pagden's words, "potentially as a cultural, moral, and finally political order with no natural frontiers" (*Lords* 30–1). In *Of Reformation* (1641) Milton appears to condemn imperial pursuits, "seeke onely *Vertue*, not to extend your Limits" (*Complete Prose Works* 1.597), restricting "this *Britannick Empire*" to the British Isles (614). Even this restricted empire is problematic since he assumes Ireland (and indeed Scotland) to be part of an organic union (596). Moreover, England's limits appear to be based on the indeterminate natural rights of an elect nation (525), and as such are extendible to its claim, in this instance, over Gascony, "our proper Colony," and the right to trade in the Dutch East Indies (587). By 1660 Milton seems to imply in *The Readie and Easie Way* that arrogance and corruption have blown the Commonwealth's chance at a revolutionary empire: foreigners will scoff, "where is this goodly tower of a Commonwealth, which the English boasted they would build to overshadow kings, and be another *Rome* in the west?" (VI.423). It seems clear that, via this invocation of the *translatio imperii*, Milton is making the distinction between a godly empire ruled by a republican Commonwealth and an antichristian one ruled by a Stuart (Barnaby "Milton and the Imperial Republic" 69).

Milton interprets and is interpellated by empire. By this I mean that Milton's rendering of an epic struggle of the Protestant crusade versus the Antichrist, and the contested subjectivities and spaces involved, necessarily takes place within a geographical imagination and idiom suffused with the history of medieval Christian and European imperialism. In the struggle against "ungodly rulers" and mobilizing a repertoire of spatial ideology to fit an imperium, Milton privileges the Protestant imperial tradition, which saw the "nation's apocalyptic renewal" (Norbrook *Poetry and Politics* 236) as inseparable from the rejuvenation of ungodly nations and peoples the world over.

Milton has no time for and gives no ground to ungodly antagonists. His *Observations on the Articles of Peace* (1649), a skilfully crafted and condescending repartee to the Royalist Marquis of Ormond, reduces the Irish to the degraded depths of humanity and the margins of civility: Ormond is "the head of a mixt Rabble, part Papists, part Fugitives, and part Savages" (*Complete Prose Works* III.315). The text not only assumes that English readers agree that the Irish are depraved, but also that the English are innately superior to the Irish: "no true borne *English-man*, can so much as barely reade them [the Articles] without indignation and disdaine ... after the mercilesse and barbarous Massacre of so many thousand *English*" (301). In view of 1641 and the formation of what amounted to a Papist army allied with Charles, Milton locates the Irish outside civil and natural rights, reversing power relations by recalling their past of "Pyracies, cruell Captivities, and the causlesse infestation of our Coast" (301–2) and their present "treasons and revolts" which "Cruelly hath dispeopled and lay'd wast [Ireland]" (304–5). It is such a history of antichristian behavior that gives the English "their right and title to that Countrey" (301). As Thomas Corns asserts "Milton's pamphlet works as a pre-emptive justification for that Cromwellian ruthlessness manifest in the storming of Drogheda" and subsequent slaughter ("Milton's *Observations*" 123). Certainly, as he steadily and derisively demolishes Ormond's arguments, Milton offers no reason for quarter to be given to this "Crew of Rebells"; he demotes their culture to an irrational backwardness or,

a disposition not onely sottish but indocible and averse from all Civility and amendment, and what hopes they give for the future, who rejecting the ingenuity of all other Nations to improve and waxe more civill by a civilizing Conquest, though all these many yeares better shown and taught, preferre their own absurd and savage Customes before the most convincing evidence of reasons and demonstration: a testimony of their true Barbarisme and obdurate wilfulnesse to be expected no lesse in other matters of greatest moment. (*Complete Prose Works* 304)

Spurning the blatant blessings of "civilizing Conquest" and the progress of humanity, the Irish lack all the proper coordinates, and abuse the natural order of things. Significantly Milton ridicules their demand for independence by juxtaposing it with their misuse of nature: the call to repeal the "Acts prohibiting to plow with horses by the Tayle, and burne oates in the straw" (303) exposes how cruel and irrational the Irish really are. Like the Irish, their language, and the spaces they inhabit, Ormond's literary style is the sign(ifier) of an infectious disorder: Milton scoffs at Ormond's "lavish pen; which feeling it selfe loose without the reines of discretion, rambles for the most part beyond all Soberness and Civility" (254). The productions of Irish culture are nothing other than literary and literal massacres; their pen and sword hack to pieces the natural logic of English cultural superiority and national rights. Milton effectively denies the Irish any legitimacy to their land due to their political and geographical mobilization and customs. Consequently he participates in the "drastic land revolution" of 1649–60, as Karl

Bottingheimer has termed it, which drove close to a million Irish out into the English empire.[12] Just as Spain's exploitation of Peru, invoked by Mammon's "bands / Of Pioners" whose "impious hands / Rifl'd the bowels of thir mother Earth / For Treasure better hid" (*Paradise Lost* 1.686–90), violates natural laws, Milton has the Irish similarly disqualify themselves from civility and rights to their cultural space. Misuse of nature is analogous to the absence of natural rights.

The struggle of the Protestant self and the control over the antichristian other finds no better venue than out in the empire, in colonial space, where the lineaments and strategies are most exposed, the stakes and arguments most clear-cut, and the glory and future most obvious. Here the many diabolians of the Atlantic world – the African, Indian, Irish, and unruly English – revealed themselves, thus the nature and extent of the crusade against them. Milton fuses the combating of those forces that seek to "dis-prepare" the Godly with his "apocalyptic and utopian excitement" (Norbrook *Poetry and Politics* 16) over the heroic adventure and promise of England's imperial enterprise. The adventurer represented national endeavor, Protestant idealism, and bourgeois industry. During the so-called "interregnum" imperialism was for the first time state-sponsored and as such represented the ascendancy of the merchant and gentry in parliament. The global mobility of imperialism not only confirmed the rule of the city over the court, but it also embodied the social mobility and religious and secular enthusiasm that had triumphed over monarchical and feudal stagnation. Utopian schemes like Harrington's Oceana, the Hartlib circles' pursuit of "Universal Reform," and scientific progress were all structured by the manifest destiny of an English empire. Milton's friend Roger Williams described the Western Design as the beginning of "greater & greater Revolutions approaching" (quoted in Kupperman *Providence Island* 352). On these grounds Milton embraces the geography of empire.[13]

Milton's armchair traveling or his satellite-like vision of the globe are testimony to what Mary Louise Pratt calls "planetary consciousness" (*Imperial Eyes* 15). *Paradise Lost* displays this ascendancy of a self-conscious spatial system and imperial sensibility – where the world is reduced to "a spot, a grain / An atom" (VIII.17–VIII.18), over which domination is more readily conceived. This confident, Ptolemic gaze combined with scientific knowledge is grounded by the geography, names, history, and exoticism avidly gleaned from chorographical projects such as Peter Heylen's *Cosmographie* (1652) and the more directly imperial breast-beating in Raleigh's *Discovery of the Large, Rich, and Beautiful Empire of*

Guiana and Purchas's collections of imperial pursuits.[14] Purchas characterizes his project as a science of empire gradually exposing the globe:
"And as in Geometricall compasses one foote is fixed in the Centre,
whiles the other mooveth in the Circumference, so is it with Purchas and
his Pilgrimes, in this Geographicall compassing" (*Hakluytus* xx.130). Just
as concerned with the God-tricks (Haraway *Simians*) of empirical standards centrifugally issuing from England, Milton uses his own set of
"golden Compasses" (*Paradise Lost* vii.225) to "partition firm and sure"
(267) the world, effectively emptying the geography outside Christen-
dom of any temporal or spatial substance.

The seventeenth century's rather paradoxical struggle to religiously
and rationally order infinite space has its parallel within the internal
contradiction of the English Revolution: the appeal for universal liberty
in the interest of particular groups and social forms. Milton displays this
balancing act of the universal and particular, with the notion of an elect
nation as a mediating agent. *Paradise Lost* signals Milton's geopolitical
wish for a divinely sanctioned map of the globe – a stable terrain
constructed and ruled over by the omniscient eye of God – at the same
time as it acknowledges the instability and anarchic liberties innate in
the formation of the individual and nation-state. The boundlessness of
God's kingdom as well as of humanism is tempered by the detailed
boundedness of contemporary trade routes and the *laissez-faire* heroism
of those "who sail / Beyond the *Cape of Hope*, and now are past /
Mozambic, [where] off at Sea North-East winds blow / *Sabean* Odors
from the spicy shore / Of *Araby*" (iv.158–63).

Yet, just as the East offers seductive, implicitly dangerous "spicy
Drugs . . . on the Trading Flood" (ii.640) – afterall it is Satan's "solitary
flight" that invokes "a Fleet" carrying such a cargo – Milton is wary of
commerce in and of itself. He admires the heroes of the Russia Company for their daring, their ambition and the way they stake England's
claim to the world, but not "the excessive love of Gain and Traffick"
(*Complete Prose Works* viii.524). The global trading system that he invokes
is of a secondary importance to Milton, indeed it represents potential
corruption. He is interested in the flow of spiritual values, how a
network laid and controlled by Englishmen will transmit Protestantism
and contract the world so it will rotate around its chosen centre,
England. Milton's attention to exotica and place-names shows him not
only to be an avid reader of Hakluyt and Purchas, but also concerned
with processing the mesmerizing circulation of information, people, and
goods to and from London. Wedded to the "geographic compassing"

required for strategic advantage is Milton's desire to regulate such a vast complex of competition, contingency, and potential for corruption.

If Milton's project is partly one of recognizing (and reconnaissance-ing) the globe for and from an English perspective, he names the world into manageable places through the acquisitive and categorizing drive of colonialism and its discursive practices. As if to unite the nascent halves of the English empire, Eve ponders what ordered repast to select from "*India* East or West, or middle shore" (*Paradise Lost* v.339) and the reader contemplates both how "*Columbus* found th' *American*" (IX.1116) and, after passing over the Ganges and "*Indian*" streams," how the "*Chineses* drive / With Sails and Wind thir cany Waggons light" (III 436–9).[15] As Milton recognizes and his text performs, "Space may produce new Worlds" (*Paradise Lost* I.650), as indeed was the case via the finally Satanic energy of mercantile capitalism and colonization. The question was who would determine production. With more than a whiff of England's manifest destiny, Milton answers that God "Intended to create, and therein plant / A generation, whom his choice regard / Should favor equal to the Sons of Heaven" (I.652–4). That this generation failed only reinforces the need to better circumscribe the self and space. The poem enacts the desire to fence what is a dangerously "fenceless World" (x.303), with its multiplicity of unstable and porous frontiers not to mention *foreign* ideas and peoples that threaten to "infect" the Godly (x.608). Just as Milton incorporates the new word "lantskip" (I.491) into his vocabulary, which connotes a particular aesthetic framing of a proprietorial command over physical space, he seeks to compress the world into an English design, albeit one fraught with internal dangers and irreconcilable tensions between personal freedom and a divine order.

Milton's "vision of England as leader of an international revolution" (Hill *Milton* 106) gains imperial substance, as opposed to the abstract invocation of God's kingdom on earth (*Paradise Lost* VII.159–61), when we look at how he, in the tradition of map-making, both identifies import-ant destinations of the colonist – for instance "*Norumbega*" (x.696) – and empties the surrounding space: "For such vast room in Nature unpossest / By living Soul, desert and desolate" (VIII.153–4). Who qualifies for a "Soul" or what qualifies for "desolate" are always up in the air, but of course whole cultures have failed to qualify in order to make "space" for "a better Race to bring / Into their vacant room, and thence diffuse / His good to Worlds and Ages infinite" (VII.189–91). That Milton is writing out of a national culture that allows him the capability, confidence, and possessiveness of global consciousness is nowhere better exemplified than when Michael takes Adam to a hill "from whose top / The Hemisphere of Earth in clearest Ken / Stretcht out to the amplest reach of prospect lay" (XI.376–80). From this vantage point Adam indeed has an imperial perspective: "His Eye might there command wherever stood / City of old or modern Fame" (XI.385–6). Tracking westward the world unfolds, like a map, revealing China, India, Russia, Persia, Africa, and Europe, to finally end up in the Americas and significantly with "unspoil'd / *Guiana*" and Raleigh's El Dorado (XI.409–11). This mouth-watering itinerary returns us to Milton's admiration for the heroic, lonely, and corruptible adventurer and his often overreaching pursuit of an ideal, which ultimately is for his country. This character clearly includes Satan: his crew expects "Each hour their great adventurer from the search / Of foreign Worlds" (X.440–1). Raleigh, and the imperial pursuits for riches in the service of Protestant England which he invokes, is a fitting conclusion (and end product) to Adam's gaze. It is an imaginary sweep that thrills Milton so that when he describes Death and Sin making their way towards earth, he not only draws on accounts from attempts at finding a North-East Passage but also includes their goal:

> As when two Polar Winds blowing adverse
> Upon the *Cronian* Sea, together drive
> Mountains of Ice, that stop th'imagin'd way
> Beyond *Pestora* Eastward, to the rich
> *Cathaian* Coast.   (X.289–93)

Similarly, his inclusion of "*Norumbega*" as representing the whole of New England at a time when the term referred only to a fixed geographical area around the mouth of the Penobscot River, perhaps signals a desire for the sixteenth-century mythography that saw Norumbega as a northern El Dorado located en route to the North-West passage.[16]

Devastated by the Restoration, disillusioned with those who had "practis'd falsehood under saintly show" (IV.122), the "incorrupt / Corrupted" (XI.56–7), and in a precarious internal exile, Milton transposes the hopes, struggles, and eventual corruption of the revolution into inherently spatial terms and the terms of empire. These terms depend upon the individual's relationship to history and social space: "The mind is its own place, and in itself / Can make a Heav'n of Hell, a Hell of Heav'n" (I.254–5). The difference between this or that state of mind – one's ideological orientation in and of society – is the difference between "The dismal Situation waste and wild, / A Dungeon horrible, on all sides round" (1.60–1) and God's "Empire." This difference has world-wide significance, since the accession of Charles II marks the total degeneration of a Godly empire: Satan and his cohorts are able to leave their "Dungeon" and "Now possess, / As Lords, a spacious World, to our native Heaven / Little inferior, by my adventure hard / With peril great achieved" (x.466–9). If Satan in part represents the corruption of the Revolution via the dangers of unbridled socio-economic expansion, this expansionary zeal is also given some legitimacy when Eve complains about spatial restrictions: "If this be our condition, thus to dwell / In a narrow circuit strait'n'd by a Foe" (IX.322–4) – a statement which equally applied to the English in Ireland.

Ultimately Milton is voicing a conflict over the possession and definition of space. Sir John Temple notes that the Irish rebellion of 1641 stems in part from the English being careless about the regulation of spatial relations: fortification is lax and the Irish have lived "promiscuously among the *British*" (*Irish Rebellion* 56, 27). A warning for all colonial elites, the English in Ireland were "suddenly swallowed up" (26) as "the whole Country began to rise about them" and civility was profaned (27). Similarly, in paradise "Such ambush hid among sweet Flow'rs and Shades / Waited with hellish rancor imminent / To intercept thy way, or send thee back / Despoil'd of Innocence, of Faith, of Bliss" (Milton *Paradise Lost* IX.408–11). As the belief in converting the Other declined on both sides of the Atlantic, the mechanisms to ensure security and vigilance became predominant. An ideology of evangelism, never pursued with any real intent, was replaced by an "emphasis . . . on the need to improve the environment" (Canny *Kingdom* 113). Thus Penn theorized his "Holy Experiment" in North America in terms of "ordered space would mean orderly and happy lives" (quoted in Meinig *Atlantic America* 133). The better management of space is at the core of *Paradise Lost*.

Satan's entrance into the garden and his threat to Adam and Eve not only invoke similar conceptions of socio-spatial relations embodied in John Locke's murderous thief (*Second Treatise* 279) or "Beast of Prey," who is always–already about to remove one from personal liberty, civility, and membership within a "chaste" community or place, but also the extremely precarious security of God's colonists in Ireland or North America. Like Locke Milton conflates individual liberty with the sanctity of property relations. Satan is cast as a "prowling Wolf" who "Leaps o'er the fence with ease into the Fold" (*Paradise Lost* IV.184–7) and in the domestic role of a thief plundering "some rich Burgher" (IV.189–

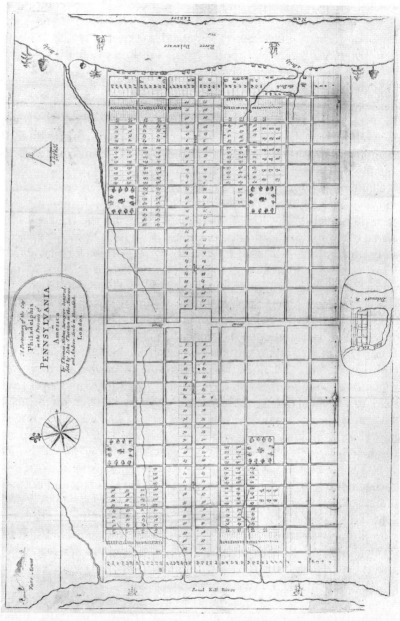

Figure 5   "A Portraiture of the City of Philadelphia in the Province of PENNSYLVANIA in America," Thomas Holme

93). Here, Milton subscribes to the spatial relations of the propertied and the colonizer, deftly uniting religious and bourgeois terminology. Seeming to return us to Temple's image of a devouring Ireland, the snake's tactics luring Eve to the apple are likened to a "delusive Light" which "Misleads th' amaz'd Night-wanderer from his way / To Bogs and Mires, and oft through Pond or Pool, / There swallow'd up and lost, from succor far" (ix.640–2). The devious nature of swamp and bog are strategic locations for Indian and Irish alike, as well as any runaway slave or servant, but are where the pursuant colonizer dare not go for fear of being consumed in this "property-less" geography, the antithesis of fence, fold, and English freedom.

Due both to the emerging geography of mercantile capitalism and the ideology of millenarianism, Milton replicates the impulse to create a homogenous globe, united under the Godly hegemony of English liberators. Or as his influential acquaintance James Harrington put it in *Oceana*: from an English garden "buds of empire, such as, with the blessing of God, may spread the arms of your commonwealth like an holy asylum into the distressed world" (323). This is an apt description of Milton's version of empire. Although Milton's design clearly began to diverge from Cromwell's Western Design, he did not relinquish the idea of England leading a world crusade and nor can he be disassociated from real imperial pursuits and a belief in English supremacy. Milton's own geographical Christiano-graphy is double-edged: it posits a brave new republican world whilst limiting such liberty to the power of an elect nation. His imagination, as shown here in the *Second Defence of the English People* (1654), contains this contradiction:

I seem to have embarked on a journey and to be surveying from on high far flung regions and territories across the sea, faces numberless and unknown, sentiments in complete agreement with mine... I seem to introduce to the nations of the earth a product from my own country, ... the renewed cultivation of freedom and civic life that I disseminate throughout cities, kingdoms, and nations. (*Complete Prose Works* iv.554–6)

Similarly, for the "buds of empire" and liberty to grow there must be instituted a strict program of spatial and ideological regulation to ensure against corruption. *Paradise Lost* maps out this conflict at both a global and domestic scale. Milton's ideal of global command and communication, which is usurped by Satan (and the antichristian Orient with whom he is so often associated), is given a more localized form within the strategic space of Paradise. It is a design that real-life colonists like Rowlandson and Behn show to be highly contested and unstable.

THE ENGLISH GARDEN ABROAD

Eve's "rape" signifies the required regimentation of people and space. In order to protect Eve (or the social order's health and the security of (re)productive territory) Milton fortifies Paradise and puts the guard into gardening.[17] Reflecting the militarization at home and in the colonies, the garden – as both private and England's domain – is more often a strategic position than a place of repose. In "Upon Appleton House" Marvell represents Lord Fairfax's gardening as a military operation replete with "vigilant patrol" (line 314. *Complete Poems*) around his property. His garden is laid out "In the just figure of a fort" (287) and flowers are arranged as regiments.[18] A metonym also for the nation, the country house garden is the vital centre about which the world moves:

> Oh thou, that dear and happy isle
> The garden of the world ere while,
> Thou paradise of four seas,
> Which heaven planted us to please,
> But, to exclude the world, did guard
> With watery if not flaming sword.
>
> ("Upon Appleton House" 321–6: *Complete Poems*)

If Marvell's ideal is exclusionary, Milton shows that, given the historical battle underway, this is not a feasible model. In Milton's garden security is tight, Gabriel's squadrons patrol the perimeter. Paradise is constructed to prevent intruders: its "enclosure green" is protected by "a steep wilderness, whose hairy sides / With thicket overgrown, grotesque and wild, / Access deni'd" (*Paradise Lost* IV.133–7). Worthy of defences by Thomas Digges, Milton then builds upon this already formidable barrier with "ranks" of gigantic trees and "higher than thir tops / The verdurous wall of Paradise up sprung" (142–3). Even Satan is temporarily thwarted by the "steep savage Hill" "thick entwin'd" with God's design (172–7). But neither armed guards – "strict Sentries and Stations thick / Of Angles watching round" (II.412–13) – nor this hostile environment can keep corruption out. Indeed, it is precisely this enclosing strategy that endangers "paradise": it concedes all the remaining space to the enemy and their (hidden) machinations to undo the godly. Exclusionary, defensive space, Milton infers, leaves the godly blind and vulnerable.

The chosen or God's revolution cannot exist in one country alone; to survive it must expand even if expansion, as Eve's wandering exemplifies, invites every danger. The placeless familiarity of paradise has its origin within English writers' sense of a multiplication of English space into a spiritual emptiness but material storehouse. Richard Eburne imagines just such a spreading of divine order in his promotional tract *A Plain Pathway to Plantations* (1624):

And if you will needs live in England, imagine all that to be England where Englishmen, where English people, you with them, and they with you, do dwell. (And it be the people that makes the land English, not the land the people.) So you find England, and an happy England too, where now is, as I may say, no land. (12)

This homogenizing vision leads Eburne to celebrate: "from England to Newfoundland, and so to the Summer Islands, and thence to Virginia, all is one tract" (25). Eburne's dream of English monopolization in the Atlantic world, later realized by the Navigation Acts, is part of the global map, owned and authored by the elect, that underwrites Milton's worldly eye.

The politics of space in *Paradise Lost* is as relevant to the estate and nation as it is to its fragile and fractious colonies. When Gabriel's squadrons arrest Satan they ask him "what boldness brought him hither / Unlicens't from his bounds in Hell Prescrib'd" (Milton *Paradise Lost* IV.908–9). The implication of the outsider, whether the poor, the Spanish or the native, trespassing on English territory or private property is evident here. Just as the debate over the right to dispossess Amerindians provides Locke with justifications for the rule of the propertied, Milton integrates specific configurations and codes of space in England with that of its colonies.[19] The corruption of the English revolution is analogous to or at least operates within the same ideological design as the threat of Indians to Cotton Mather's puritans. Perpetual vigilance over the self and its oppositional other is paramount: "leave unsearcht no nook" (IV.789). The backsliding in this surveillance leads, for Mather, to the hell-on-earth of King Philip's raids on New England settlements. This is one tactic, the other is for the godly to go on the offensive.

To achieve total control over the environment – a project studied by Bacon through to Hartlib – finds definition in the microcosm of the garden. Milton expands this project to the global level. The desire to encapsulate the world and organize it for English eyes is embodied in the Botanic Gardens at Oxford. Completed in 1641 they symbolize both the ordering of the natural world under civilized confines as well as the collecting, marketing, and reproduction of the exotic or otherwise costly. The Gardens are yet one more example of an enclosure linked to the appropriation of the natural world within a commercial network. The notion of the garden also performs as an ideological control: like the word "plantation," it obscures the origins and counterparts of the great gardens into which nobles and merchant princes, like Josiah Child, sunk the wealth obtained through colonial trade and settlement. The violence of accumulation, the slave-plantation complex, and agrarian capitalism disappear behind the benign connotations of the paradisal garden over which, following the Greek model, England serves as protectorate.

Hence lurking behind Milton's Paradise is the world of colonial exploitation and capital accumulation, forces he is wary of but which provide England with its necessary expansion. His "happy rural seat of various view" with its "Lawns, or level Downs," "Flowers of all hue," "Grots and Caves" and "murmuring waters [that] fall / Down the slope hills, disperst, or in a Lake" (*Paradise Lost* iv.247–61) bespeaks the reigning notions in England about organizing and perfecting a privately owned nature. Milton's model of ideally ordered space duplicates Bacon's prescriptions in "Of Gardens" (*Essays* 197–202), thereby uniting an English aesthetic and economic model with its opposite, the wilderness – something many of the lesser gentry, and not a few Parliamentarians, set out to do in the New World. Indeed, such an up-to-date garden, with a "wilderness," bowling green, and turreted walls incorporated into its design, was developed during the 1630s at the Earl of Cork's estate at Lismore, Ireland (Brady and Gillespie *Natives and Newcomers* 185–6). In short, the English garden is an instrument of colonialism.

Milton, therefore, conflates the utopian vision of freedom set within American/colonial plenitude with the social order and economic desires of England's elites. However, if any sort of utopia is to flourish where "Nature multiplies / Her fertile growth" (*Paradise Lost* v.318–19) opportunities for masterlessness must be curtailed by the pillars of Puritan ideology: industry, vigilance, and obedience to one's calling or station. Thus "sweet Gard'ning labor" (iv.328) is required to maintain the natural order and check the impulses to and invasions of barbarism. Milton's attention to words like "limit," "fence," and "frame" underline the dangers of too much autonomy as well as the anarchy outside the garden. Just as paradise is prone to "wanton growth" producing the "unsightly and the unsmooth" (629, 631), corruption enters the "Ill fenc't" space (372).

Aphra Behn offers a view of the latter in *Oroonoko*, where we find the Miltonic garden and its strategic set of relations surrounded not by

Satan but by the equally deadly threat to colonial property posed by
tigers, slave rebellion, and discontented Indians. Behn also offers us a
clearer view of the social relations informing and issuing from England's
gardens. Legitimizing further colonization, Behn textually counters
these dangers with a standard promotional itinerary of Surinam's
riches, including everything from "Aromaticks" to "a little Beast call'd
an *Armadilly*," with fruit, gums, and wood that "has an intrinsick Value
above common Timber" in-between (49). If only "his late Majesty, of
sacred memory, [had] but seen and known what a vast and charming
World he had been Master of in that Continent, he would never have
parted so easily with it to the *Dutch*" (48). Behn recommends herself on
these very merits: just as she was a spy for the crown, in Surinam and in
her book she acts as the eyes and ears in the service of the monarchy and
its loyal officers. She enacts the pruning-like labor needed for colonial
management. It is a service aimed to maintain the labor of colonials and
slaves on the sugar plantations. She is ultimately defeated by English
barbarism, a disease no doubt caught from the "Wild Coast" of
Surinam.

Behn connects this lost paradise with the estate of St. John's Hill, a
little England where culture and nature meet in seamless unity as if by
some providential design: "and sure, the whole Globe of the World
cannot shew so delightful a Place as this Grove was: Not all the Gardens
of *Italy* can produce a Shade to out-vie this, which Nature had join'd
with Art to render so exceeding fine" (50). Behn's description of St.
John's Hill is a celebration of a ruling class and the reproduction of their
order anywhere in the world. It is also a demarcation of paradisal and
civilized space from the ungodly, barbarous other, which includes poor
whites. In this sense Behn's description acts both as a justification of one
group's domination and their need to expand their power base in order
to maintain their superiority. The inherent instability of colonial space
and its necessarily regimented design is conveyed by Behn's noting the
situation of St. John's Hill: "it stood on a vast Rock of white Marble, at
the foot of which the River ran a vast depth down, and not to be
descended on that side" (49). The sense of size and security imply its
defensive aspect and Behn's recognition of threats to the big planters.
The "Walk or Grove of Orange and Lemon-Trees" that "hinder'd the
Sun, whose Rays are very fierce there, from entering a Beam into the
Grove" (50) gives this same sense of defence against hostile indigenous
forces. Utilizing aesthetic ideology Behn has the plantation go on the
offensive with its commanding "Prospect" and "fenc'd" landscape. The

purified nature of the garden, this oasis of peace and harmony, contains, as in *Paradise Lost*, the ideology of a privileged and besieged spot of the chosen whose birthright it is to command the land.

Just as Milton imagines Paradise within a contemporary world-system of trade, Behn does not leave this imperial outpost in the shade and "sweet Blossoms" of aesthetic ideology. St. John's Hill is clearly an instrument of colonialism and its spatial command has everything to do with the accumulation of capital through commodity production, a topic Behn for the most part displaces. Just as Behn has the grove remind the reader of the "*Mall*" in London, connecting this peripheral seat of power to its centre and entrepot in Britain, she argues that Surinam is part of "a Continent whose vast Extent was never yet known, and may contain more noble Earth than all the Universe beside; for, they say, it reaches from East to West one way as far as *China*, and another to *Peru*" (48). Behn is not limiting the colony's prospects to fruit and "Fragrancies." The reason for invoking those two symbols of unlimited wealth, China and Peru, is overtly stated a little later when Behn again interrupts the narrative, in order to promote colonialism. After meeting "*Indians* of strange Aspects" who had "with 'em Bags of Gold-Dust," Behn complains that a "Design" for exploiting "Mountains of Gold" came to nothing: "either the Design dy'd, or the *Dutch* have the advantage of it: And 'tis to be bemoan'd what his Majesty lost by losing that part of *America*" (59). To prevent similar losses in 1688 the lessons of Behn's little book must not go unheeded. And the primary lesson is the need to institute a cartography that is able to quell threats to the proper authorities – the chaos reflecting their absence – and pursue the appropriation of the resources to be had in paradise. Behn promotes herself as an agent of this design.

EXPLORING OUTSIDE PARADISE

Eve's "wand'ring vanity" (Milton *Paradise Lost* x.875) and "strange / Desire of wand'ring" (ix.1135–6) is threatened by the proverbial Indian behind every tree: "Such ambush hid among sweet Flow'rs and Shades / Waited with hellish rancor imminent / To intercept thy way, or send thee back / Despoil'd of Innocence, of Faith, of Bliss" (408–11). Through the corruption of Eve, Satan attempts to control the abundance and procreative resources of paradise, to be the one to "take" this prize: "A wilderness of sweets; for Nature here / Wanton'd as in her prime, and play'd at will / Her Virgin Fancies, pouring forth more sweet" (v.294–6). If Satan's scramble for such sweets represents "the sweep and grandeur of the emergent capitalist revolution" (Stavely *Puritan Legacies* 63) and "a class ... thrusting its way to dominance in a new age of expanding opportunity in England and in the world" (Kiernan "Milton" 168), then the wandering female signifies the dangers of unbridled socio-economic expansion and the anarchic forces it lets loose. Rowlandson is a victim of this danger as market-driven New Englanders settled ever further from the strictures of the Puritan authorities. When war came the Indians were able to take advantage of this dissolution. Behn, on the other hand, intervenes to Royally control expansion, excoriating a mercantile capitalism that enslaves, (ejects James II), and finally murders a noble like Oroonoko. The lesson of Eve is to more militantly control the conditions of social, economic, and territorial expansion.[20]

If Milton's imagining of the Fall and the demise of the Revolution draws upon the spatial dynamics of the colony, such dynamics are played out for real in the narratives of Mary Rowlandson and Aphra Behn. Whereas Eve falls from "Harvest Queen" (Milton *Paradise Lost* IX.842) to a woman "on a sudden lost, / Defac't, deflow'r'd" (900–1), Rowlandson and Behn are able to resist and challenge Satan's agents. Ultimately they are figures providing information and justifications for an overall strategy of aggressive colonization by the elect, whether that project be determined by saintly magistrates, colonial assemblies, merchants, or the crown.

Rather than a "company of sheep torn by wolves" (Rowlandson "Sovereignty and Goodness" 35), the Christians of New England had united against the Indians on the basis of a "hatred of alien races" and the need to acquire more land. King Philip's (Metacom's) War "was, in fact, the Second Puritan Conquest" (Jennings *Invasion* 298–9). The captivity narrative, whose besieged, vulnerable and tempted protagonist Milton surely incorporates, is the literary cutting edge of the Puritan's *controlled* expansion.[21] Its condemnation is directed at both Indian societies and the wayward Christian. Richard Slotkin sees the "captivity myth as a weapon for restraining the atomism and individualism reflected in the movement of people from the coast into the Indian wilderness" (*Regeneration through Violence* 115). Rowlandson's account then serves as a plumb line measuring the depths of Indian depravity and the socio-spatial breakdown of the barrier between heathen and Puritan. Her story shows how close the English have come to barbarism; it reaffirms the right of the English authorities to re-place the Indians and reorder the settlers with a stricter regime. Her victory over temptation and terror functions as a confidence-boost to New England's expansionist culture just as her narrative provides vicarious access to Indian lands that her captivity proves are legitimately English.

If Milton's topography renders the space outside saintly enclosures as essentially a wasteful territory – Satan's flights and Milton's view of the Orient typically associating non-Christian spaces with excessive mobility, wealth, arbitrary rule, and natural-historical decay – Rowlandson's Puritan imagination encounters a similar environment. A cartographer from the "Citty on a Hill" and now in the belly of the beast, she represents Indian territory as barren and violent:

When I came to the brow of the hill that looked toward a swamp, I thought we had been come to a great Indian town . . . The Indians were as thick as the trees: it seemed as if there had been a thousand hatchets going at once. If one looked before one, there was nothing but Indians and behind one nothing but Indians, and so on either hand, I myself in the midst, and no Christian soul near me. ("Sovereignty and Goodness" 45)

The war with Metacom, wherein the English lost one in ten adults, indeed threatened the basis of Puritan society. Patriarchal and commercial authority are destroyed as a wounded father begs for his life with money only to have the Indians kill him, strip "him naked, and split open his bowels" (33). This humiliation of the social order finds extended coverage within Rowlandson's "removes" from Puritan society. She interprets her misfortune in just these physically disruptive terms: "how righteous it was with God to cut the thread of my life and cast me out of his presence forever" (38). Because of the lack of regimenting their own lives and that of the Indians, God has made manifest this creeping "wilderness condition" (39) by throwing Rowlandson into the "vast and desolate wilderness"(37).

Stripped to her most vulnerable, Rowlandson is without place in this scenario; she is enclosed by a landscape in the process of being devoured by the locust-like Indians. If she is on the verge of being swallowed up in a space of bristling chaos, then the Indians are hardly at home either. Unlike the English, the Indians have a destructive and transient relationship with the land. It is they rather than trees that populate the area, hatchets ready to denature further. This is land waiting to be "replenished and subdued" by the English. Utilizing a similar cultural–spatial lexicon as Milton, Rowlandson juxtaposes Indian sterility and outlandishness – "but I in none of these / Find place or refuge" (*Paradise Lost* x.118–19) Satan complains – with a land inscribed and ordered by the productive English:

The swamp by which we lay was, as it were, a deep dungeon and an exceedingly high and steep hill before it . . . As we went along, I saw a place where English cattle had been. That was comfort to me, such as it was. Quickly after that we came to an English path which so took with me that I thought I could have freely laid down and died. ("Sovereignty and Goodness" 45)

Exposing their contradictory, self-abrogating nature, the Indians seek to tear out the "planting" of English colonies (*because* they can only destroy), although, for survival, they need to feed off English fields, further accentuating their alienation from fertility (45).[22] The unsaid cannibalism here, where even the residue of the English is gobbled up, correlates not only with Rowlandson's loss of bearings in relation to herself and her surroundings – she is temporarily consumed – but also to her potential "indianization." Food and landscape come to represent the struggle over the chastity of her body and spirit and that of English America.

If at the beginning of her account Rowlandson stands opposite the despicable appetite of the Indians, who "gaping before us with their guns, spears, and hatchets [were ready] to devour us" (34), her sojourn with her captors brings her into a position of sameness with such an appetite. It is an experience shared by Eve and Behn. The dangers of this corrupting appetite are warned against throughout the colonial world; if allowed to flourish it will indeed lead to the consuming of civility. Indeed, Eve's appetite leads to the Fall. John Temple states the case in the Irish theatre of English colonialism: "the *Irish* were resolved to . . . devour (as their very word was) the seed of the *English* out of *Ireland*, and when they had rid them there, they would go over into *England*, and not leave the Memorial of the *English* Name under Heaven" (*Irish Rebellion* 77). The appetites of the American Indians and Catholic Irish operates under the same ideological matrix; it is a basically self-satiating, bacchanalian, and *seductive* one. What lies behind the master-signifier of "cannibalism" is the accusation that the colonized are economically unproductive and socially unnatural or non-reproductive. They make no sense, they have nor crave any real presence in the world. Writing to fellow scientists at the Royal Society from New England in the 1670s, John Josselyn reports that

[the Indians are] barbarously cruel . . . Prone to injurious violence and slaughter . . . both Men and Women [are] guilty of Misoxenie or hatred of strangers, a quality appropriated to the old Brittains, all of them Cannibals, eaters of humane flesh. And so were formerly the Heathen-*Irish*, who used to feed upon the Buttocks of Boyes and Womens Paps; it seems it is natural to Savage people so to do. (*Colonial Traveler* 90)

The "filthy trash" ("Sovereignty and Goodness" 44) – bear, horse liver – that Rowlandson is forced to consume is simultaneously evidence of the failure of Indian culture (they have failed to domesticate the earth) and an agent of contagion of this bestial existence. Rowlandson's increasingly "wolfish appetite" (57) – behavior learnt from living with those she describes as "wolves" at the beginning of her narrative – signals the temptation of another life: "I was fain to take the rest and eat it [horse liver] as it was with the blood about my mouth, and yet a savory bit it was to me" (4).

New England leaders worried over the European captives who refused to return to "civilized" society, since Indian life appeared attractive to some in contrast to the discipline and drudgery of life for the majority of English colonists. The popular genre of the captivity story was harnessed by the Puritans to dissuade defections or dissension. Propagandists like Cotton Mather made certain that powerful signs of degeneration were associated with the likes of the Indian "Hope-Hood," a "hideous *loup-garou* [werewolf]" who tortures, kills and cuts up a grief-stricken English child (Vaughan and Clark *Puritans among the Indians* 140). John Gyles, another redeemed captive, even resists a fantasy of killing a number of his tormentors in the face of his probable death because he is determined to retain his Englishness. He refuses to mimick his captors because "a strange and strong impulse that I should return to my own place and people suppressed it as often as such a motion rose in my breast" (105–7).[23] Indianization to any degree was to be fiercely rebuffed.

Although Rowlandson's captivity and redemption stand for the victory of the Godly over the Satanic, there remains a nagging wolfishness about her. She informs us that she escaped with her sexual chastity intact, but cannot admit as much about her mental state. She is permanently unsettled, as if she "had been all this while in a maze and like one astonished" ("Sovereignty and Goodness" 46). Forever after she scrutinizes her own behavior and, of course, that of others. That is to say, Rowlandson is in a continual state of re-membering that her cultural identity is tied to Puritan society and not to that of her enemies: "I can remember the time when I used to sleep quietly without workings in my thoughts whole nights over together, but now it is other ways with me" (74). While super-vigilance and recalling one's role in God's design was no bad thing in light of backsliding, the necessary textual silences or unsaid "removes" of her experience, which are hinted at by her appetite for Indian fare and the "workings" of her insomnia, suggest that Rowlandson will never return to the Puritan fold. Perhaps America has marked her too deeply. This subversive undertow escapes Mather's editorial oversight. The tug-o-war over the Puritan soul leaves behind scars that permanently disfigure; redemption appears never to be complete. The "other ways" that haunt Rowlandson hint that she is forever linked to a subversion of herself and community: the possibility of going native, being radically individual, mobile, out of the authorities' reach, and enjoying new eating habits.

Rowlandson identifies this potential for degeneration and death in a traitorous "praying Indian" who wore "a string about his neck strung with Christian's fingers" (63). Similarly she later sees one of her more vicious captors at large in the very centre of the "garden": "mine eyes have seen that fellow afterwards, walking up and down Boston under the appearance of a friend-Indian" (51). During her captivity she mis-recognizes a group of Indians because they are on horseback dressed as Englishmen (58–9). This dissimulation not only underscores that ambushes abound for even the wary Puritan, but also something far worse: her own permanent state of disturbance points to the presence of the "savage within." Clearly, policies to convert and converse with the Indians have failed, and the captivity narratives conclude from the King Philip's War that, as in Ireland, total segregation and legitimate extermination or expulsion are the only solution. This is to be coupled with greater "vigilance" or discipline of the colonists, for as Satan puts it, "vigilance / I dread" (Milton *Paradise Lost* IX.157). A penetrating and discriminating oversight, both overt and covert, is a hallmark of colonial practice and intellectual imaginary.

It is not without some significance then that Behn was employed for a time as a spy for His Majesty's Government, and that she also performs this task in *Oroonoko*.[24] Like Rowlandson, however, Behn has an ambivalence about her relationship to the wilderness. Behn also develops a "wolfishness" about her as she appropriates the role of the male adventurer in her Jacobite drama. To partake of the extra-colonial and the sub-civilized, as Rowlandson and Behn essentially do, is to acquire an independence, mobility, and a closeness, if not complicity with, devouring violence. Their texts seek to erase such suspicions. Behn's reputed sexual appetite perhaps signals a deeper corruption ingested while in Surinam. Her scrutiny of herself – and often through the eyes of the Other – would seem to confirm her uncertain positionality. Rather than focus on what Margaret Ferguson has termed, "a highly unstable triangular model which . . . draws relations of sameness and difference among a black African slave, a white English-woman, and a group of Native Americans" (in Hendricks and Parker *Women, "Race," and Writing* 217), I want to emphasize Behn's surveillance of all the tense components producing colonial space and her implicit reorganizing of that space not to benefit "a community of the unjustly oppressed" (215), but the proper colonial authorities. The cases of dismemberment that occur in Surinam underscore the precarious nature of colonization and the possibilities for the eruption of the savage within.

Behn negotiates and manipulates the contesting forces. As a sentinel she performs Cotton Mather's injunction: "observe *Goings out* as well as *Breakings in*, if you would see where the *Hedge* is deficient . . ." (quoted in Slotkin *Regeneration through Violence* 88). She plays a deft game – indeed she is called upon to enact such a role by her fellow colonists (*Oroonoko* 46) – of diverting Oroonoko's power. Behn counters his threat of running away or marronage by limiting his space of action. Once he begins to seriously resist his function within the hierarchy of the plantation system and refuses to abide by its spatiality Behn steps up her surveillance and containment of Oroonoko: "I neither thought it convenient to trust him much out of our view, nor did the Country, who fear'd him." It is decided to "oblige him to remain within such a compass, and that he should be permitted, as seldom as could be, to go up to the Plantations of the *Negroes*; or, if he did, to be accompany'd by some that should be rather in appearance Attendants than Spies" (48). Behn's attention to Oroonoko makes clear that colonial order rests upon management techniques of divide and conquer. As long as she manages Oroonoko, and by extension the slaves, peace and sugar production prevail. When her techniques are overrun by irresponsible forces due to the vacuum of legitimate power then chaos ensues. The attempt at marronage in the novel is the consequence not of cruel slavery, which the Europeanized Oroonoko and Behn happily accept for the "Negroes," but of a breakdown in colonial authority. The absence of Lord Willoughby and the malevolence of Byam conspire to bring about Oroonoko's rebellion. Behn recognizes that the politics of space are crucial to keeping hell at bay.

Oroonoko begins with a shrewd description of the strategic space of

Surinam. Immediately Behn demarcates the economic functions and the cultural spaces and traditions of the different groups. She introduces us to the pragmatic though tense colonial policy toward the Indians, one of "perfect Amity, without daring to command 'em; but, on the contrary, caress 'em" (1–2). Such a policy is in the interests of trade and the colonist's initial need of the indigenous peoples.

[We live with them in] good understanding, as it behoves us to do; they knowing all the places where to seek the best Food of the Country, and the means of getting it; and for very small and unvaluable Trifles, supply us with that 'tis impossible for us to get: for they do not only in the Woods, and over the *Sevana's*, in Hunting, supply the parts of Hounds, by swiftly scouring those impassable Places, and by the mere Activity of their Feet run down the nimblest Deer . . . (4–5)

Like Caliban, the Indians of Surinam provide the colonizer with knowledge of the land, foodstuffs, and invaluable services for their maintenance in exchange for "unvaluable Trifles." Yet also like Caliban, by virtue of this knowledge and by inhabiting or having access to "impassable Places," the Indians pose a threat to the colony, which Behn is quick to point out: "So that they being on all occasions very useful to us, we find it absolutely necessary to caress 'em as Friends, and not to treat 'em as Slaves, nor dare we do other, their numbers so far surpassing ours in that Continent" (5). Behn's use of the tactical "caress" twice, like her "ennobling" infantilization of the Indians, is testament to their power.

Negotiating disturbances in paradise and at the same time placing herself in an ambiguous, dangerous, and interstitial position, Behn goes in search of the "harmless, inoffensive" Indians, who for some unexplained reason are in dispute with the English. With Oroonoko's Europeanized savagery the perfect foil, Behn enters zones that threaten to consume the whole: "we could scarce trust ourselves, without great Numbers, to go to any *Indian* Towns or Place where they abode, for fear they should fall upon us . . ." (54). The sexually charged "exchange" in the village posits the fundamental role of female bodies in the service of empire (55). Behn sets this dangerous encounter as a highly theatrical experiment. She and her maid appear to fulfil the traditional role of white women up for grabs in spaces uncontrolled by their male counterparts. However, she turns the tables on those who see women in colonial space as either about to be consumed by the natives or irresponsibly consuming the luxuries of empire. At their most vulnerable Behn makes herself and her companion valuable agents of the civilizing mission. As if playing with the feminization of imperialist capital accumulation Behn represents herself as a luxury commodity for Indian consumption. But who is seducing or consuming whom? Aware of the transgressive and sensational nature of this encounter, Behn nevertheless sees it as an exchange of sorts. In a politically fragile time she travels eight days into the wilderness and undergoes a "trial," although the Puritan genre of the captivity narrative is here reversed in that it is the Indians who are being tempted – and tempted to consume, ultimately, the trinkets of the colonist. In the interests of economic expansion and peaceful trade, Behn underlines her utility and strength in the realm of colonial space where loss of identity if not life are the norm. Venturing into the geographical interior she proves her physical and psychological interior remains unviolated. Defying customary female roles, she acquires vital knowledge about location, customs, and military might. She turns herself into a strategy of colonial expansion and the empowerment of women. It is a scene of authorization where subjecthood is reformulated via the transgression into the masculine realms and spaces of the other. In short, she embodies what is at *stake*, and the stakes of imperialism are always high, risky, and up for grabs.

Behn and her maid locate their bodies on the line between civility and savagery, and thus underscore the fragility (and temptations) of subject-hood and colonial life. While the bodies of these intrepid explorers and mediators occupy a suggestive interstitial space and invoke the tensions between the constituents of colonialism, such a positionality underscores female agency as well as the need to control such an amorphous (and amorous) space. This latter part of Behn's thinking is not only reinforced by the disfigured war-captains she meets but the Indian uprising against the Dutch. Less efficient and less legitimate colonists experience the savagery that the Indians can at any time unleash (54). The trespass of the Indians against the Dutch correlates with that of the Dutch when they took over Surinam. Behn is convinced that without the right rulers and policies the wilderness will to take over. In *Oroonoko* the savagery of the wilderness is made apparent: there are six instances of physical dismemberment – Oroonoko's killing of the tiger (52), the fate of mother, children, and a Footman during the Indian uprising (54), the "Dismemberings" of the War-Captains (57), Oroonoko's murder of Imoinda, his own disembowelling, and his death. All implicitly have their source in the self-mutilating practices of the Indians – a self-annihilation that seems to herald the ascendancy of Europeans. This is the death-dealing space that stands in contrast to the rejuvenating order of Parham-House or St. John's Hill. The absence of the central author-ity of Governor Willoughby brings about the disintegration of colonial hierarchy, within which Oroonoko occupies a key position.

As Behn distances herself from the events and retreats to more safe and civilized spaces, Oroonoko moves in the opposite direction. He moves from Trefry's Parham-House to the "little Town" of the slaves, where he rouses his subjects to rebellion, and finally into the "impass-able Woods and Rivers" (62). In short, he descends the social and spatial ladder into hell, thereby blurring the transcontinental and timeless hierarchy that he symbolizes. The "design," which once symbolized Oroonoko's total subordination to the amusement of his English female friends is now reversed. Instead of Oroonoko subduing the wilderness for the English, he now subdues the English and their slavery. Reinforc-ing the mutability of the colonial space, the word "design" changes from meaning "entertainment" to Oroonoko's "black Designs" (71) of killing colonists and Imoinda, to, finally, Governor Byam's design to execute Oroonoko. The text ends with the conflict between the colonial misrule of Byam, aided, we should note, by one "*Banister*, a wild *Irish* Man . . . a Fellow of absolute Barbarity" (76), and the savagery this misrule has produced in Oroonoko.

Oroonoko's demise and execution resonate with Locke's argument about how to treat a threat to one's property or to the social order of the propertied: "having renounced Reason, the common Rule and Measure . . . [the perpetrator] therefore may be destroyed as a *Lyon* or a *Tyger*, one of those wild Savage Beasts, with whom Men can have no Society nor Security" (*Second Treatise* 274). As long as the thoroughly Europeanized Oroonoko serves as an overseer, an instrument of main-taining a hierarchy with which he identifies, then he is given a sympath-etic portrait. When he rebels however, it quickly becomes apparent that Behn is primarily concerned with how to properly manage a colony for the crown. Akin to the name, prerogatives, and exploitation of the Royal African Company, it is "Ruler's rights – British and African – [that] are at stake" (Moira Ferguson *Subject to Others* 35).

Whipped by and stripped of civilization, Oroonoko becomes increas-ingly "some Monster of the Wood." Infected with rage and the wilder-ness, he beheads the passive Imoinda (Behn *Oroonoko* 72). It should be noted that such savagery is only ever committed by the Other or at least in the space of the Other, where European law and order are absent. Similarly, echoing the Indians from the village Behn visited, Oroonoko begins to dismember himself (75). Oroonoko is out-done by his torturers, whom Behn "vilifies [as] ... unsophisticated neophytes and parvenus holding the reins of power" (Moira Ferguson *Subject to Others* 48). "[S]o rude and wild were the Rabble" that Oroonoko cannot be saved from being systematically cut to pieces whilst being burned (*Oroonoko* 77). True to her spatial politics, Behn associates the "Rabble" with the criminalized and/or anarchic spaces of Newgate prison and the "urban" or public realm of the colony. Here again we meet the savages within, their savagery a corollary of the spaces they inhabit.

In the same way that King Philip's War "exposed virulent class antagonisms" (Slotkin *Regeneration through Violence* 81), Behn's narrative is constructed around class. Oroonoko's slavery is unjust because he is royalty. He cheerfully profits from the slave trade when a cosmopolitan African prince; in contrast to his plight, the common slave is either invisible or cowardly. In the same way, Behn and Trefry are far removed from the mass of colonials. The English villains are clearly social upstarts, non-starters, or Irish; unfortunately colonial space affords them opportunities to rise above their stations.[25] Behn's is a classic warning to the colonial elite to reform its system of governance. As Moira Ferguson persuasively concludes: "Behn affirms an abolitionist and emancipationist perspective in Oroonoko's famed speech yet ends up implicitly privileging plantocratic ideology, inflaming Eurocentric attitudes toward Africans, and bolstering the colonial status quo" (*Subject to Others* 49). If at the beginning of the novel the female colonial subject has "no place to stand" (Brown *Ends of Empire* 48) and is a vehicle for registering the instability of the individual and colonial infrastructure, then by the end she retreats behind the proper colonial authorities, in order that paradise doesn't slide into Satan's grasp.

Columbus located paradise at the source of the Orinoco River; Behn also associates Oroonoko with paradise, but a paradise produced via his control over a vital segment of colonial society. The Indians may be like "our first Parents before the Fall" (*Oroonoko* 3), but they are obviously too real and resistant to qualify for a future English-owned paradise. Clearly for Behn it is the threat to the colonial (and natural) authority from below and outside, be they Irish, Dutch, Indians, or slaves, that must be watched for and managed.[26] The inherent contest over space is better understood when we realize that Surinam was part of an incredibly vigorous and vicious mercantile capitalism, lorded over by a tiny plantocracy and fed by captives of one sort or another. Thus Stephen Dunn writes, "It would be hard to say whether the London thieves and whores rounded up for transportation to 'the Barbados Islands' or the Scottish and Irish soldiers captured in Cromwell's campaigns and sent over as military prisoners were any less hostile and rebellious than the Negroes dragged in chains from Africa" (*Sugar and Slaves* 69). In re-membering the colonial space, in that the effect of the novel is to justify and restore a more disciplined and pervasive paternalism of rightful rulers like Willoughby or the Stuarts, Behn either relegates physical violence to Indians and slaves in the wilderness or to the tyrannical rabble within the colony. In reality it was the plantocracy who was on the offensive and performed institutionalized dismemberment upon those who would or could not be obedient members of the colony. In 1694 in Barbados one Peter Boone was convicted for stealing a pig and "the Council ordered that he be cut to pieces and have his bowels burnt, and his quarters put up in the most public paths for viewing" (Beckles *Black Rebellion in Barbados* 50). In Jamaica, after yet another revolt in 1678 (there were six between 1673 and 1694), Joseph Bryan suffered the following at the hands of his English masters:

His leggs and armes was first brocken in peeces with stakes, after which he was fasten'd upon his back to the Ground – a fire was made first to his feete and burn'd uppe by degrees; I heard him speake severall words when the fire consum'd all his lower parts as far as his Navill. The fire was upon his breast (he was burning neere 3 houres) before he dy'd. (quoted in Dunn *Sugar and Slaves* 260)

Finally, therefore, Behn sides with the gentlemen who ran the labor camps which inevitably produced such a show. As this plantocracy transformed itself into the wealthiest colonials in English America, writers like Behn still sought to sell the myth of imperialism as the, albeit difficult, expansion of the English garden.[27] In his *A Trip to Jamaica* (1698–1700) Ned Ward was more truthful; he described the island as "the Dunghill of the Universe" (Dunn *Sugar and Slaves* 151). No doubt Surinam would have been described in a similar fashion.

MEMBERS OF EMPIRE

Despite their ideological differences, Milton, Rowlandson, and Behn employ a very similar historical geography in "this now fenceless World" (Milton *Paradise Lost* x.303). The new world of access and excess affords a double-edged opportunity: the mobilization of corrupting forces and the expansion of God's empire. Describing the new spatial anatomy they posit a privileged centre of an English elect about which swirls death and decay. Between these two contesting, antithetical realms lies the majority of English/colonials – an unstable mass with an ambiguous relationship to capitalism, individual liberty, and the Other. Beyond the wilderness condition is the realm of possibility, whether that be God's kingdom, an English empire, or the riches of Cathay or some El Dorado. For that possibility to become a reality the intervening spaces must be made subordinate to the centre. It is a make or break situation; like Milton, Behn and Rowlandson also describe a strategic world, a world at war. At every spatial scale, from the body and domesticated garden to the nation and globe, the elect are under siege by "the lurking Enemy / That lay in wait" (IX.1172–3). The enemy's lair – to which these texts give us access – is essentially empty of history, meaning, or (re)productivity. Through their instances of satanic dis-memberings, the texts reproduce scenarios for the systematic disappearance of whole populations, whose displacement must be accelerated to make room for a superior history and geography. Regarding the future of non-Christian space, Milton sees "a better Race to bring / Into their vacant room, and thence diffuse" (VII.189–91). In "An Horation Ode upon Cromwell's Return from Ireland" Marvell celebrates the emptying of that country of its Irish population by ironically claiming, that "Nature, that hateth emptiness, / Allows of penetration less: / And therefore must make room / Where greater spirits come" (lines 41–4: *Complete Poems*). The absence of the godly's precepts and precincts breeds destruction; it is this space of loss that the English empire will fill with its colonists and their "Lordly eyes." Without the better policing of space alienation thrives, for as Petty avers, "Thievery ... is affixt to all thin-peopled Countries, such as *Ireland* is, where there cannot be many eyes to prevent such Crimes" (*Economic Writings* 202).

England then is "paradise's only map" (Marvell "Upon Appleton House" line 768: *Complete Poems*). As God's map-maker England begins to rename/re-sign space thus making the world in its own image. Petty treats the reader in "Political Arithmetick" (1690) to the sum of England's sway:

It is not much doubted, but that the Territories under the Kings Dominions have increased; Forasmuch as *New-England, Virginia, Barbadoes,* and *Jamaica, Tangier,* and *Bumbay,* have since that time, been either added to His Majesties Territories, or improved from a *Desart condition,* to abound with People, Buildings, Shipping, and the Production of many useful Commodities. And as for the Land of *England, Scotland,* and *Ireland,* ... it is manifest, that the Land in its present Condition, is able to bear more Provision, and Commodities. (*Economic Writings* 302–3)

This imperial and mercantile composition, as we have seen, is however never free from the crisis of decomposition represented by the "Desart condition," a disease common to colony and metropole alike. Milton signifies this condition through the grotesque body of Sin, the epitome of a corrupt female body and the basis for the body politic's dissolution. Recalling Edmund Spenser's ghastly monster Errour, Sin ultimately offers an image of a society in a permanent "wilderness condition": she gives birth to her son Death, who then rapes her so that she is constantly consumed by her self: "into the womb / That bred them they return, and howl and gnaw / My bowels, thir repast" (*Paradise Lost* II.798–800). Thus it is the dismembered and dismembering Sin – consumed by a terrible appetite – that finally enters paradise in Satan's wake, to corrupt and steal away souls for Death. It is essentially a colonial struggle and appetite to which Eve succumbs, Behn explores, and Rowlandson barely resists.

Such a struggle seems a world away from the triumphalism of Dryden's "Annus Mirabilis" where Britannia reigns supreme and "The East with incense, and the West with gold, / Will stand, like supplicants, to receive her doom" (lines 1187–8: *Selection*). A similar confidence was reproduced in the streets of London. Representations of Africans and Indians and their civilization through England's benevolent commerce was the theme of the pageant for Sir James Edward's mayoralty in 1678 (Kupperman *America* 362–3). Yet this spectacle was as much about promoting England's sense of itself as an empire as it was about shoring up authority in the face of popular agitation and unrest by the savages at home. The revolution had succeeded in unleashing both a (parliamentary) state fully supportive of mercantile capitalism and empire as well as the bourgeois subject, who positively hummed with innate rights and dynamism, as well as satanic versions of itself. Increase Mather's anguished cry "*Land! Land!* hath been the Idol of many in New-England" (Slotkin and Folsom *So Dreadful a Judgement* 179) was not so much a denunciation of expansion, but a recognition of the need of those in power to orchestrate a volatile and fracturing social system which was partially fueled by the revolutionary deregulation surging throughout the English Atlantic world. Comus is the epitome of these forces; he threatens to destroy the last vestiges of a feudal order and thus release the dynamism of a fully commercial society, yet in his masterlessness he will also undermine the new order.

Locke acknowledges this problem, and balances the anarchic force of his narcissistic individual, set free to exploit the "wild woods and uncultivated wast of America" (*Second Treatise* 294), with the model of the West Indian plantocracy (237–8). Herein, the two general strands of colonialism in the English Atlantic world are fused: a free-for-all based on notions of unlimited and unpossessed land is tempered by a regulatory force made of a "community" headed by the propertied elite. Locke put such a social vision on paper in the form of *The Fundamental Constitution of Carolina*, a colony to be run by neo-feudal Lord Proprietors, a good number of whom, along with their subjects, emigrated from Barbados to Carolina where there was more room for their heirs (Dunn *Sugar and Slaves* 112–3). The need for the individual rights to be checked by a disciplinary paternalism is central to Milton, Behn, and Rowlandson. Yet, all three register a certain sympathy for that which evades authority. The ambiguous status and unsupervised liberty exhibited by Eve's independence, Rowlandson's identification with her captors, and Behn's power-play between the different racial groups is intrinsic to colonial space.

Yet one's appetite, the acquisitive and inquisitive drive of revolutionary times, can mean the difference between imperial paradise and hell; and this is what connects and concerns the three texts examined here. The texts use the female body as the bellwether of empire: she consumes its frivolous luxury items, its corrupt practices, its seductive illusions at the same time that she is mercilessly about to be consumed by the "natives," thereby, as an ideological ploy, justifying supremacist violence and repression. In Behn there is an ambiguous coalescence of the two "bodies." The gendered sensationalism exhibited, filled with barbarous violations as well as sexual *frisson* and danger, achieves three things. It gives greater legitimation and cultural access to the process of expropriating territory inhabited by indigenous peoples. Second, it reinforces spatial divisions and social hierarchies which counter a lurid chaos. And thirdly, the vulnerability of female colonists confirms that the adventure of colonialism is a masculine enterprise, that territory and colonial society must be doubly "manned," and that the patriarchal order is synonymous with civility and dominated space. This promotional, patriarchal ideology, which has folded within it the subversive image of a woman free of constraints, carries on into the eighteenth century. Moll Flanders's identity depends on how she negotiates space, whether the bedroom, London, or Carolina. Defoe has Moll move from the labyrinthine and degenerative spaces of London to a secure and prosperous life in the North American colonies.[28] At every step her appetite for autonomy and security engender both corruption, including incest, as well as new possibilities. She is also a supremely anarchic figure who ends up confirming the status quo.

What of course the texts fail to represent is the living hell created by the paragons of Christianity, commerce, and civilization, be they Company directors, Puritan ministers, or big planters. As Dunn argues in the context of Barbados:

In only one generation these planters had turned their small island into an amazingly effective sugar-producing machine and had built a social structure to rival the tradition-encrusted hierarchy of Old England. But the irony is that in accomplishing all this they had made their tropical paradise almost uninhabitable . . . Most of all they hated and feared the hordes of restive black captives they had surrounded themselves with. (*Sugar and Slaves* 116)

By murdering the land and often those who resisted their rule, the various but similar elites governed over an increasingly indivisible empire in the late seventeenth and early eighteenth centuries. The consumption of the land, labor, and bodies of its subjects, slaves, and enemies was the energy for what, at the turn of the century, John Brewer calls "an astonishing transformation in British government, one which put muscle on the bones of the British body politic, increasing its endurance, strength and reach" (*Sinews of Power* xvii). Whatever that strength, it is heartening to know that the government was never allowed to let up its vigilance for fear it might lose a "member" or two. John Winthrop had imagined a society where "the riche and mighty should not eate upp the poore, nor the poore, and dispised rise upp against theire superiours, and shake off theire yoake" (in Gunn *Early American Writing* 108). Such a utopian class system was not to be. The mighty consumed the poor, and the poor often turned the tables on their superiors. Subversive appetites persisted. An anonymous Irishman, most likely transported to the English West Indies for taking part in the Irish rebellion of 1641 and thus one of "the bloody Tygers of *Ireland*" (Corns "Milton's *Observations*" 125), "was given twenty-one lashes for remarking during dinner 'that if there was so much English Blood in the tray as there was Meat, he would eat it'" (Dunn *Sugar and Slaves* 69).

CHAPTER 5

The import and export of colonial space: the islands of Defoe and Swift

The partitioning of America was part of a vast Europeanizing process and experiment, an ongoing development of a worldwide imperialism that did much to shape modern concepts about relationships between polity and territory.   Meinig *Atlantic America* 231–2

The Vileness of the Ingredients that all together compose the wholesome Mixture of a well order'd Society.

Mandeville *Fable of the Bees* 54

It is a melancholy thing to stand alone in one's own country. I look round; not a house to be seen but mine. I am the giant of giant-castle, and have eat up all my neighbours.[1]

Thomas Coke of Holkham (quoted in Scott *Critical Essays* 278 [1785])

THE RETURN OF THE COLONIAL

Conjuring up both a Bunyanesque and Lilliputian landscape, Thomas Coke's appraisal of his estate speaks volumes about the moving forces during the late-seventeenth and early-eighteenth century in Britain and its overseas possessions. A progressive agriculturist, Coke articulates the uneasy simultaneity of vision and voraciousness, conscientiousness and ongoing colonization both at home and abroad that informed much of the thinking of this period. Further, there is something here of the "theatricality" of the social relations between the classes, as E. P. Thompson has claimed, which dictated and negotiated the limits of propriety, property, and political contests.[2] Less theatrical was the deployment and differentiation of populations into productive compartments by the numerous giants of the age. Landscape designers such as

164

William Kent, "Capability" Brown, and Humphrey Repton produced the stage, set, and scenery that conferred authority and concealed the labor that worked the land and provided the wealth. Reorganizing their estates in the interests of agrarian capitalism and bolstering their status through landscaping and palace-building, great landowners had few qualms about removing whole villages, as Viscount Cobham did to the village of Stowe. At Castle Howard Sir John Vanbrugh drowned the village of Hilderskelfe. Medieval villages and signs of labor ruined the aesthetic unity of a prospect that gazed upon the world as if it were created for the British elite to shape and rule. It is an aesthetic of having the world at one's fingertips, even in one's grasp. The Palladian Bridge at Stowe includes a depiction of the "History of Commerce and the Four Quarters of the World bringing their Productions to Britannia" (Everett *Tory View* 48).

The large landowners worked hand in hand with both the she-giant of Britannia (James Thomson's "Rule, Britannia!" appeared in 1740) and political giant Robert Walpole; together they presided over transformations in Britain's economic and spatial system. They were, what Roy Porter calls, "'amphibious,' having for generations also owned urban estates, especially in and about London" (*English Society* 57). The exploitation of credit, government positions, urban development, the enclosure of the countryside, and commercial enterprises by "a tight, self-reproducing oligarchy" (47), created social giants with fantastic castles stocked with treasure. It is the gaping distance between these families and the rest of Britain that Coke, Earl of Leicester, invokes. Or, as Porter concludes: "however complex and interdependent the society, one thing was clear: the gulfs between ruler and ruled, rich and poor, propertied and unpropertied, dominated life" (47). In *Joseph Andrews* Henry Fielding refers to "high" and "low" people who see each other as different species.

Jonathan Swift and Daniel Defoe interrogate the consequences and (dis)proportions of the abyss between the giants and mass of impoverished social pygmies. In keeping with the privileged surveillance/spying used by Milton and Behn, Swift and Defoe (another real-life spy) scrutinize social relations from revealing angles. Their omniscience resembles the bird's-eye views popularized in Kip and Knyff's *Britannia Illustrata* (1700). Overseeing reality is a desire clearly at work in Defoe and Swift. Whether as Gulliver in Lilliput and Brobdingnag or as Crusoe when he "fancy'd [him] self now like one of the ancient Giants" (*Gulliver's Travels* 179), they appropriate the power of giants to critique

Figure 6   Badminton, Gloucester, ca. 1690, Leonard Knyff and John Kip *Britannia Illustrata*, 1707

irresponsible policies and imagine an alternative polity. They use an imperialized world as a sounding-board for situations and issues affecting the British Isles. In that their imaginary is rooted in an interactive Atlantic culture system, this chapter will examine how their work resonates with colonialism and its lessons for the British Isles. Thus I argue for the links between, for instance, Africans and Indians abroad – Friday, the Yahoos – and their kin in Britain: the Irish, Highlanders, and the poachers who smeared their faces black. Similarly, I draw connections between new spatial formations and regulations at home (the workhouse, urban planning) and socio-spatial experiments in the colonies (plantations, the plans for Georgia). Literary culture both imports and interrogates the colonial experience as it returns home.

If "boundaries are drawn by mapping practices, [but] shift from within; ... [and] are very tricky" (Haraway *Simians* 201), then Swift and Defoe are cartographers conscious of mapping shifting sands. They explore new and tenuous boundaries delineating proper conduct, proper territorial rights. Perhaps we can see them as seeking to move from "a mighty maze of walks without a plan," as Pope first put it in *An Essay on Man*, to the final version: "A mighty maze! but not without a plan" (Chambers *Reinvention of the World* 68). The plan was beginning to take form through new urban arrangements and the discourse of commercial or "civic humanism" (Pocock) generated by the "public sphere" (Habermas).[3] The innovation of the coffee house epitomizes the intertwining of spatial and discursive civility. Although they are obsessed with boundaries, Defoe and Swift, like Pope, would prefer to have them erased yet invisibly upholding a coherent, naturalized master-plan. The innovation of the "fosse" or "ha-ha," magically separating garden from country-side, performs just this erasure/enforcement. Such a master-plan is what E. P. Thompson describes as a "field-of-force," where gentry and pleb theatrically act towards one another within understood boundaries (*Customs* 73). The trick was for the gentry to retain control over the theatre, script, actors, and entrance fee:

it is a structured set of relations, in which the state, the law, the libertarian ideology, the ebulliations and direct actions of the crowd, all perform roles intrinsic to that system, and within limits assigned by that system, which limits are at the same time the limits of what is politically "possible"; and, to a remarkable degree, the limits of what is intellectually and culturally "possible" also. (83)

But this social theatre depends on responsibility by all sides, as well as the judicious management of resources by the gentry. For Swift especially, irresponsibility ruled the day. Tory or Country ideology was based on this criticism: ruling class corruption and insensitivity, issuing from rampant commercialism, would topple the whole system. Any hope of a social hierarchy sanctioned by historical precedent and natural authority was dashed by the avarice and pride of the Whigs after 1714. Many Augustan writers opposed what they saw as the illusions, fraud, and luxury created by the financial revolution (1690–1740), or as we would define it, the instability produced via speculation and commodity fetishism (Brantlinger *Fictions of State* 57). Along with many of their contemporaries, Swift and Defoe negotiate what Raymond Williams calls a "crisis of values" during the late seventeenth and early eighteenth century, where the predatory was seen to have overtaken the paternalistic, where calculation undermined community, and where mythification obscured materiality. An ideology of improvement and enrichment ran rough-shod over social relations that either were or appeared to be obstacles to this modernization (*Country* 61). Hence they are concerned with limits, jurisdictions, liberties, and national and civic responsibility – the balance between Corporatism and commerce. But just as agrarian and mercantile capitalism dissolved traditional, familiar, and communitarian relations, "Free labour," as Thompson has observed, "had brought with it a weakening of the old means of social discipline" (*Customs* 42). The dissolution of obligation amongst a stable social hierarchy was most visible in London, the crucible of the nation, the cradle of empire, and constitutive of all excess.

As the eighteenth century progressed and the observation of London as "a new kind of landscape, a new kind of society" intensified (Williams *Country* 142), its perceived degeneracy, profligacy, and ominous democratic license made it an "immense wilderness" for many, including Matt Bramble in Smollett's *Humphrey Clinker*. In short, London was fast seen to be transforming itself from noble capital into nightmarish chaos. Colonies and capital increasingly resembled one another. As if simply the other side of the coin, John Gay sets his sequel to the London-based *The Beggar's Opera* in the West Indies.[4] Although *Moll Flanders* takes place amongst the coordinates of Britain's Atlantic network – from Liverpool to Virginia, Bristol to Kinsale, Bath to Carolina – it is within the labyrinthine streets of London, filled with innocents and predators, that exploration, plunder, and settlement now play themselves out. If as Judge Littleton of Barbados stated in the early 1700s that "by a kind of magnetick Force, *England* draws to it all that is good in the Plantations. It is the Center to which all things tend" (Oldmixon *British Empire* 1.xxii), many metropolitan commentators would add that all that is bad also arrives in Britain.

The adventure of cognitively mapping a deceptive and dangerous space informs Gay's *Trivia: Or, The Art of Walking the Streets of London* (1716). Making one's way through London is now a task of survival. Gay offers himself as our guide for the navigation of this *terra incognita*: "By thee transported, I securely stray / Where winding Alleys lead the doubtful Way, / The silent Court, and op'ning Square explore, / And long perplexing Lanes untrod before" (7–10). The walker must warily survey and correctly decipher the cityscape: "Let constant Vigilance thy Footsteps guide, / And wary Circumspection guard thy Side" (III.111–12); and earlier in the poem: "Be sure observe the Signs, for Signs remain, / Like faithful Land-marks to the walking Train" (II.67–8).[5] George Berkeley characterized a natural social order as similar to "plain landmarks" (Everett *Tory View* 18). Such marks are now obscured. Reconnaissance rather than a "stupid Gaze" is vital in the "Maze" or "dang'rous Labyrinth" (*Trivia* II.79, 80, 84) of Gay's London. Accuracy, crucial to both Defoe and Swift, is at a premium. Trust, charity, and naivete should be left at home if the walker – a solidly middling sort – is not to be an easy prey. It is not so much the crowds, "Link-men," beggars, and prostitutes that pose a threat to the unsuspecting and "artless," but *where* they exist. The danger can be reduced by avoiding certain areas and, ultimately, either by cleaning them up or cordoning them off. Thus Gay locates danger as place and its products: it is the "Hurry" of the crowd that barricades the street; the prostitute leads the yokel from Devon "Through winding Alleys to her Cobweb Room" (and his "Doom" [III.291–2]); and open spaces harbour ambush:

> Where *Lincoln's-Inn's* wide Space is rail'd around,
> Cross not with vent'rous Step; there oft' is found
> The lurking Thief, who while the Day-light shone,
> Made the Walls echo with his begging Tone:
> That Crutch which late Compassion mov'd, shall wound
> Thy bleeding Head, and fell thee to the Ground.   (III.133–8)

Britain as "Happy *Augusta!*" depends, therefore, on a sort of colonial intelligence. Having survived "the Perils of the wintry Town," Gay concludes, as if a Raleigh:

> Thus the bold Traveller, (inur'd to Toil,
> Whose Steps have printed *Asia's* desert Soil,
> The barb'rous *Arabs* Haunt; or shiv'ring crost
> Dark *Greenland's* Mountains of eternal Frost;
> Whom Providence, in length of Years, restores
> To the wish'd Harbour of his native Shores;)
> Sets forth his Journals to the publick View,
> To caution, by his Woes, the wandering Crew.   (III.393–406)

Gay's view is borne out by others. Exhibiting a fortress mentality or indeed the sort of viewpoint a colonist would have recording an invasion, Henry Fielding writes the following in *The Covent-Garden Journal* for 9 May 1752:

Within the Memory of many now living, the circle of the People of Fascination included the whole Parish of Covent-Garden, and a great Part of St. Giles's in the Fields; but here the Enemy broke in, and the Circle was presently contracted to Leicester-Fields, and Golden-Square. Hence the People of Fashion again retreated before the foe to Hanover-Square; whence they were once more driven to Grosvenor-Square, and even beyond it, and that with such Precipitation, that, had they not been stopped by the Walls of Hyde-Park, it is more than probable they would by this Time have arrived at Kensington. (219)

Fielding is not entirely poking fun at the paranoid migrations of "People of Fascination." Along with his fellow magistrate and half-brother John, he founded London's Metropolitan Police force and in "An Enquiry Into the Causes of the Late Increase of Robbers" (pub. 1751) he describes London as if it were a wilderness fraught with degenerates, whose very mobility, like that attributed to American Indians by hostile Europeans, is linked to thievery and violence:

Whoever indeed considers the cities of London and Westminster, with the late vast addition of their suburbs, the great irregularity of their buildings, the immense number of lanes, alleys, courts, and bye-places; must think, that, had they been intended for the very purpose of concealment, they could scarce have been better contrived. Upon such a view the whole appears as a vast wood or forest, in which a thief may harbour with as great security as wild beasts do in the deserts of Africa or Arabia; for, by *wandering* from one part to another, and often shifting his quarters, he may almost avoid the possibility of being discovered. (*Complete Works* XIII.83)

"Where then is the redress?" Fielding asks. He partially answers: "Is it not *to hinder the poor from wandering…*?" (98). An absence of supervision engenders anarchic mobility. As with colonial space, the solution is a militant stewardship. Agreeing with Fielding's colonial vision, the author of *The Tricks of the Town laid open* (1699) reduces London to "a Kind of large Forest of Wild Beasts" (quoted in Corfield *Impact of English Towns* 66). On a more civilized note, Tom Brown in his *Amusements Serious and Comical, Calculated for the Meridian of London* claims that "we daily discover in [London] more new countries" (10). This included, presumably, the warren of alleys at the west end of the Strand known as "the Bermudas" where, no doubt, "white Hottentots" roamed (Merians "What they are" 33). In *A Brief Description of the Cities of London and Westminster* (1776) John Fielding sees sailors as savages and the areas they frequent as foreign territory (Linebaugh *London Hanged* 28–9). And if planters in Barbados after 1700 referred to themselves as "Great Britain in miniature," the reverse was equally possible if at first implausible: thus Saint-Marc Girardin writes in 1831, though his sentiments are applicable to our period: "if you take any industrial town and find out the relative number of manufacturers and workers, you will be frightened by the disproportion: every factory owner lives in his factory like a colonial planter in the middle of his slaves, one against a hundred" (quoted in Hulme *Colonial Encounters* 266). As we have seen, there was a general congruence of attitudes towards the dispossessed both sides of Atlantic. Territory free of official authorization, whether wilderness, urban site, or commons, breeds degenerate or "Indian" behavior. With the influx of so many potential "Indians" to the capital and its unprecedented growth, new spatial regimes were required – regimes most readily applied to colonial spaces.[6]

In "A Proposal for Making an Effectual Provision for the Poor" (1753) Henry Fielding states: "it is not barely therefore in the numbers of people, but in numbers of people well and properly disposed, that we can truly place the strength and riches of a society" (*Complete Works* XIII.136). This well describes the interests of Swift and Defoe; both wished for the more efficient distribution of people (and therefore the wealth of the nation) through an accurate appraisal of social relations. Their advocacy of "people well and properly disposed" concurred with the generally accepted notion that manners and social reality could be transformed if subjected to reformatory practices. "The most characteristic complaint throughout the greater part of the century was," according to Thompson, citing Defoe's *Great Law of Subordination Consider'd; or, the Insolence and Unsufferable Behaviour of SERVANTS in England duly enquir'd into* (1724), "as to the indiscipline of working people, their irregularity of employment, their lack of economic dependency and their social insubordination" (*Customs* 37). The most commonly held solution was to correct, or at least contain, aberrant psychological disposition through physical positioning. For instance, the unemployed would discover reform in the new spatial regime of the workhouse (Macfarlane "Social policy and the poor" in Beier and Finlay *London* 252). There was by no means a consensus, and some poor were more deserving than others.[7] Swift might champion the cause of anglo-Irish weavers but has little sympathy for the Catholic poor.[8] And social and economic realism lay behind this more humanitarian approach to the poor (Appleby *Economic Thought* 147–57). The dynamism of capitalism could only be maintained if its destructive, devouring effluent was checked and channeled through systematized social engineering and political intervention. "The number of the poor," as Defoe states the danger, "is almost ready to eat up the rich" (*Tour* 73). However, strict supervision of social boundaries and the alleviation of the worst conditions through state institutions would keep cannibalism at bay.

The London of 1665–6, where rebellion and disease seemed inseparable, offers Defoe a chance to explore a situation that requires intensive and judicious social administration. Though he may sympathize with the poor – one critic arguing that the poor are the text's "collective hero" (Novak "Defoe" 243) – Defoe's real interest in *A Journal of the Plague Year* (1722) is how to deter the poor from rebelling. As Paul Slack shows, legislation aimed at controlling plagues targeted groups deemed subversive: "preachers' association of plague with the 'sin of the suburbs' and of the poor, and their attacks on idle vagrants, drunkards, alehouses, plays and popular games, therefore supported magistrates whose public-health regulations included control of precisely the same people and assemblies" (*Impact of Plague* 304). Indeed, unruly behaviour was often seen as the source of disease. If *Rules and Orders* is the fitting title of the plague regulations for 1666, Defoe applauds the same directorial bent in more benign terms: "the good management of the Lord Mayor and justices did much to prevent the rage and desperation of the people from breaking out in rabbles and tumults, and in short from the poor plundering the rich" (*Journal* 144). *Journal* describes an environment filled with confusion and chaos; it is only held together by savvy corporatism and the speedy negotiation of delicate spatial and social conflicts.

But *Journal* is also about empire. Indeed, isolated, racked with internal divisions, under siege, and on the brink of degeneration, the plagued city is comparable to a colony. And the evolution of capitalist society breeds numerous contagions which are often identified with colonialism. While

Fielding characterizes luxury, the idleness and crime of the poor, and the "engender[ing of] many political mischiefs" as domestic "contagion[s]" (*Complete Works* XIII.22, 28),[9] Defoe uses the plague-ridden city to criticize the corruption epitomized by the "imperialist phantasmagoria of the South Sea Bubble" (Brantlinger *Fictions of State* 57). Like the plague, empire produced "horrid delusion[s]" that "bewitched" citizens (Defoe *Journal* 50–2). The speculative mania, spectral financial transactions, and desire for consumer items can be seen as a "national infection" (53) which "began to debauch the manners of the people" (49). Such rhetoric was identical to that used by those, like Pope, Swift, and Gay anxious about the effects of empire. Well-schooled in the classics and the history of empires, Augustan writers of a Tory or Country ethos feared "the fate which had befallen Rome: persistent and uncontrolled expansion, loss of political control, and, with it, legal and cultural identity" (Pagden *Lords* 102). In light of imperial excesses beginning to transform the metropolis, Anthony Pagden concludes, "the most alarming prospect of all [was the metropolis's] final absorption by the very empire it had itself created" (106).

In order to avoid being devoured by empire's irrationalities and excrescences volatile bodies, from the colonized to the female stock jobber, need, as Swift puts it, "proper Management" (*Prose Works* IX.205). One of the most volatile bodies, as in plague literature, is the female body. Figures of commercial intercourse, uncontainable superfluities, and the illusory – behind apparent beauty lies ugliness – women embody forces of disintegration and the diseases borne of a rampant imperialism. In *Gulliver's Travels* the fraudulent surfaces of maps, company propaganda, and notions of superiority are akin to women's "beauty." Seen as the prime consumers of empire, women thus embodied its excesses. Gulliver frequently fears being consumed by the female. Like Britannia, the servant in Brobdingnag threatens to smother Gulliver in her body. At its worst, empire is a struggle between a diseased woman, Laputa, and the ineffectual and abused "Injured Lady"; the one needs reformation the latter protection. Only (male) rationality, better regulatory devices, and a reordering of social priorities, as in the context of the plague, will prevent consumption by the lures of imperial greed, grubbing, and gratuitous policies.

Vigilance and the "regulation of the city" (Defoe *Journal* 114, 56), then, are not enough to combat the madness through which "the imagination of the people was really turned wayward and possessed" (43). Defoe emphasizes that new ways of organizing and providing for the general welfare – "furnishing provisions . . . charity, and the like" (56) – are also required. In short, a different social system is needed, one which, like the classical architecture replacing vernacular styles in Britain, is structured by the balanced proportions and uniformity that bespeaks civility. To this end, both Swift and Defoe agree on certain spatial ideals which are influenced by the giant patterns that the British Empire thrust upon and circulated in its Atlantic domain.

An intricate network of colonial projects and places brought spatial experiments back to the metropole, and, ironically, to aid in the regulation of an imperialized society. For instance, the Irish New Towns of the 1640s might serve as signposts that point back to the influence on the Elizabethan conquistadors of the Spanish Empire's spatial codes, and forward to their contribution to the design of London and Philadelphia. Anne Crookshank observes of the New Towns, in her "The Visual Arts, 1603–1704," that "however irregular the shape of the surrounding fortifications, a formal street plan was prepared with roads intersecting at right angles, and, in the larger examples, with a central square, known as a 'diamond,' as a market place" (in Moody and Vaughan *History of Ireland* 472). This geometry of square and grid appears in plans for rebuilding London after the Great Fire. Further, if Philadelphia was influenced by Baroque London with its formal and spatial symmetry (Meinig *Atlantic America* 140), it was just as likely to have been influenced by Penn's knowledge of Ireland, where as an absentee landowner he had inherited 12,000 acres in Cork on his father's death in 1670.[10] Rather late and in the shadow of colonial experiments to codify and regulate space, the first model villages in England aimed at regimenting displaced "natives" only began to appear at the turn of the century.

In the same way, strategies used to organize labor abroad were exported to Britain. As the poor were increasingly needed as labor in Britain (rather than immediately shipped to the colonies), successes in social and spatial engineering in the colonies – trumpeted by reformists – returned to fill the "gaps . . . widening between successful capitalists and those they proletarianized, between patrician and plebian cultures" (Porter *English Society* 3).[11] Peter Linebaugh points out that advocates of the workhouse "often had practical experience with Irish, African and American labour conditions." Sir Matthew Hale "hoped [the workhouse] would produce the orderliness among the London poor that he had observed on a Barbados slave plantation" (Linebaugh *London Hanged* 68).[12] John Cary, founder of the society for the "Incorporation of the Poor," set up the first workhouse in Bristol based on his knowledge about techniques of "training" resistant labor in the colonies (Eric Williams *Capitalism and Slavery* 47). The belief that reformatory space (a space that *is* the process of reformation) would direct the individual to proper behavior underlay conceptions of colonies, towns, and prisons in the eighteenth century (Bender *Imagining the Penitentiary* 197). What with unification with Scotland, victory in global warfare (1689–1713), the financial revolution, the ascendancy of the Whigs and Hanovarians, and the acquisition of a more tangible imperial role, including control of the slave trade, Britain is in the midst of re-forming/identifying itself. It is the attempts to order identity and space that are incorporated into literary culture.

The formation of the subject, both national and individual, therefore, was inextricably part of being a mercantile empire and the colonial strategies to annex and work territory. If as Firdous Azim maintains the early "novel is an imperialist project, based on the forceful eradication and obliteration of the Other" by way of defining a sovereign European subject (*Colonial Rise* 37), then we might argue that the adventures written by Swift and Defoe are generally part of this project. It is this dialogic interaction that Edward Said analyzes in *Culture and Imperialism*. Whatever their different goals, both Defoe and Swift use colonial space to work through Britain's social and spatial challenges. And there was no better place than the colonies to find or set, and evaluate the objectification and negotiation of sovereignty, social orders and boundaries. Here, one could experience a magnified theatricality of social engineering. Gulliver and Crusoe undergo the reformulations of proportion and scale, not to mention identity, that so characterize colonial contact arenas. *Crusoe* is an extended crisis of proportion and definition especially at the moment of discovering the footprint and the immediate aftermath or after-mapping of self and securities. The vast differences of perspective in *Gulliver's Travels* have the same re-visioning function. It is this experience, which is thrown into relief in colonial experiments, that Defoe and Swift confront as they look, Janus-faced, toward the South Seas and the British Isles.

THE SOUTH SEA CONNECTION

In 1698 the Darien scheme to set up Caledonia and New Edinburgh on the isthmus of Central America failed. It had generated tremendous excitement and speculation, even causing the East India Company stock to suffer. The failure of the scheme, which Defoe effectively defended

via *Crusoe*, does not concern us. What the venture represented is however pertinent to understanding Defoe and Swift's conception of colonialism and the lure of Spanish America and the South Seas. England
and Spain challenged the legality of the enterprise, and it became a
symbol of Scottish independence. How it was defended against the
barrage of criticism is important. In brief, the defenders used the
language of anti-empire to bolster what was basically an attempt, as
Bridget McPhail, in "Through a Glass Darkly," puts it, "to fulfill the
thwarted colonial ambitions of the Glasgow merchants" (in Lamb
Eighteenth-Century Life 131). In *A Proposal to Plant a Colony in Darien* (1696)
William Paterson, a close friend of Defoe's, described the colony as a
"free port," although such a port would have imperial functions: "reasonable management, will of course enable its proprietors to give laws to
both oceans, and to become arbitrators of the commercial world" (in
Lamb *Eighteenth-Century Life* 129). This is the *imperial* world of Defoe and
Swift, as is the rhetoric used to defend the project. All the colony wanted
was, in the words of one staunch advocate, "a grant from, and consent
of those Indians, who were the primitive and rightful proprietors, for
their sitting down in that part of the country and for cultivating and
improving it" (138). The recognition of Indian sovereignty here is not
necessarily a cynical ploy, though it often was, but we should acknowledge that commerce, free ports, and primitive proprietors have little to
do with the evolution of a colony within the capitalist world-economy.
They have more to do with the requirements and weaknesses of a colony
in its first stages and with distinguishing British, or in this case Scottish,
colonialism from its competitors.

   The Darien scheme was part of a growing pressure for England to
expand from its Caribbean holdings into the Spanish-American Empire
and acquire the metallic wealth of the Spanish and the commercial
profits that France was presently collecting. The treasures, markets and
untold possibilities of Spanish-America exerted a powerful influence in
terms of both real and imagined travels. Even though Swift's satire takes
place in the Pacific, his imaginary still works via an Atlantic world, not
least because Ireland is at the forefront of *Gulliver's Travels* but also
because the Pacific was seen "as the western rim of Spain's American
empire" (115). The "pull" of the South Seas has yet to be fully recognized as a link between Defoe and Swift. Glyndwr Williams has noted
that

The story of English ambitions and achievements in the West Indies is a
familiar one but the attempts to approach Spain's American empire by way of

its remote but vulnerable Pacific seaboard have received far less attention. Until the mid-eighteenth century it was this motive, rather than any disinterested zeal for exploration, which sent English ships into the South Seas. ("Inexhaustible Fountain of Gold" 28)

Interest in the South Seas was kept alive by the adventures of famous buccaneers like Henry Morgan and William Dampier. Travel and adventure narratives stoked the fire. Interest was piqued due to the potential wind-fall from the Nine Years War (1688–97) and the War of the Spanish Succession (1702–13). As Williams points out: "this spate of books ... marked the beginning of the vogue for 'voyages and travels' which was to reach such enthusiastic proportions in the eighteenth century" (*Expansion of Europe* 32). Might we add *Gulliver's Travels* and *Robinson Crusoe* to the roster of narratives maintaining interests in and promoting ventures into the world of Spanish America? Their popularity and endurance surely place them among, in Williams's apt phrase "unofficial agents of imperialism" (52).

It is generally recognized that Defoe was up to his neck in colonial schemes for the Americas. *Robinson Crusoe* is the quintessential work about colonialism or as James Joyce put it, a "prophecy of empire."[13] In *An Essay on the South-Sea Trade* (1712) Defoe exclaimed: "this Trade is not only probably to be Great, but capable of being the Greatest, most Valuable, most Profitable, and most Encreasing Branch of Trade in our whole British Commerce ..." (quoted in Williams *Expansion of Europe* 37). Undaunted by the failure of the Darien Company and the bursting of the South Sea Bubble, Defoe continued to champion usurping control over the Pacific trade through settlement both in the Darien and the Pacific coast, especially in Chile.[14] The failure of the sequels to *Crusoe* are partly because trade in the Far East for the middle class readership is neither real nor exciting enough. Settlement in tropical areas of the Americas was where they could locate their economic interests, fantasies, and ideals.[15]

Although Defoe is enamoured with the colonists, merchant adventurers and heroic gentleman-pirates of yesteryear, he has his sights firmly focused on the empire of the future.[16] As Michael Nerlich argues, Defoe revives the image of the revolutionary bourgeoisie – *Crusoe* is set in 1651, amidst Navigation Acts and the Western Design – who are willing to adventure against the odds, powered by the state and a cultural dynamism. It is an anarchic energy (Nerlich *Ideology of Adventure* 268) that is necessary to shape the world in the image of Protestant England, and as attractive to Defoe as it was to Milton. But Defoe does not want to return to the good old days; a monarch like William III and his policies point to the future: "He fights to save, and conquers to set free" (*True-Born Englishman* 918), specifically against the Irish and for the commercial revolution of the 1680s and 90s (1.1000). Crusoe therefore is the spirit of English colonial and commercial daring.

It is the Pacific and South Atlantic, with their fabulously wealthy trade routes, slave trade, and potential sites for commerce and settlement, that frame Crusoe on his island. *Crusoe* is the model Defoe has in mind when in *A Plan of the English Commerce* (1728) he complains that the British "seem to have no Heart for the Adventure" (xiv) of imperialism and, in so far as they lag behind the Spanish and Portuguese, "nor can we say we have any one considerable Nation reduced to entire Obedience and brought to live under the Regularity and Direction of a Civil Government, in all our Plantations" (xiii–xiv). Invoking Elizabethan colonial projects (101–13) Defoe goes on to promote the "CONQUEST" of the West African coast (246) – an imaginary he explores in *Captain Singleton* (1720). Defoe's advocacy of commerce rather than conquest dissolves when it comes to waste land and waste people. The almost parodic rule of Crusoe becomes more serious when we listen to Defoe reproduce a familiar cant of conquest as he contemplates Africa and the African, that new standard of degenerate humanity which Swift invokes with his Yahoo:

here is not the least Use made of the Land; the fruitful Soil lies waste, a vast extended Country, pleasant Vallies, the Banks of charming Rivers, spacious Plains, capable of Improvement and Cultivation, to infinite Advantage, lie waste and untouch'd, over-run with Shrubage and useless Trees; as a Forrest trod under Foot with wild Creatures; and the yet wilder Negroes. (*Plan* 247–8)

Defoe admits that the "Negroes" plant some maize, some "Roots and Herbs," but concludes "all the rest is left naked, and thrown up to the Wilderness" (248). This begs the question: "why do they [the English and the Dutch] not enclose, fence, and set apart such lands for Cultivation, as by their Nature and Situation appear to be proper for the most advantageous Productions?" (248). Defoe views Scotland and indeed parts of England in identical terms. His "obsession with commercial expansion" (Seidel *Island Myths* 42) or Britain's dynamic "Plantation trade" is a constant throughout his life, manifesting itself in Moll Flanders's world as well as his numerous political pamphlets. He urged Harley to take over the Spanish West Indies and (in 1719) approved of the South Sea Company's proposal to set up a factory near the mouth of the "River Oroonoko," not far from Crusoe's island. If we are not so familiar with the exact geography of Defoe's colonial ambitions – Michael Seidel writes that "the places that made his colonial mouth water, were on the Chilean coast and in the area around Guiana" (42) – few would disagree with Joyce's statement that Crusoe was the "true symbol of British conquest" (quoted in Seidel *Island Myths* 54). In *Captain Singleton* the basic themes of *Crusoe* are given global scope.

Compared to Defoe Swift could not seem more removed from the quest for a British South America. Whether as Dean, Drapier or disillusioned Yahoo, he is generally regarded as a critic of colonialism. Nerlich views Swift as a savage critic of the middle class and their adventure myths, epitomized by Crusoe (*Ideology of Adventure* 275). In his justly famous attack on the process of colonization at the end of *Gulliver's Travels* Swift describes how "the Natives [are] driven out or destroyed" by "A Crew of Pyrates"; he concludes that "this execrable Crew of Butchers employed in so pious an Expedition, is a *modern Colony* sent to convert and civilize an idolatrous and barbarous People" (258). What appears to be a wholesale condemnation of Western imperialism is in fact fairly ambiguous. The process Swift describes, even with the resurgence of interest in Raleigh's plans for Guiana (Hulme *Colonial Encounters* 181), is more readily identifiable as Elizabethan imperial-piracy or traditional Spanish pursuits rather than Augustan maritime enterprise. Perhaps the conflation of past and present is the point. However, given that Britain is conducting a war against Spanish and French imperial interests, Swift is arguably invoking the increasingly popular distinction between the conquesting of Britain's competitors and its own commercial interests. I shall argue that Swift's polemic is part of the "anti-empire," where the target is not colonialism per se, but the excesses and mentality of conquest as opposed to the incorporation of the uncivilized world into an enlightened, commercial system.

There is no doubt that Swift satirizes the fanciful cartography promoted by colonial projects like the South Sea Company by referring to Herman Moll (*Gulliver* 249), who published *A View of the Coasts, Countrys, and Islands within the Limits of the South-Sea Company* in 1711. But his satire is directed at the fanciful, which he associated with the financial shenanigans and cavalier attitude of the Whigs, and not realistic colonial programs based on sound economic and foreign policy. Like Defoe in his *Reasons against a War* (1701), Swift argued in *The Conduct of the Allies* (1711) against a continental war during the crisis of the Spanish Succession in favor of a maritime campaign focused on a vulnerable

Spanish America.[17] The French were reaping massive profits in this sphere whilst the Dutch were a growing threat in the East Indies – reason enough for the extraordinary privileges and popularity bestowed upon the South Sea Company. More importantly Swift condones conquest whilst complaining that the Dutch are not upholding their share of an agreement to attack the Spanish in the "north and south seas of America": "And by the grand alliance, whatever we or Holland should conquer in the Spanish West Indies, was to accrue to the conquerors" (*Prose Works* v.88–9).

If Swift in effect cancels out the Pacific as a viable colonial arena because it is nothing but a (dangerous) distraction from real colonial relations, *Gulliver's Travels* nonetheless appropriates just these geographical areas. Swift has Gulliver warn against imperial designs aimed at the fabulous islands he encounters not so much to critique imperialism but the presumptuous and ignorant fabulation at the heart of colonial policy. Swift campaigned against the official approaches to the colonies, especially Ireland. He argued for the right use of wealth and power so that illusions, confusions, and false expectations were not created. Inaccurate and irresponsible mappings/readings of colonial space led to hazardous situations. In short, in order to avoid misapprehensions and deadly mishaps, colonial administrators must be realistic and practical.

In "On Poetry" (1733) Swift attacks the methods of conjuring meaning and form from the vacancy of corrupt poetry by referring to the tricks of cartographers: "So Geographers in *Afric*-Maps / With Savage-Pictures fill their Gaps; / And o'er unhabitable Downs / Place Elephants for want of Towns" (lines 177–80: *Writings*). Similarly "A *Statesman*, [and] a South-Sea *Jobber*" (162) use subterfuge to hide the vacancy of bankrupt government. Like Defoe, Swift saw the South Sea Bubble as *the* symbol of venal party politics and financial hocus pocus. Both shared a desire for the expansion of British commerce (Swift arguing for Ireland to be part of Britain and thus able to freely trade her resources) as opposed to bloody continental maneuvres and unscrupulous get-rich-quick schemes. In short, both argued for the creation of "Towns" rather than (white) "Elephants." As we shall see, their view of the proper development and developers of space is strikingly similar to that represented by Pope's patrician Burlington, Earl of Cork, "Whose rising Forests, not for pride or show, / But future Buildings, future Navies grow; / Let his plantations stretch from down to down, / First shade a Country, then raise a Town" ("Epistle IV: To Burlington" lines 187–90: *Poetry and Prose*). Ultimately this is an endorsement of colonialism, though of an enlightened design. *Gulliver's Travels* is a prolonged assault on the (Whig) geographers of empire with their "Savage-Pictures" and strategically placed elephants: the text speaks out against this sort of irresponsible perception of colonial spaces and peoples. At the edges of Swift's South-Sea maps, seeking to get out from under the fabrications and distortions that underwrite both Gulliver's world and Ireland, lies the real and beneficial colonial world of commerce. Swift, therefore, had one foot in an anti-imperialist camp and one firmly muddied with colonial interests, both in Ireland and abroad. He could even go so far as to praise the adventurers Defoe relished: Bristol privateers and George Anson, after he captured a Spanish treasure ship from Acapulco, were "inflamed by a true spirit of courage and industry" (*Prose Works* v.89, 79).[18]

THE EXOTIC AND SWIFT

Just as George Berkeley left Ireland for Bermuda believing reform began abroad, Swift imaginatively journeys to the South Seas in order to deal with the problems and contradictions existing in the British Isles.[19] In doing so he also affirms the journeying abroad into exotic, unknown regions which the English had been undertaking with varying degrees of success for over a century. For Swift to use colonial discourse to comment on the British Isles (as well as other adventure narratives) is natural: a reflex born of an imperial culture. There are three aspects of *Gulliver's Travels* that underscore this reflex and shed light on Swift's position as a member of the Anglo-Irish Ascendancy: the exoticism of the novel, its conception of space, and the Yahoos.

The exoticism Swift utilizes, obviously in part to mimic the mythography of early travel narratives and in part to satirize notions of supremacy and prejudice, confirms rather than undermines colonial discourse. The "redirection of the tropes of colonial discourse" (Hawes "Gulliver and Colonial Discourse" 189) are at once challenged by, for example, the inseparability of the island of Luggnagg from Japan. Exotic places of the Other, whether human, bestial, or fabulous, still act as the laboratory for testing and or critiquing British identity and values. That is to say, Swift's South Seas islands are essentially vehicles through which the British can better understand themselves and their duties. Roy Porter and G. S. Rousseau define exoticism as "all those constellations of ideas and human practices that thrive on the remote, the strange, and the unfamiliar for their essential vitality" (*Exoticism* vi). The dwarfs, giants,

flying islands, immortals, savage Yahoos, and enlightened horses represent the mobilization of standard cultural tools within the discourse of
empire. The exotic allowed the British empire "as it progressively
explored and dominated the ... globe with its guns and sails, [to]
increasingly assume[ ] the right to define human values and conduct in
their highest expression" (Porter and Rousseau *Exoticism* 6). Even if
Swift is exposing their contradictions and crises, Eurocentric values and
conduct, and their reformation, remain centerfield. The text is, as
Eagleton puts it, "a covertly imperial projection of European Man onto
the entire globe" (*Heathcliff* 155). Moreover, "thinking the exotic" is not
confined to flying islands and rational horses. Swift slides into more
realistic exoticism when he adds an orientalist "flavor" to his tall tales,
drawing on the oriental discourse that proved so successful for Dryden.
Thus we find the Lilliputian Emperor dressed in a fashion "between the
Asiatic and the European" (14); the Lilliputians' religious book is "their
Alcoran" (31); and in Brobdingnag Gulliver talks of "the Fashion of the
Kingdom, partly resembling the *Persian*, and partly the *Chinese*" (83).
There are more subtle linkages such as the inscrutable oriental mind of
the Laputians or the despotic practice on Luggnagg where supplicants
are forced to lick the dust before the throne of the King (175) which
resonates with Japan's policy of making Christians "*trampl[e] on the
Crucifix*" (186) before entering the realm of their Emperor.

On satiric terms, the corrupting and fantastical nature of the adventuring Swift targets are associated with the Orient, a typical ideological
move of those anxious about imperial excesses. In terms of colonial
discourse, the exotic is in a subordinate, if dialectical, relationship with
familiar British values and practices. In time-honored fashion, Swift
makes colonial space both exotic and anglicized, a warning and a
promise. Hence, on Pacific islands we find landscapes which are anything but exotic. Indeed, Swift's very reticence about physical space –
flora, fauna, and agrarian landscape – makes for an undifferentiated
topography that is "naturally" of one sort: British. Reminiscent of the
prospect poem, Lilliput is described in conventionally anglicized terms.
It is seen from the panoramic eye that reduces space to a stage for British
history: "the Country round appeared like a continued Garden; and the
enclosed Fields ... resembled so many Beds of Flowers. These Fields
were intermingled with Woods," and the town "looked like the painted
Scene of a City in a Theatre" (12). In Brobdingnag, the supposed
antithesis of the corrupt and hypocritical Britain, Gulliver enters a
typically English world: taking "a foot Path through a Field of Barley" to

"a Hedge" and "a Stile" (65). In the land of the Houyhnhnms Gulliver is able to recognize and coordinate his environment (193). Swift's scathing assault on the irrational and fictive, which is ironically mobilized in *Gulliver's Travels* against itself, posits and deploys a natural order inextricably British, Protestant, and hierarchical.

It is Lord Munodi's estate on Balnibarbi, as ideal and impossible as that of Crusoe, which clearly shows Swift's conception of a properly ordered geography. Munodi represents the pragmatic rather than power-mongering landowner; he is the benevolent improver beloved of Country ideology. Unfortunately, nothing but ignorance and infertility surround his "Country House . . . where his estate lay" (149). The estate is "a most beautiful Country; Farmers Houses at small Distances, neatly built, the Fields enclosed, containing Vineyards, Corn-grounds and Meadows." This most "delightful Prospect," with its "Plantations" and "Tenants," has at its center the mansion: "a noble structure, built according to the best Rules of ancient Architecture. The Fountains, Gardens, Walks, Avenues, and Groves were all disposed with exact Judgement and Taste" (150). Before returning this non-ironic utopian South Seas plantation to Ireland, where Swift was embroiled in colonial relations, I want to deal with the third aspect of *Gulliver's Travels* that has Swift shoring up colonial discourse, namely the Yahoos.

If we are allegorically implicated in the Yahoos, the colonized – be they "Hottentots," Amerindians, or Catholic Irish – were immediately identified and identifiable as the real thing. As Clement Hawes points out, the Yahoo "is indebted . . . to the racist voyage literature" ("Gulliver and Colonial Discourse" 203). Although Gulliver states that he and indeed humanity in general are little more than Yahoos, there is a moment after his expulsion by the Houyhnhnms that interrupts allegory with real imperial relations. A group of New Holland "Savages" wound a fleeing Gulliver with an arrow (Swift *Gulliver* 249). It is rather curious therefore that Gulliver then opts to "trust my self among these *Barbarians* than live with *European Yahoos*" (249). Clearly there is a distinction between corrupt civilization and barbarism. Hypocrisy is worse than barbarism. Savages are barbarians through and through, whereas European Yahoos can be reformed just as they can degenerate. The former occupy an irredeemable position of degeneracy, whereas the latter exist on a sliding scale. In the course of the novel we meet perfectly respectable European Yahoos, not least the Portuguese Captain Pedro de Mendez whose ship picks up Gulliver immediately following his encounter with real Yahoos.

It is in the accounts of the South Seas and New Holland that we find real Yahoos; William Dampier's accounts were a favorite of Swift's. In *A Voyage to New Holland* (1699; pub. 1703) Dampier introduces us to Yahoos: "their Skins [are] very swarthy. They are very dextrous and nimble, but withal lazy in the highest Degree. They are said to be dull in every Thing but Treachery and Barbarity" (182). In his earlier work *A New Voyage Round the World* (1697), Dampier characterizes the "Mindanayans" of the Philippines with "short low Noses, pretty large mouths ... their Hair black and straight, the colour of their Skin tawney ... [of] good natural wits ... but generally very lazy and thievish, [who] will not work except forced by Hunger. This laziness is natural to most *Indians*" (325).[20] Swift's tawny Yahoos more than resemble these descriptions in their despicable behavior and their features: "the face of it was flat and broad, the Nose depressed, the Lips large, and the Mouth wide" (*Gulliver* 199).

Reminiscent of the scene where Gulliver is molested by a female Yahoo, Dampier informs us that the women of the Philippines "are very desirous of the company of Strangers, especially of White Men" (*New Voyage* 327). This sexual desire to be "taken"/possessed is representative of the political desire of the native population for the "*English* to settle among them" rather than the Dutch (331). A similar craving to be dominated and saved, this time from warring cannibals and Spaniards, is played out when Friday places Crusoe's foot on his head (203–6). Domination, however, is tempered by notions of reform and the relativity of different cultures and races. We must also keep in mind that native peoples increasingly became a potential market for British manufactured goods. As they became a more integral component in the modes of production and consumption their "worth" was revised. We see this when Gulliver's belief in the innate supremacy of British society is undermined on Brobdingnag, and in Crusoe's debate over cannibalism (Defoe *Crusoe* 171) and, implicitly, slavery.[21] Further, operating in both Swift's and Defoe's view of native populations is a finely graded racial (and social) hierarchy with accompanying levels of degeneracy.[22] At the bottom are Dampier's New Hollanders and, stereotypically, the African slaves acquired from the coast of Guinea.[23] Occupying levels above them are the Hottentots and Indians. Above them, though not by much, are the "white Hottentots" of, for example, the poverty-stricken Catholic Irish. Crusoe and Friday, Gulliver and the Yahoos represent the potential mobility between the different levels of morality, civility, and value.

The point here is that Swift utilizes an ethnocentric discourse that encompasses both Hottentots and the Catholic Irish. Indeed, the Yahoos were interpreted as the Irish by Swift's contemporaries. I have focused on the Hottentot because they are the model that Swift most likely had in mind for the Yahoos; by extension they underscore how "close" or vibrant the real South Sea ventures are in *Gulliver's Travels*. Linda Merians has recently noted that the "Hottentot," who in reality were probably the Khoekhoe of the Cape Peninsula and part of the Khosian societies, were often referred to as white.[24] John Maxwell's *An Account of the Cape of Good Hope* (1707) stated: "the *Hottentots* . . . are a Race of Men . . . [whose] Hair is Wooly, Short and Frizled, their Noses flat, and their Lips thick, but their Skin is naturally White as ours" (quoted in Merians "What they are" 21). Perfect for Swift's purposes of imagining debased white people, this whiteness is often literally obscured, as Captain Rogers notes: "their chief Ornament is to be very greasy and black, so that they besmear themselves with stinking Oil . . ." (*Cruising Voyage* 308). Thus these primitives erase their "whiteness" to become, in the words of John Ovington in his *Voyage to Suratt* (1696),

> most Bestial and sordid. They are the very Reverse of Human kind . . . meaner and more filthy; so that if there's any medium between a Rational Animal and a Beast, the *Hotontot* lays the fairest Claim to that Species. They are sunk even below Idolatry . . . Nature has so richly provided for their convenience in this Life, that they have drown'd all sense of the God of it. (quoted in Merians "What they are" 21)

Significantly, "white Hottentot" was commonly used to refer to Jacobites, Papists, atheists and other undesirables like the Irish poor (33). The Yahoo refers us back to the contested site of Ireland in the same way that, as Merians persuasively argues, "the text named 'Hottentot' was being written at the same time as the British were revising their own sense of national identity" (32). Swift's use of the exotic South Seas revises, as it reissues, the identity of British colonialism, with Ireland as its nearest and most conflicted domain.

At the centre of Swift's re-visioning of imperialism is the figure of Lord Munodi, who represents a social order capable of routing destructive projectors and policy-makers as well as of reforming Yahoos. Swift would have found in Dampier's accounts of Filipino islanders similarities to the behavior and circumstances of the Irish poor under exploitative land owners allied with the Whig government in London. For instance, though the Mindanayans excel at being lazy Dampier also attributes their condition to the "severity of their Prince" who takes from them whatever they produce; this in turn "damps their Industry, so they never strive to have any thing but from Hand to Mouth" (*New Voyage* 325–6). The solution to such a state of paralyzing exploitation and poverty was not imperial domination, though when push came to shove this was often resorted to. Rather, Dampier and Swift shared the view that by introducing such decaying regions into the British commercial network civility would result. Although it is Dampier speaking it could just as easily be Swift on the future of Ireland: "as to the Product of it . . . it is very probable this Island may afford as many rich Commodities as any in the World: and the Natives may be easily brought to Commerce" (*New Holland* 224). Defoe would agree whole-heartedly. From Crusoe's island the horizon promises the limitless commercial possibilities of the Caribbean, Isthmus, South America, and Pacific. Defoe would have agreed with Woodes Rogers when he wrote of the original Crusoe's island, Selkirk's Juan Fernandez: "I have insisted the longer upon this Island, because it might be at first of great use to those who would carry on any Trade to the South-Sea" (*Cruising Voyage* 101). Underscoring the task Swift had before him with the reformation of Ireland, Erasmus Jones wrote in 1728 that the Irish were "yet so grossly Ignorant in all Matters of Religion, that the History of *Robinson Crusoe* being read to them, has pass'd current for the Legend of one of their famous Saints, and believed to be as true as Gospel" (*Trip through London* 62). It is this distortion of reality, not to mention the implicit colonization of the Irish mind by English fiction, that so angers Swift.

MANAGING AND MANIPULATING SPACE

"But where in the World should we plant?" asks Defoe in *A Plan of the English Commerce*, to which he answers:

there is Room enough still left on the Surface of the Globe . . . Places where 100,000 People may immediately plant and build, find Food, and subsist plentifully; the Soil fruitful, the Climate comfortable, the Air healthy, unmolested by Savages and Canibals, as in *North America*; unravaged by Lions and Tygers, Elephants and Monsters, as in *Africa*; fill'd with Cattle useful and eatable, tame and tractable, abounding with Fish, Fowl, Flesh, wanting nothing but to be inhabited by Christians, and ally'd to the rest of the Christian World by Commerce and Navigation. (276–7)

Swift might argue that Ireland almost fits the bill. His writings on

Ireland clearly delineate his support for the further, and more efficient, colonization by members of the Protestant Ascendancy. The imperialism he most opposed was the blunt instrument used by London. Ireland remains the touchstone in Swift's notions concerning colonialism. For instance, like his countryman Oliver Goldsmith, he denounces emigration to North America, specifically deriding William Penn's adroit advertising or "false allurements from America." He depicts Irish émigrés as exploited labor and "a Screen against the Assaults of the *Savages*" (*Prose Works* xii.78, 60) for the protection of the English. Swift's indignation is directed at the loss of labor and trade from Ireland rather than at British colonialism abroad. He believes Ireland needs the same "cultivation" as other colonies. Ireland's debilitating status as a colony, with its subsequent political instability, is a result of the irrational arrogance on the part of English and Whig imperialists, as well as an inept Ascendancy elite. Why must Ireland, with its civilized Protestant population within a stone's throw of England, be denied the relationship with England that Scotland acquired in 1707? He accuses the English of historically "look[ing] *down* upon this Kingdom, as if it had been one of their *Colonies* of *Out-casts* in America" (ix.21). But the separation of himself and the Anglo-Irish from Ireland's own set of outcasts is clearly evident when he argues:

The common objections against all this [reformation], drawn from the laziness, the perverseness, or the thievish disposition of the poor native Irish, might be easily answered, by shewing the true reasons for such accusations, and how easily those people may be brought to a less savage manner of life ... supposing the size of a native's understanding just equal to that of a dog or horse, I have often seen those two animals to be civilized by rewards, at least as much as by punishments. (xii.89)

This is not satire of the sort found in "A Modest Proposal." Swift goes on to outline what can be made of Irish Hottentots:

It would be a noble achievement to abolish the Irish language in this kingdom, so far at least as to oblige all the natives to speak only English on every occasion of business ... This would, in a great measure, civilize the most barbarous among them, reconcile them to our customs and manner of living, and reduce great numbers to the national religion ... it is almost impossible for a country gentleman to find a servant of human capacity, or the least tincture of natural honesty; or who does not live among his own tenants in continual fear of having his plantations destroyed, his cattle stolen, and his goods pilfered. (88–9)

To be sure, Swift goes on to attack absentee landowners and graziers, who are depopulating the land, but his preoccupation concerns the English policies which exacerbate the degeneracy of the natives, and put the "creole" population in increasing danger. Hence the garrison mentality exhibited by Swift at the end of the above quotation; a mentality we more readily associate with Crusoe. It is a mentality of one battling, as with the "nasty crew" of Quilca, becoming "corrupted" like the Catholic Irish and "sinking into barbarity" (VII.76). The humor of the visit to the village of Quilca does not mask the anxiety that Swift lived with in Ireland.

In her exhaustive study of Swift's landscapes, Carole Fabricant argues that the Swiftian gaze repudiates the Augustan eye and its celebration of edenic estates and bucolic landscapes. Swift's "excremental vision" not only signaled what Fabricant calls "the yawning epistemological, ideological, and literary gap" (*Swift's Landscape* 42) between Swift and the Augustans, but also accurately described the wretchedness of Ireland. But rather than "Swift's landscape tacitly den[ying] the grounds of his Augustan contemporaries' rage to order" (269–70), Swift adds a colonial perspective, thereby expanding the Augustan gaze so as to encompass the harsh realities presently beneath their rosy vision. While Fabricant is right to emphasize that Swift's sensitivity to Ireland gave him a different view of the power relations behind the written word and physical space, she pays scant attention to the Augustan figure of Munodi when discussing Swift's view of the landed classes.[25] A patrician model beset by misrule (and most likely based on the Tory MP, Robert Cope's estate in Ireland where Swift stayed whilst writing his novel [Higgins *Swift's Politics* 151–2]), Munodi contradicts Fabricant's argument that the country-house ideal is at best an abstraction for Swift. It is clear that Swift, drawing on the Virgilian reverence for the land, felt that responsible landowners made the best rulers.[26]

"A Voyage to Laputa" is the book that most directly attacks the relationship between Britannia's imperial sway (Laputa/whore) on the one hand, and Ireland (Balnibarbi) on the other. Munodi and his production of "a most beautiful Country" are under siege from the eviscerating calculations and contempt of the rulers on Laputa. While Munodi governs with "Prudence, Quality, and Fortune" (*Gulliver* 149) over a productive and well-ordered estate, which is simply an extension of his mansion and personal "Judgement," the lackeys of Laputa in the "Metropolis" of Lagado put into effect policies that create waste. Swift portrays the absurdity of the economic restrictions and exploitation of Ireland by Britain through the irrational devastation wrought by the

"Academy of PROJECTORS in *Lagado*" (151). Like Defoe, Swift is also concerned with the inflammatory nature of the South Sea Bubble (riots erupted in its aftermath). This illusory "projection" represents the arrogance and corruption of the Whig government and its imperial policies. It is fitting that Erasmus Jones recounts that because of thatched roofs sprouting green shoots, "[the Irish] live under a *Meadow*; or (as a Person said of the like Place, to which he most aptly compared the late *South Sea* Project) they have *green Ears* over their *Heads*, and a false *Ground* under their *Feet*" (*Trip through London* 55–6). The South-Sea or Balnibarbian quality of Ireland – this topsy-turvy and disintegrating world – infuriates Swift. Like Spenser, he despises the instability rife in Ireland. Both he and Swift denounce, as colonials, the absence of rational policies and practical plans for settling Ireland that leave them "in stormie surges tost" (*Faerie Queene* VI.xii.1).

Munodi's prosperous plantations and tenants contrast with Gulliver's first views of Balnibarbi: "the Houses [were] very strangely built, and most of them out of Repair. The People in the Streets walked fast, looked wild, their Eyes fixed, and were generally in Rags." The country-side is similarly out of order: "I saw many Labourers working with several Sorts of Tools in the Ground, but was not able to conjecture what they were about; neither did I observe any Expectation either of Corn or Grass, although the Soil appeared to be excellent." Despite the potential abundance of labor and produce, Gulliver concludes that "I never knew a Soil so unhappily cultivated" (149). The universal blight surrounding Munodi represents the position of the Protestant Ascendancy and underlines the need for an autonomous political and economic system. In the early decades of the eighteenth century an increasingly coherent Irish Protestant society, with its own landmarks of mansions and cultural institutions, fiercely resented the restrictions imposed by London. As J. L. McCracken comments in his "Protestant Ascendancy and the Rise of Colonial Nationalism, 1714–60": "while claiming all the privileges of freeborn Englishmen, they regarded themselves as Irish-men entitled to control the destinies of the country that had become theirs by right of conquest" (in Moody and Vaughan *History of Ireland* 107).

Although Munodi's foes seem to be projectors and policy-makers, the actual and most immediate danger is from the wild-eyed people dressed in rags that Gulliver sees in Lagado. The revolt of Lindalino, a reference to Dublin and the successful resistance to Wood's halfpence, can be read in more than one way or direction. To be sure, the revolt is against

Laputa/Britain, but the same social unrest would also threaten wealthy landowners like Munodi. Swift's aversion to violence, which Said argues sets him apart "from the reigning majority" (*The World* 84), is directed at both the imperial policies of London *and* their consequences: of placing the Catholic Irish in an untenable position which threatens to blow up in the face of the "Protestant nation" ruling Ireland. As a spokesman for the Ascendancy who recognized England's sovereignty over Ireland but balked at London's economic and legislative domination (Ferguson *Swift and Ireland* 19–20), Swift's critique of imperialism is based on this explosive situation.[27] The revolt of the city of Lindalino thus registers a complex struggle in Ireland: the resistance to Wood's halfpence – which Swift also refers to as "brass," a word associated with Catholicism – pits a Protestant nation against the corrupting influence of London at the same time as it galvanizes that constituency to take charge of Ireland's body politic and its circulation, whether of money, trade or people.

If Swift "had a low opinion of conquering armies, of colonial oppression, and of scientific schemes for manipulating people and opinion," as Said maintains (*The World* 83), it was an opinion derived from his Anglo-Irish status, directed at the schemes of Whig-controlled London, and excluded Catholics from its biting political and moral outrage. For as J. C. Beckett points out in "Literature in English, 1691–1800": "every Irish protestant, whatever his rank, felt himself to be a member of a governing society; and this sense of a common superiority to the Roman Catholic masses tended to weaken the forces of class divisions within the dominant group. It produced a kind of aristocratic egalitarianism" (in Moody and Vaughan *History of Ireland* 433).[28] This "egalitarianism," which is reminiscent of Munodi's happy estate, revealed itself in the campaign against Wood's halfpence; the Drapier's libertarian appeal to "'the whole people of Ireland' meant, quite simply, the protestants of the established church" (458–9). Using the patriotic rhetoric of the "creole nationalist" (Anderson *Imagined Communities* 14) Swift articulated the fear that the present exploitative arrangement was only producing a Balnibarbian "emptiness" that as all political commentators agreed was a recipe for disaster.

Swift's argument for the civil rights of Protestant Ireland is conjoined with and dependent upon the management and redisposing (or simply disposal) of Catholic Ireland. Swift clearly demarcates two Irelands in order for both the Irish and English elites to recognize the potential for profits and pandemonium. Protestant Ireland deserves and is identified with "the Laws of GOD, of NATURE, of NATIONS" (*Prose Works* X.63), "the

Rules of Reason, ... Spirit of Industry, and Thrift, and Honesty"
(IX.202) as well as "our *happy Situation for Commerce*" (X.149) and "the
Benefit of *Trade*" (XII.18). To deny these civilizing practices is to lock
Ireland into "an Absurdity, that a wild Indian would be ashamed of"
(18). The "absurdity" of such an unnatural state only encourages "those
Parts of this Kingdom where the *Irish* abound; ... [who] for want of
[Englishness] they live in the utmost Ignorance, Barbarity and Poverty;
giving themselves wholly up to Idleness, Nastyness, and Thievery, to the
very great and just Reproach of too many Landlords" (X.139). To his
credit Swift often cites the oppressive conditions that the "poor Popish
Natives" (IX.209) are forced to live under as an explanation for their
behavior. In any case, the incivility issues from the "Nursery [that] is the
barbarous and desert Part of the Country" (IX.203). This "Dunghill" is a
small proportion of the country, since in 1688 the Catholics held only
22% of the land, by 1703 a mere 14%. Colonization of this land was a
partial solution. The real worry however was the growing number of
mobile Catholics, usually referred to as beggars, who defied spatial
segregation as they emerged from the "desert" parts into the public eye,
an unwelcome reminder of exploitation and the ominous masses.
"[T]he Spirit of wandering" breeds "Nuisance" and "Thieves" and
wants "better regulation" (*Prose Works* XIII.133–5). Swift is particularly
concerned with delineating between the poor, who are of the established
church, and the beggars, who are Catholic and represent socio-spatial
disintegration.

In his sermon "On the Poor Man's Contentment" (IX.191) the Protestant poor, who deserve charity, are synonymous with commerce and
obedience, whereas the Catholics represent a different case altogether:
"for by the Poor I only intend the honest, industrious Artificer, the
meaner Sort of Tradesmen, and the labouring Man, who getteth his
Bread by the Sweat of his Brow, in Town or Country, and who make the
Bulk of Mankind among us" (191). Qualifying "the Bulk of Mankind" is
the key term "among us" which divides the Protestant "us" from the
Catholic "them." Relegated to little more than beasts of burden, the
Catholics are deemed inherently rebellious. They do not qualify as poor
or as sufficiently subservient to the market and Protestant nation, since
the real poor are, according to Dean Swift, "safest in Times of publick
Disturbance, in perilous Seasons, and publick Revolutions, if they will
be quiet, and do their Business" (197).

Particularly unpropitious to business are the increasing numbers of
dispossessed Catholics. As Claude Rawson has argued, Swift's view of

this group and what should be done about them dovetails with his prescription for the Yahoos. "The Question ... Whether the *Yahoos* should be exterminated from the Face of the Earth" (*Gulliver* 236) or just castrated (238), and the seeming satire of "A Modest Proposal" or "Maxims Controlled in Ireland" take on unnerving realism when we look at Swift's writings on beggars. In "A Proposal for giving Badges to the Beggars in all the Parishes of Dublin" Swift emphasizes the other-ness of "strollers, Foreigners, and sturdy Beggars" (*Prose Works* XIII.132) and states that "to say the Truth, there is not a more undeserving vicious Race of Human kind than the Bulk of those who are reduced to Beggary, even in this beggarly Country" (135). The beggars are to be demarcated: given badges and confined to their own parishes. In the current situation they "infest every Part of the Town" like "Caterpil-lars." In the dehumanizing language of the colonizer Swift rants against the oppression of this "Clan of Thieves, Drunkards, Heathens, and Whore mongers, [who are] fitter to be rooted out off the Face of the Earth, than suffered to levy a vast annual Tax upon the City" (139). The genocidal tone is tempered with the recognition that the degeneracy of the Catholics is due in part to "want of work." However, their disap-pearance would only be beneficial: for the "natives," intones Swift, "death would be the best thing to be wished for, on account both of themselves and the public" (*Prose Works* XII.136). With the barbarians already through the gates, Swift rails against a colonial policy that has the (Catholic) "natives" reproducing nothing but themselves, a practice antagonistic to civility, instead of producing surplus value under the control of the (Protestant) "public."

DEFOE'S LESSONS IN SOCIAL CONTROL

Getting the poor and discontented to "be quiet, and do their Business" (Swift *Prose Works* IX.197) was obviously the goal of the ruling elites all over the British Isles. There was fierce resistance to the turning of people into the "riches of the nation," or making them commodities of labor, as the number and character of legislation passed during this period testify. If Swift felt that *in London* "the sentiments of the vulgar" were a useful constitutional safeguard (Gilmour *Riots, Risings and Revolutions* 18), the majority of commentators found such sentiments highly toxic. Instabil-ity was rife, Popish plots and Jacobite intrigues abounded. The 1690s saw intense poverty. An estimated one quarter of the population of Scotland starved to death.[29] As Ian Gilmour observes, by the Hanover-ian accession and the Jacobite uprising of 1714/15, "Disaffection was general" (63). The legislative force brought to bear on this unrest was truly impressive: the Riot Act (1715) was followed by the Transportation Act (1719), the Combination Act (1721), the Workhouse Act, and the Black Act (1723). These legislated a new economic order and criminalized any mobilization against it.

As he moved from a rebel under Monmouth to a government spy and party hack, Defoe was a great observer of dissent and its perambulation from the margins of society to the centre. Thus it is not surprising that *Robinson Crusoe* incorporates elements of every Act. Crusoe constructs a world ruled with the paranoia, pantomime, and power of the Waltham Black Act which was designed to protect landowners' rights. The mutinous sailors violate both the Combination and Riot Acts. Crusoe's punishment for them is reminiscent of those doled out under the Workhouse and Transportation Acts. Indeed the mutiny encapsulates the struggle to control and define the production of space in the British Atlantic world. Akin to Swift's beggars, sailors were seen to defy reason and citizenship, and were often categorized as little above savages (Linebaugh *London Hanged* 135). They were the "seething mobility" who "participated in almost every port-city riot in England and America in the early modern period" (Rediker *Between the Devil* 249), formulating "ideologies of resistance" along the way (251). There were forty-eight mutinies over the period 1715–37 (228). These occurrences led Admiral Wager, First Lord of the Admiralty to warn in 1734: "we must govern the mob or they will govern us" (quoted in Gilmour *Riots, Risings and Revolutions* 76). Sailors therefore were at the cutting edge of both the promise and dangers involved in the creation of a compliant waged labor force, the usurpation of territory, and the machinations of a stable commercial network. Though Swift and Defoe eschewed wage relations for a moral economy, they shared the desire of merchants and masters to impose a contract upon Hottentots white, black, or brown, in order to create the sort of discipline sought after by the Acts. Defoe/Crusoe sees the solution to transgression in regularizing mobility and space: "to separate every thing at large in their Places" (*Crusoe* 68).

Like Munodi, Crusoe is a benevolent governor battling the wilderness and wild people (cannibals and mutinous sailors) with an ideal plantation. If Munodi must act indifferent to the irrational ravages inflicted on his island until alone with Gulliver, Crusoe must also theatrically protect his "kingdom." Both colonials worry about losing authorization (the reproduction of a social order and identity that they control) and must, as in eighteenth-century Britain, constantly and theatrically construct and dissolve, display and conceal the boundaries and forces that protect their interests. Though he is always out-numbered by those who would destroy his rule/s, Crusoe's success at improving his lot rests primarily upon his superior knowledge and utilization of space. His firepower is supplemented by the secrecy of his presence and intentions when he, Friday and the Spaniard attack and decimate a group of Amerindians (237). The mutinous sailors, however, not only have guns but are fellow countrymen and therefore must be handled with more circumspection.

The advantage of surveillance and invisibility allows Crusoe and his "army" of eight to outwit and outmaneuver the sailors: "we could see them plainly, though they could not perceive us" (263). Though they kill some of the mutineers, Crusoe's preferred method of subjugation is disorientation. He defeats the mutiny through a drama of power represented by the unseen "Governor" and his "fifty men." The conjuring up of a chain of command and thus a command of social space is intrinsic to submission. Social relations are mediated through this play of deferral, deference, and displacement, whereby the power of the ruling class rests upon a sense of its all-encompassing, natural presence. Recognizing that he gains authority through the manipulation of space, Crusoe keeps himself "out of Sight, for Reasons of State" (268). He dramatizes the situation to heighten his rule, which he admits is based on deception:

so I retir'd in the Dark from them, that they might not see what Kind of a Governour they had, and call'd the Captain to me; when I call'd, as at a good Distance, one of the Men was order'd to speak again, and say to the Captain, *Captain, the Commander calls for you*; and presently the Captain reply'd, *Tell his Excellency, I am just a coming*. This more perfectly amused them; and they all believed that the Commander was just by with his fifty Men. (269)

It is precisely because Defoe recognizes that effective government is not the apex of a natural system but rather "all a Fiction" (168), that he stresses the use of space in maintaining the rule of those who are industrious, responsible, and propertied.

The colonial vision of both Swift and Defoe – the one a colonial nationalist and the other a life-long enthusiast of colonialism and Britain's marginal societies – made them aware of the constructedness of space and thus of society.[30] Neither had much respect for arguments based on such a thing as a natural order or disposition.[31] This accounts for the anarchic energy which lies at the core of their writing. Both show the insecurity and attention to relativity and the processes of change so characteristic of those involved with expropriating and managing colonial spaces. Hence, "Swift engaged in setting up structures," Fabricant has argued, "to enclose and define at the same time that he dramatized either the futility or the impermanence of these structures" (*Swift's Landscape* 270). This definition could just as neatly be applied to the key scene in *Crusoe*: the moment Crusoe discovers the footprint. Preceding the discovery, Defoe summarizes Crusoe's idyllic set up. We review the crops, livestock, and general creature comforts maintained by his "two Plantations" (151), one of which is his cave – renamed his "Fortification" and "Castle" after the footprint (154) – and the other his "Country Seat" (152). Underscoring that there are no guarantees concerning the secure organization of self and space, the half-dozen or so paragraphs immediately prior to the discovery are saturated with, and indeed concentrate on, terms and definitions of protection. Crusoe gives us a detailed inventory of his strategic measures and his use of "Stakes or Piles" as large as trees, "Enclosures," fortifications, hedges – though of one hedge he tells us "that it was rather a Pale than a Hedge" – and numberless walls (151–3). He "spared no Pains" to construct such an Edenic bunker (153). Yet this security is turned on its head by the anonymous threat of another's trespassing presence, and Crusoe becomes his own prisoner, about to be devoured (155).

Crusoe's obsession with security seems excessive. Manuel Schonhorn has noted that of the contemporary accounts of marooned men, "None fenced, or hedged or walled ... the way Crusoe did" (*Defoe's Politics* 144). Perhaps the reason for this is that Defoe's conception of space, like Swift's, is indebted to abstract and systematic designs for expropriating territory. Moreover, as this conception constituted itself within British culture, Defoe appears to be consciously dramatizing his fascination with and endorsement of colonial enclosing. The colonial world offered him numerous blueprints and experiments to draw from. There was Penn's well-publicized colony, to promote trade and tolerance, with its "greene Country Towne" of Philadelphia. Before Penn's "Frames of Government" (1682–96, 1701) there was the absurdly metrical neo-feudal utopia of Carolina; a colony conceived and put into charter in 1669 by Shaftesbury and Locke. These designs were at once exclusionary and expansionist. In all "The New World Charters," Robert Sack points out, "the geometric lines of territorial authority become sweeping space-clearing and maintaining devices for territorially instituting communities" (*Human Territoriality* 134).

Another such community which relates more directly to Defoe and

Swift's period was the colony of Georgia. "It is probable," Jack Greene notes, "that no other early modern British colony began with a more fully articulated set of goals" (*Imperatives* 115–7). The promotional literature began to flow around 1717; the plan received incredible public acclaim and sizeable private and government sponsorship (115). The idea of Georgia worked on two inter-related fronts: as "a great national undertaking" (120) it promised to revitalize Britain's imperial capital; at the same time it would resolve the worrisome state of Britain's poor and incarcerated. Not only were the transportees going to be reformed (rather than dumped and exploited), but the colony was to be an experiment, "a model society" from which Britain itself could learn (119–20). Despite its failure as an egalitarian utopia of yeoman farmers watched over by paternal trustees, Georgia surely stood for the sort of reformist visions and Country ideology that Swift and Defoe articulate.[32] The evolution of Georgia out of prison reform represents the thematic and spatial thrust of *Moll Flanders*. An understanding of the circumstances that produce poverty and crime, and an examination of the horrors of the prison system in Britain leads to reformation, freedom, and, in theory, prosperity in the American colonies. In Defoe's novel this works; however, the founder of Georgia, James Ogelthorpe, had to resort to whipping the majority of his discontented colonists toward happiness. Reflecting the trustee's abstract theoretical perception of the colony, the design completely ignored the realities of the natural environment as well as the needs and capacities of the colonists.

This was nothing new for colonial projecting, nor for "Georgia." In his "A Discourse Concerning ... the Most delightful Country of the Universe, 1717," Sir Robert Mountgomery, an early and failed contender for a neo-feudal grant over the territory to the south of Carolina, bases his settlement on exactly the sort of security arrangements Crusoe constructs. In light of Carolina's "troubles" with Indians, Mountgomery states:

> we shall not satisfie ourselves with building here and there a *Fort*, the fatal Practice of *America*, but so dispose the Habitations, and Divisions of the Land, that not alone in our Houses, but whatever we possess, will be enclos'd by *Military Lines*, impregnable against the *Savages*, and which will make our whole Plantation one continued Fortress. (in Reese *Promotional Literature* 9)

He goes on to describe, with Defoe's attention to strategic detail, the extreme regimentation of the colony, where, very much like Jeremy Bentham's Panoptican, "the labouring People (being so dispos'd, as to

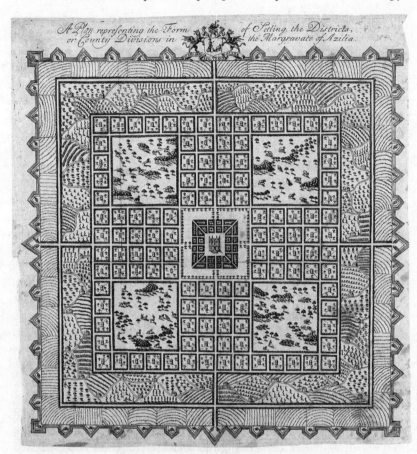

Figure 7 "A Plan Representing the Form of Setling the Districts, or County Divisions in the Margravate of Azilia," Robert Mountgomery *A Discourse Concerning the design'd Establishment of a New Colony to the South of Carolina, in the Most Delightful Country of the Universe,* 1717

be always watchfull of an Enemies Approach) are themselves within the Eye of those, set over them, and *All together* under the Inspection of their Principal" (10). The gigantic fortified square of "Azilia", geometrically divided and subdivided into farms, estates, and "Forrests," all symmetrically deployed around a central City, Fort, and the "Margraves House," is to duplicate itself in identical "Townships." This domination of space is thus enacted by a space of domination. The colony is a function of absolute authority: it is both product and producer of authorization. The perfect model of social control by the high-minded occupants of the "Margraves House," the colony is constructed to maintain a hierarchy and keep each person in their allotted station. Thus Mountgomery advertises: "and, Men once got together, 'tis as easy to dispose them regularly, and with due Regard to Order, Beauty, and the Comforts of Society, as to leave them to the Folly of fixing at Random, and destroying their Interest by indulging their Humour" (11). Encapsulating hegemonic thinking within the British Empire, Mountgomery's absolutist paternalism regards the uncertainties of freedom as destructive, while regularity is a thing of beauty.

The way Crusoe organizes space, with his strict compartmentalization of the island into areas of labor, pleasure, knowledge, and defence, mirrors the hierarchy of Mountgomery's model, giving form not just to himself but also to the Other, when or if they arrive. He defines or realizes his selfhood through the process of mapping and circumscribing the island. In other words, he revives his sense of self, his identity and well-being through possession. Indeed, as Simon Varey persuasively argues, "Once Crusoe 'get[s] a Savage into [his] Possession,' he establishes the hierarchical society that his building activity has emblematized all along" (*Space* 154). That identity is a function of space is recognized by John Evelyn when he points out that the buildings of London "are as deformed as the minds and confusions of the people" (*London Revived* 6). As if speaking directly to Mountgomery's plans for a "most Delightful Country," Evelyn argues that it is "from the asymmetrie of our Buildings, want of decorum and proportion in our Houses, that the irregularity of our humors and affections may be shrewdly discern'd" (quoted in Varey *Space* 45). It is precisely the lack of control over their environment, their isolation from a social order within which they can assert an identity, the dissonance between self and space that force Moll and Roxana, for instance, to become "entrepreneurs of the body" (Pittock *Inventing and Resisting Britain* 90). Space that produces alienation also creates the alien body – the body as (mobile) property, whose transgressive fluidity escapes the supervision so pronounced in Mountgomery, Defoe, and Swift.

I do not want to conflate the absurdly abstract and belligerent model of Mountgomery's with Defoe's much more nuanced production of space. Whereas the former's plan is absolutely visible in its deployment of power, Crusoe constructs some defences that are intentionally invisible. Defoe is ultimately interested in the strategies to incorporate or obscure the coercive structure upholding polite society. The "Wall made ... with long Stakes or Piles" (*Crusoe* 152) that are made of trees planted by Crusoe look ahead to the eighteenth-century English garden, where Nature and the artificial were seamlessly knitted together. And it was exactly the producers and owners of such estates that, in the spirit of Georgia, attempted to somewhat alleviate the rigors of the new socio-spatial reorganizing via an ideology of paternalism, utility, and a rational, public society. One of the things that links, say, William Penn with Crusoe, or Pope's Burlington to Lord Munodi is that their production of space is leavened with the patrician virtue inspired by Virgil's *Georgics*. The ideology of a moral economy at a time of rampant agrarian capitalism, speculation, and colonization depended on making visible some things whilst occluding others. Such maneuvers underpin Swift's revision of colonial relations and Defoe's examination of the individual and space. That is to say, *Gulliver's Travels* and *Robinson Crusoe* display their authors' participation in this process of arbitrating new social boundaries for an old social hierarchy. Terry Eagleton puts it in another way: "a new cultural formation is mapped on to the traditional power-structure of English society, momentarily dissolving its distinctions in order the more thoroughly to buttress its hegemony" (*Function of Criticism* 13).

A TOUR OF ORDER AND CHAOS

Near the end of *Crusoe* there is an episode that has drawn relatively little attention: when he and Friday are chased by wolves while crossing the Pyrenees. The episode reconstructs the elements of Crusoe's Caribbean trial in Europe. Caught unawares in a wilderness, he has to outwit death by marshaling his knowledge/power of organizing subordinates and creating fortifications: "I drew my little Troop in among those Trees, and placing our selves in a Line, behind one long Tree, I advis'd them all to light, and keeping that Tree before us, for a Breast Work, to stand in a Triangle, or three Fronts, enclosing our Horses in the Center" (*Crusoe* 300). Thus Crusoe's "Troop" defeat the "furious Charge" of the ravenous wolves. The wolves refer us back to cannibals not simply in that they seek to devour Crusoe and Co., but also because they refer Crusoe back to another "wild Place," that of Africa. The only sound as horrifying to Crusoe as the "Howling of Wolves" is "the Noise I once heard on the Shore of *Africa*" (297), "where whole Nations of Negroes were sure to surround us [Crusoe and Xury] with their Canoes, and destroy us;

where we could ne'er once go on shoar but we should be devour'd by savage Beasts, or more merciless Savages of humane kind" (23). The "Noise" is more than the call of the wild; it is the death-dealing totality of wilderness, beast, and savages. If barbarity sounds in the still wild spaces of Continental Europe, surely its echoes can be discerned in the unregulated regions of the British Isles and its very heart, London.

If Swift's perception of social and spatial relations is that of the Irish colonist struggling with lordly imperialists and the specter of lowlife insurrection, Defoe sees the "Whole Island of Great Britain" as a precarious collection of contact arenas, whose inhabitants and geography show just as much need of being parceled out as any colony. Defoe's eye is intrinsically colonial. One panorama takes in a landscape that "looks all like a planted Colony, every where full of People, and the People every where full of Business" (*Plan* 64–5). Defoe traces this picture of ideally apportioned space, in diminishing scale, to the parish and family itself: he describes a "whole Parish" which is "like a planted Garden, or a Colony where every Family lives as it were within it self, and by it self, for the propagating their Business" (66). As with the Munodi/Balnibarbi divide, the "planted Colony" is contrasted with non-manufacturing areas and "unemploy'd Counties" which are "waste and barren," having been let down by a "decaying wasting Gentry" (68). *Crusoe* stands as a model of efficiently organizing the environment under the most trying conditions that can, like other colonial exports, rejuvenate a "decaying" Britain.

There are the obvious "translatable" points about Crusoe's orchestration of social relations given the territoriality being implemented in Great Britain. Like an English Justice of the Peace he oversees labor relations and the law, even effectively transporting the mutineers as JPs indeed could in the early 1700s (Hill *Reformation* 143). As if a park-ranger backed by the Black Act he protects the private property of his estate against any other claims (such as rights of common).[33] The excessive juridical violence of the Act is echoed in Crusoe's treatment of the crows that ravage his corn and threaten to "devour all my Hopes" (116). Killing three "Thieves," Crusoe relates: "I took them up, and serv'd them as we serve notorious Thieves in *England*, (*viz.*) Hang'd them in Chains for a Terror to others" (117). In Crusoe's eye everyone is a transgressor, a thief until proven innocent *and* submissive. Such paranoia fit the prevailing attitudes of the elites in Britain.

Notwithstanding the parodic nature of Crusoe's "estate" it can be related back to the real-world of the landowning gentry. Adapting his views to a colonial setting, Defoe simply enacts in a primitive mode the spatial and cultural strategies deployed on British estates. Crusoe's constructions duplicate the highly visible taste in British high society for a "castle air" to their architecture. The no less ominous but "invisible" design of the "ha-ha" is also relevant here, especially with the addition of "ferocious spikes sticking out horizontally into the hollowed trench" (Franklin "The Liberty of the Park" in Samuel *National Fictions* 147). Security is balanced with an aestheticization of conspicuous power. The "new rural artillery" (Gilmour *Riots, Risings and Revolution* 199) and its designed locale aimed at the have-nots, as we shall see, has its urban parallels.[34] At a time when English gardening began to incorporate the imperial aesthetic of classical design, Defoe consciously fuses domestic and colonial space under the ideology of patrician rule – a rule characterized by the ability to (covertly) set the terms of social interaction and reproduction. It is also a rule that envelopes, knows all. Effecting the omniscience of the imperial imaginary which we have seen in Behn and Milton, Crusoe occupies, at one time or another, every class position from dispossessed to land-owning Governor. Forming a geographical hegemony also, he presides over different categories of space: the urban, rural, estate, and even the suburban.

This super-mobility counters the mobility of others. Crusoe's victory over the mutiny has the clearest relevance to Britain. His effort is part of a general attempt to impose, as in the capitalist utopias of the West Indies, a conformity of movement and behavior upon the poor. In order to provide for social stability, Fielding states in his seventeenth proposal for providing for the poor: "that it shall be lawful for any of his Majesty's subjects to seize all suspicious persons who shall be found wandering on foot, about the fields, lanes, or highways, or in the streets of any of the towns..." without a pass (*Complete Works* XIII.149). Programs to channel and contain the poor were national exercises, especially when "turnover was rapid: 'movers' outnumber[ing] 'stayers'" (Porter *English Society* 38). The great proportion of the movers migrated toward that giant magnet London, whose growth astounded and worried many in the ruling bloc.

In *Augusta Triumphans; or, The Way to Make London the Most Flourishing City in the Universe* (1728) Defoe complains that "*London*, that us'd to be the most safe and peaceful City in the Universe is now a Scene of Rapine and Danger" (quoted in Byrd *Histories* 48). As in *Moll Flanders*, London was often seen as a place of alienation and degeneration; an ungainly beast, scorning order and spawning confusion, riots, crime, and disease. The glory of the imperium's heart was praised by all, but the capital more often than not appeared to transform John Bull into the twin-headed beast of lower-class criminality and ruling-class corruption. *The Beggar's Opera* explores these two bullying and interchangeable elements of society, just as Gay's *Trivia* posits a London in need of colonial navigation. The city's regulation, especially since the Great Fire, was a priority issue speaking to both the consolidation of ruling class hegemony and the containment of the ever-swelling numbers of poor people. As Raymond Williams succinctly puts it:

For complex reasons, ranging from fear of the plague to fear of social disorder – itself a transference and concentration in London of the disturbances of the rural economy – there had been repeated attempts to limit the city's growth ... as late as 1709, when a Bill against new houses was attempted, there was a prolonged struggle, by ruling class-interests, to restrain the growth of London, and in particular to prevent the poor settling there. (*Country* 145)

The limitations, which of course did not apply to the expansion of the "West End" or houses for the "better sort," produced just the sort of chaotic, highly unsanitary, unsafe, and crowded conditions that the patrician class abhorred, though profited by as they laid out their blueprints of serene symmetry and taste, which we now admire as "Georgian" London, Bath, and Edinburgh (145). It is just this juxtaposition of order and chaos, or rather the production of a particular social order in the midst of chaos, that Defoe explores in *Journal* and *Crusoe*.

Defoe's importance lies both in the reproduction of British social relations and his objectification of its structures, institutions, and ideologies. He writes out of the moment and ideological flurry when a new hegemonic order is situating itself. His London in *A Tour*, for instance, is an abstract litany of key public and private buildings, foregrounding the city as an administrative and commercial hub kept functioning through its hospitals and prisons. Contradicting the usual celebratory tones wrapped around the capital Defoe notes, "there are in London, notwithstanding we are a nation of liberty, more public and private prisons, and houses of confinement, than any city in Europe, perhaps as many as in all the capital cities of Europe put together" (*Tour* 321). He states this not without a touch of pride; prisons – like the barracks, hospitals and dockyards in whose development, palatial aesthetic and scale Britain was a pioneer – proclaimed the nation's pragmatic and imperial nature (Girouard *Cities* 213–15). Through his inventory and categorization of the infrastructure of the city, Defoe stresses the apparatuses controlling social relations. More than this, he views freedom and power as inseparable from excess. Forever seeking a balance, Defoe recognizes that liberty and prisons are two sides of the same coin. Hence, Defoe eschews the picturesque and seeks to give "as accurate a description of [London] ... as I could do without drawing a plan, or map of the places" (*Tour* 288).[35] Like Swift with his vituperative pen, Defoe is at odds with the polite culture of consensus and aestheticized rationality promulgated by Joseph Addison and Richard Steele. Rather than this map of the rational, Swift and Defoe seek to render an *accurate* picture of social forces.

At once suggesting benign public views of society as well as prying undercover informants of private affairs, *The Spectator* and *The Tatler* spearheaded the formation of a "public sphere" which sought to standardize "rational" discourse and naturalize the state and its elites. If an exclusionary cultural system unified England's ruling bloc (Eagleton *Function of Criticism* 12), so too did the reorganization of space. Due to Swift and Defoe's essentially colonial ways of seeing, both expose the sinews of Addison's benign, self-governing milieu. Unlike Addison, who privileges rationality, Swift and Defoe make authority, and how it is mediated by space, their focus.[36] The self comes to knowledge not through the exchange of reason, but through the knowledge and appropriation of space. Thus in *Tour* Defoe examines the material basis and tensions of the public sphere and its "common standards of taste and conduct" (Eagleton *Function of Criticism* 11). Defoe would rather talk about Wren's plan for a post-Fire London centered around the Royal Exchange and not St. Paul's, than the exchange of common sense which now supposedly united Britain. Defoe's survey of the geographical regulation of disparate (and often dissident) groups was undertaken with the same goals as Addison's cultural regulation of the nation: "the classical public sphere involves a discursive reorganization of social power, redrawing the boundaries between social classes as divisions between those engaged in rational argument and those who do not" (12–13). The management of the nation therefore is taking place on two related fronts: the codifying of norms and regulating of practices carried out by the public sphere segues with the "*de facto* zoning [that was] increasingly manifest" during this period (Corfield *Impact of English Towns* 77). Of course the public sphere was inseparable from the new urban spaces of the coffee and chocolate houses.[37] The discursive community mirrored the new urban enclaves and specialized industrial towns that relegated those "outside" to irrationality, uselessness, and ignorance. Ironically, those new communities were built, like Crusoe's "estate," specifically to keep the poor in line.

Whereas Crusoe is more likely to be located in a rural/colonial context, we can relate this role model to an urban setting. John Bender writes that "Crusoe tests and revalidates forms of hegemony characteristic of urban culture, the ordering principles of the governed city" (*Imagining the Penitentiary* 56). Similarly Varey contends that "Crusoe is living out a fictional existence in a discourse that also creates the spatial disposition of a city square, because, as rentier or merchant or colonizer, he expresses the aspiration of the Whiggish middle class to possess and control a space, so raising his status and giving him a measure of political power" (*Space* 155). More explicitly, the square epitomized social mobility of the middling sort, providing them with mini-estates – townhouses resembling Palladian villas overlooking their private park. As a series of enclosures, magically merging the country and the city, the square was a retreat at the centre of things, a place of repose in the belly of the beast. It was a typically Defoeian space: a balance of the best of the worlds of business (which demanded proximity to labor) and refined leisure (which demanded separation from the masses). Moreover, it is a spatial form which flaunts the security of a hegemonic social alignment, as commanding as Crusoe on his island. Developed by titled investors and speculative builders, the "golden grids" of the West End represented at once the disengagement and distancing of the well-off from their inferiors as well as a spectacular display of power. Here was the awe-inspiring order of those who gave orders. The West End was a significant shift from the cheek-by-jowl arrangement of London in 1660. Roy Porter describes the change: "London's fashionable contrasts were not just between residential and manufacturing quarters, for the City itself was undergoing segregation and secession ... Within the City, divisions between workshops and offices, between finance and crafts, were widening all the time" (*English Society* 47). Rigid segregation by economic status and function took off after 1700. The suburb and the square embodied the removal and containment of wealth, the concealment and display of power that was as vital in the West Indies as in Britain.

The "golden grids" were the sort of spatial intervention and entrenchment in potentially threatening areas that Crusoe enacts. Developed after the Great Fire, they are the culmination of numerous schemes to remake London into what John Evelyn saw as a space "fitter for commerce, apter for government, sweeter for health, more glorious for beauty" (*London Revived* 54–5). Richard Newcourt's plan for London in 1667 envisioned the stock-in-trade of imperial experiments in Spanish

America, Ireland, and English America: central squares locating state institutions as the anchors of an infinitely reproducible grid. The plans were defeated by uncontrollable rebuilding and speculation, though the piazzas around the Exchange and St. Paul's, the centrality of churches, and the West End's geometry attest to colonial influences. Evelyn's belief that the City's design equal the status befitting a nation "which commands the Proud Ocean to the *Indies*, and reaches to the farthest *Antipodes*" (8), did eventually come about. Varey observes that the "predominant neo-Palladian style [was] ... representative of the afflu-ence of a prosperous trading nation" (*Space* 37); it was a style fit for an empire rivaling that of the Romans and the conspicuous display of wealth rendered in a "soft" and classical mold expressed the enlightened ideology of mercantile capitalism. Defoe, however, is unsatisfied with London's design; like Spenser he abhors a "straggling" plot:

> It is the disaster of London, as to the beauty of its figure, that it is thus stretched out in buildings, and as the convenience of the people directs, whether for trade, or otherwise; and this has spread the face of it in a most straggling, confused manner, out of all shape, uncompact, and unequal; neither long nor broad, round or square; whereas the city of Rome, though a monster for its greatness, yet was, in a manner, round, with very few irregularities in its shape. (*Tour* 287)

Irregularity is incompatible with a stable imperial centre. More than this, the disappearance of Rome (and other great cities) haunts imperial London. Expressive of anxieties about the fate of empire, the city as the "most glorious sight without exception, that the whole world at present can show, or perhaps ever could show" is tempered by the fate of its predecessors: "the sacking of Rome ... the burning the Temple of Jerusalem" (176–7). The swallowing up of Dunwich, which is compared to the destruction of Carthage and Rome among others, is not only "testimony of the decay of public things, things of the most durable nature" (78), but for Defoe proof that only by culturally fixing and physically staking out territory will London and its empire avoid suffer-ing a similar fate.

Defoe is positive that a discordant environment leads to fatal con-sumption: whether the Fire was due to an accident or "treachery" he is unsure, "yet nothing was more certain, than that as the city stood before, it was strangely exposed to the disaster which happened" (296). Securing space against "any wicked party" (296) is the central concern for Defoe. And the wicked are everywhere. The widespread smuggling, turnpike riots, poaching, highway robbery or simple "idleness" were all anathema to someone like Defoe, since they undermined commercial society and its communication system.[38] They avoided or negated the increasingly systematic spatial "customs" of the nation. Defoe's "circuits" in *Tour* – a perambulation that marks geographic as well as cultural boundaries – perform a rounding up of figures and areas into an equation: the integration of a national economic space. With "any wicked party" dogging his every step, coloring his every view, Defoe positively revels in the fortified, places of specialized commerce, and configurations (as well as figures) of authority.

A *Tour Through the Whole Island of Great Britain* (1724–6) virtually opens with a detailed description of "the strong fortress of Tilbury ... the key of the city of London" (52). Reminiscent of Crusoe's obsession with battlements (e.g. *Crusoe* 161), Defoe relishes the ingenious display of force at Tilbury, especially the use of nature (water in this case). Similarly, he marvels at Portsmouth's fortification with its "good counterscarp, and double moat, with ravelins in the ditch, and double pallisodoes, and advanced works to cover the place from any approach" (*Tour* 151). It is urban forms and commercial activities proscribed by regimentation that catch Defoe's fancy. Because of its "regularities" Yarmouth is "a very well governed town" lacking venues for disruptive behavior (92). The town's good government seems to stem from its grid-like shape:

streets are all exactly straight from north to south, with lanes and alleys, which they call rows, crossing them in straight lines also from east to west; so that it is the most regular town in England, and seems to have been built all at once. Or, that the dimensions of the houses, and extent of the streets, were laid out by consent. (91–2)

One of the "chief arsenals of the royal navy," the town of Rochester elicits praise due to its compartmentalization into "building-yards, docks, timber-yard, deal-yard, mast-yard, gun-yard, rope-walks and all the other yards and places, set apart for the works belonging to the navy, [all] are like a well ordered city ... you see no confusion, every man knows his own business..." (123–5). Portsmouth is perceived in the same way: its "docks and yards are now like a town by themselves, and are a kind of marine corporation, or a government of their own kind by themselves" (151). In Portsmouth's case, its military-industrial function incorporates the whole town, which Defoe deems an advantage. Not only does the fleet make "the whole place rich" and the "civil government is no more interrupted by the military," but clearly Defoe thinks a garrison town, a fundamentally *colonial* set-up effectively ruled by a governor-general, an ideal spatial formation. The regimentation of time and space, "such as being examined at the gates, such as being obliged to keep garrison hours ... things no people will count a burthen," is both commercially profitable and an inhibitor of dissent (152). Thus, Defoe promotes spatial regimes akin to the plantations and factory towns in the colonies as well as the company-town of the industrial revolution. Like Crusoe's domain, dockyard towns were inward-looking, secretive, "well-disciplined and organized in defense of their own interests and work conditions" (Corfield *Impact of English Towns* 45). Even a venue traditional for its riotous excesses, the fair, can become well governed if arranged militarily: "[Sturbridge] fair is like a well fortified city, and there is the least disorder and confusion (I believe) that can be seen any where, with so great a concourse of people" (106). On the other hand, Charelton's Horn-Fair encourages rudeness and the mob; it "ought to be suppressed, and indeed in a civilized well governed nation, it may well be said to be unsufferable" (115).

Two spatial formations are related to the garrison-town ("SHEERNESS is not only a fortress, but a kind of town" [Defoe *Tour* 127]): on the one hand, the "delicious seats of the nobility and gentry" (132) and, on the other, waste land. The former promotes a polite and commercial society, the latter engenders mutinous tendencies. Or as Defoe puts it, the seats of the nobility and gentry, when "lying so near together, make the country hereabout much more sociable and pleasant than the rest of the woody country, called the Wild" (148). Here also is the basic spatiality that Swift maps out on Balnibarbi, with Munodi's beautiful seat in opposition to the infertile madness of the rest of the island. Although the stupid imperial policies are absent from *Tour*, both Defoe and Swift agree that the "desart parts of the country" are a repository for anti-social mayhem. It is no accident that a clear reference to offences under the Black Act in *Tour* is juxtaposed with the wilderness of Bagshot-Heath. We learn that "country folks" have mistreated the benevolent Bishop of Winchester, "pulling down the pale to his park, and plundering it of the deer" (155–6). These offences, the very same that the Black Act was devised to counter, are committed not far from

a tract of land, some of it within seventeen or eighteen miles of the capital city; which is not only poor, but even quite sterile, given up to barrenness, horrid and frightful to look on, not only good for little, but good for nothing. Much of it is a sandy desert, and one may frequently be put in mind here of Arabia Deserta, where the winds raise the sands, so as to overwhelm whole caravans of travellers, cattle and people together. (156)

Defoe draws on colonial discourse to frame this wilderness and invoke images of people being devoured in unsubdued and alien terrain – one is "in danger of smothering with the clouds of sand" in a place which contains no settlements "worth remembering" (156). Furthermore, Defoe derides "the Englishmen's pride" in his beautiful country as if challenging the hyperbole of colonial promotional literature (which he does again near the border). Instead he calls for a more precise cartography. As a counter-force to the numerous places where the inhabitants are "ready to eat up the rich" (73), Defoe over-emphasizes the gentry. Indeed, commenting on his task of editing *Tour* Pat Rogers states that he was forced to leave out "many [of the stately homes Defoe included] . . . for reasons of space" (687–8). Defoe includes them for the same reason: the more space the gentry take up the better!

Defoe's fascination with the fortified or the colonial, given the garrison town's history, leads him to depict the gentry as besieged. After saluting General Pepper's success at securing Enfield Chase through his "vigilance" (*Tour* 339), we are almost immediately regaled with the "most magnificent palace or mansion house . . . in England," that of the Duke of Chandos. Chandos protects his property in time-honored fashion and as one cognizant of Enfield's experience. "In his gardens and out-houses the Duke keeps a constant night-guard, who take care to the whole place, duly walk the rounds, and constantly give the hour to the family at set appointed places and times; so that the house has some waking eyes about it, to keep out thieves and spoilers night and day" (342–3). We might easily substitute Crusoe for Chandos since they are both ever vigilant for those who would lay waste their estates.

In the face of such threats Defoe even sees the landowner as a sort of governor-general: at Wilton House the Earl of Pembroke is the "governor and law-giver . . . and the family like a well governed city" (197). Here, the country-house ideology shows its colonial politics, with all its claims to righteousness and underlying anxiety. The "true patriarchal monarch," like Locke's West Indian plantocrat, spreads his government, and of course "general beneficence," "all the country round" whilst the "poor, receive all the good they can expect, and are sure to have no injury, or oppression" (197). Defoe is in no way promoting neo-feudal social relations. Rather, he envisions a society run by a ruling bloc who represent the interests and will enforce the orderliness of a "well governed city." Through the benign power of patrician magistracy and the spectacle of majesty – a hegemony crudely embodied in Crusoe – the consolidation of a polite and commercial society would come about.[39] On the other hand, the seats of gentry and nobility are exactly what Ireland is lacking: for Swift the condition of the country is partly due to "the Ruin of so many Country-Seats and Plantations" (*Prose Works* x.130).

Thus we see how Defoe promotes the material basis to Addison's cultural consensus. The evolution of a national culture that suppressed regional autonomy was part and parcel of "the emergence of a conscious and nation-wide idiom in town housing, replacing earlier traditions of regional vernacular" (Corfield *Impact of English Towns* 174). Defoe's ideal Britain is one enveloped in a national idiom of gentrified space; when he looks back toward London from Bushy-Heath he sees, as if Gulliver in Lilliput, "a planted garden... The enclosed corn-fields made one grand parterre, the thick planted hedge rows, like a wilderness or labyrinth, divided in espaliers; the villages interspersed, looked like so many several noble seats of gentlemen at a distance" (*Tour* 343). The prospect from Lord Castlemain's estate is so unlimited "that the sight is lost in the woods adjoining, and it looks all like one planted garden as far as the eye can see" (111). The move from the country-house poem of the seventeenth century to the prospect poem of the eighteenth demonstrates the consolidation of a particular social order, one that expresses itself through the compression of territory under a landowner's imperious and possessive gaze. Defoe rightly connects the economic power of Britain in the early 1700s, which increasingly depended on colonial markets, re-export, and exotic luxury items, to the social power of the gentry. The geography of Defoe's island is coordinated by where the two work hand in hand. As "the present increase of wealth in the city of London, spreads it self into the country" (57) Defoe pursues signs of the gentry's power into the darkest corners of the nation.

Defoe is, however, frequently disappointed in his search of the gentry and their successful yoking of productive forces to the requirements of capitalism. Cornwall "may truly be said to be inhabited by a fierce and ravenous people ... charged with strange, bloody, and cruel dealings" (263). They prey on seamen and, Defoe concludes, are "a kind of barbarians" (243). A persistent debunker of myths that do not forward the interests of trade, Defoe scorns those who misrepresent reality: Northumberland, Cumberland, and Durham must be viewed with respect to "real improvements" and not "fragments of antiquity, and dressing up the wilds of the borders as a paradise, which are indeed but a wilderness" (240). With a similar contempt for inept colonial surveying he dismisses "the wonderless wonders of the Peak" (469) as preposterous especially since they have little bearing on the "improvement" of the region and obscure the main wonder: that of "the Duke of Devonshire's fine house at Chatsworth" (474). An outpost of civility, the Duke's absolute command of space manifests itself in his power to shape nature: "to make a clear vista or prospect beyond into the flat country, towards Hardwick, another seat of the same owner, the Duke, to whom what others thought impossible, was not only made practicable, but easy, removed, and perfectly carried away a great mountain that stood in the way, and which interrupted the prospect" (475). Conjuring order from chaos, it is the work of a (God-like) giant. Typically Chatsworth is surrounded by a "waste and howling wilderness." We have almost returned to a Miltonic geography. Devoid of the signposts of civility, travelers are forced "to take guides, or it would be next to impossible not to lose their way" (476). Defoe makes the familiar juxtaposition of paradisal and hellish in colonial literature when he describes the exhausted traveler's sublime view "from a frightful height, and a comfortless, barren, and, as he thought, endless moor, into the delightful valley, with the most pleasant garden, and most beautiful palace in the world" (477).

As his colonial gaze enters Scotland – an accurate perspective as opposed to "the most scandalous partiality" of Scottish observers (559) – Defoe immediately marks the country as a source of lethal transgression: he contemplates the late incursions of "Scots Highland rebels" and the rebellion of 1715, "that desperate push into England" (551–2). Scotland lacks the partitioning of space that produces civility; the "barrenness of the country" is a consequence of a "want of enclosures" (591). Defoe provides, however, useful pointers to the colonist. "Here are but a few things needful to bring Scotland" into a productive society similar to "the best counties of England" (560). Civilization depends upon, among other necessities, "A change in the disposition of the common people, from a desire of traveling abroad, and wandering from home, to an industrious and diligent application to labour at home" (560). Defoe echoes precisely the regimentation Fielding and Swift propose for the London poor, the beggars, and the "natives" of Ireland alike. Planting trees, enclosing pasture, and a stock of gentry are all needed, but first and foremost, the poor need to be spatially and economically incarcerated. The managers and masters of the new labor force need to be either English or anglicized. Defoe finds both in Dumfries. The Duke of Queensbury's estate of Drumlanrig, "like Chatsworth in Darbyshire, is like a fine picture in a dirty grotto, or like an equestrian statue set up in a barn," represents the possibility of transforming colonial spaces of "the wildest and most hideous aspect" into little Englands (591). The fortress-estate, as in England, rules the land in partnership with the commercially oriented town, which speaks the "language" of the English, empire, and mercantile capitalism:

Dumfries was always a good town, and full of merchants. By merchants, here I mean, in the sense that word is taken and understood in England (viz.) not mercers and drapers, shopkeepers, etc. but merchant-adventurers, who trade to foreign parts, and employ a considerable number of ships ... as they have (with success) embarked in trade, as well to England as to the English plantations, they apparently increase both in shipping and people. (590)

In addition to being a resource within England's Atlantic trade system, prospects are good for further investment; Defoe speculates: "and should a time come when these hidden treasures of the earth should be discovered and improved, this part of Scotland may no longer be called poor" (663).

The people of Kirkubry, for instance, are so ignorant and wasteful that they don't realize "that they have the Indies at their door" (596). Failing to recognize the "advantages that nature offers them" (598) they stand obsolete in the face of the inevitability of empire. As such they are fit only to be led or re-placed by "a people better able, and more inclined to business" (598). Defoe's overt call for the colonization of Scotland coincides with renewed efforts by the English to subdue the Scots. But because of the Union Defoe is able to characterize the latest campaign as paternal guidance rather than the conquests of Cromwell and the Romans. Hence George I invades "not as a foreigner and conqueror, but as a sovereign, a lawful governor and father of the country, to deliver from, not entangle her in the chains of tyranny and usurpation" (650–1). Defoe prefers the "prudent management [that] prevented" larger "tumults and disorders" over the Union, but it is clear that conquest is in order for the "north land of Scotland," where he has never seen a people "so wild, untaught, or untractable" (673). Defoe's distinction between Cromwell and George I is of course a matter of semantics. Management and conquest are two sides to the same coin, just as the allegiance everyone pledges to Crusoe and his paternalism are inseparable from his monopoly of violence and resources. Thus Defoe continually acknowledges the Roman roads throughout his tour: their timeless reality is an index – a universal measurement – of technical and organizational skill, ingenious design and solid imperial practice, law and order, unification and communication, and the regulation of territory and inhabitants. The road is the symbol not just of the route to a civilized empire, but, more specifically, the absolutely necessary and rational imposition of a way that authorizes a particular group's economic, political and cultural supremacy. Like the city square, the dockyard town, or the country estate, the Roman road is important to Defoe because it represents control of space by those with the right disposition.

PROSPECTS FOR SCOTLAND

The spread of Britain's commercial network in the early part of the eighteenth century was a two-pronged affair. Defoe's prescription for Scotland neatly summarizes the policy and ideologies of mercantilism and conquest. On the one hand, Scotland, now incorporated into the English economy, "is so noble a prospect, of what business, and commerce might ... do for it" (*Tour* 595), but on the other, because of "inhabitants so wild and barbarous" (663), commerce will probably have to be forced by garrisons stationed "for the better regulating the Highlands" (661). Even if rationality became the mark of the cultured "public," the absolutes of authority were again and again called upon to deal with resistance to the most reasonable systems of government imposed near and far by London. The savage reinstatement of authority by the "bloody Assizes" in the aftermath of Monmouth's Rebellion in 1685, had its counterpart in the barbarity of the Duke of Cumberland's campaign against the Highlanders in 1746. The Black Act shows that the authorities did not necessarily restrict their savagery to the colonies or to times of outright rebellion. Underlining the coloniality of the ruling bloc's control of space, the Black Act, as Thompson points out, "together with the Riot Act ... establish an armory of sanctions to be used, in subsequent terrorist legislation against disaffected Highlanders [and] Irish agrarian rebels" (*Whigs and Hunters* 197). The profitable but at times anarchic "pan-Atlantic interchanges" (Linebaugh *London Hanged*) of the empire, both forced and allowed the colonial elites to produce an increasingly homogeneous conception of managed space.

Literary culture processed these conceptions and practices. The extremely popular Inkle and Yarico narrative represented both the access to empire that literature offered the populace as well as a moral lesson about the excesses of imperialism.⁴⁰ In this way, the tale serves a function similar to that of *Gulliver's Travels* and *Robinson Crusoe*. Like Hobbes's, Locke's and Rousseau's "fables of origin" that are located in the Americas (Hulme *Colonial Encounters* 187), Swift and Defoe strip "man" of his pretensions and presumptions only to reconfirm a certain social order. Inkle and Yarico, Gulliver and Crusoe, and Locke's Every-man all serve to reinscribe a particular class's or nation's moral suprem-acy and social codes while registering anxieties about the costs of expansion and government abroad. Formulations of space are yet another import from abroad, as I have tried to show. Defoe's reproduc-tion in *Tour* of Lord Godolphin's plan for re-peopling the New Forest in Hampshire is a carbon-copy of numerous colonial urban projects. Moreover, the "disappearing act" (Porter *English Society* 45) or ostenta-tious visibility (Williams *Country* 105) of the landowners, the "theatrical style" of the elites and the "countertheater" of the plebs (Thompson *Customs* 45, 67) are as much a product of negotiating colonial arenas as they are of class antagonism in Britain.

We can say that Swift and Defoe appropriate countertheater – for instance exposing the nitty gritty of social relations – only to reaffirm the boundaries that enforce what Raymond Williams describes as "the many miles of new fences and walls, the new paper rights, [that] were the formal declaration of where the power now lay" (*Country* 107). If Moll Flanders "resists the ideological demand for conformity expressed ... by such spaces as Grosvenor Square or Bath's North Parade," as Varey points out (*Space* 146), then her resistance is dissolved when she surely conforms to the colonial regulation of space in the wider world of the British Atlantic system. True to the interests of the ruling class and mercantile capitalism, Defoe makes Moll alien in Grosvenor Square but at home in Carolina. She is finally made to conform to the spatial segregation and more systematic use of colonies and troublemakers promoted by the government. Ultimately Moll, like Crusoe, is an example of the "regularization of work practices" and space, "[that] was prompted by growing economic specialization and the increasing subdivision of labour" (Corfield *Impact of English Towns* 33).

Defoe and Swift saw the new economic developments as forces of good, if coupled with ruling class paternalism. They both agreed with Thorowgood's view, in George Lillo's *The London Merchant* (1731): "See how [trade] is founded in reason, and the nature of things; how it has promoted humanity, as it has opened and yet keeps up an intercourse between nations, far remote from one another in situation, customs and religion; promoting arts, industry, peace and plenty; by mutual benefits diffusing mutual love from pole to pole" (52). To which Trueman adds the benefits that "tame the fierce and polish the most savage; . . . teach them the advantages of honest traffick" (52). Steele's character Sir Andrew Freeport was a popular embodiment of such principles and intentions. Pope's Burlington another example. In "Windsor-Forest," Pope praises "Albion's" liberatory trade. But Pope, Defoe, and Swift all concede that commerce and Britannia's liberty are inseparable from her appropriation of space. The multiple spaces, the "Imperial Works" each invokes are ultimately connected by the organizing force of empire. All focus on the rejuvenation of "Realms commanded" by "*Britannia's* standard" ("Windsor-Forest" lines 32, 110: *Poetry and Prose*).

Finally, we should recognize that Defoe's depiction of the Highlanders, not unlike Swift's Yahoos and Irish Catholics, dovetailed with the aftermath of Culloden in 1746. He describes West Highlanders as "some of the worst, most barbarous, and ill governed of all . . . desperate in fight, cruel in victory, fierce even in conversation, apt to quarrel, mischievous, and even murderers in their passion" (676). This view was shared by the officers in charge of subjugating the Highlands once and for all. The logical consequence of Defoe or Swift's "natives" was the policy of extermination decided upon in advance of Culloden (Gilmour *Riots, Risings and Revolutions* 126). As if striving to produce that dream of the colonist, the *tabula rasa* or *terra nullia*, the English troops performed so that "in a little time, for the space of fifty miles, nothing was to be seen but silence, ruin and desolation" (quoted in Jennings *Empire* 4). This is not to say Defoe would have endorsed such slaughter, but Defoe's view of the Highlanders and *Robinson Crusoe* surely endorsed colonialism. Similarly, it is not surprising that *Gulliver's Travels* would be the one book in Daniel Boone's knapsack as he went about the adventure of opening up the interior of the North American continent (Slotkin *Regeneration through Violence* 298).

Rational argument and the incentives of commerce often, when the usually unwilling recipients resisted the imperatives of capital, had to be shelved whilst cleaning-up operations restored order. And it is here, between the appropriation and domination of space that we find Defoe and Swift. Both pursued more efficient colonial policies and commercial networks. To this end, proportions and potentials had to be accurately acknowledged. As Defoe contemplates the Highlands he laments that our geographers seem to be almost as much at a loss in the description of this north part of Scotland, as the Romans were to conquer it; and they are obliged to fill it up with hills and mountains, as they do the inner parts of Africa, with lions and elephants, for want of knowing what else to place there. Yet this country is not of such difficult access, as to be passed undescribed, as if it were impenetrable. (*Tour* 663)

Swift says the same thing about the strategic stationing of elephants in "On Poetry." Both authors are advocates of replacing myths with the facts of colonialism. Only accurate, enlightened, and responsible geopolitics in proportion to the task of subjugating the "natives" would provide Britain and its colonies with stability. Too many white elephants abound, the South Sea Bubble being only the most infamous. Defoe and Swift, however, meet under the sign of the displaced elephant and toast to a better management.

CHAPTER 6

1745 and the systematizing of the Yahoo

All my lousy life I've crawled about in the mud! And you talk to me
about scenery!
Beckett *Godot* 39

In the Works of the DIVINE ARCHITECT of all Things, we find
nothing but perfect Figures, consisting of the utmost *Regularity*, the
sweetest *Harmony*, and the most delightful *Proportion*.
Wood *Origin of Building* (pub. 1743)

Let this Third Region or Wilderness be Natural-Artificial.
Nourse *Campania Faelix*

The crisis of values that Defoe and Swift negotiate gradually built into
the *Sturm und Drang* of rebellion during the second half of the eighteenth
century. The combined dislocating dynamos of agrarian and industrial
revolution produced the self-governing free market. However, the burgeoning territorial sway and social burdens won by imperial wars, the
economic interloping of the colonies, and the decline of customary
society laid siege to the rule of natural law. The weight of self-interest,
which spawned the decadence of elites and dissent of the lower orders,
made for a tottering empire. While religious revivalism and the enthusiasm of the lower classes was one response, another was the rationalization of systems of control by the elites. It was this side of the Enlightenment, rather than the secular project of individual liberty, that Defoe
had proposed for the Highlands. Sixty-six years after the Union, however, Samuel Johnson observed that Scotland still languished with "no
visible boundaries," "in uniform nakedness" (Johnson and Boswell
Journey 39), rural folk living like "Hottentots" (51), and lacking any
accurate method to measure and understand its language, history or
topography.[1] In his *A Journey to the Western Islands of Scotland* (1773) he

announces that the country was "unconnected with the general system" of English standards (65). It was, as *Humphry Clinker* informs us "more and more savage the further we advance [north]" (Smollett 275). Nonetheless, by the middle of the eighteenth century Britain was quickly developing a "general system" through which the empire could more effectively deal with the growing incivility directed at London's rule throughout the Atlantic world. Scotland, and specifically the counter-attack against the Forty-Five Rising, was the testing ground for technologies of colonial control. This chapter is about the web of spatial strategies issuing from the events of the 1740s.

THE "RULE OF TASTE" AND FORCE

During the first half of the eighteenth century the "Rule of Taste" coincided with the growth of the military–fiscal state determined to impose its own harmony among its Isles and colonial holdings. Simultaneously boasting empire and mystifying its true designs, the classical cool of Palladianism was well suited for the imperial belligerence of the governors-general. The commonality between the two systems was in large part due to the fact that it was never possible to uncouple the Godly order envisaged by John Wood in the epigraph above, designed by the "DIVINE ARCHITECT" and His chosen, from the excremental dissonance of the Yahoo. Forty-eight years after Swift coined the term, a genteel Scotswoman on a journey to the West Indies was horrified to discover a group of Highland emigrants secretly stowed away on her ship. Janet Schaw writes in her *Journal of a Lady of Quality; Being the Narrative of a Journey from Scotland to the West Indies, North Carolina, and Portugal, in the years 1774 to 1776*: "never did my eyes behold so wretched, so disgusting a sight. They looked like a Cargo of Dean Swift's Yahoos newly caught" (28). As imperialism brings disparate groups into proximity with one another, strategies must be created to ensure that proximity does not slide into familiarity or transgression. Increasingly the question for empire was how to utilize yet keep segregated the Yahoos, savages, natives, and hottentots that are supposedly British subjects. As the British Empire, via the Seven Years War, engrosses itself beyond its wildest dreams and then loses its thirteen colonies, the concern with managing excess territory, wealth, populations, and sentiments becomes paramount. The age old colonial process of tying up loose ends and tying down loose cannons takes on critical proportions.

Schaw's exclamation articulates the disjunction between the imagined community of Britannia's domains – anchored via patrician, plantation, and paternalism – and the conflicted colonies, awash with social, political, and racial promiscuity. Many of the major writers of the eighteenth century share Schaw's navigation between the myths of empire and the struggles to shore up or subvert them. Literary culture works through this fracture between an empire based on liberty, homogeneity, commerce, and natural laws as opposed to the reality of dissenting politics, alterity, conquest, and systematized exploitation. In "Of Plantations and Colonies" in *Cato's Letters* (No. 106, 1722) John Trenchard and Thomas Gordon voice the type of empire Swift and Defoe as well as later commentators like Johnson supported. There was an alternative, they argued, to sheer force: "the other Sort of Colonies are for Trade, and intended to encrease the Wealth and Power of the native Kingdom; which they will abundantly do if managed prudently, and put and kept under a proper Regulation" (in Jehlen and Warner *English Literatures* 827). This trading commonwealth, which is reminiscent of the Darien scheme, is clearly dependent upon and controlled by regulations set by Britain. Further, "put and kept" give management a rather ominous ring. Here is an attempt, via an anti-empire discourse, to set up a more effective hegemony throughout Britain's Atlantic world. This period particularly exposes the necessary vacillation between consent and coercion characteristic of colonizing power (Eagleton *Heathcliff* 98). The key plank in this program was natural law; the key problem was the law's constant denaturalization. As the century progressed the hierarchy through which empire functioned began to unravel: the Yahoos appeared to be gaining power and audacity. As James Otis put it as the American Revolution broke out: "when the pot boils the scum will rise" (quoted in Greene and Pole *American Revolution* 623). Dissent threatens to expose and sweep aside, as J. Hector St. John de Crèvecoeur put it, all "mechanisms of subordination" (*Letters* 343), unleashing the lowest orders of society in an orgy of anarchy.

The various mechanisms of subordination, which ideally remain part of reflex rather than repression, were coordinated under a general "systematizing of nature" (Pratt *Imperial Eyes* 30). Such systematicity comes into being in the latter half of the eighteenth century and was perfected by the military and the "science" of Natural History. As far as military organization, cartography, topographic sketching, population control, the development of communications, and colonial policy go, the battle of Culloden in 1746 and its bloody aftermath provided crucial space and time for experimentation. The years 1745–6 are, I shall argue, the beginning of the standardization of both the instruments of imperial military power and a way of seeing populations within contact arenas that reverberated around the globe. The epitome of empire's failure to civilize, the '45 cast its fearful shadow on British culture. The Rising lurks in the background of Fielding's *Tom Jones* (pub. 1749); the "banditti" (336) threaten the stability and natural hierarchy represented by Allworthy's estate, which is aptly called "Paradise-Hall" (104). It also, by bloodily thrusting the entirety of Scotland into the British Empire, impacted on inter-colonial relations. In the North American colonies, as the corporatist tradition declined, wages replaced contractual labor, free and slave populations grew rapidly, and market forces and violent expansionism boomed, the widespread unrest and uprisings from the late 1740s up to the Revolution were perceived and often dealt with through the lens of the '45 (Greene and Pole *American Revolution* 98, 186).[2] Moreover, many on both sides of the conflicts were veterans of the Highland rebellion and its aftermath.

Swift died in the year the northern Yahoos rose in rebellion and invaded England. One legacy of Culloden was simply the ability to conjugate the Highlanders as Yahoos.[3] To think of Yahoos is already to situate oneself, as indeed Swift's global imagination intends, in an international context and a superior vantage point. The pre-eminent colonized subject, the "Yahoo" is as much a social label as a spatial one. Underscoring Janet Schaw's conflation of the emigrants and the physiological results of sea sickness and cramped space, Yahoos are people who produce and live in waste. As a taxonomic term positioning an individual or group perilously close to the bottom of the league-table of civility, Yahoo would seem to be a dead-end state of being. Yet empire offers redemption. Absolute subordination to and service in the cause of imperialism can lift the Yahoo into the realms of the civilized. Thus the policy of recruiting Highlanders into the British army in huge numbers, effectively exploiting the discipline of clan loyalties and structure, was a post-'46 development.[4] The British army became truly British, former colonial populations incorported under the banner of Britannia. Just as we see in certain strains of Romanticism, a fierce loyalty to different (British) locales is fused with a global mission, a duty to protect universal values. For the Yahoo the army was at once a mechanism of subordination and a place where different cultural codes were given recognition. Thus Scots, Irish, and Welsh, not to mention the English laborer became the cutting edge of the British Empire.

In addition to manpower, Culloden produced officers and skills that subsequently had a major impact on colonial affairs. Culloden enabled the Duke of Cumberland to become Commander-in-Chief of the British Army and spread his belligerence, arrogance and incompetence in large doses around the globe, serving to bolster the power of the metropolitan center through military control over the periphery.5 As Francis Jennings, in *Empire of Fortune*, points out with respect to America, Cumberland's officers, many of whom were with him at Culloden, "were to enlarge the crown's prerogatives and repress the powers of colonial assemblies" (5).6 More than this, Cumberland's appointees represented a hawkish policy to standardize the framework of colonial life. While John Campbell, 4th Earl of Loudon, veteran of Culloden and Commander-in-Chief in North America failed to defeat the French or keep the colonial assemblies in line, he did accomplish "the systematization of military organization and supply" (286).7 General James Wolfe was trained at Culloden and on "police duty" in the Scottish Highlands (205). In 1751 Wolfe advocated genocide of the clans; the same icy logic was evident when he ravaged the Gaspé peninsula and ordered his men "to burn and lay waste the country" surrounding Quebec (205). What he had learned in the Highlands was exported, with not a little success, to the North American continent. Empire evolves through such a surprisingly closeknit network. The skills Captain James Cook learnt during the Seven Years War charting the St. Lawrence (which helped Wolfe gain victory) voyaged into the furthest reaches of the South Seas.

In the same year that Bonnie Prince Charlie rallied his Highlanders and marched south, the largest assault ever attempted on the fulcrum of France's North American empire was staged. The attack upon the fortress of Louisbourg on Cape Breton Island, guarding the approach to the St. Lawrence River, can be coupled with the outcome of '45 for one basic reason: Culloden and Louisbourg are indicative of a single and more coherent imperial system militarily willing and able to facilitate primitive accumulation and the subsequent command of colonial populations and productivity. The Jacobites and the French Empire represented two forces amongst many that the British imperialists strove to dominate. Defeating rivals and rebels whilst retaining Britannia's beneficent poise is the central anxiety for the British during the latter half of the eighteenth century, when the empire appeared to roller-coaster between stupendous global domination and the doldrums of decadence.

More benign but no less effective instrumentalities of colonialism issued from subduing the Highlands. Bernard Smith claims that one can trace the rise of empirical naturalism in art to the cartographic technologies worked out in Scotland. "Basic techniques of survey and topographic description were developed in the Scottish Highlands"; later these skills well served British expansionism (*Imagining the Pacific* 29). The colonial enterprise has always harnessed (and furthered) the powers of persuasion, information, and legitimation that art and science can bestow, as John White and Thomas Harriot in the attempts to settle Roanoke prove. But this means of obtaining accurate knowledge in the service of imperial power (28) becomes increasingly institutionalized and popularized as the eighteenth century wears on. As with geography, drawing develops in the shadow of military purposes. It was taught in naval and military schools. As Smith points out, "topography came to exercise a commanding influence upon landscape as a fine art because of its continuing importance to the army and navy" (28). A figure like Paul Sandby, founding member of the Royal Academy, underlines this relationship. He refined his perspective and line whilst serving in Scotland as chief military draughtsmen, mapping out Scotland's "modernization" via road and bridge building. As with Petty's survey of Ireland almost a hundred years earlier (the Down Survey was conducted in the 1650s), Sandby's task was to put Scotland *down* on paper, to give the territory its official imprimatur. "In Scotland," Smith elaborates, "he developed those skills that led him to become a key figure in British art in the shift towards naturalism that flourished towards the end of the eighteenth century" (30).

After the Highlands Sandby goes on to naturalize metropolitan power, depicting Windsor Castle and its environs whilst in the employment of Cumberland who became Ranger of Windsor Park. Essentially Sandby, whether in colonial Scotland or the heart of England, aestheticizes dominated geography in the name of the picturesque and the naturalistic. The picturesque knitted together topographic information with aesthetic taste. Regimented territory was given a natural veneer and cultural value which allowed the ownership, production, and domination of such landscape to be pleasantly overlooked. Captain John Bernard Gilpin (1701–76), father of the theoretician of the picturesque and inspiration for the Romantic movement, William Gilpin, spent more than twenty years involved in the occupation of Scotland; his "passion for landscape sketching, which he passed on to his son, developed ... in the context of military topography" (64). A greater definition or valuation of space entered into every aspect of eighteenth-century culture.

Figure 8   "View of Strath Spey, County Perth, 1747" Paul Sandby

THE AESTHETICS OF FORTIFICATION

If the sentimental intrinsic to neo-classicism, the Gothic, and the Romantic begin to dominate the conception and perception of space after 1760, the period preceding this aesthetic of the natural and originary witnessed an anxious reshuffling of the coercive and consensual faces of hegemony. After 1715 John Vanbrugh's emotive Gothic was replaced with the "cold, elaborate finality" (Summerson *Architecture* 334) of Palladianism, which swiftly permeated the nation. Yet the Roman rationalization promoted by Burlington and Kent, which would seem to advertize the imperial project, coincided with a mystification of empire through an emphasis on antiquity or the archaeology of the British nation. More importantly, the "sentiment for 'nature'" offset "the repressive discipline of classical purism" (322). If the architecture of the elite proclaimed imperial control, their geometric gardens were replaced by the "nature" of parks.

Landscape gardening provides an illuminating example of this transitional period where force and finesse reformulated themselves so as to naturalize structures of power. Yet the lineaments of military force remained embedded within or visible in the wings of these theatrical scenes of gentle retirement. If the Tudor garden was designed as a fortified space, then the "aesthetic premises implicit in fortification" (Kruft *Architectural Theory* 103) remained a potent force. Even if culture was increasingly called upon to do the regulatory work of explicit power, the politics of fortification continued to inscribe itself upon the land-scape, from the garden to the city. Just as Marvell describes Fairfax's seventeenth-century garden as a military arena ("Upon Appleton House"), the landscape of Blenheim Palace was designed to depict the battle of Blenheim, with each plantation representing a battalion. As all the authors from Spenser to Swift recognize, space that most closely resembles paradise (from the point of view of English elite) must be protected from the envious, the devious, and the venomous. Their politics of space is based on an insurgency against blessed enclosures, which therefore must take on a territorially aggressive stance. The ideology of landscaping in Britain is fraught with this fundamentally colonial outlook.

As we have seen, the "ha-ha" is only the most obvious example of garden design which is simultaneously a quasi-military tool and a perceptual trick to soften brute property rights. The lay out of many estates and gardens from a bird's eye point of view resemble forts. Representations of Stowe exhibit a fortress design. In Batty Langley's *New Principles of Gardening* (1728) a curiously fortified island and arbor seem to hark back to *Robinson Crusoe*. The military air could be subtle or quite public. The innovation of the "eye-catcher," often a distant tower or monument, perhaps ruined, forced the gaze to appreciate the extent and design of a landscape, yet it also promoted self-surveillance under what could be seen as observation towers keeping an eye on both estate and wanderer. On the other hand, around 1725 Vanbrugh designed the park wall at Castle Howard with crenellated bastions. At Duncombe he also had a hand in the wall dividing park from garden, which is half bastion-type wall and half a sunken fence. There is a sense of defending property as well as a sort of colonizing impulse; after all, Kent's "ha-ha" was created to allow private property, so apparent in the garden, to become indistinguishable from the natural world. This seamlessness, which dominates the country-house and prospect poem, is often disrup-ted by an uneasy negotiation between the systematic and the natural. A painting by Edward Haytley neatly exemplifies this apparent conflict, although in reality one is simply seeing both sides of the coin of hegemonic domination.

Two years before Culloden Haytley finished *Sandleford Priory* (1744). It depicts the Montagu family enjoying – indeed we're also invited to enjoy

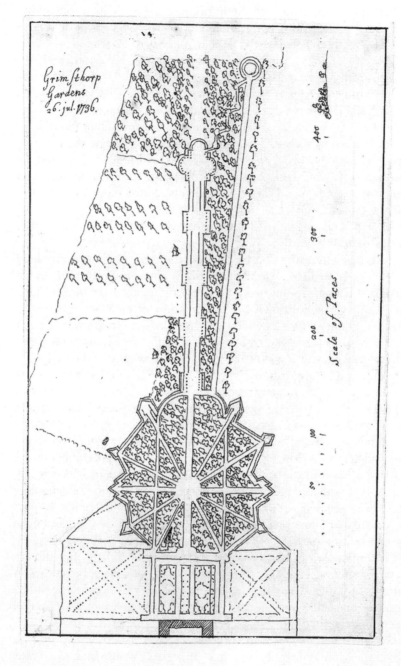

Grim∫thorp
Gardens
26. jul. 1736.

Scale of Paces

50   100   200   300   400

Figure 9a Stephen Switzer's plan of the Bastion Gardens, Grimthorp (drawn by William Stukeley), 1736

The Duchesses Bastion in Grimsthorp gardens. Aug. 10. 1736.

Figure 9b William Stukeley's sketch of the Duchess's Bastion, 1736

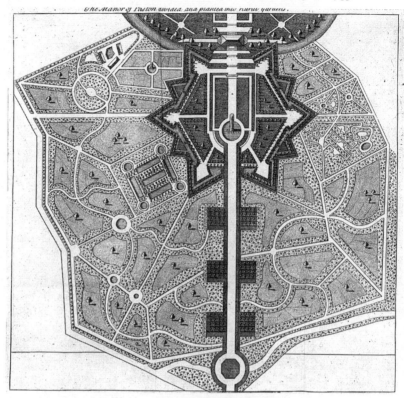

Figure 10 "The Manor of Paston divided and planted into Rural Gardens,"
Ichnographia Rustica, vol. II, 1718

– the bucolic prospect: the manicured lawns leading to fields wherein haymakers work against the tranquil backdrop of a village and distant hills. The viewer is looking from what must be the country house, as it commands a subordinate countryside. The Montagus with their telescope embody polite supervision over the land. It is a fairly good example of a Georgic landscape painting, where ownership, rural labor, pastoral amusements, and an ordered landscape are celebrated.[8] But this apparently harmonious and holistic microcosm, the *ferme ornée*, exudes an ominous sense of potential disruption. The very staginess of Haytley's painting seems to be an attempt to fix spatial relations in the face of danger. The geometric structuring of the picture is enforced by the almost symmetrical pattern of the trees and haystacks. Further, the scene and its actors are compartmentalized; manual labor is divided from mental labor/leisure of the Montagus, class division mirroring the

Figure 11 "Frontispiece of Trellis Work...," Batty Langley
New Principles of Gardening, 1728

division of space. Even though there are no visible fences (bar one very rustic remnant) the Montagus are separated from the haymakers by an elaborate system of terraces and lakes. Alternatively, the family are *protected* by a series of ramparts, escarpments, and moats designed against transgression. If labor appears regulated (even choreographed) as picturesque peasantry, then the fortified nature of the Montagu garden would suggest that laborers cannot be contained within this wished-for role. Turbulence seems to bubble just off stage. The overturned chair and the nearby bowls resembling cannonballs underscore a latent tension to the scene. Instead of one of the women inviting us to enjoy the landscape, perhaps she is gesturing for help. Or perhaps she has spied, and wants us also to see, the peasant in the center of the prospect who may or may not be asleep, but is certainly out of place.

That paradisal space should be fortified and clearly an exclusive place – a condition pointing to the unequal distribution of God's bounty – was an irony William Cobbett, in 1823, clearly relished when he discovered in Kent:

At UP-STREET I was struck with the words written upon a board which was fastened upon a pole, which pole was standing in a garden near a neat little box

Figure 12 "Sandleford Priory" Edward Haytley, 1744

of a house. The words were these. "PARADISE PLACE. *Spring guns and steel traps are set here.*" A pretty idea it must give us of Paradise to know that spring guns and steel traps are set in it! (*Rural Rides* 207)

Significantly, one of the most influential texts about the paradisal retreat and "a Rural life" is set within a military context, in a siege in fact. More than this, Addison's play *Cato* (1713) simultaneously sings the virtues of retirement to the classical estate, which is immune to corruption, and advises that in the face of "dark Design" (68) – a phrase which echoes Oroonoko's "black Designs" (Behn *Oroonoko* 76) – leaders must formulate a "Plan of Power" (*Cato* 63: III.v).9

What constitutes a plan of power, or what Spenser would call a sound "plott," are summarized for us in an early text on "gardening," or what might more accurately be called the ideology of proprietorial and colonial desire. Intrinsic to Henry Wotton's imaginary garden in *The Elements of Architecture* (1624) is a supervisory power over the natural world that pervades literary culture as Britain becomes the global empire. Wotton advocates a paternal overview with an ability to manipulate or transform space as if one were its divine creator. Here is the lordly impulse in Milton and Defoe. Wotton's garden must include a place where the landowner can see "a generall view of the whole *Plott*" and its design be such that as one wanders its tasteful wildness one has the feeling of being "*Magically* transported into a new Garden" (in Hunt and Willis *Genius* 48). This theatrical power, the control over space and perception, and the securing of knowledge about a landscape's history structures the texts we have studied from Spenser through to Swift. Only colonialism could perform such tricks. Whilst they were usually deadly abroad as the tools of colonial strategy they could be delightful at home in the picturesque country estate. The English garden was the preeminent symbol of the nation's innate liberty. Yet whether the Jacobean Mannerist garden, whose popularity coincided with the first wave of Atlantic colonial projects, or the eighteenth-century "park," the landscape of liberty was underwritten by the speculation, wealth, and ideology of imperialism.

LAYING DOWN THE LINE

The "Rule of Taste," therefore, had a conformity built into it that gave little quarter to dissent. The martial and palatial of Vanbrugh's gothic – which was inseparable from real military exigencies and buildings (for example the barracks at Berwick upon Tweed built in 1717 after the Jacobite invasion of 1715) – was refined into the polite Roman militarism of the stripped classicism that dominated until the late eighteenth century. The latter is best exemplified by John Wood the elder's "restoration" of Bath to its former Roman glory. A national code of orthodoxy that was most obvious in architecture and landscape design laid down the rule of a Patrician oligarchy, a group who transcended Whig and Tory divisions. Even if Burlington and his disciples like Pope argued that the country house should not command and exhibit utility rather than luxury, the building boom from the 1720s to mid-century simply reinforced in new ways the division of space in the interests of the elite; a group whose perception of country and city was always imbued with an imperial consciousness which had "scene(ic)" and "obscene" space (Lefebvre *Production*) as its central guiding ideology. As Raymond Williams puts it, "one of the last models of 'city and country' is the system we now know as imperialism" (*Country* 279). In his *The Art of Architecture: A Poem, In Imitation of Horace's Art of Poetry* (1742) John Gwyn considers "*Nature's* Laws" and concludes:

> On that alone, on *Nature's* perfect Plan,
> I form my SYSTEM, as I FIRST began.
> By You inspir'd, I boldly lay the Line,
> And ev'n am vain to call the Subject mine.
> So ORPHEUS, once by more than human Sway,
> Tam'd *Savage Beasts*, or Men as wild as they.   (31)

London's architecture, as well as classical literature, is linked to another project of subordination to natural codes: the subjugation of native peoples.

The ongoing project of surveying and appropriating North America throws into relief the division of space in eighteenth-century Britain. William Byrd's advocacy in 1728 of an enlightened stewardship over a compartmentalized, taxonomically ordered America is a carbon copy of the prevailing attitude in the British Isles, especially toward Scotland and Ireland. The quintessential Augustan aristocratic and naturalist-surveyor, Byrd is aghast at the chaotic blur of distinctions when natural divisions based on class, race, and nation should prevail. The North Carolinian backcountry "Borderers" are "Porcivorous" "Infidels," as isolated as, he states, Crusoe, and showing their degenerative bent by offering succor to runaway slaves (*Histories* 58–72). The Indians, he reports, are "like the wild Irish" (262), which points both to the coalescence of European and Indian as well as the urgent necessity to draw the line. In such conditions not even a Crusoe can be trusted to produce order. Byrd's *Histories of the Dividing Line betwixt Virginia and North Carolina* is part of the transatlantic project of constructing a social hierarchy synonymous with "a Compleat Rural LANDSCAPE" that "ha[s] a most agreeable Effect upon the Eye" (296). Byrd represents an attempt to "controvert" unfixed territory and peoples in the name of the civic humanism and a "balanced" commonwealth.[10] Increasingly, the woods or the city as a "place of encounters" (Lefebvre *Production*) between the rational rulers and the Yahoo is ruled out. The task is to turn spaces of proximity and obscurity into the "structured space of separation" (Harvey *Urban Experience* 178).

Byrd's "Compleat" space is akin to what Crèvecoeur would later wistfully call a "system of happiness" (*Letters* 226). It is a system that naturalizes a socially produced topography and typology in the interests and moral authority of the propertied. "But what means shall be employed," as Lord Kames asks, "for bringing to light this natural standard?" His answer is, in a word, space. In the "Gardening and Architecture" section of *Elements of Criticism* (pub. 1762), an influential book both sides of the Atlantic, he first observes that "Rough uncultivated ground, dismal to the eye, inspires peevishness and discontent." He continues "may not this be one cause of the harsh manners of savages?" (451). This is followed with some concrete examples of how geography may be used to inspire a taste for obedience:

In Scotland, the regularity and polish even of a turnpike-road has some influence of this kind upon the low people in the neighborhood. They become fond of regularity and neatness; which is displayed, first upon their yards and little inclosures, and next within doors. A taste for regularity and neatness, thus acquired, is extended by degrees to dress, and even to behaviour and manners. (465)

We also learn that the "fierce ... plebeians of Bern" learnt their manners with the construction of "public buildings ... particularly a fine town-house, and a magnificent church" (465). Of course, the reorientation of plebs most often came in forms less to do with inspiration than with incarceration. Gary Nash points out that as poverty and insecurity grew for all classes in the urban centers of the thirteen colonies attempts to head off the crisis were made through the containment of the most troublesome groups:

It was hard to ignore the fact that in all the cities the largest buildings erected after 1765 – cloth manufactories, almshouses, and prisons – were constructed to contain the impoverished, a growing criminal element spawned by poverty, and a non criminal middle-class group whose only offense against society was an inability to weather the economic storms of the period. (*Urban Crucible* 218)

As the ability to regulate labor or malcontents became more of a necessity so projects representing a definitive version of space, of "real" geographical information grew in size and urgency. The bird's eye view, which seeks domination, is supplanted by the cartographic eye, which codifies domination. The official conspectus provided elites with the capacity for swift and efficient action against dissent. It also ruled out anti-hegemonic versions of space and time, marking them as unrealistic. The 1740s saw a number of significant cartographies appear confirming the spatial hegemony of those who control the production, dissemination, and instruments of knowledge and power.

The '45 stimulated map production and the empire's will to totalize in accordance with its world view and to ensure a proprietary claim over realism. Symbolic of this move to stake out reality and a precursor to the Ordnance Survey, the Great Military Survey was started in 1747. As I have already pointed out this survey provided techniques, training, and skills which evolved into the naturalism of the picturesque. In addition, Emanuel Bowen brought out his aptly named book, *The Complete System of Geography* (1744–7), later followed by *The Complete Atlas or Distinct View of the Known World* (1752). Like Milton's apocalyptic geography, a world view, a particular historical ordering is implicit in these geographical systems. Imperial systematizing came in both global form, as with Bowen, and in local form: in 1746 John Roque brought out his famous large scale plan of London in twenty-four sheets as well as the *Environs of London* in sixteen sheets. Roque's gigantic and meticulous representation of London seems to boast of a city of imperial status, a capital whose scale challenges that of the world. The minute detail and painstaking precision of this world-city advertizes verisimilitude and rationalizes a particular form of knowledge. Ichnography has grown from the ground plan of one house to that of the largest city on earth, a city that is on the cusp of encapsulating the earth. My point here is not to try to argue that these and other contemporaneous endeavours to accurately map and scientifically claim space all issue from the campaign against the Highlands. Rather, I want to argue that these cartographies are inseparable from a general systematizing of nature in which Culloden marked a turning point.

This brings us finally to the point that has been implicit throughout, which is that the identity, cultural production and practices of empire and its inhabitants are determined by, in the words of Edward Said, the "disposition of power and powerlessness" (*Orientalism* 332) and therefore the deployment of the powerful and the powerless: the way they are arranged in history and geography, time and space. Imperialism, Paul Carter argues, seeks to represent its "fixed and detachable facts" as part of a natural–historical order rather than acknowledge "the material uncertainties" of spatial locality and practices, wherein the Other's "spatial command of the country" is evident (*Botany Bay* xvi, 335–6). As efficient and brutal as colonialism could be its spatial command over territory did not always prevail. Despite Culloden and its aftermath of "modernization" along the lines of English standards, an irritated Samuel Johnson could report: "stones [that] were placed to mark the distances" along military roads in the Highlands were being removed; he continues in disgust, "the inhabitants have taken [them] away, resolved, they said 'to have no new miles'" (Johnson and Boswell *Journey* 148).

TOWARD THE SYSTEM OF ROMANTICISM

But if a systematized empire is necessary it must at once be mystified. As the military were called upon to police the American colonies and the 1740s saw a shift from trade to conquest in India (thereby contradicting the eighteenth century's celebration of Britannia's love of freedom and commerce), empire is filtered through common sense, the sentimental, civic virtue, and the Romantic aesthetics of Nature and Selfhood. Increasingly empire's ills become a function of individual, class, or government immorality and effeminacy. The rot had set in. As popular in Boston as it was in London John Brown's jeremiad, *An Estimate of the Manners and Principles of Times* (1757) located decay "in Britain's own internal divisions and moral corruption" (Colley *Forging the Nation* 87). According to Brown decadence was spawned by, amongst others, the governing classes (whose effeminate, Francophile tendencies showed their true colours) and nabobs returning to sport their ill-gotten fortunes. Those who wore empire on their sleeves and thus provoked resentment and emulation by inferior groups were countered in Britain by the rise of middle class clubs and a reformist sensibility that paraded a manly, robust, and no less imperialist patriotism. The backbone of Britannia with their middle class pieties felt caught between the irresponsible use of power by elites and the innumerable yahoos just waiting for the governing classes to disappear up their own decadence. What many a writer grapples with during the eighteenth century, particularly during and after the American Revolution, is the denaturalization of the empire *by* the empire's unrestrained accumulation of land and capital. From mid-century on, deregulation of the always precarious balance between community and commerce picked up speed even in the American colonies where corporate values had stronger roots.

Central to the crisis of empire then was this unsettling change in the way Anglo-American society knew and governed itself. As Nash says of the colonies:

Part of the adjustment to change was a halting acceptance of a new system of values that legitimated private profit seeking, rationalized the abandonment of economic regulation, and projected a future economic world in which men's energies, cut loose from age-old mercantilist controls instituted to promote the good of all, would produce a common good far better. (*Urban Crucible* 97)

The decline was more advanced in Britain. Whether in the colonies or in Britain the self-sufficient moral economies of the disinterested, patrician landowner and yeomen (the still resilient core of the country-house ethos) is posited as the alternative to imperial/urban decadence. The popularity of Addison's play *Cato* (1713) is evidence that for many a Tory/Country and Evangelical reformer the cities and commerce spawned divisiveness and destruction. The basic tenets of this critique common to much early Augustan writing found more urgent representation in the novels of Fielding and Smollett, where the purgatorial city is contrasted with the solace of rural retirement, as well as in the Romantics. This ideological construct at once defends the social relations of the landowning classes whilst it mystifies and mitigates the true extent of the commercialization and colonial investment which also dominated the countryside.

Either offstage or, as in *Cato*, implicit within the main critique of overweening ambition, venality, and aggrandizement without a restraining moral code, lurks the anti-empire. The anti-empire comes into its own in the last decades of the eighteenth century and the turmoil of revolution, reaction, and Romanticism. With the structures of the empire both changing and increasingly evident, the anti-empire argues for "a self-adjusting system [which] aligns the supervisory functions of a patrician class together with a laissez-faire rhetoric of natural evolution" (Simpson *Romanticism* 59). But the anti-empire of Romanticism, most

forcefully put by Wordsworth, with its critique and solutions rooted in
an agrarian republicanism, the autonomous individual, and a return to
a mythical community bound by blood and soil, begins to appear
mid-century. In fact the thrust of Wordsworth's work continues the
social relations of the country-house ethos, leading the poet in his
Burkeian tract *To the Freeholders of Westmorland* (1818) to endorse the great
landowners like the Lowther family as best suited to rule Britain.
Lowther is cut from the same cloth as Pope's enlightened Burlington.
The nostalgia for a lost social order of paternalism is as apparent in
Johnson's "London: A Poem In Imitation of the Third Satire of Juven-
al" (1738) as it is Wordsworth's "Salisbury Plain" (composed 1793–4)
where the female vagrant remembers a Golden Age of rural self-
sufficiency, faith and community beloved of republican ideology (lines
238–9, 246–7: *Wordsworth*). Furthermore, like Johnson Wordsworth
yokes this virtuous society to a sense of manifest destiny – embodied
either as a personal mission or as past patriots who gloriously and
morally expanded British dominion. In *Cato* Addison also connects the
rural retreat of the virtuous to a benevolent version of empire. In a
typical imperial move, Addison has the Europeanized African prince,
Juba, endorse European conquest; imperialism is a project

> To civilize the rude unpolish'd World,
> And lay it under the Restraint of Laws;
> To make Man mild, and sociable to Man;
> To cultivate the wild licentious Savage
> With Wisdom, Discipline, and lib'ral Arts;
> The Embellishments of Life.   (28: I.iv)

It is left to the evil Syphax to state the consequences of such a project
from the point of view of the colonized: "in short, to change us into
other Creatures...?" (28: I.iv). But then Syphax is full of unhealthy
"Numidian Temper" and "Wiles" (25, 47: II.v). He is not to be trusted.

As in the latter part of the century, expansion was seen by British
critics as a double-edged sword: the liberating capacity of empire was
accompanied, or more often than not forgotten for the "growing excrescences" (Smollett *Humphrey Clinker* 65) of unfettered capitalism. A distinction perhaps between responsible power-broking and irresponsible
power-mongering. Addison makes this distinction through the characters of virtuous Cato and greedy Caesar. In 1734 Robert Morris decried
a Britain with her traditional monopoly of liberty ruined by an "Excess
of Indolence, and *ennervated* by Luxury." Linking the spatial design of the

elites to social well-being, his *Lectures on Architecture* warn that a decline in villas in ancient Rome led to awful consequences: "at length the whole Empire became a Seat of *wild Desolation*" (in Hunt and Willis *Genius* 235). In the same spirit, Pope juxtaposes the villas of Burlingtion and Bathurst with the corrupting and trivializing luxuries mocked in "The Rape of the Lock" (1712–14). If the "glitt'ring spoil" of empire (1.132) and the greedy Whig Sir Balaam go hand-in-hand, so to do the villas of Jacobite/Tory landowners and the virtuous imperial Britannia at the end of "Windsor Forest." But as we approach mid-century even the natural superiority and utility of the country house is deemed infected with corruption. Joseph Warton, for example, abandons Britannia altogether in *The Enthusiast: or, The Lover of Nature* (1744). Rather than repositories of genius and history, the height of ordered nature and culture, Warton sees both Versailles and Stowe, like the city, as tortured places in comparison to the wilderness. In "Excess and endless riot doom to die" (line 126) seems to be his diagnosis for Britain. Virtue and its "immortal train / Forsake Britannia's isle . . ." (189–90) for America.

Foreshadowing the fantasies of America as a Rousseauian model for new citizens, Wharton has the Enthusiast plan to set off for "western climes" and live "With simple Indian swains, that I may hunt / The boar and tiger through the savannahs wild" (195–9). George Berkeley comes to a similar, though more Caribbean conclusion in 1752. His "On the Prospect of Planting Arts and Learning in America" wishes to leave the British Isles behind, and cross the Atlantic to "another golden Age" (in Jehlen and Warner *Literatures of America* 1060). By mid-century many believed that manifest destiny had moved west across the Atlantic; History now resided in North America. Later, Coleridge and Southey would conjure up their Pantisocracy, and before the Terror exposed the Jacobin savage necessitating the strong hand of a natural leader, visions of the noble Euro-American Indian and the primitive republican reigned in the hot house of the Godwin circle.

If North America increasingly beckoned to the Jacobite–Republican spirit, its ethos of discovering one's individuality and God's order through territorial exploration had long been a feature of British society. *Culturally* the Puritan and Anglican rejection of all that was incorporated under the label "wilderness," was replaced by a spirit of adventure in the pursuit of liberating the internal and external wildness. The imperatives of capitalism and its imperial fix (expansion),[11] meant that repression of one's self in the service of God, community, and crown was replaced by the secession of one's self – secession into the wilderness and in quest of an independence guaranteed by land-ownership removed from the corrupting forces of cities, commerce, and their elites, but in the name of "America."[12]

In Britain a similar, more polite form of secession went by the name of tourism. The haunts that Wordsworth immortalized – the Lake District, the Wye Valley, Snowdonia, and the Scottish Highlands – were all tourist stamping grounds by the 1760s. In a classic example of how a culture born of colonialism produces new spaces (and how colonialism reproduces itself in domestic forms), the publication of Paul Sandby's water-colours of 1747–52 made the Falls of the Clyde a popular tourist site in the 1790s (Thomas *Natural World* 266).

The pursuit of self-interest and the interior was, therefore, carried out in Britain's wilder areas (the Lake District) and former colonial contact arenas (the Highlands and Wales). Here the aesthetically primed and privileged could conjure up the picturesque and "enjoy the *frisson* of being lost, 'a-mazed,' [or] 'be-wildered'" (Andrews *Search for the Picturesque* 62). The quest was conducted to the strains of nature's liberating medicine for the soul while also functioning as a no less reassuring act of dominating space; in other words, a domesticated version of colonialism. The walking tour offered a feeling of ownership over the natural world through an exclusive aesthetic experience. Whether in Britain or its former colonies, the experience of plugging into the moral and historical force of Nature generated an independence based on a revelatory connection to a divine order of things. Moreover, this belief was disseminated on both sides of the Atlantic via narratives of conversion and personal triumph (over persons and places wilder than the Euro-American) through the imperially inflected pursuit of mastering nature or finding mastery within nature.[13]

James Thomson had imagined this new national identity based on an empathy with nature and the authentic in *The Seasons* (1730). It is an identity issuing from a middle class desirous of the affirming powers and balms of the natural. Invoking in *Spring* what can only be described as a Romantic sensibility in 1730, where self-authorization is a corollary of nationhood and empire-building, Thomson writes:

> You wander through the Philosophic World;
> Where in bright Train continual Wonders rise,
> Or to the curious of the pious Eye.
> And oft, conducted by Historic Truth,
> You tread the long Extent of backward Time:
> Planning, with warm Benevolence of Mind,

> And honest Zeal unwarp'd by Party-rage,
> *Britannia's* Weal; how from the venal Gulph
> To raise her Virtue, and her Arts revive.

("Spring" lines 923–31)

Renovation of the nation is a function of renovating oneself by possessing History and Nature. If national unity, economic prosperity, and the maintenance of the established social and political order "could not be accomplished without an empire," they also required a hegemonic "process [that] reflected a divine harmony" (Williams *Contours* 71). Wordsworth, the architect of a new Albion, continued the tradition of deferring to an-other worldly force that was as much Providence – as partial to the English as in the days of Spenser – as it was Empire.

BUILDING A NEW NATION

The new nationalism that rooted itself to one soil and clarified "questions of Britishness" during this period (Colley *Forging the Nation* 145), was a process of uniting particular social and spatial ensembles in the "peripheries" to the "center." It was also a cultural process whereby "The unfenced regions of society" (Wordsworth *The Prelude* VII.62) – a phrase invoking Milton's dangerously "fenceless world" (*Paradise Lost* x.303) – are enclosed by universal symbols of nationhood. As if the "ha-ha" was applied to British culture, lines and boundaries were dissolved under the rubric of one nature, one nation, one empire. However, at the same time as this cultural (as well as geographical and industrial) unification is taking place, methods of dividing one class from another, one race from another intensify. The colonial tactics of mapping a hinterland and subjugating resistant populations not only nurtured scientific typology and classification of an "empirical" reality, but also produced an increasingly systemic process of assigning order and rank – a specific class identity – to people. This compartmentalization of people began in the 1740s and takes off in the 1790s (Langford *Polite and Commercial People* 652). Class consciousness increasingly became a matter of space.

The spatial/architectural theories of the 1740s and 50s came to fruition at the turn of the century (Batty Langely "discovered" the lost rules of the Gothic in 1742). The Romantic and Regency period mediated social relations with idyllic geographies – model villages for laborers, sub-urban communities for the middle class, the *rus in urbe* of parks with their "villas" (rather than mansions), and the valorization of the primitive. In order to offset and facilitate a Bullish empire the mystifying aesthetics of an idealized countryside and national spirit were brought to bear on the muscular athletics of capital. The fact that the creator of Regency London and one of the foremost theorists of the picturesque worked together in the same government department in 1806 surely underscores this partnership. Uvedale Price introduced John Nash to the picturesque's linking of architecture and landscape (Fox *London* 78). Central to both their theoretics of spatial relations (and for a romantic like Wordsworth) was the naturalizing of a hierarchical division of society in the face of increasingly turbulent class politics. Generally there was a return to the primal or essential Britain during this period: the popularity of medieval architecture, woods as primitive churches, the "rustic" style, a taste for wild landscape and gardening styles, domestic tourism, and the theory of merging the formal with the informal. To embrace the wild was a mark of civility, as if behind the soft critique of cities and other "modern" ills there was a proclamation of how in control of nature the British were. The anti-systemic anti-industrialism embodied in the enthusiasm for the ancient and wild closely resembles the anti-empire in that its critique of modern society serves as an ameliorating device.

Influential theorists and practitioners like James Gibbs and John Wood the elder traced pure spatial design to the organic forms of the primitive hut, Moses's Tabernacle, Solomon's Temple, and ancient Rome. The return to the first forms and primal designs and the incorporation of the individual within either a natural or architectural monumentality is a combination we see in both the urban regularity of Wood's development of Bath and Romanticism's personal embrace of the nation's nature. Arguably the desire for the organic and the colossal arise from the experience of being an imperial nation. Golden Age spaces were for the most part those undergoing or recently ravaged by colonization. Idyllic villages were never far removed from the "quasi-colonial" purpose of planned villages in the internal contact arenas of the British Isles, especially the Highlands and Ireland (Kearny *The British Isles* 193–4). The village was being appropriated as either a method of control or mystification. Thus, the latter part of the eighteenth century saw the development of a national space where inequalities and contest succumb to cottaged communities for laborer and bourgeoisie alike, each group immersed in "proprietorial desire"; a desire at once thankful for the superior civility of the British and eager to extend their indigenous liberty to the rest of the world.

While musing on the genius of the British, who are characterized as "Benefactors of Mankind," and praising the estate of Stowe as the epitome of taste, Gilbert West makes a pertinent though unintended link. In his poem "Stowe, the Gardens of the Right Honorable Richard Viscount Cobham" (1732), he claims the same muse for "The *Planter's* Spirit and the *Poet's* Fires" (Hunt and Willis *Genius* 215–8). The gardens of Stowe do indeed represent, both in practice and through the theatrical review of Britain's imperial past and destiny, a colonization of space and the disguising of that fact by numerous poets. Stowe and its celebrants engage in a relationship duplicated at a global level. It is therefore apt that perhaps the leading light of spatial design in the first half of the eighteenth century, William Kent, had the greatest impact on Stowe's development and, to return to imperial origins, designed illustrations for *The Faerie Queene*. Moreover, Spenser's imagery inspired Kent's garden designs; thus, colonial Ireland inserted itself at the very heart of English landscaping. By introducing wildness into the pattern of the English garden via sunken fences and raising Palladianism, with its ethos of patrician utilitarianism and enlightenment, to a national level, Kent's work represents the fundamental theatrics that secured the power and property of the elite. Kent brought to fruition what Henry Wotton almost a hundred years earlier had called the ideal garden's "wilde *Regularitie*."

The movement of systematizing – from an overtly classificatory and coercive regime to its mystification through the ascendancy of natural spaces and organic cultural forms – is straddled by a key mid-eighteenth century text, Samuel Johnson's *Dictionary* (1755). The categorization of the English language is a further effort to naturalize a particular version of reality. But Johnson's project is more than this: in keeping with the times his preface describes what is essentially a colonial campaign or exhibits what Jane Jacobs calls the "not-so-hidden histories and not-so-absent geographies of imperialism" (*Edge of Empire* 4).

Johnson wishes to purify the language of its "wild exuberance ... the tyranny of time and fashion, ... the corruptions of ignorance, and caprices of innovation" (*Dictionary* 3). This "struggle for our language" against the foreign (27) and excessive should use the same strategies as those used to reterritorialize Scotland and re-landscape Stowe. Johnson's "survey" will enable "rules" to establish "order," "confusion to be regulated," and the "boundless" to be framed. His "established principle of selection" (4) of a pure English lexicon declares war on the domestic threat posed by the diction of "the laborious and mercantile part of the people" as well as the international threat posed by foreign dialects which commerce brings to Britain's shores (23, 25). As if hunting down surviving Highlanders and their culture after Culloden, Johnson proclaims that "fugitive cant," in other words language in some way subversive to an official lexicon, "must be suffered to perish with other things unworthy of preservation" (23). In the interests of the whole nation and a pure, strong language, the Other must be eradicated. Finally, Johnson ends with the dream of a benevolent empire. As "teachers of truth" secure within their ordered and unified domain, the English will teach "foreign nations" the blessings of civility (27). But there is an ironic twist to this imperial project, disguised as classification of language. Johnson unwittingly underscores that the natural, the national, and the essentialized identity are never independent of the Other, the opposite or the oppositional. Plumbing "the wells of English undefiled" Johnson cites a poet who was wholly dependent for poetry, as well as property, on the non-English: Edmund Spenser (18–19). Demonstrating how empire works through the interdependence of colonizer and colonized, Johnson partially draws his "untainted" English, his encyclopedia of Britannia's civility from colonized Ireland and "the wilde fruit, which salvage soyl hath bred" (*Faerie Queene* "To the Right Honourable the Earle of Ormond and Ossory").

CHAPTER 7

Conclusion: the politics of space

Daughter: Is it true that these poor men can't swim in the sea here?

Lawyer: Yes, not even with their clothes on. Only people caught trying to drown themselves get away without paying a fine. But I hear the police beat them up later in the station house.

Daughter: Why don't they go where the beaches aren't private?

Lawyer: All the beaches are private.

Daughter: But I mean outside of town, in the country, where the land doesn't belong to anyone.

Lawyer: It all belongs to someone.

Daughter: Even the sea? The great, open...

Lawyer: Everything! If you're out on the sea in a boat, you can't even come ashore without getting permission and paying a fee. Beautiful, isn't it?

. . . .

Daughter: (*covering her face as she leaves*) This is no paradise!

Coal Heavers: No, it's hell, that's what it is!

Strindberg *A Dream Play* 253-4.

I have tried to close the gap between literary criticism and the hurly burly of defining and dividing up "real" geography (Jacobs *Edge of Empire* x). To study the production of knowledge is to study the production of space. At the core of this project is the thesis that "the spatial organization of society," in Doreen Massey's words, "is integral to the production of the social, and not merely its result. It is fully implicated in both history and politics" (*Space, Place, and Gender* 4). Further, within the saturating context of imperialism, I have focused on the "spatial forms and fantasies through which a culture declares its presence" (Carter *Road to Botany Bay* xxii). The texts analyzed here demonstrate how significant the organization and representation of space is to hegemony, and how the interpretation and development of space cannot be understood without recognizing the impact or infusion of the experiences and experiments of imperialism.

The world historical force of the imperial enterprise renovated the earth just as it surely renovated metropolitan culture and the cultures it invaded. The archetypal imperialist, Robinson Crusoe, springs from the same heroic world that Defoe, in the *Review* of May 1, 1711, describes as trade's theatre of operations: "trade carries the very soil away and transposes the world in parts, removing mountains and carrying them over the sea into other countries" (*Best of Defoe* 126). To achieve such territorial feats, imperial might has to accompany this sort of "trade." The Spanish Empire's infamous excavation of Potosi's silver with the bodies of enslaved Indians was as loudly deplored as it was secretly envied. The English were transfixed by such Satanic energy. This mammoth exploitation of space, of the earth's natural resources, served as a beacon for the early adventurers for an English Empire. Its repercussions energized merchants hungry for new markets and consumer goods, and the financial mechanisms to support them. At home English noblemen and gentry were already mining their estates for black gold.[1] The commodification of land, natural resources, and labor sent the dispossessed and the discontented to urban areas and overseas in huge migratory flows. It is this earth-shattering, society-shaking movement in spatial forms and relations which suffused literary culture with its dynamic/demonic force.

I have traced the development of the way traditional and new spaces are perceived by Renaissance Humanism, Puritanism, and the Rationalism of the Enlightenment. Perhaps the notion of stewardship is too benign for the way territory was expropriated and redesigned. Yet the term does invoke the benevolent empire that intellectuals on both sides of the Atlantic believed could exist. At the bottom of the desire for a more humane and efficient empire was James Harrington's distinction, derived from Cicero, between *imperium* and *patrocinium* (Marshall *Eighteenth Century* 53). That England/Britain in contrast to the Catholic empires was innately benevolent and commercial, offering protection rather than exploitation, was a bedrock assumption never seriously challenged. From the country house to the colony the notion of benign patronage by an elect prevailed. The British Isles was, if properly managed, "the Centre of the Worlds good things" (Purchas *Hakluytus* 1.3).

Samuel Purchas described his completed project as "having out of Chaos of confused intelligences framed this Historicall World, by a New way of Eye-evidence..." (xxxvii). Management by the elect strove for similar ends, although objectivity was supplemented by the omniscient eye. Throughout this book I have endeavored to show how stewardship, under colonial pressures, slips into an oppressive super-vision: the Lordly eye which proclaims control and superiority while it spies out threats to itself. Even in its subversive state, where women like Aphra Behn and Mary Rowlandson are a witness to events ordinarily beyond their purview, the ability to have a super-vision carries imperial overtones. On the one hand, Eliza Hayward and her *The Female Spectator* (1744–46) are subversive because the goal is to occupy a traditionally all-male space and "secure an eternal fund of intelligence" about its "mysteries" and "secrets" (5). But on the other hand, the will to omnipresence and the imagination of transgressing boundaries cannot in this case be divorced from an imperial culture. The politics of sight is inseparable from the politics of site; witness the definition of "site" by Roger de Piles, in 1708: "the word *site*, or situation, signifies the view, prospect or opening of a country" (in Hunt and Willis *Genius* 113).

The lordly eye is also a dissatisfied eye – it strains to get beyond myth and delusion, falsehood and perversion to a more accurate version of socio-spatial relations. It is as if Spenser or Swift seek to remove the absurd proportions of Elizabeth in the Ditchley Portrait, which pretends a national and global domination, in order to see more of Saxton's careful cartography below her feet. Attention to real geography has been a concern throughout this study. The period the book covers is roughly framed by two significant cartographic events: William Camden's map of *Britannia* in 1586 and the Great Military Survey of 1747 (precursor of the first Ordnance Survey of Britain in 1794). The first represented the broad outlines of the British kingdoms as a sovereign and hierarchical nation-state. The second represented in minute detail and, as Foucault might have it, "politico-strategic term[s]" (*Power/Knowledge* 69) the bureaucratic naturalization of national space by the authorities. The two mappings of space symbolize the general time–space compression and process of "great Confinement"[2] that colonization engendered during the period.

In that real geography is a cultural plot or a particular version of coordinates, symbols, rights, and social practices, it is revealing to read Samuel Johnson's *Dictionary* as a plotting of the nation, a chorographical map of a sovereign territory's means of signification. Johnson's project is therefore similar to that of Christopher Saxton and his late sixteenth-century county maps. Both establish and seek to codify a naturalized form of communication whereby the disparate and incoherent are fashioned into a recognizable and unified tabulation. Like the colonial process of "ground-clearing," both projects "institute one system of memorialization at the expense of another" (Carter *Lie* 6). Classification and cultural centralization establishes a mental geography that reinforces a particular narrative of nation. If in Saxton's maps "Places were transformed from a state of separation to one of proximity" (Tyacke *Map-Making* 25) and viewers were encouraged "to think spatially" (27), then Johnson's plotting of the English language seeks to perform a similar task: rendering English exclusive, the nation unified in its lexicon, and bringing the English-speaking world into some sort of order centered on the metropole's code. The spatial implications of a text like Johnson's dictionary need to be foregrounded in order for its imperial character to be recognized.

Like the culture we study for a living, we are subjects of and to empire. It is the underlying contention of this project that when we are studying works that have at their core ideologies stemming from, what Raymond Williams termed, "the long dream of a simple Rural England" (*Resources* 225) or the myth of a Golden Age unsullied by industrialism or territorial aggrandizement, we are also studying the long dream and shadow, if not the actual machinery of empire. As Robert Young concludes, we may believe the opposite, but we cannot escape "the colonial legacy" (*Colonial Desire* 182) nor, in Stuart Hall's words, "the language of empire ... [which] still constitute a massive ideological repertoire in British history" (in Nelson and Grossberg *Marxism and the Interpretation of Culture* 65). William Appleman Williams would of course state the same for US history. In the same spirit, the historian Stephen Saunders Webb argues that "much of our unwillingness to face the contemporary fact of American empire and to acknowledge that we are constituents of a world culture lies in our ignorance of the imperial origins of our politics and of our world view" (*1676* xv). Whilst noting the "explosion" in the study of imperialism and its domination of culture, Michael Sprinker asks why there is "an extraordinary amnesia concerning the actual record of their past?" Sprinker elaborates this way:

the discussion of the culture of empire has emanated principally from departments of literature and language, where training in and thoroughgoing knowledge of history are rarely required. The disciplinary bias of cultural studies has consequently tended to underplay or ignore altogether the complex material determinations of imperialism's history. (in De la Campa, Kaplan, and Sprinker *Late Imperial Culture* 7)

The study of empire's cultural productions has been too textually based and formulated, thus tending toward an ahistorical, discursive understanding of imperialism. Too often when it comes to imperialism we are, in Lefebvre's wonderful phrase, "mere wordmills" (*Production* 51), ignoring the fact that imperialism "is an act of geographical violence through which ... space ... is explored, charted, and finally brought under control" (Said *Culture* 225). This project has hopefully contributed to a more politically and geographically specific rendering of imperial pursuits, its uneven development, and its differentiation of territory (and its inhabitants) into productive and non-productive, civilized and backward, peaceful and murderous, superior and rightfully subordinate.

The pursuit of a more materialist exploration of imperial culture – an even bigger picture of EMPIRE – is not however to further privilege imperial history or its teleological inevitability to the detriment of other histories. We should of course beware of depicting a monolithic, all pervasive system that as much as we might expose its ugly designs and detest its consequences we end up providing no evidence for viable alternative societies in the past and for the future. As Jane Jacobs points out empire always had competition: "One of the key contributions to be made by postcolonial studies is to demonstrate the vulnerability of imperialist and colonialist power... [These dominant cultures] are always anxiously regrouping, reinventing, and reinscribing their authority against the challenge of anticolonial formations but also against their own internal instability" (*Edge of Empire* 14). Hopefully this book has not only shown that empire is riven with contradictions, crises, and dissent, but that anti-hegemonic spatial and social structures have always been both the thorn in the side of empire and the catalyst for its every development. The authors I have studied display the anxiety, inspiration, and empowerment that issued from this volatile historical process. All of this is to underscore that empire is not something that happened in the past and imperialism something that happens over there. Imperialism cannot take place without the elaborate preparations at home made by the hegemonizing apparatus of culture. It is a way of perceiving and ruling over space that takes place (literally) on the doorstep of the imperial centre.

Sir William Petty claimed in the seventeenth century "declining all Military means of setling and securing *Ireland* in peace and plenty, what we offer shall tend to the transmuting one People into the other, and the thorough union of Interests upon natural and lasting principles" (*Economic Writings* 1.157). Without such methods estates like his 50,000 acre plot in County Kerry would remain illusory. Spenser and Swift advocated the same strategy of transmutation rather than the mutations and distortions produced by inept colonial policies. Swift does not satirically locate Gulliver in a "never-never land" like that of *Terra Australis Incognita* (in Lamb *Eighteenth Century Life* 123) to show that colonialism is irrational. Swift and Spenser, who uses the concept of a fairy land to a similar end, attack unrealistic colonial policies that pursue illusions and produce untenable societies. At the same time, however, their savage critique, born of living in Ireland, undermines the "natural and lasting principles" Petty speaks of, showing how constructed and mutable they really are.

These naturalized principles became the Enlightenment's emancipatory ideal for the world; principles which are not reducible to European imperialism, but are not separable from it either, as post-colonial studies has clearly shown. As the American Revolution showed, ideals such as "universal Benevolence," human rights, and simple, patriotic "habits" can, as Abigail Adams argued, be weapons against imperialism and the "Luxury of Foreign Nations" (in *American Writing* Gunn 508–9). But without the acknowledgement of how such principles produce space (and vice versa), empire under a different guise of a "thorough union of Interests" is free to go about its business. Too often the "rest" are simply expected to fit into the West's map of the world, and like the cartographic handkerchiefs popular around 1700 to remain in the West's pocket.

This book has attempted to denaturalize principles and geographies that veil the practices of imperialism. One final example will serve to underline how the imperial ethos often mutates into "trade" and moral management. William Hogarth's painting of Captain Coram (1740) captures just such a move.[3] Combining the best of the country squire with urban-based accumulation of capital, Coram is celebrated for his wealth from overseas trade and how he has channeled it into charity (the Foundling Hospital). William Hogarth, the progressive, relishes painting one so obviously from lowly origins in a manner usually reserved for the aristocracy, underscoring that the mercantile middle class are the natural successors of the aristocracy. But if Hogarth immortalizes Coram for all the right reasons, all the wrong reasons for his success are also included in the painting: charity and trade are indeed meaningless without recognizing that empire facilitated Coram's rise. Just as it was for the managerial class of empire, the globe, turned to "THE WESTERN OR ATLANTICK OCEAN" is at the feet of this ruddy servant of the public and nation. With its hardly legible inscription the globe is at the margin of the composition and the ships in the background have faded. Coram and pious success are center stage. We must work not only to connect the two, but bring empire into full focus the better to remove it from the picture all together.

Notes

1 In the first documented tree-planting, Burghley had thirteen oaks planted in Windsor Park.
2 Similarly, Albrecht Dürer's utopian city in his influential treatise on fortification in 1527 closely resembles the woodcut of Tenochtitlan included in the recently published Latin edition of Cortes's letters. In turn, Dürer's design very likely influenced the design of New Haven, Connecticut.
3 Burke is referring to the Indianism of Asia rather than America.
4 The more secular "Britannia," who appeared on coins in 1665, begins to replace the notion of a Chosen nation at the end of the seventeenth century (Greene in Marshall *Eighteenth Century* 214.)
5 For an excellent example see Makdisi, *Romantic Imperialism*.
6 For a cogent and critical overview of postcolonial studies see Dirlik "The Postcolonial Aura" 328–56. A convenient anthology of critical essays is provided by Williams and Chrisman *Colonial Discourse and Post-Colonial Theory*.
7 Perhaps a sign of the times is Gikandi *Maps of Englisness*, Jacobs *Edge of Empire*, Blunt *Travel, Gender, and Imperialism*.
8 A fine example of the former is Brantlinger *Rule of Darkness*.
9 For summaries on geography and its historical and critical development see Livingstone *Geographical Tradition*, and Gregory *Geographical Imaginations*.
10 In emphasizing a spatial analysis I am at the same time heedful of Lefebvre's warning: "when codes worked up from literary texts are applied to space – to urban spaces, say – we remain, as may easily be shown, on the purely descriptive level. Any attempt to use such codes as a means of deciphering social space must surely reduce that space itself to the status of a *message*, and the inhabiting of it to the status of a *reading*. This is to evade both history and practice" (*Production* 7).
11 Numerous historians and cultural theorists point out the difficulty in using the multivalent term "empire." See for example Pagden *Lords of all the World*, 12–28; Canny *Origins* 1–2; 103; and Benita Parry in Pearson, Parry and Squires *Cultural Readings* 227.

12 I take this phrase from Knapp *An Empire Nowhere*. My use of the phrase should not be seen as a specific critique of Knapp's thesis.

13 Craddock was in fact in the minority; there was relatively little overlap between company merchants and colonial merchants up until the 1640s.

14 See also Wood "Agrarian Origins" 14–31.

15 Armitage footnotes mostly new historicist texts when describing literary theory's obsession with empire. New historicism however focuses on the micro-politics of (usually elite) subjectivity and power rather than the material practices and forms of imperialism.

16 For more on "moral capitalism" in New England see Innes *Creating the Commonwealth*.

THINKING TERRITORIALLY: SPENSER, IRELAND, AND THE ENGLISH NATION-STATE

1 See Julia Reinhard Lupton's discussion of "plot" in Bradshaw, Hadfield, and Maley *Representing Ireland*, 97.

2 Robins was pelted with rocks from an Irish castle when inquiring for topographical information and his fellow surveyor Francis Jobson wrote that he felt "every hour in danger to lose my head" as indeed was the fate of another surveyor at this time (Andrews *Plantation Acres* 44).

3 For example see the essays on Spenser in Bradshaw, Hadfield, and Maley *Representing Ireland*.

4 Other recent studies include Cullen and Roche eds., *Spenser Studies* and Fogarty *Spenser in Ireland*.

5 Chris Highely goes so far as to call approaches that place Spenser in an Atlantic world of colonial endeavors and desires anachronistic, trading in "an over-totalized and speciously unified 'discourse of colonialism'" (*Shakespeare* 7).

6 See also *View* 125.

7 *View* was entered in Stationers' Register on the 14 April 1598, but was only published in 1633. For a discussion over why the text failed to appear see Hadfield *Spenser's Irish Experience* 78–84.

8 For more on adventure and adventurers see Nerlich *Ideology of Adventure* 108–34.

9 *A Discourse of the Common Weal of this Realm of England* (written 1549; pub. 1581), went through eleven editions between 1583 and 1640. The very common sensical dialogue blames the "dearth" or inflation on over-specialization in agricultural production, lack of regulation when enclosing, and, most importantly, economic isolation. He advocated entering the transformative arena of international trade.

10 For the best account of mercantilism and its development see Williams *Contours* 27–74.

11 See Canny, "The permissive frontier" in Andrews, Canny, and Hair *Westward Enterprise* 18–19.

12 As Hill puts it, "its [the North-West Passage] historical importance is that it

led to scientific, nautical, and commercial enterprises, which linked John Dee with Sir Humphrey Gilbert and George Cascoigne, Gresham College (Briggs, Gunter) with practical explorers like Foxe and James, with Hakluyt, with the Virginia Company, with big City financiers like Sir Thomas Smith and Sir John Wolstenholme, and with Parliamentarians like Sir Dudley Digges" (*Intellectual Origins* 44).

13 The first Gresham Professor of Geometry, Henry Briggs, was an active member of the Virginia Company and wrote a *Treatise on the North-West Passage* (Hill *Intellectual Origins* 40).

14 For Harriot's connections with imperialists, writers, scientists and colonial companies see Hill *Intellectual Origins* 124–5.

15 For a debate on Spenser's strategy for Ireland's subjugation and the degree of violence advocated see Canny "Spenser's Irish Crisis" 201–9; and Ciaran Brady's reply, "The Road to the *View*" 210–15.

16 Dee is credited with first coining the phrase "Brytish Impire." For more on Dee and his place within the Renaissance see Sherman *John Dee*.

17 The preface was to Henry Billingsley's translation of Euclid, published in 1570.

18 For Dee, the security of the nation includes domestic foe: the navy will also act as a rapid deployment force "against such of Ireland, Scotland, or England, who shall, or will traitorously, rebelliously, or seditiously assemble in Troops, or Bands, within the Territories of Ireland, or England" (*General and Rare Memorials* 6).

19 This actually refers to a female monster associated with Spain's warring in the Lowlands.

20 In 1569, Spenser was admitted to Pembroke Hall, Cambridge as a "sizar": a poor scholar who had to perform servant's duties.

21 One might place both poets in the historical moment just before, as Marx put it, the drowning of "the most heavenly ecstasies of religious fervour, of chivalrous enthusiasm, of philistine sentimentalism, in the icy water of egotistical calculation" (*Manifesto* 16).

22 See *View* 107–8 and *Faerie Queene* v.xii.24–v.xii.27.

23 See Shepherd and the "grubby stories about Spenser's property deals" (*Spenser* 22).

24 Administratively, culturally, and militarily the Irish were extremely hard to dominate because of the way they used, saw, and moved through space. The solution became a policy of "wiping out of two significant and overlapping elements in Irish society, the traveling craftsmen, messengers, and entertainers and the learned class of brehons and poets" (Quinn *Elizabethans* 125–6).

25 See Canny *From Reformation to Restoration* 121.

26 For the connection between Spenser's dialogue and the colonization of language, see Anne Fogarty in Coughlan *Spenser and Ireland* 90.

27 Sheila Cavanagh discusses the strategic and ideological bearing of Irish dress and appearance in Bradshaw, Hadfield, and Maley *Representing Ireland* 101–2.

28 For a discussion of Spenser and gender see Cavanagh *Wanton Eyes and Chaste Desires*. For a good overview of the development of patriarchy within early modern society see Hamilton *Liberation of Women*.

29 See Shepherd *Spenser* 23. Landowners were required to fill their estates with English rather than Irish tenants and labourers; the latter, however, were deemed more subservient and were used by many landowners.

30 Sheehan argues that the "Blatant Beast typifies the potential for degradation contained in nature, the very substance of the anti-principle in life" (*Savagism and Civility* 77).

31 In fact, the colonizers openly provoked retaliation by native landowners in the hope that any retaliation would result in forfeiture of the landowners land.

32 In *View* Spenser notes the Scythian or Old Scottish war-cries as "howls" (54–6).

33 The spatial scale outlined here, from the body to the castle, is obviously complicated in that Elizabeth's body and her virginal state was also used to represent the territory of the English nation-state and its colonial spaces, i.e. Virginia.

34 See Sheehan *Savagism* as well as Hamlin *Image of America*. For a more general survey of savagism and representations of the "wild man" see Dudley and Novack *Wild Man Within*.

35 After the first Florida colony in 1562, its founder Jean Ribault went to England.

36 For more on the colony of Roanoke see Quinn *Set Fair for Roanoke*.

37 This extract is from a letter to Sir Edward Stafford on 21 July 1584. See Quinn *Roanoke Voyages* 90.

38 See Andrews, Canny, and Hair *Westward Enterprise* 18–19. The younger Thomas Smith was killed by his own servants in Ireland in 1573.

39 Spenser's *View* is, however, quite different from the vast majority of promotional literature which simply sought to depict the colonial space in as alluring a light as possible.

40 Interestingly the plague, famine, and war of 1582 in Ireland left the population seriously depleted, and promotional literature called upon Englishmen, as their duty, to repopulate the South (MacCarthy-Morrogh *Munster Plantation* 26).

41 *Discourse* was only meant for Elizabeth's eyes, and was not published until recently.

42 This is particularly evident after the Munster rebellion in 1598 and the so-called Indian massacre in Virginia in 1622. Potentially reformable savages become beasts.

43 Books 1–3 were published in 1590, and 4–6 in 1596.

44 Simon Shepherd elaborates that Spenser was "accused by his Anglo-Irish neighbour Lord Roche of falsely dispossessing the lord of castles and ploughlands, and of beating up the lord's servants and bailiffs. Spenser's answer does not deny this, but accuses Lord Roche of disloyalty . . ." (22).

45 Stephen Greenblatt argues that "the whole of *The Faerie Queene* is the expression of an intense craving for release, which is overmastered only by a still more intense fear of release" (*Renaissance Self-Fashioning* 173).

46 For a review of how Spenser's *View* fares in academia today see Breen "The Empirical Eye" 44–52.

CONTRACTING GEOGRAPHY FROM THE COUNTRY HOUSE TO THE COLONY

1 For an analysis of the country-house poem see Williams *Country and City* 12–59; McClung *Country-House*; Kenny *Country-House Ethos*; and Don Wayne, *Penshurst*. For a more general survey of the ideologies fuelling the country-house ethos see Patterson *Pastoral and Ideology*.

2 Royal proclamations ordered the gentry to their estates in 1603, 1622–4, 1626–7, 1638, 1632, 1639 and 1640 (Fitter 240). James and Charles I promoted traditional (rural) society through the *Book of Sports*.

3 See "Virgideriarum," book 5, satire II in Woudhuysen *Renaissance Verse* 407. Underling the essentially unEnglish state of the countryside, Hall links the absence of hospitality to the Escorial in Spain.

4 Fitter states that "Country House poetry carries th[e] 'unseen hands' view of natural fertility as spontaneous, sybaritic providence to an extreme. Nature as pleasuring, freely producing agency" (*Poetry, Space, Landscape* 246).

5 See Hobsbawm, "The General Crisis of the European Economy in the Seventeenth Century"; and De Vries *Economy of Europe*.

6 Innes refers this crisis to the years 1590–1650.

7 Immanuel Wallerstein argues that this period, beginning in 1540, is one of

> class *formation*, a capitalist agricultural class (whose wealthier members are called "gentry" and whose lesser members are called "yeomen"). The social process of land consolidation in England at this time is one of increasing income to this class as a whole including to the lesser members of it, while it involves the beginnings of the creation of a proletariat, most of whom was still not firmly settled in the towns but rather were "vagabonds," seasonal wage workers with subsistence plots, and lumpenproletariat in the towns. (*Modern World-System* 256)

8 As Richard Ligon points out, the houses of the gentry in the English West Indies were ill-suited for a tropical climate. Ligon went to great lengths to design alternatives. The impracticality of the houses underlines not only the strength of the planters' cultural self-image, but also how far they would go to remain "English Gentlemen" and thus mimic their counterparts back home.

9 This is taken from "Skialetheia," Satire 5 (1598).

10 See Canny's essay "The permissive frontier" in Andrews, Canny, and Hair, *Westward Enterprise* 17–44.

11 For the truly resistant, even revolutionary Caliban see Retamar *Caliban and Other Essays*.

12 The numerous cross-referencing of Indians with the Irish, usually via clothing, implicitly recognizes the humanity and cultural space of the Indians. In *Mourt's Relation* the Indians wear "long hosen [which] ... were altogether like the Irish-trousers" (53). George Percy in his "Observations" (1606) likens "a path-way ... to an Irish pace" (Purchas xvIII.413).

13 This is from "Virginia Verger: Or a Discourse shewing the benefits which may grow to this Kingdome from American English Plantations, and specifically those of Virginia and Summer Ilands."

14 For more on the English and their relationship with the ecology of America see Merchant *Ecological Revolutions*.

15 Purchas summarizes all of England's claims thus:

> so that England may both by Law of Nature and Nations challenge Virginia for her owne peculiar propriety, and that by all right and rites usuall amongst men ... also, first discovery, first actual possession, prescription, gift, cession, and livery of seisin, sale for price, that I mention not the naturall Inheritance of the English their naturally borne, and the Unnatural outcries of so many unnaturally murthered, for just vengence of rooting out the authors and actors of so prodigious injustice. (*Hakluytus* ixx.224–5)

16 Donne was also frustrated when a storm prevented an expedition setting off for Guiana in 1597. Whilst Raleigh and Essex tried to persuade Elizabeth to let them go to Guiana instead of chase a Spanish fleet, Donne, still at Plymouth, wrote "To Mr. R.W."

17 Rabb saw the gentry's contribution as "an unprecedented phenomenon in European history" (*Merchant and Gentry* 68).

18 Williams asserts "Th[e] concept of an overseas economic empire as the means to improvement at home synthesized the mercantilist's concern for agriculture with his support for commerce" (*Contours* 46).

19 For more on what the revolution achieved see Hill *Intellectual Origins*, chapters 7, 8, and 11.

20 Canny claims that Munster was "probably the wealthiest English overseas settlement that had developed anywhere by the middle of the seventeenth century" (*Kingdom* 77).

21 Other views differed from that of Johnson and his obvious promotional eyesight. Colonel George Cartwright in 1665 saw Boston with "houses [that] are generally wooden, their streets crooked and unpaved, with little decency and no uniformity" (quoted in Cressy *Coming Over* 32).

22 See Jennings *Invasion* 144–5.

23 MacCarthy-Morrogh states that "the Winthrop web of intermarriage in Suffolk and the eastern counties caught up a number of other families and spun them over to Ireland in this period" (*Munster Plantations* 200).

24 See Bridenbaugh and Bridenbaugh *No Peace* 94–6; and Dunn, *Sugar and Slaves* 336–7.

25 David Cressy claims that the "best figures indicate that 69,000 emigrant Britons crossed the Atlantic in the 1630s, of whom only 21,000 went to New England. Even at its peak the settlement of New England accounted for just

30 per cent of the departing migrants, with most of the rest going to the Chesapeake and the Caribbean. Approximately 540,000 people left England during the period 1630 to 1700, of whom roughly 377,600 went to the New World. Many of the others migrated to Ireland to populate the Protestant plantations of Ulster, or to other places in Europe" (*Coming Over* 69). Bernard Bailyn brings Ireland more firmly into the picture when he writes, referring to the Great Migration between 1630 and 1642: "three times that number left England for other colonies in America and the West Indies, and almost six times that number of Englishmen and Scots (120,000) migrated to Ireland. In one 24–*month* period in the 1630s, at least 10,000 Scots migrated to Ireland, roughly half the total of the entire Puritan migration" (*Peopling of America* 26).

26 See Jennings for the use and histories of terms such as "savage" and "settlement," and specifically for the turning point of 1622 (*Invasion* 77).

27 See Canny, "The Permissive Frontier," in Andrews, Canny, and Hair *Westward Enterprise* 40–4. Also Meinig *Atlantic America* 144–50.

28 One of course should be aware that Morton's text is highly mediated by the fact that he was transported back to England by the "Christians" he subsequently attacks.

29 John Winthrop confirms social hierarchy in his Atlantic-crossing sermon "A Modell of Christian Charity," when he unequivocally states: "God Almightie in his most holy and wise providence hath soe disposed of the Condicion of mankinde, as in all times some must be rich some poore, some highe and eminent in power and dignitie; others meane and in subjeccion" (76).

30 Winslow died in 1656 on the return voyage from Jamaica to England.

31 For the exploits of first three see Martin *Profits in the Wilderness* 46–79. For more on Pynchon see Innes *Labor in a New Land.* John Winthrop Jr. had a lucrative career in speculation and town founding. By the time he was elected governor of Connecticut in 1657 (which he was hired to set up), "he had lived in Boston, Salem, Ipswich, Saybrook, New London, New Haven, and Hartford. Three of these towns he had founded himself" (Martin *Profits in the Wilderness* 54). At the end of his life, he had amassed a huge amount of property in land (56).

32 Jennings states that up until "King Philip's War … In an oversimple way, one might say that all intercolonial relations were motivated or shadowed by efforts to acquire Narrangansett land" (*Invasion* 179).

33 Mathew Cradock, the largest investor in the Massachusetts Bay Company, was granted most of Medford. In the 1630s "Cradock's plantation" was run by Cradock employees, tenants, and agents (Martin *Profits in the Wilderness* 35). Cradock never set foot in North America.

34 For more on the term "inhabitant" – which had next to nothing to do with residing in a place – see Martin *Profits in the Wilderness* 217–28. Martin uses the phrase "splintered society" to describe the "several different communities exist[ing] within each town" (235).

35 See Cronon *Changes in the Land* 141.

36 Although Denham celebrates the natural prerogative of Charles I to rule, his poem is as "progressively" chorographical and ideologically compatible with the country-house genre because of the way he represents space. The only difference from other chorographical poems is that the king is the natural heir to national space rather than the gentry.

OVERSEEING PARADISE: MILTON, BEHN, AND ROWLANDSON

1 In Virginia two successful planters offered a plan to construct a six-mile wall running from the Charles to the James Rivers, manned with their own servants (Breen *Puritans and Adventurers* 124). This proposed palisade, ignored by the mass of land-hungry tobacco growers, did in fact materialize in 1634. In Ireland John Temple envisioned the British replanting behind "a wall of separation set up betwixt the *Irish* and the *British* [so that] it will not be in their power to rise up ... to destroy and root them [the English] out in a moment" (*Irish Rebellion* Preface).

2 See Kolodny *The Lay of the Land*, and her follow up *The Land Before Her*.

3 Gayatri Spivak rightly notes that Foucault's notion of the regimented body elides its formation within the context of imperialism. See Spivak's "Can the Subaltern Speak?" (in Nelson and Grossberg *Marxism* 271–313).

4 For an examination of Behn's relationship to the systems of the marketplace, colonialism, and sexual/racial politics see Ferguson "News from the New World" 151–89.

5 *Comus* and *Paradise Regained* are taken from *Complete English Poems*. For more on the political meanings and context behind "Comus," see Brown *John Milton's Aristocratic Entertainments*.

6 See Kendrick "Milton and Sexuality." Kendrick's "politico-cultural reading" of the "chastity cult" has chastity as a "political statement and instrument of control, as generalized sexuality" which "appear under the aspect of the reification imposed by emergent capitalism" (43–4).

7 During the 1660s there were strikes and mutinies in the dockyards, weavers' riots, and the first organizing of combinations or unions for higher wages.

8 See also Linebaugh's essay "All the Atlantic Mountains Shook."

9 *Britannia* (1675) and *Itinerarium Angliae:or, A Book of the Roads* (1675).

10 For more on Milton's relationship to providential and systematic geography see my essay "The 'Lordly eye': Milton and the Strategic Geography of Empire," in *Milton and the Imperial Vision*, eds. Rajan and Sauer. This volume is a good representative of the present state of Milton studies.

11 Besides *Observations on the Articles of Peace*, see Lipking on "Lycidas," "The Genius of the Shore," 205–21.

12 The years 1649 to 1660 saw the massive transference of land to Protestants and a new colonial class, who had the "monopolies of trade, local and national power" (Barnard *Cromwellian Ireland* 304). Barnard estimates that the "Catholic share of land fell from 59 per cent in 1641 to 20 per cent in

1660, of which the bulk was in Connaught" (11). Eleven years of war and subsequent transportation of soldiers to France and Spain and civilians to the colonies, especially the West Indies, reduced the population of Catholics by nearly a million. The vacated and fertile land was to meet the demands of Cromwell's dangerously radical army, his supportive adventurers or investors, as well as the fiscal needs of the Commonwealth (Bottingheimer *English Money* 53, 134).

13 With respect to Milton's use of colonial discourse, see Evans *Milton's Imperial Epic* and Stevens *"Paradise Lost* and the Colonial Imperative" 3–22. For a general discussion of geography and literature see Gillies *Shakepeare and the Geography of Difference*.

14 For more on the chorographical influences within Milton's writing see Cawley *Milton and the Literature of Travel*.

15 Gauri Viswanathan in "The Naming of Yale College: British Imperialism and American Higher Education," points out that Cotton Mather in the 1670s, as part of his strategy to persuade Elihu Yale to sponsor what became Yale College, refers to the colonies as "parts of western *India*" (in Kaplan and Pease *Cultures* 87).

16 See Baker *et al. American Beginnings*.

17 For more on gardens see Hill *The English Bible* 153.

18 In "An Horatian Ode Upon Cromwell's Return From Ireland" Marvell represents Cromwell as another gardener, intent on bringing fertility and order to the British Isles. In this context, it is interesting that Kiernan notes that Heaven is "a totally militarized realm" ("Milton" 165).

19 See Arneil *John Locke and America*.

20 For discussions of gender, Milton's sexual politics, and whether Eve is a patriarchal or progressive character of femininity, see Walker *Milton and the Idea of Woman*; McColley *Milton's Eve*; and Turner *One Flesh: Paradisal Marriage and Sexual Relations in the Age of Milton*.

21 For a good overview of the genre see Derounian-Stodola and Levernier *The Indian Captivity Narrative, 1550–1900*.

22 Sir John Temple, like other colonial propagandists, also argues that the colonized are jealous of the civility, amenities, and progress the English communities enjoy. Thus a motive of an uprising is the colonized's wish to be like the English, thereby proving the superiority and right to rule of their oppressors.

23 Mather does point out in "A Narrative of Hannah Dustan's Notable Deliverance from Captivity" that Indian-like behavior can be safe in some cases. In Dustan's case he argues that her scalping of her captors is legitimate: it is "not forbidden by any law to take away the life of the murderers by whom her child had been butchered" (Vaughan and Clark *Puritans among the Indians* 164).

24 For more on Behn see Todd *Aphra Behn Studies*.

25 For a post-colonial reading of *Oroonoko* see Azim *Colonial Rise*. She argues that "Oroonoko is the prototype of the colonized subject, the Third World

bourgeoisie of modern times, whose commercial, economic and political welfare are dependent on the fortunes of international finance" (50). Also see Andrade "White Skin."

26 Dunn reminds us that around 1660 "Irish Catholics constituted the largest block of servants on the island, and they were cordially loathed by their English masters" (*Sugar and Slaves* 69).

27 Dunn notes that in the 1680 census of Barbados, 175 big planters represented 7% of property holders, yet owned 54% of the property on the island (*Sugar and Slaves* 96–7).

28 It is still necessary, however, for Moll to be on her guard against deception in the colonies as her marriage to her brother (in Virginia) testifies.

THE IMPORT AND EXPORT OF COLONIAL SPACE:
THE ISLANDS OF DEFOE AND SWIFT

1 Coke is most immediately referring to his resiting of the hamlet of Holkham.

2 See *Customs*, 42–83.

3 See Habermas *Structural Transformation*; and Pocock *Virtue, Commerce and History*. For a review of the Habermasian concept see, Calhoun, ed., *Habermas and the Public Sphere*. For a succinct discussion of these developments see Eagleton *Function of Criticism* 9–27.

4 Gay published *Polly* in 1729.

5 The attention to surveillance also manifests itself in *The Spectator*, Eliza Hayward's *The Female Spectator*, and Bentham's panoptican; see Bender's *Imagining the Penitentiary* and Foucault's essay "Panopticism" in Rainbow, ed., *The Foucault Reader* 206–13.

6 Ironically the most notorious case of "Indians" terrorizing the capital was the group of aristocrats who called their gang the "Mohocks."

7 For example, Timothy Nourse in his *Campania Faelix* (1700) argued that poverty was good because the poor were then "inur'd to all manners of Hardships, prove excellent good Labourers, where they are kept in order; and as they are exceeding serviceable for the Country Affairs in Times of Peace, so are they most useful in Time of War, for the same reason of being bred hardy, and when reform'd by Discipline will make good rough, cross-gained Soldiers enough, fit to kill or be kill'd" (quoted in Varey *Space* 36).

8 Claude Rawson makes the distinction between Swift's contempt for the Yahoos and his compassion for "some generalized or typical category of oppressed 'harmless' people'" (*Order from Confusion* 75). He goes on to explain the distinction and seeming ambiguity: "the compassion for the 'harmless People,' like the pity for the Irish, exists in order to highlight Swift's loathing for the oppressor rather than as a sign of tenderness for the oppressed" (77).

9 Luxury also corrupts the rich, but its consequences, according to Fielding, when it trickles down to the poor are far worse: "it reaches the very dregs of the people, who aspiring still to a degree beyond that which belongs to

them, and not being able by the fruits of honest labour to support the state which they affect, they disdain the wages to which their industry would entitle them..." (*Complete Works* XIII.22).

10 See Dunn and Dunn, eds. *The World of William Penn*. Penn also took a trip to Ireland, leaving London on 15 September 1669 and returning to Dublin on 1 July 1670. The trip is recorded in "My Irish Journal," in Dunn and Dunn, eds. *The Papers of William Penn*.

11 After 1660 the traditional plantation solution for the indigent was increasingly criticized. As the economy expanded and slowly "industrialized" emigration (forced or otherwise) to the colonies where wages were often higher, was attacked as a drain on the labor pool. See Appleby *Economic Thought* 135–47.

12 See Heward *Matthew Hale* especially 59.

13 Peter Hulme has argued, however, that interpretations of *Robinson Crusoe* have ignored its setting in the Caribbean (*Colonial Encounters* 176).

14 Hulme points out that "there is no evidence that Defoe's commitment to his own pet project of a South Sea trading area based on a new English colony in South America with an entrepot on the Pacific coast – clearly akin to the Darien idea – was in the least reduced: his plans remain remarkably consistent from the 1690s through to 1727, well after the bursting of the Bubble" (*Colonial Encounters* 181).

15 The sequels do not represent a progression in Defoe's thinking, from supporting colonialism in *Crusoe* to a commercial policy. Rather the sum of the three books is a realistic portrayal of Britain's spheres of action in the world as well as a marketing ploy to cover those spheres.

16 In *A Plan of the English Commerce* Defoe exemplifies English "Genius" with reference to the first settlers in New England (228–9). Hulme writes that "by looking back beyond the great merchant companies to the age of Raleigh, Defoe could endow Robinson Crusoe with something of the heroism of the adventurer who risked life and limb as well as capital, therefore, adventitiously, providing a link between the Elizabethan era and the true age of adventure in the second half of the nineteenth century" (*Colonial Encounters* 184).

17 Swift points out that "while we, for ten years, have been squandering away our money upon the continent, France hath been wisely engrossing all the trade of Peru, going directly with their ships to Lima, and other ports, and their receiving ingots of gold and silver for French goods of little value" (*Prose Works* v.79).

18 Anson's South Sea jaunt was an unmitigated failure until he captured the Acapulco galleon on its way to Manila and bagged one of the richest treasure troves taken by the English, worth more than £400,000.

19 Swift supported Berkeley's "romantic design" for setting up a college in Bermuda, writing that the plan "is very noble and generous." See Fraser, ed., *Works of George Berkeley*, 345. Swift's hero Bolingbroke dreamt of "... buying the Dominion of Bermuda, and spending the remainder of my

days as far as possible from those people with whom I have past the first and greater part of my life." He goes on to ask Swift: "will you ... transport yr self with me into the middle of the Atlantick ocean? we will form a society, more reasonable, and more useful than that of Dr. Berkley's Colledge..." (quoted in Fabricant *Swift's Landscape* 4).

20 Dampier shows an open mindedness uncommon among most colonial "surveyors"; for example he disparages reports of cannibalism (485) and inherent barbarity (484) and comments on the "natural beauty" of the Hottentots (537), who are almost universally used as the standard of degenerate humanity.

21 Hulme observes that Defoe is "negotiating the unspeakable – and eventually uncloseable – gap between the violence of slavery and the notion of a moral economy" (*Colonial Encounters* 222). Defoe's relationship with Xury and Friday blur the line between slave and servant.

22 Woodes Rogers lists eleven types of racial mixes ranging from Spaniard to Sambo (Negro and Indian) in his *Cruising Voyage* (1712).

23 In *A New Voyage Round the World* Dampier is sympathetic toward Moskito Indians and the "poor Americans" (457) who have suffered under the yoke of Spanish rule, and the Hottentot rank above the New Hollanders, for whom he has little more than disgust.

24 For more on the Hottentot, see Pratt *Imperial Eyes*, especially 38.

25 For instance, see 95–129. Fabricant juxtaposes Pope's reverence of Richard Boyle, 3rd Earl of Burlington and 4th Earl of Cork with Swift's open contempt for this wealthiest and most ostentatious of absentee landowners (109–11).

26 See for instance his letter to Pope in 1721 in *The Correspondence of Jonathan Swift*, II.372.

27 Although the Protestants had become more secure due to the Penal Laws that barred Catholics from office and property ownership, they grew increasingly resentful of the economic servitude legislated through the Navigation Acts (1660–3), the Cattle Act (1666), and the Woolen Act (1699).

28 Beckett's observation, I think, speaks to Said's warning that we not "ally Swift too closely with the real holders of those basically reactionary values, the great landed aristocracy, the established church, the imperial monarchy... Swift himself was not a property owner" (*The World* 83). Moreover, not that one has to own property in order to defend Munodi-like landowners, but Fabricant notes that Swift had his own tenants and agents, both of whom gave him financial headaches (101).

29 The pioneer statistician Gregory King estimated that in 1700 half the families in England lived below the subsistence level.

30 Here I am referring to Defoe's interest in the criminal underworld of London (Moll Flanders, Jonathan Wild), pirates and adventurers (Raleigh, Captain Singleton, Crusoe, Colonel Jack), as well as his own precarious position as both insider (spy, government hack) and outsider (dissenter, debtor).

31 Schonhorn reinforces this point when he writes that Defoe's belief in patriarchal power "derives from institution and education, not from biology" and that "Defoe seems to insist on the non-filial, artificial origins of government" (*Defoe's Politics* 160).

32 Despite the euphoria of the British press and public, reports about Georgia's failure filtered back to Britain. Likened to living under a Turkish or Russian government, the colonists were denied rum, slaves, and rights, so that a contemporary account avers that "for some time there were more imprisonments, whippings, etc., of white people, in that *colony of liberty*, than in all British America besides" (quoted in Greene *Imperatives* 124).

33 See E. P. Thompson *Whigs and Hunters*.

34 The "new rural artillery" included spring guns and man-traps, the latter with names such as "The Body-squeezer" or "The Crusher" (Gilmour *Riots, Risings and Revolution* 199). See also Jill Franklin's "The Liberty of the Park" in Samuel *National Fictions* 152–4.

35 Defoe does give us a standard picturesque view of London when looking back toward the capital from Bushy-Heath (*Tour* 343).

36 The switch from bird's-eye panoramas to views at the ground level, especially after 1750 (Franklin in Samuel *National Fictions* 144), mirror that from authority to the rational "sight" promoted as the "public sphere."

37 For more on the significance of the coffee houses and the production of bourgeois civil society see Stallybrass and White *Politics and Poetics* 94–100.

38 Gilmour estimates that 20,000 people were "regularly engaged in smuggling in Sussex and Kent alone" (*Riots, Risings and Revolution* 163). Linebaugh states that "The tension between the commercial society represented by turnpikes and the subsistence economy associated with waste, weald and common was profound, and could upon occasion burst forth in mass direct action, as occurred in the Hereford Turnpike Riot of 1736 (206).

39 For more on Defoe's views on magistracy see Schonhorn *Defoe's Politics*. On majesty, see Hay, "Property, Authority and the Criminal Law" 26–39.

40 The story first appeared in Richard Ligon's *A True and Exact History of the Island of Barbadoes* in 1673. It was popularized to become "one of the most often repeated and most popular narratives of the eighteenth century" (Hulme *Colonial Encounters* 227) by Richard Steele's version in *The Spectator* (No. 11, Tuesday 13 March) in 1711. Goethe planned a play in 1766, and the tale only began to fade away after 1810. Earlier, Aphra Behn's *Oroonoko*, via Thomas Southerne's play of the same title in 1695, was also extremely popular in eighteenth-century England.

1745 AND THE SYSTEMATIZING OF THE YAHOO

1 Johnson states at one point, "These countries have never been measured, and the computation by miles is negligent and arbitrary" (*Journey* 75).

2 On contractual labor see Nash *Urban Crucible* 164; on population growth see Greene *Intellectual Construction* 83–4.

3 For more on Culloden see Prebble *Culloden*.
4 See Prebble *Mutiny: Highland Regiments in Revolt, 1743–1804*.
5 See Speck *The Butcher: The Duke of Cumberland and the Suppression of the '45*.
6 Jennings also directly connects the development of colonial relations in North America with Culloden and its aftermath. My own thinking was both confirmed and greatly advanced by his work in this area.
7 Another veteran was Brigadier General John Forbes who was sent to take Fort Duquesne in 1758.
8 Another good example would be Balthasar Nebot's Hartwell House Series done in the 1730s.
9 Also like Oroonoko, the young Numidian prince, Juba, is at heart a European: he has a "*Roman* Soul" (Addison *Cato* 73).
10 See Kramnick *Republicanism and Bourgeois Radicalism*.
11 For more on this spatial fix see Harvey *Limits to Capital* 431–8, 442–5.
12 The secession of the individual as opposed to serving the corporate whole was not of course new, as Thomas Morton amply testifies and William Bradford recognized, but it only became a dominant ideology at the time of American independence.
13 Slotkin outlines three basic types of personal narratives, that of conversion, of captivity, and of personal triumph (*Regeneration through Violence* 279). He states that captivity narratives waned "as the demand for an image of emergent American power and dominance grew" (296).

CONCLUSION: THE POLITICS OF SPACE

1 See Stone *Crisis of the Aristocracy* 339.
2 Here I am appropriating and widening the meaning of Foucault's phrase; see *Madness and Civilization* 38–65.
3 For a perceptive reading of this painting see Colley *Forging the Nation*, 56–60.

Works cited

Addison, Joseph. *Cato. A Tragedy*. 13th edn. London, 1733.

Ahmad, Aijaz. *In Theory: Classes, Nations, Literatures*. London: Verso, 1992.

Anderson, Benedict. *Imagined Communities: Reflections on the Origin and Spread of Nationalism*. London: Verso, 1983.

Andrade, Susan Z. "White Skin, Black Masks: Colonialism and the Sexual Politics of *Oroonoko*." *Cultural Critique* 27 (Spring 1994): 189–214.

Andrews, J. H. *Plantation Acres: an Historical Study of the Irish Land Surveyor and his Maps*. Omagh: Ulster Historical Foundation, 1985.

Andrews, K. R. *Trade, Plunder and Settlement: Maritime Enterprise and the Genesis of the British Empire, 1480–1630*. Cambridge University Press, 1984.

Andrews, K. R., N. P. Canny and P. E. H. Hair, eds. *The Westward Enterprise: English Activities in Ireland, the Atlantic, and America, 1480–1650*. Detroit, MI: Wayne State University Press, 1979.

Andrews, Malcolm. *The Search for the Picturesque: Landscape Aesthetics and Tourism in Britain, 1760–1800*. Stanford, CA: Stanford University Press, 1982.

Appleby, Joyce Oldham. *Economic Thought and Ideology in Seventeenth-Century England*. Princeton, NJ: Princeton University Press, 1978.

Arneil, Barbara. *John Locke and America: the Defence of English Colonialism*. Oxford: Clarendon, 1996.

Azim, Firdous. *The Colonial Rise of the Novel*. London: Routledge, 1993.

Bacon, Francis. *The Works of Francis Bacon*. Vol. 2. Philadelphia, PA: 1851.

The Essays. Ed. John Pitcher. Harmondsworth: Penguin Classics, 1985.

Bailyn, Bernard. *The Peopling of British North America: An Introduction*. New York, NY: Vintage, 1988.

Baker, Emerson W., Edwin A. Churchill, Richard S. D'Abate, Kristine L. Jones, Victor A. Konrad, and Harald E. L. Prins, eds. *American Beginnings: Exploration, Culture, and Cartography in the Land of Norumbega*. Lincoln, NE: University of Nebraska Press, 1994.

Barnaby, Andrew. "'Another Rome in the West?' Milton and the Imperial Republic, 1654–1670." *Milton Studies* 30. Ed. Albert C. Labriola. Pittsburgh, PA: University of Pennsylvania, 1993.

Barnard, T. C. *Cromwellian Ireland: English Government and Reform in Ireland, 1649–60*. Oxford University Press, 1975.

Beaud, Michel. *A History of Capitalism, 1500–1980*. New York, NY: Monthly Review Press, 1983.

Beckett, Samuel. *Waiting for Godot: a Tragicomedy in Two Acts*. New York, NY: Grove Weidenfeld, 1982.

Beckles, Hilary. *Black Rebellion in Barbados: the Struggle Against Slavery, 1627–1838*. Bridgetown, Barbados: Carib Research and Pub. Inc., 1987.

Behn, Aphra. *Oroonoko or, The Royal Slave*. New York, NY: Norton, 1973.

Beier, A. L. and Roger Finlay, eds. *London 1500–1700: the Making of the Metropolis*. London: Longman, 1986.

Belsey, Catherine. *John Milton: Language, Gender, Power*. London: Basil Blackwell, 1988.

Bender, John. *Imagining the Penitentiary: Fiction and the Architecture of Mind in Eighteenth-Century England*. Chicago, IL: University of Chicago Press, 1987.

Benevolo, Leonardo. *The European City*. Trans. Carl Ipsen. Oxford: Basil Blackwell, 1995.

Berkeley, George. *The Works of George Berkeley*. Vol. 4. Ed. A. C. Fraser. Oxford: Clarendon, 1901.

Blackburn, Robin. *The Making of New World Slavery: from the Baroque to the Modern, 1492–1800*. London: Verso, 1997.

Blaut, J. M. *The Colonizer's Model of the World: Geographical Diffusion and Eurocentric History*. London: Guilford Press, 1993.

Blunt, Alison, *Travel, Gender, and Imperialism: Mary Kingsley and West Africa*. London: Guilford Press, 1994.

Blunt, Alison and Gillian Rose, eds. *Writing Women and Space: Colonial and Postcolonial Geographies*. New York, NY: Guilford Press, 1994.

Bondi, Liz. "Locating Identity Politics." *Place and the Politics of Identity*. Eds. Michael Keith and Steve Pile. London: Routledge, 1993.

Bottingheimer, Karl S. *English Money and Irish Land: the 'Adventurers' in the Cromwellian Settlement of Ireland*. Oxford: Clarendon, 1971.

Bradford, William. *Of Plymouth Plantation, 1620–1647*. New York, NY: Modern Library, 1981.

Bradshaw, Brendan, Andrew Hadfield, and Willy Maley, eds. *Representing Ireland: Literature and the Origins of Conflict, 1534–1660*. Cambridge University Press, 1993.

Brady, Ciaran. "The Road to the *View*: on the Decline of Reform Thought in Tudor Ireland." In *Spenser and Ireland: an Interdisciplinary Perspective*. Ed. Patricia Coughlan. Cork: Cork University Press, 1989.

Brady, Ciaran and Raymond Gillespie, eds. *Natives and Newcomers: Essays on the Making of Irish Colonial Society, 1534–1641*. Dublin: Irish Academic Press, 1986.

Brantlinger, Patrick. *Rule of Darkness: British Literature and Imperialism, 1830–1914*. Ithaca, NY: Cornell University Press, 1988.

Fictions of State: Culture and Credit in Britain, 1694–1994. Ithaca, NY: Cornell University Press, 1996.

Braudel, Fernand. *The Perspective of the World*. Vol. 3. *Civilization and Capitalism,*

Fifteenth to Eighteenth Century. Trans. Siân Reynolds. New York, NY: Harper and Row, 1979.

Breen, John. "The Empirical Eye: Edmund Spenser's *A View of The Present State of Ireland*." *The Irish Review* 16 (Aut/Winter 1994): 44–52.

Breen, T. H. *Puritans and Adventurers: Changes and Persistence in Early America*. Oxford University Press, 1980.

Brenner, Robert. *Merchants and Revolution: Commerical Change, Political Conflict, and London's Overseas Traders, 1550–1653*. Cambridge University Press, 1993.

Brereton, John. *A Briefe and True Relation of the Discoveries of the North Part of Virginia . . . made in this present year, 1602*. Readex Microprint, c. 1966.

Brewer, John. *The Sinews of Power: War, Money and the English State, 1688–1783*. Cambridge, MA: Harvard University Press, 1990.

Bridenbaugh, Carl and Roberta Bridenbaugh. *No Peace Beyond the Line: the English in the Caribbean, 1624–1690*. Oxford University Press, 1972.

Brown, Cedric C. *John Milton's Aristocratic Entertainments*. Cambridge University Press, 1985.

Brown, John. *An Estimate of the Manners and Principles of Times*. 2nd edition. London: 1757.

Brown, Laura. *Ends of Empire: Women and Ideology in Early Eighteenth-Century English Literature*. Ithaca, NY: Cornell University Press, 1993.

Brown, Tom. *Amusements Serious and Comical, Calculated for the Meridian of London*. Ed. Arthur L. Hayward. New York, NY: Dodd, Mead and Co., 1927.

Bunyan, John. *The Holy War*. Ed. James F. Forrest. New York, NY: New York University Press, 1967.

Miscellaneous Works. Vol. 2. Oxford University Press, 1976–.

Burke, Edmund. *The Works of the Right Honorouble Edmund Burke*. Vol 6. London: 1881.

Byrd, Max. *London Transformed: Images of the City in the Eighteenth Century*. New Haven, CT: Yale University Press, 1978.

Byrd, William. *Histories of the Dividing Line betwixt Virginia and North Carolina*. 1728. New York, NY: Dover, 1967.

Cabeza de Vaca, Alvar Nuñez. *Adventures in the Unknown Interior of America*. Trans. and ed. Cyclone Covey. Albuquerque, NM: University of New Mexico Press, 1986.

Calhoun, Craig, ed. *Habermas and the Public Sphere*. Cambridge, MA: MIT Press, 1992.

Canny, Nicholas. *The Elizabethan Conquest of Ireland: A Pattern Established, 1565–76*. New York, NY: Barnes, 1976.

Kingdom and Colony: Ireland in the Atlantic World, 1560–1800. Baltimore, MD: Johns Hopkins University Press, 1988.

"Spenser's Irish Crisis: Humanism and Experience in the 1590s" *Past and Present* 120 (1988): 201–209.

From Reformation to Restoration: Ireland 1534–1660, Dublin: Helicon Ltd., 1987.

Canny, Nicholas, ed. *The Origins of Empire*. Vol. 1. *The Oxford History of the British Empire*. Oxford University Press, 1998.

266 *Works cited*

Carew, Thomas. *The Poems of Thomas Carew*. Ed. Rhodes Dunlap. Oxford: Clarendon, 1949.

Carter, Paul. *The Road to Botany Bay: an Essay in Spatial History*. London: Faber, 1987.

The Lie of the Land. London: Faber, 1996.

Cavanagh, Shelia T. *Wanton Eyes and Chaste Desires: Female Sexuality in* The Faerie Queene. Bloomington, IN: Indiana University Press, 1994.

Cawley, Robert Ralston. *Milton and the Literature of Travel*. Princeton, NJ: Princeton University Press, 1951.

Chambers, Douglas. *The Reinvention of the World: English Writing 1650–1750*. London: Arnold, 1996.

Clark, Peter and Paul Slack. *English Towns in Transition, 1550–1700*. Oxford University Press, 1976.

Cobbett, William. *Rural Rides*. Ed. George Woodcock. Harmondsworth: Penguin, 1985.

Colley, Linda. *Britons: Forging the Nation, 1707–1837*. New Haven, CT: Yale University Press, 1992.

Corfield, P. J. *The Impact of English Towns 1700–1800*. Oxford University Press, 1982.

Cormack, Lesley B. "'Good Fences Make Good Neighbors': Geography as Self-Definition in Early Modern England." *ISIS* 82 (1991): 639–661.

Charting an Empire: Geography at the English University, 1580–1620. Chicago, IL: University of Chicago Press, 1998.

Corns, Thomas N. "Milton's *Observations upon the Articles of Peace*: Ireland under English eyes." In *Politics, Poetics, and Hermeneutics in Milton's Prose*. Eds. D. Lowenstein and James Grantham Turner. Cambridge University Press, 1990.

Coughlan, Patricia, ed. *Spenser and Ireland: an Interdisciplinary Perspective*. Cork: Cork University Press, 1989.

Cramb, J. A. *The Origins and Destiny of Imperial Britain*. Toronto: Musson Book Co. Ltd., 1915.

Cressy, David. *Coming Over: Migration and Communication Between England and New England in the Seventeenth Century*. Cambridge University Press, 1987.

Crèvecoeur, J. Hector St. John de. *Letters From An American Farmer and Sketches of Eighteenth-Century America*. Ed. Albert E. Stone. Harmondsworth: Penguin Classics, 1986.

Cronon, William. *Changes in the Land: Indians, Colonists, and the Ecology of New England*. New York, NY: Hill and Wang, 1983.

Cronon, William, George Miles and Jay Gitlin, eds. *Under an open Sky: Rethinking America's Western Past*. New York, NY: Norton, 1992.

Cullen, Patrick and Thomas P. Roche, eds. *Spenser Studies: a Renaissance Poetry Annual* 12. New York, NY: AMS Press, 1998.

Dampier, William. *A New Voyage Round the World*. London: 1717.

A Voyage to New Holland, etc. in the Year 1699. London: 1703. Gloucester: Alan Sutton, 1981.

Davies, John. *A Discoverie of the True Causes Why Ireland Was Never Entirely Subdued.* London: 1612.

Deane, Seamus. *A Short History of Irish Literature.* Notre Dame, IN: University of Notre Dame Press, 1986.

De Grazia, Margreta, Maureen Quilligan and Peter Stallybrass, eds. *Subject and Object in Renaissance Culture.* Cambridge University Press, 1996.

De la Campa, Roman, E. Ann Kaplan and Michael Sprinker, eds. *Late Imperial Culture.* London: Verso, 1995.

De Vries, Jan. *Economy of Europe in an Age of Crisis 1600–1750.* Cambridge University Press, 1976.

Dee, John. *Preface to the English Euclid.* London: 1570.
General and Rare Memorials Pertayning to the Perfect Arte of Navigation. London: 1577.

Defoe, Daniel. *A Plan of the English Commerce.* Oxford: Basil Blackwell, 1927.
The Best of Defoe's Review: *an Anthology.* Compiled and edited by William L. Payne. New York, NY: Columbia University Press, 1951.
A Tour Through the Whole Island of Great Britain. Abridged and edited by Pat Rogers. Harmondsworth: Penguin, 1971.
Captain Singleton. Ed. Shiv K. Kumar. Oxford University Press, 1973.
Robinson Crusoe. Ed. Donald J. Crowley. Oxford University Press, 1981.
A Journal of the Plague Year. Eds. Anthony Burgess and Christopher Bristow. London: Penguin, 1986.
Moll Flanders. Ed. David Blewett. London: Penguin, 1989.
The True-Born Englishman and Other Writings. Eds. P. N. Furnbank and W. R. Owens. Harmondsworth: Penguin, 1997.

Denham, John. "Cooper's Hill." *The Penguin Book of Renaissance Verse, 1509–1659.* Ed. H. R. Woudhuysen. Harmondsworth: Penguin, 1992.

Derounian-Stodola, Kathryn Zabelle and James Arthur Levernier. *The Indian Captivity Narrative, 1550–1900.* New York, NY: Twayne, 1993.

Dirlik, Arif. "The Postcolonial Aura: Third World Criticism in the Age of Global Capitalism." *Critical Inquiry* 20 (Winter 1994): 328–56.

Donne, John. *John Donne.* Ed. John Carey. Oxford University Press, 1990.

Drayton, Michael. *Works.* Vols. 3 and 4. Ed. J. William Hebel. Oxford: Basil Blackwell, 1933–.

Dryden, John. *Dryden: a Selection.* Ed. John Conaghan. London: Methuen, 1978.

Duden, Barbara. *The Woman beneath the Skin.* Cambridge, MA: Harvard University Press, 1991.

Dudley, Edward and Maximillian E. Novack, eds. *The Wild Man Within: An Image in Western Thought from the Renaissance to Romanticism.* Pittsburgh, PA: University of Pittsburgh Press, 1972.

Dunn, Richard S. *Sugar and Slaves: the Rise of the Planter Class in the English West Indies, 1624–1713.* Chapel Hill, NC: University of North Carolina Press, 1972.

Dunn, Richard S. and Mary Maples Dunn, eds. *The World of William Penn.* Philadelphia, PA: University of Pennsylvania Press, 1986.

Eagleton, Terry. *The Function of Criticism: from the Spectator to Post-Structuralism.*

London: Verso, 1984.

Heathcliff and the Great Hunger: Studies in Irish Culture. London: Verso, 1995.

Eburne, Richard. *A Plain Pathway to Plantations.* 1624. Ed. L. B. Wright. New York, NY: Cornell University Press, 1962.

Evans, J. Martin. *Milton's Imperial Epic: Paradise Lost and the Discourse of Colonialism.* Ithaca, NY: Cornell University Press, 1996.

Evelyn, John. *London Revived: Consideration for its Rebuilding in 1666.* Ed. E. S. De Beer. Oxford: Clarendon, 1938.

Everett, Nigel. *The Tory View of Landscape.* New Haven, CT: Yale University Press, 1994

Fabricant, Carole. *Swift's Landscape.* Baltimore, MD: Johns Hopkins University Press, 1982.

Fanon, Frantz. *The Wretched of the Earth.* Trans. Constance Farrington. New York, NY: Grove Weidenfeld, 1968.

Ferguson, Margaret, "News from the New World: Miscegenous Romance in Aphra Behn's *Oroonoko* and *The Widow Ranter*." *The Production of English Renaissance Culture.* Eds. David Lee Miller, Sharon O'Dair, and Harold Weber. Ithaca, NY: Cornell University Press, 1994.

Ferguson, Moira. *Subject to Others: British Women Writers and Colonial Slavery, 1670–1834.* New York, NY: Routledge, 1992.

Ferguson, Oliver Watkins. *Jonathan Swift and Ireland.* Urbana, IL: University of Illinois Press, 1962.

Fielding, Henry. *The Complete Works of Henry Fielding.* Vol. 13. New York, NY: Croscup and Sterling Co., 1902.

Tom Jones. Ed. R. P. C. Mutter. Harmondsworth: Penguin, 1985.

The Covent-Garden Journal and a Plan of the Universal Register-Office. Ed. Bertrand A. Goldgar. Oxford: Clarendon, 1988.

Fitter, Chris. *Poetry, Space, Landscape: Toward a New Theory.* Cambridge University Press, 1995.

Flaubert, Gustave. *Sentimental Education.* Harmondsworth: Penguin, 1987.

Fogarty, Anne, ed. *Spenser in Ireland: The Faerie Queene, 1596–1996.* Dublin: The Irish University Review 26.2, 1996.

Foucault, Michel. *Madness and Civilization.* Trans. Richard Howard. New York, NY: Random Press, 1965.

Discipline and Punish: The Birth of the Prison. New York, NY: Vintage Books, 1979.

Power/Knowledge: Selected Interviews and Other Writings, 1972–1977. New York, NY: Pantheon, 1980.

"Panopticism." In *The Foucault Reader.* Ed. Paul Rainbow. New York, NY: Pantheon, 1984.

Fox, Celina, ed. *London–World City, 1800–1840.* New Haven, CT: Yale University Press, 1992.

Gay, John. *Trivia: Or, The Art of Walking the Streets of London.* London: 1716.

Gillies, John. *Shakespeare and the Geography of Difference.* Cambridge University Press, 1994.

Gilmour, Ian. *Riot, Risings and Revolution: Governance and Violence in Eighteenth-Century England*. London: Pimlico, 1993.

Gikandi, Simon. *Maps of Englishness: Writing Identity in the Culture of Colonialism*. New York, NY: Columbia University Press, 1997.

Girouard, Mark. *Cities and People*. New Haven, CT: Yale University Press, 1985.

Greenblatt, Stephen. *Renaissance Self-Fashioning: from More to Shakespeare*. Chicago, IL: University of Chicago Press, 1980.

Greene, Jack P. *Imperatives, Behaviors and Identities: Essays in Early American Cultural History*. Charlottesville, VA: University Press of Virginia, 1992.

    The Intellectual Construction of America: Exceptionalism and Identity from 1492 to 1800. Chapel Hill, NC: University of North Carolina Press, 1993.

Greene, Jack P. and J. R. Pole, eds. *The Blackwell Encyclopedia of the American Revolution*. Oxford: Blackwell, 1991.

Gregory, Derek. *Geographical Imaginations*. Oxford: Blackwell, 1994.

Greville, Fulke. *Life of Sir Philip Sidney*. 1652. Oxford: Clarendon, 1907.

Grove, Richard H. *Green Imperialism: Colonial Expansion, Tropical Island Edens and the Origins of Environmentalism, 1600–1860*. Cambridge University Press, 1995.

Gunn, Giles, ed. *Early American Writing*. Harmondsworth: Penguin, 1994.

Gwynn, John. *The Art of Architecture: a Poem, In Imitation of Horace's Art of Poetry*. 1742. Los Angeles, CA: UCLA, 1970.

Habermas, Jürgen. *The Structural Transformation of the Public Sphere: An Inquiry into a Category of Bourgeois Society*. Cambridge University Press, 1962.

Hadfield, Andrew. *Spenser's Irish Experience: Wilde Fruit and Salvage Soyl*. Oxford: Clarendon, 1997.

Hakluyt, Richard. *The Principal Navigations, Voyages, Traffiques and Discoveries of the English Nation*. Vol.1. Glasgow: James MacLehose and Sons, 1903.

Hamilton, Roberta. *The Liberation of Women: a Study of Patriarchy and Capitalism*. London: Allen and Unwin, 1978.

Hamlin, William M. *The Image of America in Montaigne, Spenser, and Shakespeare: Renaissance Ethnography and Literary Reflection*. New York, NY: St. Martin's Press, 1995.

Haraway, Donna J. *Simians, Cyborgs, and Women: the Reinvention of Nature*. New York, NY: Routledge, 1991.

Harrington, James. *The Commonwealth of Oceana*. In *The Political Works of James Harrington*. Ed. J. G. A. Pocock. Cambridge University Press, 1977.

Harriot, Thomas. *A Briefe and True Report of the New Found Land of Virginia*. 1590. New York, NY: Dover, 1972

Harvey, David. *The Limits to Capital*. Chicago, IL: University of Chicago Press, 1982.

    The Urban Experience. Baltimore, MD: Johns Hopkins University Press, 1989.

    Justice, Nature, and the Geography of Difference. Oxford: Blackwell, 1996.

Hawes, Clement. "Three Times Round the Globe: Gulliver and Colonial Discourse." *Cultural Critique* (Spring 1991): 187–214.

Hay, Douglas, Peter Linebaugh and E. P. Thompson, eds. *Albion's Fatal Tree*.

London: Allen Lane, 1975.

Hayward, Eliza. *The Female Spectator*. Book 1. London: 1744.

Helgerson, Richard. *Forms of Nationhood: the Elizabethan Writing of England*. Chicago, IL: University of Chicago Press, 1992.

Hendricks, Margo and Patricia Parker, eds. *Women, "Race," and Writing in the Early Modern Period*. New York, NY: Routledge, 1994.

Herrick, Robert. *Hesperides*. London: George Newnes, 1905.

Heward, Edmund. *Matthew Hale*. London: Robert Hale, 1972.

Heylyn, Peter. *Microcosmus or A Little Description of the Great World*. London: 1621.

Higgins, Ian. *Swift's Politics: a Study in Disaffection*. Cambridge University Press, 1994.

Higginson, Francis. *New-Englands Plantation (or A Short and True Description of the Commodities and Discommodities of that Countrey)*. 1630. *Massachusettes Historical Society*. Vol. 62. Boston, MA: MHS, 1930.

Highely, Chris. *Shakespeare, Spenser and the Crisis in Ireland*. Cambridge University Press, 1997.

Hill, Christopher. *Intellectual Origins of the English Revolution Revisited*. Oxford: Clarendon, 1997.

　Reformation to Industrial Revolution. London: Weidenfeld and Nicholson, 1967; Harmondsworth: Penguin Books, 1992.

　Milton and the English Revolution. New York, NY: Viking, 1977.

　The Century of Revolution, 1603–1714. New York, NY: Norton, 1980.

　A Nation of Change and Novelty: Radical Politics, Religion and Literature in Seventeenth-Century England. London: Routledge, 1990.

　The English Bible and the Seventeenth-Century Revolution. London: Allen Lane, 1993.

Hobbes, Thomas. *Leviathan*. Ed. C. B. MacPherson. Harmondsworth: Penguin, 1988.

Hobsbawm, E. H. "The General Crisis of the European Economy in the Seventeenth Century." In *Crisis in Europe, 1560–1660*. Ed. Trevor Aston. New York, NY: Basic Books, 1965.

Hulme, Peter. *Colonial Encounters: Europe and the Native Caribbean, 1492–1797*. London: Routledge, 1992.

Hunt, John Dixon and Peter Willis, eds. *The Genius of the Place: the English Landscape Garden, 1620–1820*. Cambridge, MA: The MIT Press, 1993.

Innes, Stephen. *Labor in a New Land: Economy and Society in Seventeenth-Century Springfield*. Princeton, NJ: Princeton University Press, 1983.

　ed. *Work and Labor in Early America*. Chapel Hill, NC: University of North Carolina Press, 1988.

　Creating the Commonwealth: the Economic Culture of Puritan New England. New York, NY: Norton, 1995.

Jacobs, Jane M. *Edge of Empire: Postcolonialism and the City*. London: Routledge, 1996.

Jameson, Fredric. "Modernism and Imperialism." In *Nationalism, Colonialism, and Literature*. Terry Eagleton, Fredric Jameson, and Edward W. Said.

Minneapolis, MN: University of Minnesota Press, 1990.

Jehlen, Myra and Michael Warner, eds. *The English Literatures of America, 1500–1800*. London: Routledge, 1997.

Jennings, Francis. *The Invasion of America: Indians, Colonialism, and the Cant of Conquest*. New York, NY: Norton, 1976.

Empire of Fortune: Crowns, Colonies and Tribes in the Seven Years War in America. New York, NY: Norton, 1988.

Johnson, Edward. *Johnson's Wonder-Working Providence, 1628–1651*. Ed. J. Franklin Jameson. New York, NY: Scribners, 1910.

Johnson, Samuel. *Johnson's Dictionary: a Modern Selection*. Eds. E. L. McAdam and George Milne. London: Cassell, 1995.

Johnson, Samuel and James Boswell. *A Journey to the Western Islands of Scotland* and *The Journal of a Tour to the Hebrides*. Ed. Peter Levi. Harmondsworth: Penguin, 1984.

Jones, Erasmus. *A Trip through London*. London: 1782.

Jonson, Ben. *The Complete Poems*. Ed. George Parfitt. Harmondsworth: Penguin, 1975.

Josselyn, John. *John Josselyn, Colonial Traveler*. Ed. Paul J. Lindholdt. Hanover, NH: University Press of New England, 1988.

Kames, Lord (Henry Home). *Elements of Criticism*. 1762. New York, NY: 1838.

Kaplan, Amy and Donald E. Pease, eds. *Cultures of United States Imperialism*. Durham, NC: Duke University Press, 1993.

Kearny, Hugh. *The British Isles: A History of Four Nations*. Cambridge University Press, 1989.

Kendrick, Christopher. "Milton and Sexuality: a Symptomatic Reading of *Comus*." In Nyquist, Mary and Margaret W. Ferguson, eds. *Re-Membering Milton: Essays on the Texts and Traditions*. London: Methuen, 1988.

Kenny, Virginia C. *The Country-House Ethos in English Literature, 1688–1750: Themes of Personal Retreat and National Expansion*. Sussex: The Harvester Press; New York, NY: St. Martin's Press, 1984.

Kiernan, V. J. "Milton in Heaven." *Reviving the English Revolution*. Eds. Geoff Eley and William Hunt. London: Verso, 1988.

Eight Tragedies of Shakespeare. London: Verso, 1996.

Knapp, Jeffrey. *An Empire Nowhere: England, America, and Literature from* Utopia *to* The Tempest. Berkeley, CA: University of California Press, 1992.

Kolodny, Annette. *The Lay of the Land: Metaphor as Experience and History in American Life and Letters*. Chapel Hill, NC: University of North Carolina Press, 1975.

The Land Before Her: Fantasy and Experience of the American Frontier, 1630–1860. Chapel Hill, NC: University of North Carolina Press, 1984.

Kramnick, Isaac. *Republicanism and Bourgeois Radicalism: Political Ideology in Late Eighteenth-Century England and America*. Ithaca, NY: Cornell University Press, 1990.

Kriedte, Peter. *Peasants, Landlords and Merchant Capitalists: Europe and the World Economy, 1500–1800*. Cambridge University Press, 1983.

Kruft, Hanno-Walter. *A History of Architectural Theory from Vitruvius to the Present.* London: Zwemmer, 1994.

Kupperman, Karen Ordahl. *Providence Island 1630–1641: the Other Puritan Colony.* Cambridge University Press, 1993.

Kupperman, Karen Ordahl, ed. *America in European Consciousness, 1493–1750.* Chapel Hill, NC: University of North Carolina Press, 1995.

Lamb, Jonathan, ed. *Eighteenth-Century Life.* 18.3 (Nov. 1994).

Lang, James. *Conquest and Commerce: Spain and England in the Americas.* New York, NY: Academic Press, 1975.

Langford, Paul. *A Polite and Commercial People: England, 1727–1783.* Oxford University Press, 1992.

Lefebvre, Henri. *The Production of Space.* Trans. Donald Nicholson-Smith. Oxford: Basil Blackwell, 1991.

Ligon, Richard. *A True and Exact History of the Island of Barbadoes.* 1673. London: Frank Cass and Co. Ltd., 1970.

Lillo, George. *The London Merchant.* Ed. A. W. Ward. London: Heath, 1906.

Linebaugh, Peter. "All the Atlantic Mountains Shook." In *Reviving the English Revolution.* Eds. Geoff Eley and William Hunt. London: Verso, 1988.
   The London Hanged: Crime and Civil Society in the Eighteenth Century. London: Penguin, 1991.

Lipking, Lawrence. "The Genius of the Shore: Lycidas, Adamastor, and the Poetics of Nationalism." *PMLA* 2.111 (March 1996).

Livingstone, David N. *The Geographical Tradition: Episodes in the History of a Contested Enterprise.* Oxford: Basil Blackwell, 1992.

Locke, John. *Two Treatises of Government.* Ed. Peter Laslett. Cambridge University Press, 1989.

MacCarthy-Morrogh, Michael. *The Munster Plantation: English Migration to Southern Ireland 1583–1641.* Oxford: Clarendon Press, 1986.

Makdisi, Saree. *Romantic Imperialism: Universal Empire and the Culture of Modernity.* Cambridge University Press, 1998.

Maley, Willy. *Salvaging Spenser: Colonialism, Culture and Identity.* London: Macmillan, 1997.

Mandeville, Bernard. *The Fable of the Bees.* 1714. Ed. Phillip Harth. London: Penguin, 1989.

Marshall, P. J., ed. *The Eighteenth Century.* Vol. 2. *The Oxford History of the British Empire.* Oxford University Press, 1998.

Martin, John Fredrick. *Profits in the Wilderness: Entrepreneurship and the Founding of New England Towns in the Seventeenth Century.* Chapel Hill, NC: University of North Carolina Press, 1991.

Marvell, Andrew. *The Complete Poems.* Ed. Elizabeth Story Donno. Harmondsworth: Penguin Classics, 1985.

Marx, Karl. *Capital: A Critique of Political Economy.* Ed. Frederick Engels. Vol. 1. New York, NY: International Pub., 1967.
   Manifesto of the Communist Party, New York, NY: International Pub., 1983.

Marx, Karl and Fredrick Engels. *The German Ideology*. Ed. C. J. Arthur. New York, NY: International Pub., 1989.

Massey, Doreen. *Space, Place, and Gender*. Minneapolis, MN: University of Minnesota Press, 1994.

Mather, Cotton. *Decennium Luctuosum*. Boston, MA: B. Green and J. Allen, for Samuel Phillips, 1699.

Magnalia Christi Americana. 1702. Ed. K. B. Murdock. Cambridge, MA: Belknap Press, 1977.

McClung, William A. *The Country House in English Renaissance Poetry*. Berkeley, CA: University of California Press, 1977.

McColley, Diane Kelsey. *Milton's Eve*. Urbana, IL: University of Illinois Press, 1983.

McLeod, Bruce E. J. "The 'Lordly eye': Milton and the Strategic Geography of Empire." *Milton and the Imperial Vision*. Eds. Balachandra Rajan and Elizabeth Sauer. Pittsburgh, PA: Duquesne University Press, 1999.

McVeagh, John, ed. *All Before Them: English Literature and the Wider World*. Vol. 1: *1660–1780*. London: The Ashfield Press, 1990.

Meinig, D. W. *Atlantic America, 1492–1800*. Vol. 1: *The Shaping of America: a Geographical Perspective on 500 Years of History*. 2 vols. New Haven, CT: Yale University Press, 1986.

Merchant, Carolyn. *Ecological Revolutions: Nature, Gender, and Science in New England*. Chapel Hill, NC: University of North Carolina Press, 1989.

Merians, Linda E. "What they are, who we are: Representations of the 'Hottentot' in Eighteenth-Century Britain." *Eighteenth-Century Life* 17 (1993): 14–39.

Mendyk, Stan A. E. *"Speculum Britanniae": Regional Study, Antiquarianism, Science in Britain to 1700*. University of Toronto Press, 1989.

Milton, John. *Complete Prose Works of John Milton*. Don M. Wolfe, ed. 8 vols. New Haven, CT: Yale University Press, 1953–62.

Paradise Lost. Ed. Merritt Y. Hughes. New York, NY: Macmillan, 1962.

Complete English Poems, Of Education, Areopagitica. Ed. Gordon Campbell. London: Everyman, 1993.

Mitchell, W. J. T., ed. *Landscape and Power*. Chicago, IL: University of Chicago Press, 1994.

Montaigne, Michel de. *The Essays: a Selection*. Ed. M. A. Screech. Harmondsworth: Penguin, 1993.

Moody, T. W. and W. E. Vaughan, eds. *A New History of Ireland*. Vol. 4. Oxford: Clarendon Press, 1986.

Morgan, Edmund S. *American Slavery, American Freedom: the Ordeal of Colonial Virginia*. New York, NY: Norton, 1975, 1995.

Morton, Thomas. *New English Canaan*. 1632. *Tracts*. Vol. 2. Ed. Peter Force. Washington, DC: 1838.

Moryson, Fynes. *The Itinerary of Fynes Moryson*. Vol. 4. Glasgow: James MacLehose and Sons, 1908.

Mourt's Relation. 1622. New York, NY: Corinth Books, 1963.

Nash, Gary. *The Urban Crucible: the Northern Seaports and the Origins of the American Revolution.* Cambridge, MA: Harvard University Press, 1986.

Nelson, Cary and Lawrence Grossberg, eds. *Marxism and the Interpretation of Culture.* Urbana, IL: University of Illinois Press, 1988.

Nerlich, Michael. *Ideology of Adventure: Studies in Modern Consciousness, 1100–1750.* Vol. 1. Minneapolis, MN: University of Minnesota Press, 1987.

Norbrook, David. *Poetry and Politics in the English Renaissance.* London: Routledge and Kegan Paul, 1984.

Nourse, Timothy. *Campania Faelix, or a Discourse of the Benefits and Improvements of Husbandry.* London: 1700.

Novak, Maximillian E. "Defoe and the Disordered City." *PMLA* 92 (1977): 241–252.

Nussbaum, Felicity. *Torrid Zones: Maternity, Sexuality, and Empire in Eighteenth-Century English Narratives.* Baltimore, MD: Johns Hopkins University Press, 1995.

Nussbaum, Felicity and Laura Brown, eds. *The New Eighteenth Century: Theory, Politics, English Literature.* London: Methuen, 1987.

Oldmixon, John. *The British Empire in America.* 2 vols. London: 1708.

Pagden, Anthony. *Lords of all the World: Ideologies of Empire in Spain, Britain and France c. 1500–1800.* New Haven, CT: Yale University Press, 1995.

Patterson, Annabel. *Pastoral and Ideology: Virgil to Valery.* Berkeley, CA: University of California Press, 1987.

Pearson, Keith Ansell, Benita Parry, and Judith Squires, eds. *Cultural Readings of Imperialism: Edward Said and the Gravity of History.* New York, NY: St. Martin's Press, 1997.

Penn, William. *The Papers of William Penn,* Vol. 1 [1644–1679]. Eds. Mary Maples Dunn and Richard S. Dunn. Philadelphia, PA: University of Pennsylvania Press, 1981.

Petty, William. *The Economic Writings of Sir William Petty.* Vol. 1. Ed. Charles Henry Hill. Cambridge University Press, 1899.

Pile, Steve and Nigel Thrift, eds. *Mapping the Subject: Geographies of Cultural Transformation.* London: Routledge, 1995.

Pittock, Murray G. H. *Inventing and Resisting Britain: Cultural Identities in Britain and Ireland, 1685–1789.* London: Macmillan, 1997.

Pocock, J. G. A. *Virtue, Commerce, and History: Essays in Political Thought and History, Chiefly in the Eighteenth Century.* Cambridge University Press, 1985.

Pope, Alexander. *Poetry and Prose of Alexander Pope.* Ed. Aubery Williams. Boston, MA: Houghton Mifflin, 1969.

Porter, Roy. *English Society in the Eighteenth Century.* London: Penguin, 1990.

Porter, Roy and G. S. Rousseau, eds. *Exoticism in the Enlightenment.* Manchester University Press, 1990.

Pratt, Mary Louise. *Imperial Eyes: Travel Writing and Transculturation.* New York, NY: Routledge, 1992.

Prebble, John. *Culloden.* Harmondsworth: Penguin Books, 1967.

Mutiny: Highland Regiments in Revolt, 1743–1804. New York, NY: Penguin, 1977.

Purchas, Samuel. *Hakluytus Posthumus or Purchas His Pilgrimes*. 20 vols. Glasgow: James Maclehose and Sons, 1905–1940.

Quilligan, Maureen. *Milton's Spenser: the Politics of Reading*. Ithaca, NY: Cornell University Press, 1983.

Quinn, D. B. *The Elizabethans and the Irish*. Ithaca, NY: Cornell University Press, 1966.

　　Set Fair for Roanoke: Voyages and Colonies, 1584–1606. Chapel Hill, NC: University of North Carolina Press, 1985.

Quinn, D. B., ed. *The Roanoke Voyages 1584–1590; Documents to Illustrate the English Voyages to North America under the Patent Granted to Walter Raleigh in 1584*. Vol. 1. London: Hakluyt Society, 1955.

Quinn, D. B. and A. N. Ryan. *England's Sea Empire, 1550–1642*. London: George Allen and Unwin, 1983.

Rabb, Theodore K. *Merchant and Gentry Investment in the Expansion of England, 1575–1630*. Cambridge, MA: Harvard University Press, 1967.

Rawson, Claude. *Order from Confusion Sprung*. London: George Allen and Unwin, 1985.

Rediker, Marcus. "Stout Hands and Fast Feet: the History and Culture of Working People in Early America." In *Reviving the English Revolution*. Eds. Geoff Eley and William Hunt. London: Verso, 1988.

　　Between the Devil and the Deep Blue Sea: Merchant Seamen, Pirates, and the Anglo-American Maritime World, 1700–1750. Cambridge University Press, 1989.

Reese, Trevor R., ed. *The Most Delightful Country of the Universe: Promotional Literature of the Colony of Georgia, 1717–1734*. Savannah, GA: The Beehive Press, 1972.

Reps, John W. *Town Planning in Frontier America*. Columbia, MO: University of Missouri Press, 1980.

Retamar, Roberto Fernandez. *Caliban and other Essays*. Minneapolis, MN: University of Minnesota Press, 1989.

Rich, Adrienne. *Blood, Bread, and Poetry: Selected Prose*. New York, NY: Norton, 1986, 1994.

Rogers, Woodes. *A Cruising Voyage Round the World*. 1712. London: Cassell and Co. Ltd., 1928.

Rose, Gillian. *Feminism and Geography: the Limits of Geographical Knowledge*. Minneapolis, MN: University of Minnesota Press, 1993.

Ross, Kristin. *The Emergence of Social Space: Rimbaud and the Paris Commune*. Minneapolis, MN: University of Minnesota Press, 1988.

Rowlandson, Mary. "The Sovereignty and Goodness of God." *Puritans Among the Indians: Accounts of Captivity and Redemption, 1676–1724*. Eds. Alden T. Vaughan and Edward W. Clark. Cambridge, MA: The Belknap Press of Harvard University Press, 1981.

Sack, Robert. *Human Territoriality: Its Theory and History*. Cambridge University Press, 1986.

Said, Edward W. *The World, the Text, and the Critic*. Cambridge, MA: Harvard University Press, 1983.

"Opponents, Audiences, Constituencies and Community." *The Anti-Aesthetic: Essays on Postmodern Culture*. Ed. Hal Foster. Port Townsend, WA: Bay Press, 1983.

Culture and Imperialism. New York, NY: Knopf, 1993.

Orientalism. New York, NY: Vintage, 1979, 1994.

Samuel, Raphael, ed. *National Fictions*. Vol. 3. *Patriotism: the Making and Unmaking of British National Identity*. 3 vols. London: Routledge, 1989.

Schaw, Janet. *Journal of a Lady of Quality; Being the Narrative of a Journey from Scotland to the West Indies, North Carolina, and Portugal, in the years 1774 to 1776*. Ed. Evangeline Walker Andrews. New Haven, CT: Yale University Press, 1922.

Schonhorn, Manuel. *Defoe's Politics: Parliament, Power, Kingship and* Robinson Crusoe. Cambridge University Press, 1991.

Scott, John. *Critical Essays on Some of the Poems of Several English Poets*. London: 1785.

Seidel, Michael. Robinson Crusoe: *Island Myths and the Novel*. Boston, MA: Twayne, 1991.

Shakespeare, William. *The Tempest*. Ed. Robert Langbaum. New York, NY: Signet, 1987.

Shammas, Carole. *The Pre-industrial Consumer in England and America*. Oxford: Clarendon, 1990.

Sheehan, Bernard W. *Savagism and Civility; Indians and Englishmen in Colonial Virginia*. Cambridge University Press, 1980.

Shepherd, Simon. *Spenser*. Atlantic Highlands, NJ: Humanities Press, 1989.

Sherman, William H. *John Dee: The Politics of Reading and Writing in the English Renaissance*. Amherst, MA: University of Massachusetts Press, 1995.

Sidney, Philip. *Miscellaneous Prose of Sir Philip Sidney*. Ed. Katherine Duncan-Jones and Jan Van Dorsten. Oxford: Clarendon, 1973.

Sir Philip Sidney: Selected Prose and Poetry. Ed. Robert Kimbrough. Madison, WI: University of Wisconsin Press, 1983.

Simpson, David. *Romanticism, Nationalism, and the Revolt Against Theory*. Chicago, IL: University of Chicago Press, 1993.

Skelton, R. A., ed. *The Theatre of the Whole World*. Amsterdam: Theatrum Orbis Terrarum, 1968.

Slack, Paul. *The Impact of Plague in Tudor and Stuart England*. London: Routledge and Kegan Paul, 1985.

Slotkin, Richard. *Regeneration through Violence: the Mythology of the American Frontier, 1600–1860*. Middletown, CT: Wesleyan University Press, 1973.

Slotkin, Richard and James K. Folsom, eds. *So Dreadful a Judgement: Puritan Responses to King Philip's War 1676–1677*. Middletown, CT: Wesleyan University Press, 1978.

Smith, Bernard. *Imagining the Pacific: In the Wake of the Cook Voyages*. New Haven, CT: Yale University Press, 1992.

Smith, Charlotte. *The Poems of Charlotte Smith*. Ed. Stuart Curran. Oxford University Press, 1993.

Smith, John. *The Complete Works of Captain John Smith*. 3 vols. Ed. Philip L. Barbour. Chapel Hill, NC: University of North Carolina Press, 1986.

Smith, Neil. *Uneven Development: Nature, Capital and the Production of Space*. Oxford: Basil Blackwell, 1984.

Smith, Neil and Cindi Katz. "Grounding Metaphor: Towards a Spatialized Politics." In *Place and the Politics of Identity*. Eds. Michael Keith and Steve Pile. London: Routledge, 1993.

Smith, Sir Thomas. *A Discourse of the Common Weal of this Realm of England*. Ed. Elizabeth Lamond. Cambridge University Press, 1954.

Smollett, Tobias. *Humphry Clinker*. Ed. Angus Ross. Harmondsworth: Penguin, 1985.

Soja, Edward W. *Postmodern Geographies: the Reassertion of Space in Critical Social Theory*. London: Verso, 1989.

Speed, John. *The Theatre of the Empire of Great Britaine*. London: 1627.

Speck, W. A.. *The Butcher: The Duke of Cumberland and the Suppression of the '45*. Oxford: Basil Blackwell, 1981.

Spenser, Edmund. *A View of the Present State of Ireland*. Ed. W. L. Renwick. Oxford: Clarendon Press, 1970.

The Faerie Queene. London: Penguin, 1978.

The Works of Edmund Spenser. Vol. 9. Eds. Edwin Greenlaw *et al.* Baltimore, MD: Johns Hopkins University Press, 1949.

Complete Poetical Works. Eds. J. C. Smith and E. De Selincourt. Oxford University Press, 1970.

Stallybrass, Peter and Allon White. *The Politics and Poetics of Transgression*. Ithaca, NY: Cornell University Press, 1986.

Stavely, Keith. *Puritan Legacies*. Ithaca, NY: Cornell University Press, 1987.

Stevens, Paul. "*Paradise Lost* and the Colonial Imperative." *Milton Studies* 34 (1996): 3–22.

Stone, Lawrence. *The Crisis of the Aristocracy, 1558–1641*. Oxford: Clarendon, 1965.

Strindberg, August. *Dream Play*. In *Strindberg: Five Plays*. Ed. Harry G. Carlson, New York, NY: Signet, 1983.

Summerson, John. *Architecture in Britain 1530–1830*. 8th revised edn. London: Penguin, 1991.

Swift, Jonathan. *Prose Works*. 12 vols. Ed. Herbert Davis. Oxford: Basil Blackwell, 1941–8.

The Correspondence of Jonathan Swift. Vol. 2. Ed. Harold Williams. Oxford: Clarendon, 1963.

The Writings of Jonathan Swift. Eds. Robert A. Greenberg and William B. Piper. London and New York, NY: Norton, 1973.

Gulliver's Travels. Eds. Peter Dixon and John Chalker. London: Penguin, 1985.

Taylor, E. G. R. *The Original Writings and Correspondence of the Two Richard*

Hakluyts. Vol. 2. London: The Hakluyt Society, 1935; 2nd Series. Vol. 77.

Temple, John. *The Irish Rebellion: Or An History Of the Beginnings and First Progress of the General Rebellion.* London, 1679.

Todd, Janet, ed. *Aphra Behn Studies.* Cambridge University Press, 1996.

Thomas, Keith. *Man and the Natural World: Changing Attitudes in England 1500–1800.* London: Penguin, 1984.

Thompson, E. P. *Whigs and Hunters: The Origins of the Black Act.* New York, NY: Pantheon, 1975.

Customs in Common. London: Merlin Press, 1991.

Thomson, James. *The Seasons and The Castle of Indolence.* Ed. James Sawbrook. Oxford: Clarendon, 1984.

Turner, James G. *The Politics of Landscape.* Oxford University Press, 1979.

One Flesh: Paradisal Marriage and Sexual Relations in the Age of Milton. Oxford: Clarendon, 1987.

Twombly, Robert. *Power and Style: a Critique of Twentieth-Century Architecture in the United States.* New York, NY: Hill and Wang, 1995.

Tyacke, Sarah, ed. *English Map-Making, 1500–1650.* London: The British Library, 1983.

Urry, John. *Consuming Places.* London: Routledge, 1995.

Varey, Simon. *Space and the Eighteenth-Century English Novel.* Cambridge University Press, 1990.

Vaughan, Alden T. and Edward W. Clark, eds. *Puritans among the Indians: Accounts of Captivity and Redemption, 1676–1724.* Cambridge, MA: The Belknap Press of Harvard University Press, 1981.

Viswanathan, Gauri. *Masks of Conquest: Literary Study and British Rule in India.* New York, NY: Columbia University Press, 1989.

Walker, Julia M., ed. *Milton and the Idea of Woman.* Urbana, IL: University of Illinois Press, 1988.

Wallerstein, Immanuel. *The Modern World-System I: Capitalist Agriculture and the Origins of the European World-Economy in the Sixteenth Century.* New York, NY: Academic Press, 1974.

Ward, Ned. *The London-Spy Compleat, In Eighteen Parts.* 1698. London: Casanova Society, 1924.

Warton, Joseph. "The Enthusiast: or, The Lover of Nature." *Eighteenth Century Poetry and Prose.* Eds. Louis I. Bredvold, Alan D. McKillop, and Lois Whitney. 2nd edn. New York, NY: The Ronald Press Company, 1956.

Wayne, Don. *Penshurst: the Semiotics of Place and the Poetics of History.* Madison, WI: University of Wisconsin Press, 1984.

Webb, Stephen Saunders. *The Governors-General: The English Army and the Definition of the Empire, 1569–1681.* Chapel Hill, NC: University of North Carolina Press, 1979.

1676: The End of American Independence. New York, NY: Knopf, 1984.

West, Cornel. *Keeping Faith: Philosophy and Race in America.* New York, NY: Routledge, 1993.

Wigley, Mark. "Untitled: The Housing of Gender." *Sexuality and Space.* Ed.

Beatriz Colomina. Princeton, NJ: Princeton Architectural Press, 1992.

Williams, Eric. *Capitalism and Slavery*. Chapel Hill, NC: University of North Carolina Press, 1944; repr. 1994.

Williams, Glyndwr. *The Expansion of Europe in the Eighteenth Century*. New York, NY: Walker and Company, 1966.

"'The Inexhaustible Fountain of Gold': English Projects and Ventures in the South Seas, 1670–1750." In *Perspectives of Empire*. Eds. John E. Flint and Glyndwr Williams. London: Longman, 1973.

Williams, Patrick and Laura Chrisman, eds. *Colonial Discourse and Post-Colonial Theory: A Reader*. New York, NY: Columbia University Press, 1994.

Williams, Raymond. *The Country and the City*. Oxford University Press, 1973.

Marxism and Literature. Oxford University Press, 1977, 1989.

Resources of Hope: Culture, Democracy, Socialism. Ed. Robin Gable. London: Verso, 1988.

Williams, William Appleman. *The Contours of American History*. New York, NY: Norton, 1988.

"Empire as a Way of Life." *Radical History Review* 50 (Spring 1991): 71–102.

Wilson, Kathleen. *The Sense of the People: Politics, Culture and Imperialism in England, 1715–1785*. Cambridge University Press, 1995.

Winthrop, John. "A Modell of Christian Charity." 1630. *Winthrop Papers*. Vol. 2. Boston, MA: MHS, 1931.

Wood, Ellen Meiksins. "The Agrarian Origins of Capitalism." *Monthly Review* 3.50 (1998): 14–31.

Wood, John. *The Origin of Building, or, the Plagiarisms of the Heathen Detected*. London: 1743.

Wood, William. *New England's Prospect*. 1634. New York, NY: Burt Franklin, 1967.

Wordsworth, William. *William Wordsworth*. Ed. Stephent Gill. Oxford University Press, 1990.

Woudhuysen, H. R. ed. *The Penguin Book of Renaissance Verse*. Selected by David Norbrook. Harmondsworth: Penguin, 1992.

Wren, Stephen. *Parentalia: or Memoirs of the Family of the Wrens*. London. 1750. Facsimile repr. Farnborough, 1965.

Young, Robert J. C. *Colonial Desire: Hybridity in Theory, Culture and Race*. New York, NY and London: Routledge, 1995.

Zevi, Bruno. *Architecture as Space: How to Look at Architecture*. Trans. Milton Gendel. New York, NY: Da Capo Press, 1993.

Index